ADAPTIVE ORIGINS

ADAPTIVE ORIGINS

Evolution and Human Development

Peter LaFrenière

Psychology Press
Taylor & Francis Group

New York   London

Psychology Press
Taylor & Francis Group
270 Madison Avenue
New York, NY 10016

Psychology Press
Taylor & Francis Group
27 Church Road
Hove, East Sussex BN3 2FA

© 2010 by Taylor and Francis Group, LLC
Psychology Press is an imprint of Taylor & Francis Group, an Informa business

Printed in the United States of America on acid-free paper
10 9 8 7 6 5 4 3 2 1

International Standard Book Number: 978-0-8058-6012-2 (Hardback)

Library of Congress Cataloging-in-Publication Data

LaFreniere, Peter.
    Adaptive origins : evolution and human development / Peter LaFreniere.
      p. cm.
    Includes bibliographical references and index.
    ISBN 978-0-8058-6012-2 (hardcover : alk. paper)
    1. Evolutionary psychology. 2. Developmental psychology. I. Title.

BF698.95.L34 2011
155.7--dc22
                                                                2010020434

Visit the Taylor & Francis Web site at
http://www.taylorandfrancis.com

and the Psychology Press Web site at
http://www.psypress.com

CONTENTS

PREFACE

The origins of this textbook can be traced back twenty-five years to my efforts in teaching developmental psychology within the wider theoretical framework of evolutionary theory. This was always problematic because most developmental textbooks barely mentioned Darwin until recently, and they completely failed to convey the necessary integration of ontogeny and phylogeny essential to understanding the organism's adaptation. By the choice of the phrase *Adaptive Origins* as the title, I invite students to view these processes as interdependent. Development cannot be fully understood except in the light of evolutionary theory, and the best proof of the theory is the fact of development. For students of evolutionary psychology, all the central topics, such as evolved mental modules for theory of mind or language, require an understanding of the developmental processes that lead to their expression. Genes, as important as they are, are never the whole story.

Another reason for writing this book is the pressing need to organize and integrate new knowledge from the neurosciences, genetics, genomics, evolutionary developmental biology, ethology, primatology, psychology, paleoanthropology, and archaeology. It is unrealistic to expect an undergraduate student to synthesize such diverse information on human adaptation scattered across so many disciplines and specialized areas of inquiry. An interdisciplinary textbook on human development may help counter the trend in American higher education towards increasingly narrow and technical specialization.

Existing textbooks on evolutionary psychology are too often an expression of this trend, and they have been criticized by evolutionary scholars in recent years as too narrow in their focus. In this book I adopt a broad definition of this important field beginning with the idea that evolutionary and developmental processes work together to solve problems of adaptation. Because of the developmental perspective that informs this evolutionary vision, there will be less talk of "stone-age minds" and more discussion of the epigenetic processes that wire the brain via endogenous signals from our DNA and exogenous signals from the environment.

☐ Plan of the Book

The book begins with a series of chapters that introduce students in the social sciences to biological theories and concepts. The first chapter provides a historical treatment of evolutionary theory and classical ethology and concludes with a brief introduction to evolutionary developmental biology. The second chapter introduces sociobiology and evolutionary psychology, with an emphasis on the maturation of the principal concepts of these fields. Chapter 3 addresses two fundamental questions: how genes construct the organism and how they influence behavior. After a brief survey of molecular genetics, epigenetics, and gene–environment interaction, there is a detailed treatment of behavioral genetics with respect to temperament and personality. Twin studies provide an important window on the direct influence of genes on whole organisms and compliment studies in molecular genetics and genomics.

Chapter 4 introduces physical anthropology, archaeology, population genetics, and the study of modern human origins. Evidence of the physical and cultural remains of the hominid expansion out of Africa, including recent discoveries on the Island of Flores, will be presented, as well as modern genetic analyses of the fossil record where it has been possible to obtain DNA samples. The next chapter treats a unique and complex aspect of human evolution: the evolution of the brain, its development, and its functions. In Chapter 6, the student is introduced to the hormonal system and its organizing impact on prenatal development and activating influences on pubertal development and human growth, including the contemporary problem of obesity. These first six chapters on different facets of human biology will likely be the most challenging material for students in the social sciences, thus they are written at an introductory level primarily with these students in mind.

The next series of chapters will likely be more familiar to students of developmental psychology than students of evolutionary psychology. However, the treatment of several major topics of emotional, cognitive, and social development is organized within the framework of evolutionary theory. The unity of development and its connection to evolution and phylogenetic adaptation will become clear. Students should be able to describe how evolved systems emerge from earlier precursors and the process by which they are transformed and reorganized over the lifespan. Students will also learn how these evolved systems are related to adaptive biological, motivational, and social processes that have functional significance for the organism.

Chapters 7 and 8 present evidence for evolutionary continuity in facial expression, nonverbal communication, and attachment, while Chapter 9 stresses relative discontinuity in symbolic thought, theory of mind, and language. Chapter 10 focuses on sex differences highlighting universal features of human behavior that derive from sexual selection and parental investment theory and present old topics to psychologists in a new light.

The last series of chapters address three central problems of human adaptation and illustrate the integrative value of a broad evolutionary model to understand topics in psychology. Chapter 11 reviews a wealth of recent research on mate selection, reproductive strategies, and parental investment. Chapter 12 introduces the exciting new field of Darwinian medicine, including evolutionary perspectives on physical diseases and mental illness. Finally, Chapter 13 reviews research on cooperation and competition, including topics like game theory, kin selection, reciprocal altruism, the free-rider problem, and multilevel selection.

The first wave of evolutionary psychology textbooks was crucial in establishing courses within required psychology curricula and conveyed the promise and excitement of this emerging field. I hope that this textbook, as part of the second wave, will broaden and expand the integration of evolutionary perspectives within the curriculum.

Evolutionary Theory

The modern theory of evolution owes its existence to two remarkable 19th-century scientists, Charles Darwin and Gregor Mendel. It is widely recognized as one of the greatest accomplishments of the human mind, with implications that have still yet to be fully grasped. After 150 years and many challenges, Darwin's theory of evolution by natural selection has revolutionized our thinking about the natural world and the place of humans in it. It has restructured and energized the biological and behavioral sciences, and its impact on psychology has never been stronger than it is today. Its relation to the many diverse and expanding fields of biology was summed up succinctly by Dobzhansky (1973, p. 125): "Nothing in biology makes sense except in the light of evolutionary theory."

☐ Darwin and Natural Selection

Darwin's theory embraces a vision of immense grandeur, but it can also be reduced to relatively few explanatory principles. This stunning achievement had its roots in Darwin's five-year voyage aboard the H.M.S. *Beagle* where the young naturalist sought to account for the marvelous adaptive fit between species and their environments and to explain the origins of the diverse forms of life he encountered. His extraordinary powers of observation and deduction resulted in one of the most influential scientific works ever produced, *"The Origin of Species* (Darwin, 1859). In essence this work can be abstracted to the principles of variation, selection, and retention and summarized in just five points:

1. Despite the fact that offspring in any generation outnumber parents, the total number of individuals in a species remains somewhat stable across generations. One may thus deduce that a certain percentage of offspring die and/or never reproduce (Malthus, 1826).
2. Individuals within any species vary in terms of their morphology, physiology, and behavior.
3. Certain variants are more likely to survive and leave more offspring than others as a function of the demand characteristics of the environment that they inhabit. This is Darwin's principle of natural selection.
4. Offspring somehow inherit the characteristics of their parents. Certain characteristics will be retained more often than others, and natural selection ensures retention of those characteristics that best fit the environment.
5. Throughout the history of life on earth, environmental conditions changed and different species moved into new environments, and species gradually changed to fit the new conditions. All life forms are thus related and can be traced through a series of common ancestors back to the origin of life.

Although Darwin had formulated this solution to the problem of adaptive design and the origin of species relatively early in his career, he was reluctant to publish his ideas knowing that they would create quite a stir. For 20 years he labored to build the empirical evidence to substantiate his theory. When he received a letter from another British naturalist, Alfred Russel Wallace, working on similar ideas, he arranged for a joint presentation of their views on natural selection at the Linnaean Society in London in 1858.

In retrospect the publication of Darwin's *The Origin of Species* in 1859 was the scientific event of the century, but at the time it was received with mixed reviews. In the popular press and among the general public the idea of evolution aroused immense controversy and generated much confusion. Among scientists the concept of evolution aroused little controversy, but was still poorly understood by many scientists at that time, in part because the idea had a long pedigree. Prior to an evolutionary view, species were viewed as immutable creations with a divine purpose: early evolutionary views tended to incorporate this purposeful attribution in viewing species as progressive with humans at the top, just below angels (Charlesworth, 1992). In contrast to previous theories of evolution, Darwinian evolution was not teleological or inherently progressive towards some ideal. Instead, it simply proceeded by chance opportunities and the necessary demands of the environment that inevitably winnowed out less fit organisms from the gene pool (Figure 1.1). As Darwin (1871)

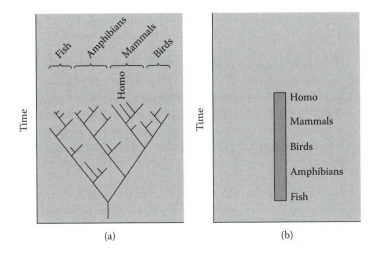

FIGURE 1.1   Darwin's model (a) replaces previous teleological models (b) of evolution.

explained, the purpose of writing *The Origin of Species* was twofold: "I had two distinct objects in view; first to show that species had not been separately created, and secondly, that natural selection had been the chief agent of change (1859, p. 61)." However, it was just this design capability of natural selection that many 19th-century scientists did not fully appreciate.

It was Darwin's particular genius to grasp the full significance of natural selection as an answer to the question of adaptive design in nature. Adaptation is a central concept in evolutionary biology; it refers to the characteristics of living organisms that enable them to survive and reproduce in a particular environment. Recollecting his key discovery in his autobiography Darwin commented:

> It was equally evident that neither the action of the surrounding conditions, nor the will of the organisms, could account for the innumerable cases in which organisms of every kind are beautifully adapted to their habits of life—for instance, a woodpecker or tree frog to climb trees, or a seed for dispersal by hooks or plumes. I had always been much struck by such adaptations, and until these could be explained it seemed to me almost useless to endeavor to prove by indirect evidence that species have been modified. (Darwin, 1958, p. 34)

Because adaptations are common to all living things by dint of natural selection, examples of such adaptations surround the naturalist regardless of which species interests him or her. One of Darwin's favorite examples of adaptive design was the woodpecker.

The woodpecker's most obvious adaptation is its powerful, characteristically shaped beak. It enables the woodpecker to excavate holes in trees. They can thus feed on the year-round food supply of insects that live under bark, insects that bore into the wood, and the sap of the tree itself. Tree holes also make safe sites to build a nest. Woodpeckers have many other design features as well as their beaks. Within the beak is a long, probing tongue, which is well adapted to extract insects from inside a tree hole. They have a stiff tail, that is used as a brace, short legs, and their feet have curved toes for gripping on to the bark; they even have a special type of molting in which the strong central pair of feathers is molted last. The beak and body design of the woodpecker is adaptive. The woodpecker is more likely to survive, in its natural habitat, by possessing them. (Ridley, 2004, p. 6)

In observing two of the most common species of woodpeckers here in Maine, the Downy and Hairy woodpeckers, you will notice that the male of each species sports a bright red head patch, though females do not. Indeed, in many bird species, the male has bright plumage especially in the spring, while the female is cryptically colored. Her cryptic coloration is easily explained as a product of natural selection since camouflage is one of the most ubiquitous forms of defense against predation found in nature. But is what is good for the goose, not also good for the gander? Apparently not. As a keen naturalist, well acquainted with the details of sexual dimorphism in the animal world, Darwin knew there must be a mechanism besides natural selection to account for such a pervasive characteristic of different species.

He developed his answer to this question in *The Descent of Man and Selection in Relation to Sex* (1871). In this work, Darwin introduces sexual selection as a specific form of natural selection that arises "from the advantage that certain individuals have over other individuals of the same sex and species, in exclusive relation to reproduction" (p. 256). Darwin identified two processes: (1) intrasexual: competition of members of the same sex for mates (e.g., the male lion's greater size, strength, and mane), and (2) intersexual— members of one sex choose as mates members of the other sex, whose phenotypes differ in some heritable fashion (e.g., the peacock's tail).

☐ Mendel and the Laws of Inheritance

As originally proposed in 1859, Darwin's theory had one remaining weakness. While Darwin could observe individual variation in species-typical characteristics, he had no persuasive explanation for their transmission from one generation to the next. If natural and sexual selection determined which traits were adaptive, how were these traits retained in the species? Because the complex characteristics that interested Darwin appeared to blend in the offspring, producing an intermediate form, he speculated that the hereditary material was some fluid-like substance that could be blended in various proportions. Such was the practical knowledge of naturalists in his era who, after all, had been successfully breeding traits in dogs and other domestic species for many years. While this solution was reasonable and seemed to fit the facts, it was nevertheless incorrect. The problem of retention in Darwin's model was to be remedied by simple experiments: growing peas in the garden of an Austrian monk.

Key breakthroughs in science are often made when scientists choose to tackle simpler problems first, and there is no better example of this principle of the "art of the soluble" than the research of the Austrian monk Gregor Mendel. Mendel chose to work with simpler organisms and focused his research on characteristics that were expressed as simple dichotomies in both parent and offspring. Unlike crossbreeding in dogs, crossbreeding different pea plants produced offspring that were either yellow or green, with no intermediate forms. Working with such simple structures allowed Mendel to use straightforward quantitative methods to test his ideas about heredity.

After a series of ingenious breeding experiments, Mendel was able to provide a more parsimonious account of the origin of individual characteristics and their transmission to the next generation. Mendel realized that each individual's characteristics or phenotype results from the unique combination of genes that are contributed by each parent, referred to as the individual's genotype. The key observation that Mendel made was that crossbreeding plants of different pure genotypes (yellow vs. green plants) resulted in first generation offspring of only one type, yellow, referred to as dominant. However, the next generation of crossbreeding resulted in 75% yellow plants (the dominant form) and 25% green plants (the recessive form). From this experiment, Mendel correctly deduced that the dominant gene when paired with itself or with the recessive gene would yield the dominant phenotype. Only the recessive gene paired with itself (a 25% probability) would yield the recessive phenotype. Simple experimentation enabled Mendel to discover the laws of inheritance that Darwin had postulated as necessary but was unable to find through naturalistic observation. This illustrates an important methodological point that remains just as true today: the combination of fieldwork and laboratory experimentation can be extremely effective in generating and testing scientific hypotheses. Despite the fact that no scientist in Mendel's era had ever seen a gene, their existence could be derived from careful observation and systematic experimentation.

☐ The Modern Synthesis

Though Mendel was a contemporary of Darwin they were unaware of each other's work. Without an Internet or other means of connection, Mendel's ideas lay dormant in the scientific world until they were rediscovered in the early 20th century. Initially, they were put forward in opposition to Darwin's theory, rather than as a complement to it. The modern synthesis arose in the 1930s as a result of the efforts of Wright, Fisher, and Haldane, who proposed a workable integration of Darwin's theory of evolution with Mendelian, or population, genetics. This integration posits that (1) evolution proceeds in a gradual manner, (2) heritable traits are determined by genes, (3) natural selection of these traits is the principal means of evolution, and (4) these processes explain both the evolution of a species over time and the origin of new species, accounting for the great diversity of life forms living and extinct.

The importance of the incorporation of Mendel's model of particulate inheritance to Darwin's theory of evolution by natural selection cannot be overstated. Indeed, natural selection would not be viable under Darwin's original assumption of blending inheritance, a fact that was pointed out by his critics before the synthesis. In a very real sense, Darwin's theory required Mendel's theory. Let us look at the logic underlying this state of affairs.

When we say that Mendelism is a particulate theory of inheritance, we mean that individual genes are preserved during development and transmitted unaltered to the next generation, except in the rare event of a mutation. In Darwin's original idea of blending inheritance, individual genes are not preserved intact, but rather altered when the parents' sets of genes are blended together. Thus a particular gene that conferred an advantage would not be preserved and could not spread in a population because it would be blended with less advantageous genes. Mendelian genetics rescues Darwin's concept of natural selection from this serious criticism by providing a mechanism whereby discrete genes are preserved within the population. If they are then "selected for," over time they would become increasingly widespread within the gene pool.

☐ Early Scientific Evidence

Much of the evidence for Darwin's theory of evolution was lying about in pieces before he supplied the connecting concept of natural selection. Animal breeders had a practical understanding of how selection worked and could "select for" various characteristics in the pigeons, dogs, or domestic livestock they bred for various purposes. The term *natural selection* was derived from this existing use of the term *selection*. Naturalists already had a fine understanding of how various species were related in terms of shared morphological characteristics, and as early as 1735 Carolus Linnaeus had developed a taxonomic classification that is still used today. In the early 19th century, the English morphologist Richard Owen developed the concept of homologues, and across the channel in France, Jean-Baptiste Lamarck developed a theory of evolution, as had Darwin's grandfather, Erasmus. Early paleontologists provided an extensive fossil record showing the appearance and disappearance of species over geologic time periods. But nobody had supplied the mechanism that accounted for this accumulating empirical evidence. Darwin was working on connecting the evidence to his theory when another British naturalist, Alfred Russel Wallace, hit upon virtually the same mechanism as Darwin. In 1858 Joseph Hooker presented both of their papers to the Linnaean Society. But it was the logic and evidence provided by Darwin that would be so influential in the long run.

Darwin drew upon the following four independent sources of evidence to support his claim that all species evolved by natural selection:

1. Paleontology
2. Biogeography
3. Morphology
4. Embryology

The fossil record revealed the existence of many different extinct species in Darwin's time. It was well understood by geologists and paleontologists that more recent strata were layered atop more ancient rock, and that the fossils the rocks contained could be dated as a result. Darwin observed that species that shared similar characteristics were clustered together in adjacent strata. From these facts he reasoned that closely allied species altered some characters and succeeded one another in time because they are related by common descent.

Darwin was particularly impressed by a similar clustering pattern in the biogeographical distribution of living species. Hares and rabbits lived in dry scrubland, whereas beavers and muskrats inhabited wetlands. Moreover, similar species tended to be found on the same continent in neighboring areas. Thirteen species of finches nest in the Galapagos, and 44 species of wood warblers nest in North America, all of them exhibiting species-typical preferences for nesting sites, food sources, and habitat. In contrast, animals found in very similar habitats on different continents are not closely allied. The observation that ecologically different species found in the same geographical area are more similar than ecologically similar species found in different areas led Darwin to deduce that species that are nearby in space are similar because they are related by common descent.

A stunning modern example of this is found in the case of "ring species" such as the Californian salamander *Ensatina* (Ridley, 2004). A ring species contains a set of intermediate forms that are distributed geographically in the shape of a ring. At one end of the ring only one species is found, while at the other, two distinct species are seen, with the intermediate forms found in between. For example, the salamander *Ensatina* is distributed in a ring in California as shown in Figure 1.2. In the northern range there is just one species. As we move south the distribution splits to form a continuous ring around the San Joaquin valley. On the coastal side of this ring the salamanders vary in form and are lightly pigmented and have been given different taxonomic names. On the inland side of the ring the salamanders are blotched and are given a different series of taxonomic names. At the southern tip of this ring the blotched and unblotched variants meet and coexist as separate species; *that is, they do not interbreed*. Because species are defined by phenotypic differences in form and inability to interbreed, the salamanders at the southern tip of the ring qualify as distinct species. Ring species are significant because they show that the process of anagenesis, or the gradual transformation of a species by natural selection, can in some cases lead to speciation (also called cladogenesis), or the evolution of reproductively isolated populations into distinct species. Modern evidence reveals that new species can also be produced experimentally through artificial selection, as is the case for many agricultural and horticultural varieties of plants, such as irises, tulips, dahlias, etc.

In Darwin's era morphologists grouped different species together by observable design features using a hierarchical taxonomic classification system developed by Linnaeus that is still used today, as shown in Figure 1.3. The basic unit of the classification system is the species, always identified by the genus name and the species name, as in *Canis lupus* or Homo sapiens.

Darwin went a step beyond mere classification by reasoning that groups of species share these similar designs because they have a common origin. The number of characteristics that they share may be used to indicate how closely they are related. However, a fundamental distinction in the comparative analysis of morphology must be made between a similarity between species that can be traced to a common origin (homology), and one that has been produced through independent but convergent lines of evolution (analogy). Analogous features often appear to be similar in their function, but differ in terms of underlying mechanism. Butterflies, birds, and bats all fly, but the similarities end there, since bats, as mammals, belong to a different taxonomic group than birds or butterflies. Although they all have wings that sustain intricate patterns of flight, their wings differ markedly in the neural and muscular mechanisms responsible for flying. In contrast, the wings and flight patterns of different species of bats (or birds, or butterflies) are homologous (Figure 1.4). Homologous

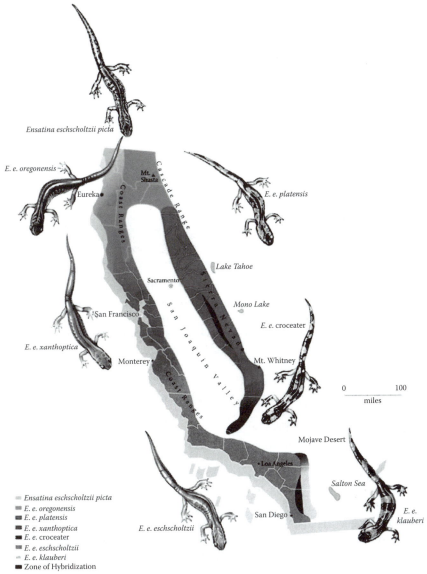

Ensatina eschscholtzii picta

E. e. oregonensis

Eureka

Mt. Shasta

Coast Ranges

Cascade Range

E. e. platensis

Lake Tahoe

Sacramento

Sierra Nevada

San Francisco

San Joaquin Valley

Mono Lake

E. e. croceater

E. e. xanthoptica

Monterey

Mt. Whitney

Coast Ranges

0   100
miles

Mojave Desert

Los Angeles

Salton Sea

- Ensatina eschscholtzii picta
- E. e. oregonensis
- E. e. platensis
- E. e. xanthoptica
- E. e. croceater
- E. e. eschscholtzii
- E. e. klauberi
- Zone of Hybridization

E. e. eschscholtzii

San Diego

E. e. klauberi

Color gradation show zones of intergradation of subspecies

FIGURE 1.2 Ring species show how new species originate from progressive changes in a population according to demands from different habitats. (From Ridley, M. [2004]. *Evolution* [3rd ed.]. Cambridge, MA: Blackwell Science. With permission.)

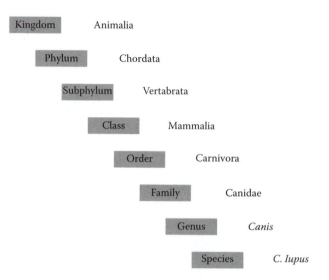

FIGURE 1.3 The Linnaean system of taxonomic classes.

features, such as the bone structure of the forelimbs of humans and other mammals including whales, may sometimes differ in outward appearance and even function, but they always retain underlying similarities in the details of their construction owing to a common genetic foundation, even if later evolution creates substantial divergences.

The discipline of embryology is similar to morphology but concerns itself exclusively with the comparative study of organisms before they are born. The embryos of mammals all resemble one another in their early stages of development and differentiate from one another later. Similarly the larvae of beetles, moths, and flies are more similar to one another than they are to their respective adult forms. Darwin reasoned that such patterns could not be explained by coincidence but revealed the structures laid down by descent from a common ancestor.

An excellent example of the role of embryology as distinct from morphology is seen in the analysis of the phenotypically different limbs of tetrapods (four-legged vertebrates). Tetrapods such as reptiles, birds, and mammals occupy quite different habitats, and their limbs have been adapted by natural selection to serve diverse functions. There is no functional reason why they should have a pentadactyl (five digit) limb at all. Three digits or seven would be equally functional. Indeed the limbs of horses and some lizards have fewer than five digits. However, in all cases tetrapod limbs pass through an embryological stage in which five digits are seen, demonstrating the vestige of the common ancestral pentadactyl state. As Darwin (1859, p. 434) commented,

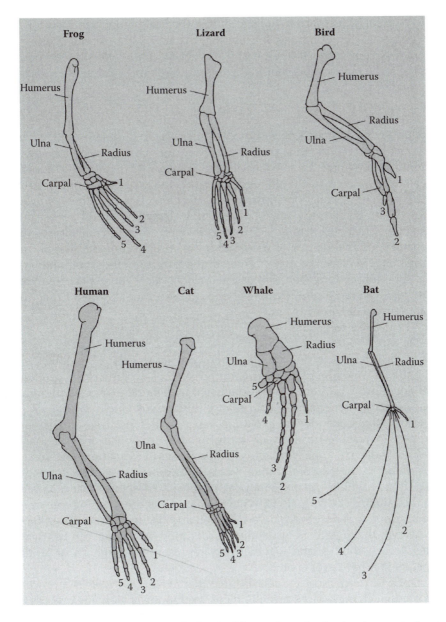

FIGURE 1.4   A classic morphological homology is the basic pentadactyl (five digit) forelimb common to all modern tetrapods. (From Ridley, M. [2004], *Evolution* [3rd ed.]. Cambridge, MA: Blackwell Science. With permission.)

What could be more curious than that the hand of man formed for grasping, that of a mole, for digging, the leg of a horse, the paddle of a porpoise and the wing of a bat, should all be constructed on the same pattern and should include similar bones and in the same relative position?

The key point in making the case for descent from a common ancestor is that the basic structure observed is the same in all related organisms *and that it is arbitrary*, thus there is no other compelling reason for why it should be the same. The most basic homology found in nature is thus the genetic code. As Crick (1968) demonstrated, the code is essentially arbitrary; the coding relationships are pure accident. But once they evolved, they would remain the same, because any deviation would be fatal—a situation Crick refers to as a "frozen accident." The universality of the genetic code is thus one of the most compelling arguments that all life forms have a common origin. Indeed, the precision and computational capacities of modern computer-assisted biochemical and genetic analyses provide even more compelling evidence for evolutionary theory than the data sources of Darwin's era.

Key debates following the widespread scientific acceptance of the synthetic theory of evolution have focused on the concept of species (Mayr, 1970), the level of selection (i.e., the gene, organism, or group; Dawkins, 1976; Hamilton, 1964; Mayr, 1970; Williams, 1966), and evolution as a gradual, continual process or one that is dominated by long periods of equilibrium punctuated with periods of rapid change (Eldredge & Gould, 1972).

Most textbooks depict evolution as a branching tree, suggesting an ever-increasing diversity of life forms. But this view of evolution is flawed. Indeed, it appears that five major phases of extinction have struck the planet in the past 500 million years, and we have currently entered a sixth phase with estimates of approximately 27,000 species lost each year in the rain forests alone (E. O. Wilson, 1992). Thus, a branching tree must be redrawn to reflect both "diversification and decimation" (Gould, 1989). Whatever the final form of the model, all living organisms can be traced back to one another and together they represent less than 1% of all the species that have ever evolved.

Since Darwin, most models assume that evolution involves a process of gradual change. More recently many evolutionists view the process as long stable eras punctuated with abrupt periods of change or *punctuated equilibrium* (Eldridge & Gould, 1972). An important difference between these two models of evolution involves the causal theories underlying them. The traditional gradualist view of evolution invokes the process of adaptation to explain the origin of new species as the result of the accumulation of small changes produced by natural selection over long periods of time. In contrast, the punctuated equilibrium model posits adaptation as a consequence of speciation, with major changes occurring after populations are separated geographically and genetically. It is likely that both models have operated throughout evolutionary history. Certainly evolution does not always proceed at a constant rate. For example, each major phase of extinction has been followed by a rapid radiation of new species that quickly restored the level of diversity to a new high (Lewin, 2004). Typically, a new group of species becomes dominant. A characteristic pattern of rapid evolution, referred to as adaptive radiation, often follows the introduction of an important evolutionary innovation, such as feathered flight in birds or placental gestation in mammals. A relatively empty ecology following mass extinction provides an opportunity for these innovative life forms to adapt new variations and multiply via descendant species as each finetunes its adaptation to a particular niche. Bipedal locomotion provided a similar opportunity for hominids to adapt to a changing east African landscape when dense forests gave way to open savannah grasslands.

☐ Modern Scientific Evidence

Competing concepts about the nature of the evolutionary process are central to scientific progress. As with scientific theories in general, the synthetic theory of evolution continues to be refined and reexamined in light of new evidence. Modern biology provides a number of distinct sources of evidence in support of Darwin from the following scientific disciplines that did not exist in his day:

1. Biochemistry
2. Molecular biology
3. Population genetics
4. Genomics

As the synthetic theory of evolution gained prominence after the 1940s, earlier debates were revisited and older positions began to be challenged by these new methods. For example the relationships between humans and the great apes was put under the scrutiny of the microscope. Since the 1920s, the great apes (gorillas, chimpanzees, and orangutans) were viewed as a natural grouping of closely related relatives, with humans regarded as more distant. This conception replaced the earlier view of Darwin and Haeckel and remained ascendant until the molecular biologist Morris Goodman challenged it with new data in 1963. His research on blood proteins clearly demonstrated that humans and the African apes were more closely related, with the Asian great ape (orangutan) a more distant relative, as was originally conceived by Darwin and Haeckel (Goodman, 1963). More recent work in genomics, the study of genomes using DNA sequence data, further establishes that humans are more closely related to chimpanzees (even more than are gorillas) since they share 98.6% of their mitochondrial DNA. These new data have led to changes in classification and nomenclature as well, with the term *hominin* gradually replacing the older term *hominid* to reflect the molecular evidence that we are a subfamily. Subsequent analyses using molecular biological data reveal that the origin of the human line is remarkably recent (Sarich & Wilson, 1967). We shall introduce and discuss modern genetic analyses and human origins in greater detail in Chapters 3 and 4.

Probably no more dramatic evidence for evolution exists today than the study and treatment of microbial diseases like HIV/AIDS, Ebola, SARS, and other viruses that can spread directly and quickly from person to person. Biomedical research to combat the spread of these diseases makes use of information derived from biochemistry and molecular biology. The key difficulty that is common to all these diseases is their inherent capacity to quickly evolve mutant strains that are resistant to the antibiotics used to treat them. Thus, an evolutionary perspective is vital for understanding, preventing, and treating these infectious diseases.

Recently we have seen an Ebola virus in Africa kill half of those who fell ill. Another example is Legionnaires' disease, so named because of its rapid spread via a hotel air-conditioning system that infected a conference of Legionnaires visiting from all parts of the United States. Currently, an avian flu virus endemic in Asia appears to be evolving in ways that increasingly heighten the possibility of a pandemic. However, no other infectious disease has received more public attention in our generation than HIV/AIDS. We shall discuss pandemics at length in Chapter 12, but let us now examine this one case in more detail to illustrate the evolutionary process in action at the molecular level.

HIV/AIDS

Over the past 30 years we have witnessed the worldwide spread of the human immunodeficiency virus (HIV) which has resulted in the deaths of over 30 million people worldwide from AIDS while another 40 million people are infected with the virus (UNAIDS, 2005). Unlike most viruses, HIV does not attempt to escape detection by the immune system, it attacks it instead. The immune system's T-cells that coordinate the counterattack against the virus are continuously destroyed by the HIV. Following infection, an individual with HIV typically remains healthy for a time. During this period, the body produces enough T-cells to offset the losses to HIV. But over time the system is overwhelmed and T-cells are eventually destroyed at a faster rate than they are produced. This leaves the body vulnerable to any other pathogens that may be around. Although these pathogens may cause only mild infections in healthy individuals they can be serious or fatal to an individual with an advanced case of HIV, producing an acquired immune deficiency syndrome or AIDS.

HIV uses RNA as its hereditary material. It reproduces inside a human cell by producing a DNA copy from its RNA, a process of replication that is actually aided by enzymes supplied by the host cell. One key enzyme, called reverse transcriptase, is supplied by HIV to convert RNA into DNA, which is the reverse of the DNA to RNA conversion process normally found in humans. Anti-HIV drugs are designed to inactivate the reverse transcriptase. One such drug, 3TC, acts initially to quickly devastate an HIV population inside the human body. But within the first few days, resistant strains evolve and spread quickly via the selection pressures created by the presence of 3TC within the body. Only resistant strains of the original HIV survive and reproduce, providing a microcosm of all evolution on the planet. In a matter of a few weeks, the percentage of drug-resistant strains will increase to 100% in most patients, as the original strain is selected against (Schuurman et al., 1995). Molecular biologists can study the precise molecular changes that arise to provide the new strain its resistance to 3TC, one of many examples of evolution as an observable fact of nature.

Understanding the evolutionary process by which HIV acquires its resistance to an antiviral drug has been the key to improving treatment by means of more effective multiple drug "cocktails" that greatly slow the evolution of the virus within the patient. The same evolutionary logic applies to other similarly futile attempts of human technology to control nature through the production of various antibiotics, insecticides, and herbicides. In each case, modern technology is outpaced by the rapidity of the evolution of resistant forms of the bacteria, viruses, insects, and weeds, as the case may be.

☐ Classic Ethology: Lorenz and Tinbergen

Historically, the term ethology has been widely employed since the 1930s, as the branch of biology that concerns the naturalistic observation and description of animal behavior, although the development of this science was clearly anticipated by Darwin much earlier. Darwin was the first to appreciate that behavioral adaptation is realized through the same process of natural selection as that which led to the morphological and physiological characteristics that support the behavior pattern.

Darwin shows in the most convincing manner that analogous processes (to the evolution of organs) have taken place in the evolution
of motor patterns, as for instance, in the case of snarling, in which
an expressive movement with a purely communicative function
has developed out of the motor pattern of actual biting which, as a
means of aggression, has practically disappeared in the human species. (Lorenz, 1965, p. xii)

Although it is clear that an ethological approach owes much to Darwin
and the subsequent work of zoologists like Heinroth, Whitman, and
Craig around the turn of the century, it was not until the publications
of Lorenz and Tinbergen (Lorenz, 1935, 1941; Lorenz & Tinbergen, 1938;
Tinbergen, 1951) that ethology emerged as a systematic and coherent discipline. In his early publications Lorenz focused on species-typical behaviors that could be used for taxonomic purposes, much like morphological
characteristics, to compare different species and trace ancestral relationships (Eibl-Eibesfeldt, 1989). As we shall see, the line of inquiry initiated
by Darwin into the homologous nature of human facial expressions was
to become a central battleground between those who viewed humans as
purely cultural beings and those who viewed human behavior in comparative perspective as shaped by evolution. Unlike Darwin, the classical
ethologists chose to focus their investigations on simpler organisms.

According to Ernst Mayr, "the major contribution of the leaders of biological thought has been the development and refinement of concepts
and occasionally the elimination of erroneous ones. Evolutionary biology
owes a remarkably large portion of its concepts to Charles Darwin, and
ethology to Konrad Lorenz" (Mayr, 1982, p. 42).

Konrad Lorenz is best known for his work on imprinting in the gray-
lag geese; Niko Tinbergen studied aggression in species of fish like sticklebacks; and Karl von Frisch was interested in communication in bees.
Together these three scientists were awarded the 1973 Nobel Prize for
establishing the foundations of ethology. In 1935 Lorenz published "Der
Kumpan in der Umwelt des Vogels" or "The Companion in the Bird's
World." In this seminal paper, Lorenz introduces the new science of ethology, articulates its basic concepts and methods and provides a comprehensive discussion of the different types of relationships systematically
observed among birds. These relationships are organized from the bird's
point of view and include the parental companion, the infant companion,
the sexual companion, the social companion, and siblings. According to
Lorenz, these relationships are all essential for survival and reproduction and as a result they are highly stereotyped by natural selection. The
bird's individual experience plays a key role in its emergence, but there are

important elements of each of them that are not learned. As Lorenz later asserted in response to his American critics, to say that they are innate is about as much of an exaggeration as to say that the Eiffel Tower is made of metal.

By 1935, Lorenz was able to formulate the basic concepts of ethology, including the idea of an innate template by which specific behaviors (fixed action patterns) are released by triggers (sign stimuli). A classic example of such a lock-key mechanism is the release of aggressive behaviors involved in territorial defense in the male stickleback (a small fish common to Europe) by the red underbelly of other male sticklebacks (Tinbergen, 1951).

Naturalistic observation of sticklebacks during the breeding season revealed that males build and defend a nest from encroachment by other male sticklebacks, relentlessly attacking them if they approach too close to the nest. In his classic experiments, Tinbergen tested the hypothesis that male aggression was released by the bright red coloration of the male's underbelly (which is gray outside the breeding season). He presented various models to male sticklebacks that were defending their nest (Figure 1.5). Some of the models closely resembled a male stickleback in size and shape, but without red coloration, while other models did not look anything like a stickleback, but did have a red belly. These experiments clearly demonstrated that males only attacked the models with a red underbelly. Later research showed that this aggression was context-specific and could not be elicited in males outside their home territory.

Several important points can be drawn from this classic example of ethological research. First, it illustrates that an ethological approach is not synonymous with naturalistic observation. Tinbergen's hypotheses were generated as a result of careful fieldwork guided by evolutionary theory, and subsequently tested in experiments. Rather than identifying ethology with a particular method, the discipline is more appropriately defined according to its questions. Tinbergen provides a succinct account of an ethological orientation to the study of behavior in his fourfold scheme of basic questions concerning (1) evolution, (2) development, (3) causation, and (4) function (Table 1.1). Within this framework, an ethologist seeks to understand behavior from a broad perspective that combines the concerns of developmental psychologists (How does a particular behavior develop?

TABLE 1.1 Tinbergen's Four Basic Questions about Behavior

	Proximate	Ultimate
How?	Development	Evolution
Why?	Causation	Function

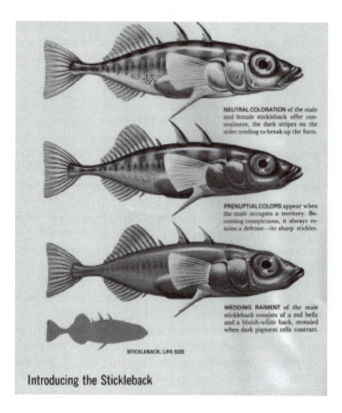

Introducing the Stickleback

FIGURE 1.5   Tinbergen's models demonstrated that the proximate cause of intermale stickleback aggression was the male's red underbelly. (From Tinbergen, N. [1951]. *The study of instinct.* London, UK: Oxford University Press. With permission.)

What causes it to occur?) with those of the zoologist (How did a particular behavior evolve? What are its adaptive functions?). In the example of stickleback territorial defense, the proximate cause of male aggression is the sign stimulus (the intruding male's red underbelly during breeding). This type of territorial aggression is unique to males and occurs only when they are in their home territory and another male approaches. In other words, the aggressive response has evolved in the male of the species as a conditional strategy and shows much greater flexibility than a simple reflex. Its adaptive function is to protect the male's reproductive investment and ensure the survival of his offspring.

An important philosophical foundation of classic ethology is the notion of critical realism (Eibl-Eibesfeldt, 1989; Lorenz, 1973; Popper, 1965), which assumes that species-typical adaptations mirror external reality. As an

FIGURE 1.5   (continued). Nesting habits of the stickleback and male territorial defense.

epistemological system, the idea of critical realism builds upon Kant's transcendental idealism in the following manner. Kant understood that an organism's knowledge of the external world is determined not solely by the features of external reality, but also by its perceptual faculties. This philosophical view is expressed by Karl Popper in *The Logic of Scientific Discovery* (1965): "The thing-in-itself is unknowable: we can only know its appearances, which are to be understood (as pointed out by Kant) as resulting from the thing-in-itself and from our own perceiving apparatus. Thus appearances result from a kind of interaction between the things-in-themselves and ourselves" (cited from Lorenz, 1973, p. 18). But Kant did not see how the organism's perceptual faculties were related to the features of external reality. Lorenz realized that the sensory/perception systems and brains of organisms must have evolved in order to respond to those features of external reality that were critically involved in their survival and reproduction.

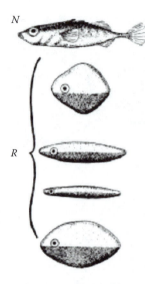

FIGURE 1.5   (continued).

These phylogenetic adaptations, from the finch's beak to the human eye, are "shaped" over time by environmental demands and opportunities. Likewise behavioral adaptations represent the accumulation of information about features of the environment that have at some time been critical in enhancing survival and reproductive success. Lorenz viewed the innate structures of thought, language, and emotional expression in humans to be excellent examples of phylogenetic adaptations, foreshadowing the emergence of evolutionary psychology. Now many neurobiological studies support this view by identifying specific structures in the human brain that map onto these important functions. Darwin supplied the two key mechanisms by which such evolution occurs: natural selection and sexual selection. The behavior patterns that have proven to be successful in terms of inclusive fitness became codified genetically and this "information" is transmitted to future generations. Responses that have been shaped by critical environmental stimuli include neurological, physiological, motivational, perceptual, and cognitive components of the system. Ultimately, natural selection can operate only on the behavioral consequences of the system for the individual organism. For this reason, ethologists have been primarily interested in the functional significance of behavior rather than the investigation of unobservable psychological states (Charlesworth, 1982).

The key insight of ethology is to extend the operation of natural selection beyond physical features to behavior. According to Lorenz (1978/1981), the

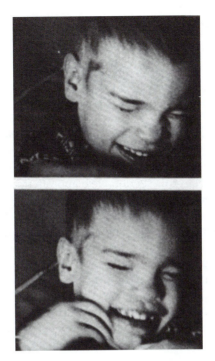

FIGURE 1.6   Facial expressions of a deaf and blind child. (Photos courtesy of I. Eibl-Eibesfeldt.)

discovery that behavior patterns are homologous is the point from which ethology marks its origin. A good example of a homologous expressive behavior that has been selected for in human infants is smiling. As a congenitally organized behavior, the smile requires no prior learning in its production and functions to elicit care giving immediately after birth, before the expression is fully integrated into an emotion system. One means to dramatically illustrate the inborn nature of the infant's expressive repertoire is to observe the facial expressions of children born deaf and blind. These children exhibit the full range of facial expressions, though they may be less refined than those of sighted children (Eibl-Eibesfeldt, 1973; see Figure 1.6). They smile when their mother caresses them, laugh excitedly during stimulating play, cry when hurt, and frown and clench their teeth when angered. These expressive behaviors exhibited by deaf and blind children are the same as those that have been shown to be universal across cultures.

From an ethological point of view, the child is not born a tabula rasa or blank slate upon which the environment acts. Rather the child is capable of actively engaging the environment from birth, with inborn

predispositions, preferences, and reflexes that have been bestowed by natural selection to provide an adaptive advantage at the start of life.

☐ Evolution and Development

The general theme of this book is that evolution and development are not
separate forces governing the origin of life forms, but rather interdependent biological processes. This is expressed in the title and briefly discussed in the preface. In this section we elaborate upon this theme.

Integrating developmental and evolutionary perspectives is no small
task, in large part because the various disciplines related to each topic
have grown up apart. Yet development is directly linked to evolution by
two unavoidable facts: (1) it is the phenotype that is the target of selection,
and (2) the phenotype is a product of development involving both genetic
and environmental determinants (Mayr, 1970; West-Eberhard, 2003).
Thus, evolution involves the generation of variable phenotypes, then the
screening of these individual variants by selection, and finally the retention and transmission of the selected variants in future generations.

Genetic Sources of Phenotypic Variation

At the beginning of this chapter you were introduced to this tripartite process of variation-selection-retention. Now we examine more precisely the
sources of variation that selection acts upon (Figure 1.7). Many biologists

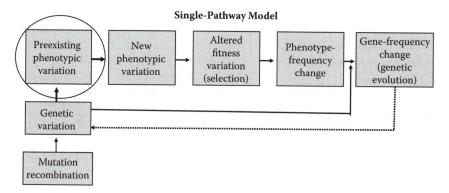

FIGURE 1.7 Causal relations between environment, genes, phenotype, and selection in adaptive evolution. New phenotypic variation can
begin with genetic change (bottom). Dashed arrows indicate feedback
among variables. (Adapted from West-Eberhard, 2003.)

would name mutation as the *only* genuine source of the evolutionary novelty that underlies genetic change. According to this view, variations occur from time to time in the individuals of a population, as a result of genetic mutations that occur to some extent naturally, by copying errors, but can also be caused by chemicals or radiation. While often fatal, some mutations confer a reproductive advantage and, aided by the processes of crossing over and assortative mating, the genetic structure of a breeding group gradually changes. This largely random process of mutation that must occur in the gametes (or stem cells that make them) is widely regarded as the key source of variation for natural selection to work on. As an example, the blood groups found in human populations originated as mutations, as have many other polymorphisms.

Other examples of genetically induced variation are recombination and drift, though few documented cases exist of either as a source of evolutionary novelty (West-Eberhard, 2003). Of course, sexual recombination is an important source of genetic variation. Via sexual reproduction the genes of the male and female are mixed (after half of the mixture has been discarded) ensuring that no two siblings will be alike, except for identical twins. Despite its minimal effect on novelty, sexual recombination is very important in the spread of alleles and their testing in different combinations. We will have much more to say about this in Chapter 3.

In theory, drift has been viewed as a potential source of evolutionary novelty since the introduction of Sewall Wright's (1932) shifting balance theory. Wright proposed that drift can initiate change due to chance combinations of existing genes, as for example, the founder effect whereby a small, genetically isolated population produces a novel developmental response that is locally favored by selection. Temporary barriers initially protect the novel combination from erasure by gene flow, then later, after barriers are removed, the consolidated adaptive trait spreads. Despite the compelling logic of Wright's theory, surprisingly little empirical evidence exists to substantiate it. Of the three possible contributors to genetically induced variation, mutation, rather than recombination and drift, seems to have the greatest importance.

Another surprising result of recent research is that the biodiversity of body plans and morphology in many organisms is not necessarily reflected in their genetic diversity, at least at the level of the sequences of genes. Even within a species, the occurrence of novel forms does not generally correlate with levels of genetic variation sufficient to account for all morphological diversity. A major question is: If the novelty of life forms we observe in nature is not always reflected in the genome, where does it come from?

Apart from mechanisms such as mutation and duplication, novelty may also arise by mutation-driven changes in gene regulation. The finding that much biodiversity is not due to differences in genes, but rather to alterations in gene regulation, has introduced an important new element into evolutionary theory (Carroll et al., 2004). Diverse organisms may have similar developmental genes but highly divergent regulatory mechanisms for these genes. Such changes in gene regulation are second-order effects of genes, resulting from the interaction and timing of activity of gene networks, as distinct from the functioning of the individual genes in the network.

The discovery of the homeotic Hox gene family in vertebrates in the 1980s allowed researchers in developmental biology to empirically assess the relative importance of gene regulation to the evolution of morphological diversity. Several biologists argue that variations in the level, pattern, or timing of gene expression may provide more variation for natural selection to act upon than changes in the gene product alone (Carroll, 2000). Only a small fraction of the genes in the genome are involved in development. Hox genes determine where limbs and other body segments will grow in a developing embryo or larva.

In addition, the organism's developmental history conditions the impact of later developmental inputs. Experiments demonstrate that the timing of an event may be critical to the development of a limb.

Consider for example the development of a chick embryo. If, at an early stage when leg and wing buds are just emerging, one removes a bit of tissue from the base of the leg bud and places it at the tip of the wing bud, there can be an interesting result. This tissue, which if left alone would have differentiated to become part of a thigh, now becomes a normal looking part of the wing tip. This is an environmental or contextual effect, because the surrounding cells "induce" it to become part of the wing by turning certain genes on or off (Rutter, 2006). It is also interesting that if such a transfer is done a bit later, it does not take; that is, one gets an anomalous glob of flesh at the tip of the wing. This is because the tissue was already "committed" to becoming leg tissue at this later phase in development. Most interesting, if the transfer is done at a precise point—not very early and not too late—one can get an amazing result. The tissue becomes not normal wing and not anomalous leg tissue, but a claw! How can this be? It is because at this point the incipient thigh tissue is already committed to becoming leg tissue, but it is not fully committed to becoming thigh. The surrounding cells can still induce it to become a tip, not the tip of a wing but rather the tip of a leg, a claw. This simple illustration supports each of the three features of development. Genes are, of course, involved. The tissue does not become a fin no matter when you transfer it. Context too is always important, in this case the surrounding cells. But so is past development, that is the timing or developmental phase. The intervening event has a notably different impact depending on when it happens; that is, depending on the prior development of the organism. (Sroufe, 1997, p. 3)

Sroufe argues on this basis that it is not genes and environment, but genes, environment, and time, or *organism* and environment, that determine growth. Genetic effects are influenced by past experience and the environmental changes it creates.

In a wide-ranging synthesis of recent work in evolutionary developmental biology West-Eberhard (2003) explores how environmentally induced variation affects development. She makes a strong case that environmental induction has the greatest potential to contribute to evolutionary novelty. Before we examine her theory of developmental plasticity let's take a brief look at previous theories of environmental sources of evolutionary novelty.

Environmental Sources of Phenotypic Variation

The idea that environmentally produced variation could fuel evolutionary change was first proposed by Jean-Baptiste Lamarck. Lamarck (1809), who preceded Charles Darwin as a major evolutionary theorist, argued that evolution was driven by the interaction of organisms with their environment, by the use and disuse of characters, a process known as *inheritance of acquired characteristics.*

In every animal which has not passed the limit of its development, a more frequent and continuous use of any organ gradually strengthens, develops and enlarges that organ, and gives it a power proportional to the length of time it has been so used; while the permanent disuse of any organ imperceptibly weakens and deteriorates it, and progressively diminishes its functional capacity, until it finally disappears. All the acquisitions or losses wrought by nature on individuals, through the influence of the environment in which their race has long been placed, and hence through the influence of the predominant use or permanent disuse of any organ; all these are preserved by reproduction to the new individuals which arise, provided that the acquired modifications are common to both sexes, or at least to the individuals which produce the young. (Lamarck, 1809, p. 113)

While widely believed in Lamarck's time, the concept of the inheritance of acquired characteristics was subsequently rejected by August Weismann

(1893), who developed a theory of inheritance in which "germ-plasm" (the hereditary material passed from parents to offspring) remained separate and distinct from "soma" (the material composing the body of an organism). According to Weismann's germ plasm theory inheritance only takes place by means of the germ cells or gametes (egg cells and sperm cells). All of the other cells of the body—somatic cells—do not function as agents of heredity. The effect is only one way: germ cells produce somatic cells but remain completely unaffected by anything the somatic cells learn or any ability the body acquires during its life. Genetic information thus cannot pass from soma to germ plasm and on to the next generation, as Lamarck proposed. This state of affairs is referred to as the Weismann barrier and is a central component of the modern evolutionary synthesis.

In the preface to one of Weismann's books, Darwin stated that "the manner in which the environment acts is as yet quite unknown. At the present time there is hardly any question in biology of more importance than this of the nature and causes of variability ..." (Darwin, 1882, p. vi, cited in West-Everhard, 2003). Notwithstanding the general demise of the theory of inheritance of acquired characteristics, scientists have continued to assert that the environment is crucial to evolutionary novelty. Ethologists and other naturalists since Baldwin (1902) have remarked that "behavior takes the lead in evolution" and that genetically based morphological changes often follow the path initiated by behavioral innovations. In this view behavior helps to create the environmental conditions under which morphological traits are selected (Wcislo, 1989). Form follows function and the resulting specialized morphological feature amplifies or enhances the initial functional behavioral pattern. A key proponent of this view that behavior takes the lead in evolution was Ernst Mayr, who believed that "behavioral shifts in the utilization of the animate and inanimate environment are by far the most important factors in macroevolution. They are involved in all major adaptive radiations and in the development of all major evolutionary novelties" (Mayr, 1974, p. 657).

The Baldwin effect, named after its originator, James Mark Baldwin, emphasized the fact that the recurring behavior of individual members of a species can shape the evolution of that species. The "Baldwin effect" is a trait change that occurs in an organism as a result of its interaction with its environment that becomes gradually assimilated into its genetic/ epigenetic repertoire. This happens because of the differential survival of individuals who learn to respond appropriately to novel, adverse, and recurring environment conditions (Baldwin, 1902).

For example, suppose a species of squirrel is threatened by a new predator (automobiles) and there is a behavior that makes it more difficult for these four-wheeled predators to kill squirrels (monitoring approaching cars). Individuals who learn the behavior more quickly will obviously be at an advantage. As time goes on the ability to learn the behavior will improve (by genetic selection), and at some point it may even appear to be an instinct. In Chapter 7 we will examine just such a case in our discussion of whether monkeys' widespread fear of snakes is learned or innate. Another oft-cited example is the evolution of lactose tolerance in human populations with a long tradition of raising domesticated animals for milk. This argument holds that a feedback loop operates whereby a dairy culture increases the selective advantage for this genetic trait, while the spread of the trait within a tribal population increases the collective rewards of a dairy culture. While still controversial after more than 100 years, the "Baldwin effect" should not be confused with Lamarck's concept of the "inheritance of acquired characters" discussed previously. It does not imply that the advantageous response somehow becomes genetically determined (as implied by Lamarck), but only that the genes underlying the ability to produce the response spread in a population due to selection.

Of course, modern day evolutionists have not been idle regarding the evolutionary role of the environment; we next explore contributions from the field of evolutionary developmental biology.

☐ Evolution of Development

The emerging discipline of evolutionary developmental biology gained impetus from the discovery of genes regulating embryonic development. Evolutionary developmental biology (EDB) is the branch of biology that compares the developmental processes of different species in order to understand the nature of development itself and how it evolved. It addresses the origin and evolution of embryonic development, how modifications of developmental processes lead to the production of novel features, and the role of developmental plasticity in evolution.

We have seen how evolution proceeds by "tinkering," shuffling the deck of genetic material and recombining what is already available in novel ways. Just as evolution tends to create new genes from parts of old genes, evolution also rearranges developmental processes to create novel structures, often conserving a similar program or module in a host of organisms.

EDB came of age with the advent of high-speed computers that permitted more detailed understanding of the molecular basis of developmental mechanisms. Current studies examine how the dynamics of development determine the phenotypic variation arising from genetic variation and how that affects the direction of evolution. EDB can be distinguished from earlier approaches by its focus on a few crucial ideas. One of these is modularity: the organization of the organism into anatomically distinct parts. Often these parts are repeated, such as fingers or ribs. Researchers are exploring the genetic and evolutionary basis for the division of the embryo into distinct modules and for the partly independent development of such modules.

Another central idea is that some gene products function as switches whereas others act as diffusible signals. Genes specify proteins, some of which act as structural components of cells and others as enzymes that regulate various biochemical pathways within an organism. It is no longer plausible to assume that an organism is a straightforward reflection of its component genes. Because traits are regulated by switches, they can be turned on and off and recombined with other modules by very minor changes in the genome. This accounts for the fact that phenotypically diverse organisms share a large percentage of their component genes.

The birth of EDB might be traced to a 1961 discovery by Jacques Monod, Jean-Pierre Changeux, and François Jacob. They discovered within a bacterium a gene that functioned only when "switched on" by an environmental stimulus (Monod, Changeux, & Jacob, 1963). Later, scientists discovered specific genes in animals, including a subgroup of the genes, called Hox genes, that act as switches for other genes, and could be induced by other gene products, morphogens, that act analogously to the external stimuli in bacteria. These discoveries drew biologists' attention to the fact that genes can be selectively turned on and off, rather than being always active, and that highly disparate organisms (for example, fruit flies and human beings) may use the same genes for embryogenesis, just regulating them differently.

In addition to providing new support for Darwin's assertion that all organisms are descended from a common ancestor, this finding suggested that the crucial distinction between different species may be due less to differences in the content of their gene products than to differences in spatial and temporal expression of their genes. The implication that major evolutionary changes in body morphology are associated with changes in gene regulation, rather than the evolution of new genes, suggests that the action of natural selection on promoters responsive to Hox and other "switch" genes may play a major role in evolution.

Another focus of EDB is developmental plasticity or the recognition that phenotypes are not uniquely determined by their genotypes. If the generation of phenotypes is conditional, and dependent on external or environmental inputs, evolution can proceed by a "phenotype-first" route with genetic change following, rather than initiating, the formation of morphological and other phenotypic novelties. We shall discuss the specifics of "neural plasticity" in the construction of the brain in Chapter 5.

Summarizing the various means by which evolutionary novelty may be introduced we now see that the model presented earlier in Figure 1.7 is incomplete. What must be added is a pathway from environmental

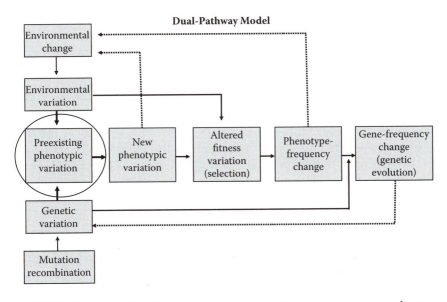

FIGURE 1.8   Causal relations between environment, genes, phenotype, and selection in adaptive evolution. New phenotypic variation can begin with either environmental change (top) or genetic change (bottom). Dashed arrows indicate feedback among variables. (Adapted from West-Eberhard, 2003.)

variation to phenotypic variation. Thus, West-Eberhard (2003) presents a dual pathway model for the introduction of variation that fuels adaptive evolution (Figure 1.8).

The initiation of a novel trait in the organism (the phenotype) could be due to genetically driven processes (mutation, genetic recombination, or new genetic combinations caused by drift) or to environmentally driven processes. "Environmentally induced novelty can spread without positive selection due to spread or recurrence of the conditions inducing them, without special restrictions as to population structure or developmental linkage to other traits. They can be heritable if there is genetic variation in the developmental capacity to produce them in response to an environmental input" (West-Eberhard, 2003, p. 144). Moreover, environmentally induced traits may be immediately recurrent because of the prevalence of the inducing feature of the environment, and more likely to spread than mutations that can be quickly eliminated by natural selection. As a result of modularity and plasticity, the organism has the capacity to respond to new situations that recur with a novel trait, which then is able to spread throughout a population via selection for the ability required to produce the trait. For these reasons, West-Eberhard considers environmental induction to have greater potential in introducing adaptive traits in a species.

☐ Chapter Summary

The modern theory of evolution owes its existence to two remarkable 19th-century scientists, Charles Darwin and Gregor Mendel, who provided the key mechanisms of evolution by natural selection and heredity, respectively. In contrast to previous theories of evolution, Darwinian evolution was not teleological or inherently progressive towards some ideal. Instead, it simply proceeded by chance opportunities and the necessary demands of the environment that inevitably winnowed out less fit organisms from the gene pool. Darwin was the first to grasp the full significance of natural selection as an answer to the question of adaptive design in nature. Adaptation is a central concept in evolutionary biology; it refers to the characteristics of living organisms that enable them to survive and reproduce in a particular environment. Darwin also introduced the concept of sexual selection as a specific form of natural selection that arises "from the advantage that certain individuals have over other individuals of the same sex and species, in exclusive relation to reproduction" (1871, p. 256).

The modern synthesis arose in the 1930s as a result of the efforts of Wright, Fisher, and Haldane, who proposed a workable integration of Darwin's theory of evolution with Mendelian genetics. This integration posits that heritable traits are determined by genes and that natural selection and sexual selection, rather than mutation, is the principal means of evolution.

Darwin drew upon the following four independent sources of evidence to support his claim that all species evolved by natural selection: paleontology, biogeography, morphology, and embryology. Ring species are especially significant because they show that the process of anagenesis, or the gradual transformation of a species by natural selection, can in some cases lead to speciation, or the evolution of reproductively isolated populations into distinct species. Contemporary biology also provides a number of distinct sources of evidence in support of Darwin from the following scientific disciplines that did not exist in his day, including biochemistry, molecular biology, population genetics, and genomics. Molecular biologists can now resolve debates about human origins or study the precise molecular changes that arise to provide new strains of HIV, one of many examples of evolution as an observable fact of nature. Understanding the evolutionary process by which HIV acquires its resistance to an antiviral drug has been the key to improving treatment by means of more effective multiple drug "cocktails" that greatly slow the evolution of the virus within the patient. The same evolutionary logic applies to other similarly futile attempts of human technology to control nature through the production of various antibiotics, insecticides, and herbicides.

The key insight of the classical ethologists was to extend the operation of natural selection beyond physical features to behavior. Within the framework provided by evolutionary theory, ethologists address four basic questions concerning behavior: evolution, development, causation, and function. A fundamental distinction is made regarding a similarity between species that can be traced to a common origin (homology) and one that has been produced through independent but convergent lines of evolution (analogy). From an ethological perspective, the child is not assumed to be born a tabula rasa, or blank slate, upon which the environment acts. Rather the child is capable of actively engaging the environment from birth, with inborn predispositions, preferences, and reflexes that have been shaped by natural selection to provide an adaptive advantage.

Development is directly linked to evolution by two unavoidable facts: (1) it is the phenotype that is the target of selection, and (2) the phenotype is a product of development involving both genetic and environmental determinants. Thus, evolution involves the generation of variable phenotypes, then the screening of these individual variants by selection, and finally the retention and transmission of the selected variants in future generations. A surprising result of recent research is that the biodiversity of body plans and morphology in many organisms is not necessarily reflected in their genetic diversity, at least at the level of the sequences of genes. Several biologists argue that variations in the level, pattern, or timing of gene expression may provide more variation for natural selection to act upon than changes in the gene product alone.

The idea that environmentally produced variation could fuel evolutionary change was first proposed by Jean-Baptiste Lamarck (1809), who preceded Charles Darwin as a major evolutionary theorist. He argued that evolution was driven by the interaction of organisms with their environment, by the use and disuse of characters, a process known as "inheritance of acquired characteristics." This was later rejected by Weismann's germ plasm theory.

The "Baldwin effect" is a trait change that occurs in an organism as a result of its interaction with its environment that becomes gradually assimilated into its genetic/epigenetic repertoire. Its underlying mechanism is the differential survival of individuals who learn to respond appropriately to novel, adverse, and recurring environment conditions (Baldwin, 1902).

According to contemporary evolutionary developmental biologists, the initiation of a novel trait in the organism (the phenotype) could be due to genetically driven processes or to environmentally driven processes. Evolutionary developmental biology (EDB) is the branch of biology that addresses the origin and evolution of embryonic development; how modifications of developmental processes lead to the production of novel features; and the role of developmental plasticity in evolution. Developmental plasticity implies that phenotypes are not uniquely determined by their genotypes. If the generation of phenotypes depends on both genetic and environmental inputs, evolution can proceed by a "phenotype-first" route with genetic change following, rather than initiating, the formation of morphological and other phenotypic novelties.

☐ For Further Inquiry

Carroll, S. B., Grenier, J. K., & Weatherbee, S. D. (2004). *From DNA to diversity: Molecular genetics and the evolution of animal design* (2nd ed.). New York, NY: Norton.

Ridley, M. (1996). *Evolution* (2nd ed.). Cambridge, MA: Blackwell Science.

West-Eberhard, M. J. (2003). *Developmental plasticity and evolution*. London, UK: Oxford University Press.

Videos and information for teachers and students by PBS: http://www.pbs.org/wgbh/evolution/index.html

CHAPTER 2

Contemporary Evolutionary Perspectives

☐ Sociobiology

Another discipline to emerge from the modern synthesis and classical ethology was sociobiology, a term made at once popular and controversial with the publication of E. O. Wilson's comprehensive opus, *Sociobiology: The New Synthesis*. Wilson (1975) defined *sociobiology* as the "systematic study of the biological basis of social behavior." If Wilson had confined his analysis of social behavior to nonhuman animals there would have been no controversy. Indeed, many of the principles of sociobiology were initially worked out in both logical and empirical terms within the traditional biological disciplines of entomology and zoology. Like Darwin and Lorenz before him, Wilson got into hot water for daring to suppose that the principles of sociobiology also applied to humans, a position that is now both widespread and not particularly controversial.

In contrast to the popular media, including unfortunately many college textbooks, I will not jump into a discussion of political or ethical considerations that are presumed (often incorrectly) to stem from applying evolutionary theory to human behavior. Besides the illogic of "putting the cart in front of the horse," the other problem with this common approach is that it presumes that a scientific theory should be judged on its alleged political implications rather than on the basis of the standards of scientific methodology and empirical evidence. Even these necessary and valid critiques must await the even-handed presentation of the core concepts of the theory, which is my sole intent here in Chapter 2. So, just what is sociobiology and what was all the fuss about?

Sociobiology builds directly on the foundations of the modern synthesis, which have not been seriously questioned by biologists since they were established by the work of Fischer, Haldane, and Wright before the mid-20th century. This is not to say that evolutionary theory has not advanced. Indeed, many of the key theoretical advances that have been incorporated into 21st-century evolutionary thought were summarized by Wilson in 1975. In this brief account, I shall focus on four key concepts that were all part of the theoretical biologists' toolkit 30 years before the advent of evolutionary psychology. These key advances were made by the sociobiologists William D. Hamilton and Robert Trivers.

Inclusive Fitness and Reciprocal Altruism

Considered by many as one of the most important evolutionary theorists since Darwin, Hamilton (1964) is most well known for his concept of kin altruism or inclusive fitness. The characterization of animal behavior as "red in tooth and claw" does not acknowledge the widespread presence of altruism in the animal world where an individual can be observed helping others, sometimes at its own expense. But if evolution programs animals to behave out of self-interest how can evolutionary theory account for altruism?

As many naturalists before him, Hamilton recognized that such apparent acts of altruism were most common between kin. He therefore devised a formula $c < rb$, where c equals the cost to the actor, r is the degree of genetic relatedness between the actor and the recipient, and b is the benefit. It is important to remember that both costs and benefits are calculated in the currency of reproductive success. The direct fitness of the individual (direct offspring) plus the gain in reproductive success from indirect fitness (the offspring of relatives weighted by their degree of relatedness) equals *inclusive fitness*. Rather than always behaving out of self-interest, evolutionists view animals as behaving in ways that maximize inclusive fitness.

Following Hamilton's rule, evolutionists expect animals to help those with whom they share genes "by common descent." A coefficient of relatedness can be calculated so r in the formula can be assigned to different relatives. Identical twins share 100% their genes, parents share 50% with their offspring as do biological siblings and fraternal twins, grandparents-grandchildren, aunts/uncles-nieces/nephews share 25% and so on. The more genes that are shared, the greater the likelihood of altruism. A common misinterpretation of kin altruism is that animals (including humans) must be able to perform these calculations in their head or are constantly trying to figure out some aspect of the equation. This is definitely not the case in nonhuman animals, and even with respect to humans, there is no assumption that such calculations are conscious.

The problem of altruism in evolutionary theory stimulated Harvard theorist Robert Trivers (1971) to work out an additional explanation for the existence of altruism. Rather than the widespread nepotism in animals where parents are observed to provide care and even sacrifice their lives for their offspring, Trivers focused his attention on human acts of altruism directed towards nonkin. Could these acts, which seem to contradict the "selfish gene" view of individual selection, be explained by evolutionary theory as well?

Trivers begins his analysis by borrowing Hamilton's rule and removing the "kin" from kin altruism. Thus the formula $c < rb$ reduces to $c < b$. In other words, for nonkin altruism to exist the cost to the actor must be less than the benefit to the recipient. Two other prerequisites are needed to establish Trivers' concept of *reciprocal altruism*. First, individuals must be able to recognize each other in order to "keep accounts." This allows the individual to reciprocate with "honest players" and to detect and punish "cheaters." Second, individuals should have a reasonably long lifespan to allow for the reciprocal relationship between two individuals to establish itself in repeated contacts.

These prerequisites of reciprocal altruism make it unlikely that mosquitoes engage in reciprocal altruism. Indeed, although reciprocal altruism is possible among animals and various examples in species like dolphins, birds, and primates have been documented, the consensus among zoologists is that such occurrences are relatively rare (Slater, 1994). As Trivers recognized, however, reciprocity among humans is more the rule than the exception.

Parental Investment and Parent–Offspring Conflict

The cost/benefit analysis that gave rise to the concepts of kin altruism and reciprocal altruism can also be fruitfully applied to the problem of parental investment. It is obvious from the preceding discussion that it is in the genetic self-interest of parents to provide care for their own offspring. Robert Trivers' contribution stems from his recognition that there are limits to what parents should be willing to invest. Thus, *parental investment* is defined as "any investment by the parent in an individual offspring that increases the offspring's chance of surviving at the cost of the parent's ability to invest in other offspring" (Trivers, 1972).

Trivers went on to specify that there is typically a difference in the degree of parental investment in offspring favoring females that results in a marked asymmetry in roles. Mating competition would be expected to be greater in the lower-investing sex, while mate choice would be expected to be greater in the higher-investing sex. Thus, most, but not all, examples of sexual selection involve either male-male competition or female choice. These forces are thought to account for much of the observable sexual dimorphism across a wide variety of species. We will have a great deal more to say about the implications of sexual selection and parental investment theory when we discuss the evolution of mate choice and female and male reproductive strategies in Chapter 12.

Shortly after outlining the evolutionary logic of parental investment, Trivers (1974) realized that from the standpoint of maximizing inclusive fitness an inevitable conflict of interest arises between the parent and offspring. In examining his conceptualization of parent-offspring conflict it is important to understand that the biological imperative of maximizing fitness operates differently on the two generations involved. Let us examine each perspective using the example of weaning.

The primate reproductive strategy is one of high investment in few offspring, usually only one at a time. A primate mother expends considerable care on her newborn, including the biological costs of providing milk. While it "pays" for her to invest greatly, it would not pay for her to invest absolutely. There comes a time, late in infancy, when the offspring is better prepared to feed herself, and the mother is biologically ready to breed again. At a certain point in time, the mother's optimal strategy is to wean the first infant in preparation for reproducing another. Now here's the catch. *This point in time arrives sooner for the mother than for the infant since she shares 50% of her genes with both offspring.* From the older sibling's perspective it would be beneficial to entice her mother to continue to invest in her well-being up to the point when her new sibling would benefit twice as much as herself, *since she shares 50% of her genes with her sibling but 100% with herself.* Moreover, if the fathers were different between siblings as is common in nonhuman primates, they would then share only 25% of their genes by common descent, and parent-offspring conflict and sibling rivalry would then be predicted to be still greater.

Together these four concepts: (1) inclusive fitness, (2) reciprocal altruism, (3) parental investment, and (4) parent-offspring conflict enabled sociobiologists to reframe an evolutionary account of social behavior of all animals from insects to elephants that rested squarely on the new view of natural selection at the level of the individual. As Oxford biologist Richard Dawkins (1976) expounded in *The Selfish Gene*, social behavior could be best accounted for if one decentered and viewed genes as the center of the biological universe, with the organism relegated to a temporary vehicle for transmitting genes from one generation to the next. In his *Sociobiology: The New Synthesis*, the eminent Harvard entomologist, E. O. Wilson (1975) was the first to develop a comprehensive explanation for the evolution of social behavior of all species great and small, simple and complex, that rested upon the ideas developed in the Modern

Synthesis of evolutionary biology, together with the conceptual advances of Hamilton and Trivers.

☐ Multilevel Selection Theory

During the heyday of sociobiology during the 1960s, 1970s, and 1980s the question of altruism rose to the forefront of evolutionary thinking. Indeed, it would be difficult to overestimate the theoretical importance of altruism in sociobiological accounts of behavior. Altruism appears to be deeply problematic from certain evolutionary perspectives because, by definition, it implies that individuals engage in behavior that benefits others at one's own expense and thus would be selected against. Such behavior could not evolve if selection operates only at the level of the individual—the selfish gene principle (Dawkins, 1976). However, altruism could evolve as the result of natural selection at the level of the group, and indeed, beginning with Darwin, several influential theorists have put forward this possibility (Darwin, 1871):

> It must not be forgotten that although a high standard of morality gives but a slight or no advantage to each individual man and his children of the same tribe, yet an increase in the number of well-endowed men and advancement in the standard of morality will certainly give an immense advantage to one tribe over another. A tribe including many members who, possessing in a high degree the spirit of patriotism, fidelity, obedience, courage, and sympathy, who were always ready to aid one another, and to sacrifice themselves for the common good, would be victorious over most other tribes; and this would be natural selection. (p. 500)

In two sentences Darwin announces a fundamental problem of social life and provides for its solution in evolutionary terms. This quote is the starting point for most arguments in favor of multilevel selection theory. It is universally recognized that the chief difficulty with the spread of altruistic genes within any group of individuals is that genes for group advantageous behavior are seldom advantageous for the individual who acts to benefit the group and consequently they are generally selected against within groups. For Darwin, the solution was to recognize that natural selection can operate at more than one level, including the level of selection between competing groups. In short, *selfishness beats altruism within groups. Altruistic groups beat selfish groups.*

Thus, multilevel selection theory is a theory of evolution by natural selection that recognizes possible trade-offs in the selection of heritable traits at different levels of selection. At the within-group level, a trait for morality, that increases the fitness of other group members at the expense of the individual's own fitness, will decline to extinction over time within the group. Multilevel selection theory solves this dilemma by positing that the same trait will increase in the total population if groups possessing the trait are more likely to out-compete groups that do not possess the trait. Ultimately selection for the trait within the total population (species) will depend upon the relative speed and potency of within- and between-group selection. As we shall see in Chapter 13 this rather simple equation is complicated by many factors.

But do group-level adaptations actually exist? In historical terms, the answer is emphatically yes (1871–1965), emphatically no (1966–1996), and emphatically yes again (1997–present). See for example a recent article entitled "The Rise, Fall, and Resurrection of Group Selection" (Borrello, 2005). The full details of this dialectic are beyond the scope of this introductory text, but the interested reader can consult a brief historical treatment of this central issue in evolutionary biology written by two well-known scholars who helped shaped the debate over the past three decades, D. S. Wilson and E. O. Wilson (2007). In short, they conclude that group selection, once vilified as heresy within the ranks of sociobiologists, has made a startling comeback based upon further review of the evidence.

Group selection refers to the idea that genes (alleles) can spread in a population because of the benefits they bestow on groups (in competition with other groups), regardless of their effect on the fitness of individuals within that group. Group selection was used as a popular explanation for adaptations, especially by V. C. Wynne-Edwards (1962, 1986). For several decades, however, critiques, particularly by George C. Williams (1966), John Maynard Smith (1976), and Richard Dawkins (1976, 1982) cast serious doubt on group selection as a major mechanism of evolution, and only recently have group selection models been resurrected.

The theoretical models of the 1960s implied that the effect of group selection was negligible for two reasons. First, alleles are likely to be held on a population-wide level, leaving nothing for group selection to select for. Second, generation time is much longer for groups than it is for individuals. Assuming opposite selection pressures, individual selection will occur much faster, swamping any changes potentially favored by group selection (Ridley, 2004).

The comeback began in the late 1970s when experimental results demonstrated that group selection was far more effective than extant theoretical models ever would have predicted. A review of this experimental work has shown that the early group selection models were flawed because they assumed that genes acted independently, whereas in the experimental work it was apparent that gene interaction, and more importantly, genetically based interactions among individuals, were an important source of the response to group selection (e.g., Wade, 1977). As a result many began to recognize that group selection, or more appropriately multilevel selection, could be a potentially important force in evolution.

Spatial populations of predators and prey have also been shown to show restraint of reproduction at equilibrium, both individually (Rauch, Sayama, & Bar-Yam, 2003) and through social communication (Werfel & Bar-Yam, 2004), as originally proposed by Wynne-Edwards. While these spatial populations do not have well-defined groups for group selection, the local spatial interactions of organisms in transient groups are sufficient to lead to a kind of multilevel selection. There is, however, as yet no evidence that these processes operate in the situations where Wynne-Edwards posited them; the analysis by Rauch et al. (2003) is of a host-parasite situation, which was recognized as a context where group selection was possible earlier by E. O. Wilson (1975), in a treatise broadly hostile to the whole idea of group selection.

In more recent years, the limitations of earlier models have been addressed, and newer models suggest that selection may sometimes act above the gene level. David Sloan Wilson and Elliot Sober have long argued that the case against group selection had always been overstated. They focus their argument on whether groups can have functional organization in the same way individuals do and, consequently, if groups can also be "vehicles" for selection. Echoing Darwin, they hold that groups that were able to cooperate effectively may have out-reproduced those that did not. Wilson and Sober's new version of group selection is usually referred to as multilevel selection theory (Sober & Wilson, 1998; Wilson & Sober, 1994).

Multilevel selection theory has also been invoked to explain what Maynard Smith & Szathmary (1995) refer to as *major transitions in evolution*—transitions that shift the unit of selection from solitary replicators to networks of replicators enclosed within compartments. A number of authors have explored the question why lower-level selection did not disrupt the formation of the higher-level unit using multilevel selection theory (Frank 1999; Maynard Smith & Szathmary, 1995; Michod, 1997, 1999; Wilson & Wilson, 2007). The concept of such *superorganisms* or groups of cooperating organisms that transform themselves into a single organism has a long lineage (Wheeler, 1911) but it has reemerged as a viable concept in recent years. In her pioneering account of the evolution of the eukaryotic cell, Margulis (1970) argued that this advanced type of nucleated cell (common to all plants and animals) did not evolve by incremental steps from the more basic prokaryotic cell (common in bacteria). Rather a transition occurred in which symbiotic associations of bacteria became so fully integrated as a unit that they emerged as single organisms.

Throughout the evolution of life forms, major transitions have involved shifts from independent genes to chromosomes, from prokaryotic cells to eukaryotic cells containing organelles, from unicellular to multicellular organisms, and from solitary organisms to colonies. Some of these transitions occurred in the distant evolutionary past, others much more recently. In each case, a number of smaller units, originally capable of surviving and reproducing on their own, coalesced into a single larger unit, thus generating a new level of biological organization. The challenge is to understand *why* it was advantageous for the lower-level units to cooperate with one another, and form a larger unit, not *whether* such transitions took place.

In the transition to multicellularity, for example, we need to know why selection between competing cell lineages did not disrupt the integrity of the emerging multicellular organism. One possibility is that selection acted on the higher-level units themselves, leading them to evolve adaptations that minimize conflict and increase cooperation among their constituent parts. Thus, in the case of multicellularity, Bass (1988) and Michod (1997) argue that early sequestration of the germ line may be one such adaptation, for it reduces the probability that mutant cells, arising during ontogeny, will find their way into the next generation. Another idea is that passing the life cycle through a single-celled stage, as occurs in most animal and plant species, is an adaptation for minimizing within-organism conflict, for it increases the relatedness, and hence decreases the competition, between the cells within an organism. These particular examples have both been contested, but the general idea that the major transitions involve an interaction between selection at different levels is now widely accepted (Okasha, 2004).

It follows that levels of selection other than that of the individual organism *must* have existed in the past. Thus, the argument that individual selection is "all that matters in practice" is no longer tenable. The very concept of major transitions refutes the once common dogma that higher-level selection is always weaker than lower-level selection (Wilson & Wilson, 2007). Okasha (2005) offers this succinct summary of the theoretical implications of this view for sociobiology:

> Since cells and multi-celled creatures obviously have evolved, and function well as adaptive units, the efficacy of group selection cannot be denied. Just as the blanket assumption that the individual organism is the sole unit of selection is untenable from a diachronic perspective, so too is the assumption that group selection is a negligible force. For by "frameshifting" our perspective downwards, it becomes apparent that individual organisms are cooperative groups, so are the *product* of group selection! (p. 1008)

Even in the earlier discussions, it was recognized that entities at different levels of hierarchical organization form a temporal sequence, that is, lower-level entities must evolve before higher-level ones much as they do in ontogeny. Consider, for example, Richard Dawkins' (1982) brief discussion of how independently replicating units may originally have become grouped into compartments. Dawkins says that it is "easily understood" why independent replicators might have gained an advantage by "ganging up together" into cell-like compartments, because their biochemical effects might have complemented each other (p. 252). This is a plausible idea, but does it not in effect invoke group selection? Replicating molecules combining themselves into compartments is strictly analogous to individual organisms combining themselves into colonies or groups. But Dawkins remains an implacable *opponent* of group selection, insisting that it is negligible as an evolutionary force (Okasha, 2004).

☐ Evolutionary Psychology

The most recent step in the Darwinian revolution was taken by the school of evolutionary psychology, which is the direct descendant of sociobiology. We have already seen that Darwin developed the idea that natural selection systematically shaped the characteristics of living organisms that enable them to survive and reproduce in a particular environment. Lorenz (1973) realized that the sensory/perception systems and brains of organisms must have evolved in order to respond to those stable features of external reality that were critically involved in their survival and reproduction. Lorenz viewed the innate structures of thought, language and emotional expression in humans to be excellent examples of phylogenetic adaptations. Contemporary evolutionary psychologists focus their research on understanding the design features of the cognitive abilities of the human mind and the organic structures of the human brain that support mental operations.

Basic Assumptions

Like their predecessors, evolutionary psychologists articulate an alternative framework to the Standard Social Science Model (SSSM) or the prevailing notion that the contents of human minds are social constructions, and the view that the social sciences are autonomous and disconnected from any evolutionary or biological foundation (Tooby & Cosmides, 1992). According to the SSSM view the human mind resembles a blank slate, virtually free of content until written on by the hand of experience. Domain-general mechanisms are thought to govern all aspects of the mind, including reasoning, learning, memory, and language. Because these mechanisms are assumed to operate uniformly, according to unchanging principles, regardless of the content they are operating on or the larger domain involved, they are described as *domain-general*.

In contrast to the SSSM, evolutionary psychologists assume that "all normal human minds reliably develop a standard collection of reasoning and regulatory circuits that are functionally specialized and, frequently, domain-specific. These circuits organize the way we interpret our experiences, inject certain recurrent concepts and motivations into our mental life, and provide universal frames of meaning that allow us to understand the actions and intentions of others" (Tooby & Cosmides, 1992, p. 3).

Below are five basic principles that evolutionary psychologists Cosmides and Tooby apply to any topic in psychology in their attempts to understand the design of the human mind:

1. The brain is a physical system. It functions as a computer. Its circuits are designed to generate behavior that is appropriate to your environmental circumstances.
2. Our neural circuits were designed by natural selection to solve problems that our ancestors faced during our species' evolutionary history.
3. Consciousness is just the tip of the iceberg; most of what goes on in your mind is hidden from you. As a result, your conscious experience can mislead you into thinking that our circuitry is simpler than it really is. Most problems that you experience as easy to solve are very difficult to solve—they require very complicated neural circuitry.
4. Different neural circuits are specialized for solving different adaptive problems.
5. Our modern skulls house a Stone Age mind.

The same functionalist perspective that guides research in ethology and sociobiology guides research questions in evolutionary psychology. They all share the view that only natural and sexual selection can introduce complex functional organization into a species' phenotype (Dawkins, 1986; Williams, 1966). This functional level of explanation is essential for understanding how selection pressures design brains. The primary function of the brain is to generate adaptive behavior, behavior that is sensitively contingent upon information from an organism's environment. The patterning of information can vary along a continuum ranging from patterns that are stable across generations to patterns that can fluctuate within a short amount of time. Three-dimensional space is an example of a stable, universal pattern of information and the visual system has evolved to provide animals with relevant perceptual faculties to navigate this space. If distinguishing color is critical to the organism, color vision is also likely to evolve. Predatory hunters like hawks and eagles would evolve especially keen vision to detect small movements from long distances, and so on. In this manner invariant conditions that are of importance to the organism create the selection pressures for the evolution of modularized brain and cognitive systems (Geary & Huffman, 2002; Tooby & Cosmides, 1995), whereas dynamic conditions create pressures for plasticity and the evolution of less modularized, domain-general systems (Chiappe & MacDonald, 2005; Geary, 2005).

As shown in Figure 2.1, human cognitive modules can be organized with respect to the domains of folk psychology, folk biology, and folk physics (corresponding to selection pressures from the social, biological, and physical ecology of human adaptation). There is evidence for plasticity within these modularized domains, as well as evidence for domain-general brain and cognitive systems that operate on information patterns generated by modularized brain and cognitive systems (Geary, 2005). These domain-general systems are known as general fluid intelligence (Cattell, 1963).

In this textbook, we make no assumptions regarding the extent to which the human mind is modular by design. Although there is certainly some degree of modularity for specialized functions like language and

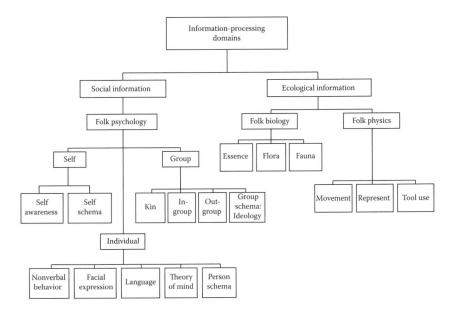

FIGURE 2.1 Evolutionarily salient information processing domains and associated cognitive modules that compose the domains of folk psychology, folk biology, and folk physics. (Adapted from Geary, D. C. (2005). *The origin of mind: Evolution of brain, cognition, and general intelligence*. Washington, DC: American Psychological Association. With permission.)

facial recognition, it is also apparent that much of our capacity for adapting to novel problems encountered in our modern environment relies upon domain-general information processing. Elsewhere I have argued that while pursuing their agenda of documenting domain-specific mechanisms, evolutionary psychologists must retain a central role for domain-general human adaptations, particularly those adaptations that rely upon cortical processing (LaFreniere, 2005). Domain-general mechanisms are the hallmark of human adaptation and give our species its unique flexibility to successfully adapt to a wide range of environmental demands. By their very nature, domain-general mechanisms are better suited than domain-specific mechanisms in environments where individuals face novel and fluctuating problems requiring flexibility and insight (Chiappe & MacDonald, 2005; Geary, 2005). In the end, the relative degree of domain specificity versus generality of the human mind remains an open and essentially empirical question.

The especially long developmental period that evolved in humans provides opportunities for adjusting and fine-tuning folk modules and knowledge. The necessity for this developmental plasticity derives from the complexity of social relationships and the wide range of biological and ecological niches occupied by humans. In each domain, there is evidence for both inherent constraints that guide attention to invariant information patterns, such as human voice patterns (Freedman, 1974), and experience-based modifications of the associated systems to accommodate variation, such as recognition of individual voices (Pascalis, de Haan, & Nelson, 2002). From this perspective, developmental plasticity functions to adapt modular systems to nuances of the local ecology (Geary, 2005).

Geary introduced the concept of soft modularity as a recognition of the inherent plasticity of human development and adaptation even when evolved modules provide the necessary starting point for development. Soft modularity can take three different forms: (1) mechanisms that allocate brain resources depending on particular environmental demands, (2) mechanisms that enable the creation of new categories according to environmental demands, and (3) modules that have evolved an invariant range of domain-specific information (e.g., human speech sounds). Interaction with the environment is often essential to hone adaptation of evolved phylogenetic systems to specific circumstances, and we will discuss examples of how domain-specific systems are open to environmental modification throughout this book.

Because different theorists use the term "module" somewhat differently, Geary and Huffman (2002) outline four hierarchical levels of modular organization. The most basic level of organization is the neural module, which may be described as a region of the sensory cortex. Next, perceptual modules arise from the activity patterns of neural modules and provide a complex and abstracted representation of the environment as perceived by the organism through their sensory apparatus. Recall that what the organism sees depends on the type of visual system a particular species has evolved, which in turn depends upon the adaptational needs of the organism in the visual realm. The next level of abstraction moves from sensory perception up to a meaning-based representation or cognition and thus is referred to as a cognitive module. Finally, a functional module integrates the information coming from the lower-level modules with the affect and motivation of the organism to guide its behavior in pursuit of evolutionary significant goals. Notice that although natural selection operates on the behavioral output, it also has the power to shape the evolution of all the lower-level modules upon which the behavior is based.

In addition, once a lower-level module has evolved it can be used as a building block to assemble a new, complex cognitive module without needing to evolve all of the constituent parts de novo. In this way evolution acts as a "tinkerer" perpetually adjusting templates derived from lower-level modules in assembling new higher-level modules, without having to "reinvent the wheel" each time (Geary, 2005; Marcus, 2004). In more formal terms, new functional modules can emerge with rather minor evolutionary changes in the underlying genotype by reorganizing existing lower-level modules into new functional units.

A functionalist perspective places a great deal of emphasis on the search for evidence of adaptive design, but as Darwin himself recognized, while nature's designs may be intricate and ingenious, they are not perfect. Natural selection can only select from existing alternative designs on the basis of how well each solves adaptive problems. This process of selection has produced intricate designs that solve all sorts of adaptive problems from stereoscopic color vision to optimal foraging algorithms, designs that can exceed the reach of any human engineer. But not all species-typical characteristics are functional products of natural selection. Some are merely spinoffs and byproducts of functional designs; others may simply reflect noise in the system. Certainly one can never assume that all existing traits of organisms are currently functional.

An especially important caveat regarding evolved cognitive modules is that these mechanisms may not necessarily generate adaptive behavior today, because they evolved during the Environment of Evolutionary Adaptedness or EEA. As a relatively new species, the human EEA is sometimes specified as the African savannah during the Pleistocene. However, strictly speaking, the EEA is not a specific place or time, but rather the composite of all selection pressures that produced an adaptation. Thus, the EEA for one human adaptation may be different from that for another. The limbic system that governs our basic emotions evolved during the mammalian radiation over 200 million years ago (MYA), but the biology underlying human male provisioning of offspring is not shared with other mammals and arose during the human EEA within the past two million years. Many human adaptations, particularly those mediated by the neocortex and exclusive to us (e.g., language), must have evolved relatively recently, since the constellation of design features that make human speech possible exists in no other species.

To the extent that the present-day environment of humans has changed from that of our EEA, some mechanisms may actually be a source of maladaptation. We will refer to this possible state of affairs as the *mismatch hypothesis*. An example of such a mismatch would be our tendency to enjoy sweets. Such a taste may have once been adaptive in an environment where fruit was scarce, but it can now generate maladaptive behavior in an environment with a ready supply of sugar and artificial sweeteners. Despite such problems such a tendency is likely to persist indefinitely in the future of our species, since there is no mechanism available for the rapid de-evolution of once adaptive traits. We will return to the mismatch hypothesis in greater detail in our discussion of Darwinian medicine in Chapter 12.

□ Evidence of Adaptive Design

A major challenge of evolutionary psychology is to specify the criteria necessary for discriminating the features of the human mind that represent phylogenetic adaptations from other characteristics of the mind. What would constitute conclusive evidence for an evolved psychological mechanism?

This problem of identifying adaptations was initially considered by George Williams (1966) in his classic work *Adaptation and Natural Selection*. The first criterion for identifying a potential evolved psychological mechanism is the same as for any phylogenetic adaption: it must solve a specific and recurring problem of adaptation. Finding that it solves an adaptive problem with "reliability, efficiency, and economy" is then prima facie evidence that one has located an adaptation (Williams, 1966).

Williams was acutely aware of the problem of overattributing evolved adaptations to behavior that did not require such explanations, and this conservative posture reached an extreme in the writings of Gould and Lewontin (1979) who argued that evolutionary psychologists are prone to see adaptations everywhere, often in the absence of empirical evidence. Other critics point out weaknesses in the current evolutionary psychology paradigm that stem from an overemphasis on modularity or domain-specific mechanisms of the mind at the expense of domain-general views.

Evolutionary psychologists contend that "the mind is organized into modules or mental organs, each with a specialized design that makes it an expert in one arena of interaction with the world. The modules' basic logic is specified by our genetic program. Their operation was shaped by natural selection to solve the problems of the hunting and gathering way of life led by our ancestors in most of our evolutionary history" (Pinker, 1997). Because evolutionary psychologists claims that there are "hundreds or thousands" of such modules, this view of the mind has been dubbed the "massive modularity thesis."

To build a case for a domain-specific module we must first identify the properties of such a mechanism. David Buss (2008) has outlined the following six properties of an evolved psychological mechanism:

1. It exists in its current form because it has successfully solved a recurring and specific adaptive problem.
2. It is designed to take in only a narrow slice of information.
3. Its input informs the organism of the particular adaptive problem it is facing.
4. It is transformed through decision rules into output.
5. Its output can be physiological, information to other psychological mechanisms, or manifest behavior.
6. It is directed toward the solution to a specific adaptive problem.

The beginning of such an analysis is often described in terms of "reverse engineering" the organism. For example, in reverse-engineering sonar in bats, Dawkins proceeds as follows: "...I shall begin by posing a problem that the living machine faces, then I shall consider possible solutions to the problem that a sensible engineer might consider; I shall finally come to the solution that nature has actually adopted" (1986, pp. 21–22). Engineers figure out what problems they want to solve, and then design machines that are capable of solving these problems in an efficient manner. Evolutionary biologists figure out what adaptive problems a given species encountered during its evolutionary history, and then ask themselves, "What would a machine capable of solving these problems well under ancestral conditions look like?" Because there may be more than one way of solving a given problem, empirical studies are needed to determine which solution natural selection has engineered.

☐ Chapter Summary

Sociobiology is defined as the systematic study of the biological basis of social behavior. It builds directly on the foundations of the modern synthesis by adding four key concepts chiefly developed by William D. Hamilton and Robert Trivers. Together these four concepts: (1) inclusive fitness, (2) reciprocal altruism, (3) parental investment, and (4) parent–offspring conflict enabled sociobiologists to reframe an evolutionary account of social behavior of all animals from insects to elephants that rested squarely on natural selection at the level of the individual.

Hamilton (1964) is most well known for his concept of kin altruism or inclusive fitness. The direct fitness of the individual (direct offspring) plus the gain in reproductive success from indirect fitness (the offspring of relatives weighted by their degree of relatedness) equals inclusive fitness. The more genes that are shared between individuals, the greater the likelihood of altruism.

The problem of altruism stimulated Harvard theorist Robert Trivers to work out an additional explanation for the existence of altruism. Trivers focused his attention on human acts of altruism directed towards nonkin. For nonkin altruism to exist the cost to the actor must be less than the benefit to the recipient. Two other prerequisites are needed to establish the Trivers' concept of reciprocal altruism. First, individuals must be able to recognize each other in order to "keep accounts." This allows the individual to reciprocate with "honest players" and to detect and punish "cheaters." Second, individuals should have a reasonably long lifespan to allow for the reciprocal relationship between two individuals to establish itself in repeated contacts.

The cost-benefit analysis that gave rise to the concepts of kin altruism and reciprocal altruism can also be fruitfully applied to the problem of parental investment, defined as "any investment by the parent in an individual offspring that increases the offspring's chance of surviving at the cost of the parent's ability to invest in other offspring" (Trivers, 1972). Trivers specified that there is typically a difference in the degree of parental investment in offspring favoring females that results in a marked asymmetry in roles. Mating competition would be expected to be greater in the lower-investing sex, while mate choice would be expected to be greater in the higher-investing sex. Thus, most, but not all, examples of sexual selection involve either male-male competition or female choice.

Trivers (1974) also realized that from the standpoint of maximizing inclusive fitness an inevitable conflict of interest arises between the parent and offspring. In his conceptualization of parent-offspring conflict it is important to understand that the biological imperative of maximizing fitness operates differently on the two generations involved.

Multilevel selection theory is a theory of evolution by natural selection that recognizes possible trade-offs in the selection of heritable traits at different levels of selection. It is universally recognized that the chief difficulty with the spread of altruistic genes within any group of individuals is that genes for group advantageous behavior are seldom advantageous for the individual who acts to benefit the group and consequently they are generally selected against within groups. For Darwin, the solution was to recognize that natural selection can operate at more than one level, including the level of selection between competing groups. In short, *selfishness beats altruism within groups. Altruistic groups beat selfish groups.* Ultimately selection for a trait within the total population (species) will depend upon the relative speed and potency of within- and between-group selection.

The most recent step in the Darwinian revolution was taken by the school of evolutionary psychology, which is the direct descendant of sociobiology. Evolutionary psychologists assume that "all normal human minds reliably develop a standard collection of reasoning and regulatory circuits that are functionally specialized and, frequently, domain-specific. These circuits organize the way we interpret our experiences, inject certain recurrent concepts and motivations into our mental life, and provide universal frames of meaning that allow us to understand the actions and intentions of others" (Tooby & Cosmides, 1992, p. 3).

Contemporary evolutionary psychologists focus their research on understanding the design features of cognitive abilities of the human mind such as language, theory of mind and facial recognition, and the structures of the human brain that support these mental operations.

Geary introduced the concept of soft modularity as recognition of the inherent plasticity of human development and adaptation even when evolved modules provide the necessary starting point for development. Soft modularity can take three different forms: (1) mechanisms that allocate brain resources depending on particular environmental demands, (2) mechanisms that enable the creation of new categories according to environmental demands, and (3) modules that have evolved an invariant range of domain-specific information (e.g., human speech sounds). Interaction with the environment is often essential to hone adaptation of evolved pylogenetic systems to specific circumstances.

Geary and Huffman (2002) outline four hierarchical levels of modular organization. The most basic level of organization is the neural module, which may be described as a region of the sensory cortex. Next, perceptual modules arise from the activity patterns of neural modules and provide a complex and abstracted representation of the environment as perceived by the organism through their sensory apparatus. The next level of abstraction moves from sensory perception up to a meaning-based representation or cognition and thus is referred to as a cognitive module. Finally, a functional module integrates the information coming from the lower-level modules with the affect and motivation of the organism to guide its behavior in pursuit of evolutionarily significant goals. Notice that although natural selection operates on the behavioral output, it also has the power to shape the evolution of all the lower-level modules upon which the behavior is based. New functional modules can emerge with rather minor evolutionary changes in the underlying genotype by reorganizing existing lower-level modules into new functional units.

An important caveat regarding evolved cognitive modules is that these mechanisms may not necessarily generate adaptive behavior today, because they evolved during the Environment of Evolutionary Adaptedness or EEA. As a relatively new species, the human EEA is sometimes specified as the African savannah during the Pleistocene. To the extent that the present-day environment of humans has changed from that of our EEA, some mechanisms may actually be a source of maladaptation. We will refer to this possible state of affairs as the mismatch hypothesis.

A major challenge of evolutionary psychology is to specify the criteria necessary for discriminating the features of the human mind that represent phylogenetic adaptations from other characteristics of the mind that may only appear to do so. The first criterion for identifying a potential evolved psychological mechanism is the same as for any phylogentic adaptation: it must solve a specific and recurring problem of adaptation. Finding that it solves an adaptive problem with "reliability, efficiency, and economy" is then prima facie evidence that one has located an adaptation.

Although one must certainly accept the modularity thesis for some specialized functions (language and facial recognition are well documented), it is apparent that much of the human capacity for adapting to a wide range of novel problems encountered in our modern environment relies upon domain-general information processing. Domain-general mechanisms are the hallmark of human adaptation and give our species its unique flexibility to successfully adapt to a wide range of environmental demands, particularly novel and fluctuating problems requiring flexibility and insight.

☐ For Further Inquiry

Alcock, J. (2001b). *The triumph of sociobiology*. Oxford, UK: Oxford University Press.

Barkow, J. (Ed.) (2006). *Missing the revolution: Darwinism for social scientists*. Oxford, UK: Oxford University Press.

Buss, D. M. (Ed.). (2005). *The handbook of evolutionary psychology*. Hoboken, NJ: Wiley & Sons.

Dunbar, R. I. M. & Barrett, L. (Eds.) (2007).*The Oxford handbook of evolutionary psychology*. Oxford, UK: Oxford University Press.

Geary, D. C. (2005). *The origin of mind: Evolution of brain, cognition and general intelligence*. Washington, DC: American Psychological Association.

Human Behavior and Evolution Society Web site: Retrieved 2010 from http://www.hbes.com/

Wilson, D. S. & Wilson, E. O. (2007). Rethinking the theoretical foundation of sociobiology. *The Quarterly Review of Biology, 82*(4), 327–348.

The Genetic Basis of Evolution and Behavior

☐ How Genes Help Construct the Organism

All plants and animals share the same basic building blocks of eukaryotic cells. This shared characteristic is homologous, meaning that all of these multicellular organisms derived this structure from a common ancestor as life forms began to evolve and speciate over the past 4000 million years. This tree of life is depicted in Figure 3.1.

Eukaryotic cells differ from prokaryotic cells found in simpler organisms like bacteria in that eukaryotic cells contain many membrane-bound organelles, small membrane-bound structures inside the cell that carry out specialized functions. For example, the nucleus is surrounded by a nuclear membrane and contains most of the hereditary material (DNA) of the cell. Notice that not all life forms have this type of cell. Prokaryotic cells are found in simpler organisms like bacteria. As shown in Figure 3.2, prokaryotes are much simpler structures that do not have the distinct nucleus or the complex organization of the eukaryotes.

Both of these types of cells, and thus all living organisms, contain the molecule deoxyribose nucleic acid, or DNA, which provides the essential mechanism for heredity. As seen in Figure 3.2, eukaryotic DNA is contained within the cell's nucleus, except for a much smaller amount of DNA contained in certain organelles such as mitochondria. Mitochondria are minute, sausage-shaped structures found in the clear cytoplasm of the cell. Mitochondria are responsible for energy production. They contain enzymes that help to convert food material into adenosine triphosphate (ATP), which can be used directly by the cell as an energy source.

51

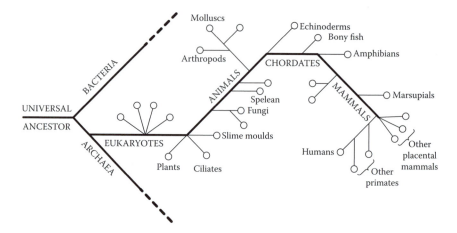

FIGURE 3.1 Darwin introduced a branching tree of life that would become the standard metaphor for speciation.

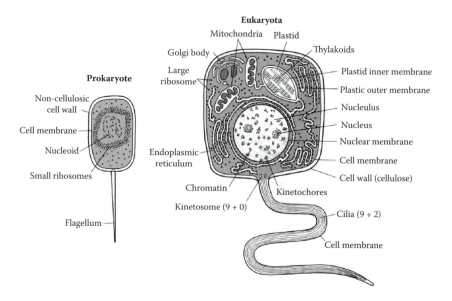

FIGURE 3.2 Eukaryotic cells found in all plants and animals evolved from prokaryotic cells found in simpler organisms like bacteria. Eukaryotic cells contain many membrane-bound organelles or small membrane-bound structures inside the cell that carry out specialized functions. (From Ridley, M. [2004]. *Evolution* [3rd ed.]. Cambridge, MA: Blackwell Science. With permission.)

Mitochondrial DNA

Mitochondrial DNA (mtDNA) is typically passed on only from the mother; thus mitochondria are clones. This is important to geneticists because the only source of change in the mtDNA from generation to generation is mutation, unlike nuclear DNA which changes by 50% each generation because of the recombination of sexual reproduction. Because its mutation rate may be more easily estimated than DNA, mtDNA can be used as a kind of "molecular clock." Similarly, the Y chromosomal DNA that is paternally inherited may also be used to trace lineage. Molecular geneticists use both techniques to estimate the degree of relatedness between different populations and to reconstruct patterns of evolution, as will be discussed in Chapter 4.

DNA, RNA, and Chromosomes

The much larger amount of DNA found within the cell's nucleus is located in structures called chromosomes, which are large enough to be seen through a light microscope. The nucleus of each animal cell contains at least one chromosome, a strand of coiled DNA.

The entire human genome was sequenced for the first time in 2001 with the aid of high-speed computers. Preliminary estimates from the Human Genome Project indicate that it is about 3 billion nucleotides long organized on 46 chromosomes that contain approximately 30,000 genes. The average length of a human gene is about 5000 nucleotides, thus only about 5% of human DNA actually codes for genes (Ridley, 2004). Because of increased computational capabilities, rapid advances are now being made in molecular genetics and genomics (gene sequencing) that would not have been possible in previous decades. Nevertheless, the impressive results of the Human Genome Project represent just the beginning of our understanding of the role genes play in constructing the organism, the topic of this section.

Genes can be thought of as indivisible units of heredity and are more formally defined as a segment of DNA that contains the code for constructing one specific type of protein molecule. Genes accomplish this through replication of one strand of the DNA as RNA, as shown in Figure 3.3.

The molecular structure of DNA, comprised of pairs of complementary strands arranged in a double helix, was discovered by Watson and Crick in 1953. DNA is a double helix formed by base pairs attached to a sugar-phosphate backbone. Each DNA molecule is composed of a sequence of units. Each unit or nucleotide consists of a phosphate and a sugar, connected to one of four bases, adenine, thymine, cytosine, and guanine (A, T, C, and G). These four bases code for the production of amino acids, which form the building blocks of various proteins, which in turn help structure

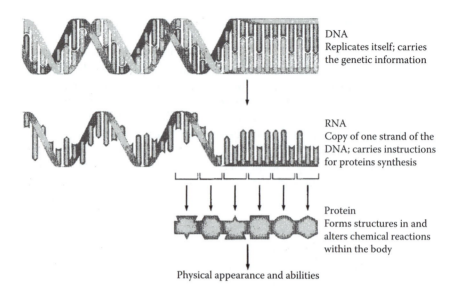

DNA
Replicates itself; carries
the genetic information

RNA
Copy of one strand of the
DNA; carries instructions
for proteins synthesis

Protein
Forms structures in and
alters chemical reactions
within the body

Physical appearance and abilities

FIGURE 3.3 How genes construct the organism. Genes are composed of DNA, which can replicate one strand of itself called RNA, which contains instructions for synthesizing protein. Proteins represent fundamental building blocks of physical structures of the body and are capable of altering the body's chemistry to aid in processes like digestion. (From Kalat, J.W. [1999]. *Introduction to psychology* [5th ed.]. Pacific Grove, CA: Brooks/Cole. With permission.)

the organism's physiology, morphology, physical appearance, and abilities. Genes are replicated in each parent and recombined in infinite variety in each offspring, except identical twins who inherit the exact same genotype from their parents. This fact alone makes twin research critical to a scientific understanding of heritability in humans, as we discuss later in this chapter.

☐ How Genes Influence Behavior and Development

As shown in Figure 3.4, the route by which genes influence behavior and development is indirect and always influenced by interaction with the organism's internal and external environment. Virtually every aspect of an organism's phenotype is the joint product of its genes and its environment. A common misunderstanding of the relationship between genes (the genotype) and the organism (the phenotype) is the analogy of genes as a

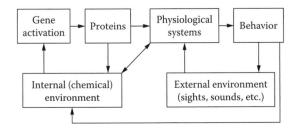

FIGURE 3.4   How genes influence behavior. The proteins produced by genes directly affect physiological systems in the organism, which in turn influence behavior. All aspects of this process are open to inputs from the internal or external environment as indicated by the arrows.

blueprint for the organism. Rather than following a blueprint, the genome does not actually specify a final product in intricate detail. Instead of a *blueprint*, Dawkins (1982) proposes the metaphor of genes providing a *recipe* for development. While the metaphor of blueprint is clearly misleading, the recipe metaphor is too static an image to capture the dynamic qualities of a responsive phenotype.

West-Eberhard (2003) points out that while metaphors capture some important qualities of development, they are deficient as general guides to thinking about development and evolution, and no substitute for theory. The development of the organism from the genotype is an epigenetic process that serves to specify methods of construction rather than a finished product. In addition, genes work in combination with, rather than in isolation from, one another, and make use of the same master instructions over and over again, allowing genes to be expressed to different extent in different locations. These are precisely the processes that would allow a relatively small number of genes (30,000) to create the myriad and complex potentials of the human mind (100 billion neurons at birth). As Gary Marcus concluded in *The Birth of the Mind* (2004), "A brain built by pure blueprint would be at a loss if the slightest thing went wrong; a brain that is built by individual cells following self-regulating recipes has the freedom to adapt" (Marcus, 2004, p. 158). Because of its special importance to human behavior, as well as its complexity, we reserve further discussion of the evolution and development of the human brain for Chapter 5.

☐ Gene–Environment Interactions

In the past philosophers and scientists often pitted genetic and environmental factors against one another, as if a strong case for one resulted in a weak position for the other. Nativists battled empiricists and psychologists reformulated these old debates in terms of nature versus nurture. An important theme of this book is that nature and nurture collaborate in producing the visible characteristics of the phenotype. A strong case for heritability of a trait in no way undermines the belief that the environment critically influences the development of the organism. Rather than viewing genes and environment as separate forces acting on the child, developmentalists view genes and the environment as acting together, often in highly complex ways. Moreover, the responsive phenotype responds to both internal and external signals in much the same way. Because of this genetic and environmental influences can be interchangeable rather than somehow opposed to each other.

An epigenetic perspective considers developmental change as an interactive function of internal structures and the ecology in which these structures are embedded. Behavioral development never takes place in the absence of ecological support. Some epigenetic rules are conditional on environmental cues and were designed by natural selection to produce different phenotypes in different environments. In certain species of fish (e.g., blue headed wrasse) if the solitary male of the social group dies, the largest female is transformed into a male. In this particular ecology an epigenetic program evolved a conditional response to sex determination, enabling a female to change sex in response to a social cue—the absence of a male in the group.

Recent advances in epigenetics have led to a more detailed understanding of the chemical scaffolding that supports DNA and activates or deactivates genes. For example, in a 2007 paper presented at the National Academy of Sciences, scientists demonstrated that female rats exposed to high levels of the fungicide vinclozin had male offspring who were likely to be sterile and to develop various diseases, including cancer, as adults. What makes the study noteworthy is that the propensity for diseases persisted in the male rats over four generations (Crews et al., 2007). The rats' genes had not been altered by the fungicide and no genetic change occurred. Rather the fungicide altered the chemistry of early development by influencing the expression of the genes. DNA methylation is one type of chemical modification of DNA that can be inherited without changing the original DNA sequence. As such, it is part of the epigenetic code and can cause diseases associated with environmental agents to be transmitted across generations.

An important example of epigenetic modification of gene expression in humans is the *developmental-origins hypothesis*, sometimes called the Barker hypothesis after David J. P. Barker, a researcher at the University of Southampton (Barker, 1992, 1997). The theory states that reduced fetal growth is strongly associated with a number of chronic conditions (obesity, coronary heart disease, stroke, diabetes, and hypertension) later in life. This increased susceptibility results from adaptations made by the fetus in an environment limited in its supply of nutrients. This means that in poor nutritional conditions, a pregnant female can modify the development of her unborn child such as to prepare for survival in an environment in short supply of resources, resulting in a thrifty phenotype (Hales & Barker, 1992). Individuals with a thrifty phenotype have a smaller body size, slower metabolic rate, and are less active, which may be seen as adaptations to an environment that is chronically short of food (Bateson & Martin, 1999). The above examples illustrate the concept of *developmental plasticity*, the phenomenon by which any given genotype can give rise to a range of different physiological or morphological types in response to different environmental conditions during development.

Because the action of genetic material is involved in the metabolic processes of every cell, genetic influence, like environmental influence, is also relevant to every developmental process. As the Zen Buddhist D. T. Suzuki commented, "once you have taken nature and nurture apart, how will you ever put them back together?" Such processes can only be taken apart in the mind of the theorist or on the page of a text, but never in the day-to-day functioning of the organism in its habitat. Noted evolutionary developmental biologist West-Eberhard offers the following comment:

> There is no known method to estimate the proportional total influence of environment versus genes on individual or trait development. Measures like heritability and genetic versus environmental variance do not come close to a true assessment of the relative contribution of environment and genes to development. They refer only to causes of variation in particular quantitative traits, measured under specified environmental conditions and within a single generation. (West-Eberhard, 2003, p. 101)

In several influential papers, Sandra Scarr (Scarr, 1992; Scarr & McCartney, 1983) has developed a comprehensive model of the different types of *gene–environment interaction* that construct an individual's phenotypic characteristics like personality traits. The authors begin with a position that is universally accepted by developmentalists: a child's phenotype (observable characteristics) is a product of the child's genotype and rearing environment. In their model, illustrated in Figure 3.5, the child is cast as an active agent in his or her own development, in addition to the genetic contributions of both parents, and the shaping influence of the environment that they create for their child.

Three types of genotype–environment effects are proposed: passive, active, and evocative. A *passive effect* refers to the rearing environment provided by genetically related parents. The assumption here is that the parents' genetic characteristics influence what type of environment they create for themselves and their children. Rowe (1994) argues that genes

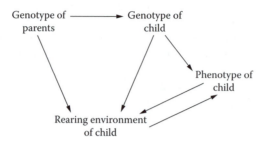

FIGURE 3.5   Gene–environment interactions. (Adapted from Scarr & McCartney, 1983.)

can certainly influence variation in child-rearing styles via their organizing effects on the parents' central nervous system. He cautions social scientists against overinterpreting environmental influences in studies using biological families that relate parental child-rearing with childhood personality traits.

Parents and their children are a coevolving system in which passive genotype–environment correlations are of great importance. For example, there may be correlations between children's genotypes and the environments provided by their biological parents. Intelligent parents have children with a high genetic potential for intelligence and they also provide optimal environments for the facilitation of their children's intelligence. Children would be expected to differentially benefit from the environments provided by high-investment parents depending on their genotype. Thus far the evidence does indeed indicate that, in early childhood at least, passive genotype–environment correlations are more important contributors to the correlations between measures of IQ and measures of the environment than are active or evocative genotype–environment correlations (Plomin, 1994).

An *active effect* refers to the child's own choices to selectively attend to a specific aspect of the general environment. It is well known that individuals engage in a great deal of active "niche-picking," partly creating their own environment, which in turn influences the course of their development. Scarr and McCartney (1983) propose that the child's genotype contributes to the choices that the child makes.

Evocative effects refer to the various responses by a child's parents, teachers, peers, and others that are elicited by the child because of some aspect of his or her genotype. For example, if a child who is naturally shy by temperament is overprotected by well-intentioned parents, that child's environment may be substantially different from that of a bold child whose parents provide a wide range of social experiences. Peers as well may cease to initiate contact with a child who is unresponsive to social overtures out of shyness, creating a less stimulating social environment than that evoked by a more gregarious child. Again the question concerning evocative effects is not whether the child influences the responsive social environment (this should be obvious), but whether individuals are responding to *genetically* determined child characteristics.

As noted earlier, demonstrating heritability in a child's temperament or personality does not rule out environmental influences. Similarly, demonstrating associations between a biological parent's child-rearing style and childhood outcomes does not rule out a genetic contribution to the association, particularly via gene–environment interaction effects.

For example, research has consistently demonstrated stable individual differences in biobehavioral responses to stress in rhesus monkeys (Suomi, 2003). Approximately 10% of these monkeys consistently exhibit impulsive and/or inappropriately aggressive responses to mildly stressful situations throughout development; those same individuals also show chronic deficits in their central serotonin metabolism. These patterns emerge early in life, remain stable from infancy to adulthood, and have been shown to be highly heritable. At the same time, the response pattern is open to major modification by specific early experiences involving early attachment relationships.

Genetic and early experience factors often interact in dramatic fashion. For example, a specific polymorphism in the serotonin transporter gene is associated with deficits in serotonin metabolism, extreme aggression, and excessive alcohol consumption among monkeys who experienced insecure early attachment relationships, but not in monkeys who developed secure attachment relationships with their mothers during infancy. According to Suomi, daughters tend to develop the same type of attachment relationships with their own offspring that they experienced with their mothers early in life. He concludes that early experiences in attachment quality provide a possible nongenetic mechanism for transmitting these patterns to subsequent generations. The parallels of Suomi's research with longitudinal research on mother–infant attachment and child developmental outcomes are striking and will be discussed further in Chapter 8.

☐ Behavioral Genetics

Behavioral geneticists are interested in the extent to which individual differences between people in a given environment can be accounted for by differences in their genes. The quantitative evidence for genetic effects on behavior (*heritability*), derives from two principal sources, twin studies and adoption studies. In general, adoption studies that have attempted

TABLE 3.1 Percentage of Genetic Relatedness in Different Relations

Relationship	Percent Relatedness
Identical twins	100
Fraternal twins	50
Full brothers or sisters	
Parent/child	
Half brothers of sisters	25
Grandparent/grandchild	
Aunt or uncle/niece or nephew	
First cousins	12.5
Second cousins	6.25

to demonstrate links between the temperament of parents and their biological and adopted children have demonstrated only minimal heritability. Twin studies are generally viewed as more conclusive. According to Bouchard (1996), twin studies provide an important window on the direct influence of genes on whole organisms and will continue to complement studies in molecular genetics.

How does the study of twins inform us about genetic influences? We shall begin our discussion with research on the heritability of infant temperament. The logic for investigating the heritability of any trait that we can measure begins by recalling that *monozygotic* or *identical* twins have the same genotype. They share 100% percent of their genes, unlike *dizygotic* or *fraternal*, twins who share only 50% of their genotype. See Table 3.1 for the percentage of genes shared in different types of kin relations.

☐ Heritability of Infant Temperament

Temperament refers to individual differences in behavior and emotionality, such as activity level, attentiveness, adaptability, and mood, that appear early in life and are assumed to be inborn *traits* of the infant. These traits are generally measured as continuous dimensions that are expected to have a high degree of stability over time and across situations, and a biological basis, both in terms of neurophysiological underpinnings and heritability. As shown in Table 3.2, theorists may differ in their definition of various traits that make up the infant's temperament; however, they all agree that it represents the biological contribution to personality.

TABLE 3.2 Models of Temperament

Thomas & Chess (1977)	Rothbart (1981)	Buss & Plomin (1984)
1. Activity	1. Activity	1. Activity
2. Rhythmicity	2. Smiling and laughter	2. Emotionality
3. Approach-withdrawal	3. Fear	3. Sociability
4. Adaptability	4. Soothability	
5. Intensity	5. Distress to limitations	
6. Threshold	6. Undisturbed persistence	
7. Mood		
8. Distractibility		
9. Persistence of attention		

In practice, heritability estimates of temperament may vary depending on (1) assessment technique (parental ratings vs. observation), (2) which dimension of temperament is being assessed, (3) what developmental period is being examined, and (4) the assumptions of the model used to generate the estimates.

Table 3.3 displays comparisons of correlations based on parental ratings of Rothbart's six dimensions of temperament for identical and fraternal twins based on data from studies by Goldsmith and colleagues (Goldsmith, Losoya, Bradshaw, & Campos, 1994). The first column of the table shows the concordance (degree of similarity) between parental reports for monozygotic (MZ) and dizygotic (DZ) twins. *The degree of the genetic influence is reflected by the difference in the two concordance estimates between MZ and DZ twins.* Across the six scales of the Infant Behavior Questionnaire (IBQ), concordances are substantially higher for activity level and the two negative affect scales, but more equivocal for positive scales. This suggests that negative emotionality has a greater genetic basis than positive mood.

TABLE 3.3 Twin Similarity for Rothbart's Infant Behavior Questionnaire (IBQ)

IBQ Scales	Identical *R*	Fraternal *R*
Activity level	.69	.35
Fear	.67	.43
Distress to limitations	.71	.29
Smiling and laughter	.72	.66
Soothability	.69	.71
Duration of orienting	.76	.57

Note: Adapted from Goldsmith (1978, 1986), Goldsmith and Campos (1986).

TABLE 3.4 Twin Correlations and Heritability
Estimates for Infant Temperament and Emotion

Measure	MZ	DZ	h²	h²
Temperament				
Observational				
Inhibition	.57**	.26**	.62**	.56**
Shyness	.70**	.45**	.49*	
Parental Report				
CCTI-Emotion	.35**	−.02**	.72**	.28**
CCTI-Shyness	.38**	−.03	.82**	.28**
Emotion				
Observational				
Positive	.53**	.37**	.33	
Negative	.11	.06	.10	
Overall Mood	.19**	.02	.34	.16
Empathy PC	.42**	−.03	.89**	.36**
Frustration PC	.26**	.19	.15	
Parental Report				
Positive	.84**	.82**	.05	
Negative	.71**	.39*	.68**	

$*p < .05; **p < .01.$
Source: From Plomin et al. (1993).

The MacArthur Longitudinal Twin Study (Emde et al., 1992; Plomin et al., 1993) also supports this conclusion. Results from this study, which assessed 200 identical and fraternal twin pairs at 14 months, are presented in Table 3.4.

The data indicate much greater variability in the estimates of genetic heritability of infant temperament and emotion than in comparable data in older subjects. Similar to previous findings, this research indicates that the tendency to express negative emotions is highly heritable, but only for parental reports, and only when uncorrected estimates are used. In contrast, positive emotionality did not show significant heritability for either parental report or observational measures. This is because both MZ and DZ twins were rated as highly similar, especially by parents. Remember that the key to showing genetic heritability lies in the *differences* in concordances between MZ and DZ twins. Notice, for example, that the high heritability estimate for empathy (.89) derives primarily from the lack of any concordance between DZ twins (-.03), rather than exceptionally high concordances between MZ twin pairs (.42). Because a negative correlation between DZ twins violates the model's assumptions, the second, more conservative estimate of .36 is probably more accurate than the uncorrected estimate (.89). Other important findings are the significant genetic loadings for behavioral inhibition and shyness, further establishing the viability of these measures as temperament constructs.

Measurement error in assessments of infant temperament necessitates that conclusions be drawn from many different studies using different samples and different methods, rather than the results of any single study. This is equally true for most psychological research. Taken together, twin studies tend to support three broad patterns in the database. First, there is moderate heritability of temperament shown when parental reports are used (Buss & Plomin, 1984), but only minimal evidence for heritability when using observational measures of temperament (Emde et al., 1992; Goldsmith & Campos, 1986; Goldsmith & Gottesman, 1981; Matheny, 1989). Second, heritability estimates are consistently higher for indices of negative emotionality (defined variously as behavioral inhibition, shyness, fear, or distress) than positive mood (Emde et al., 1992; Goldsmith, 1993). Third, heritability estimates in one developmental period do not necessarily generalize to other ages. For example, little evidence has been found for heritability for temperamental dimensions in neonates, including such behaviors as irritability, soothability, and activity level, though these traits show at least some genetic influence at the end of the first year.

Because behavioral genetics research on temperament clearly indicates the presence of genes operating on the development of neural and neurochemical structures, psychobiological models of inherited temperament and personality traits must consider the evolutionary basis and adaptive significance of these individual differences. We now turn our attention to the question of why personality traits evolved.

□ Personality as an Evolved System

The area of personality deals with some of the most basic systems underlying behavior. Imagine that you were designing an animal (or human) to be able to survive in a world filled with dangers (like poisonous snakes) and opportunities (like attractive mates). What systems would you need? That would depend on which species you were designing, because each species has a different ecology. Different species need different resources, and they face a different mix of opportunities and dangers.

Natural selection is the great designer that has produced the systems that people and animals use to make a living in the world. Even the most primitive animals would need systems designed to obtain resources (Panksepp, 1998). The most common behavioral approach systems are designed for obtaining food and mates, but more advanced species might also be designed with systems for obtaining social status or dominance within the group. Because the world is never a completely safe and benign place for any species, there must also be systems designed to deal with threats, the most important of which are fear systems that have been studied in a wide range of animals (Gray, 1987; LeDoux, 1996). Moreover, a well-designed animal would also be able to regulate its arousal. It is certainly adaptive to be aroused when one is confronting dangers or opportunities. (Think how weird it would be if people were stone-faced and impassive when they found out they just won the lottery, or found themselves being chased by a hungry crocodile.) But arousal is very costly—people who are stressed out all the time would quickly become exhausted and vulnerable to disease. So there must also be a system of arousal regulation designed to energize the animal to meet environmental challenges or opportunities, but also designed to turn off when things return to normal. Without an arousal system, the animal (or person) would either be permanently aroused and prone to exhaustion and disease; or it would be permanently underaroused and unable to deal with environmental challenges like hungry crocodiles.

Virtually all mammals have behavioral approach systems, fear systems, and arousal regulation systems. But some species, especially humans, have some other important systems designed by natural selection as part of our personalities. Humans and some other species have systems that promote pair bonds and other types of close relationships involving love and affection between mates and nurturing of offspring. And some species—perhaps only the most advanced primates—must be able to carry out projects requiring attention to detail and inhibiting present pleasures for long-term gains—the conscientiousness system.

When we say that someone is conscientious, we are implicitly thinking in terms of a dimension of conscientiousness, with some people on the high end, some people in the middle, and some on the low end. In fact, personality dimensions do approximate bell-shaped normal curves, with most people toward the middle and a decreasing percentage of people as you get farther away from the average.

Individual differences are a very important part of personality, and they are certainly important in everyday life. For example, with the trait of conscientiousness, we all recognize and appreciate the differences between a dependable, responsible overachiever and an irresponsible, unreliable person who can't get to work on time. (Employers are especially likely to notice and value these differences!) But individual differences in personality are compatible with the idea that first and foremost personality should be thought of as a universal set of evolved systems designed to solve problems of living during our evolutionary past. In the same way, all humans have a respiratory system and a circulatory system that are designed to carry out fundamental biological functions. These are human universals, and our first interest should be to understand the general, universal features of these systems. However, people vary in these systems, so that, for example, some people, like Lance Armstrong, have relatively high lung capacity while others have relatively low lung capacity. All humans have respiratory systems, but some of us have larger, more efficient respiratory systems than others—marathon runners compared to couch potatoes.

This also suggests that as we move out toward the extremes of personality dimensions, we are more likely to see pathological conditions (Costa & Widiger, 1994). From this point of view, several important types of psychopathology can be understood as being extreme on personality dimensions. For example, being afraid of real dangers is highly adaptive. But it's maladaptive if you are prone to phobias in the absence of real danger to the point where it interferes with everyday life. And it's maladaptive to have no fear at all, to the point of recklessness. We take up this topic in more detail in Chapter 12.

Five-Factor Model of Personality

Thus, personality systems are evolved systems designed to deal with life's dangers and opportunities. Research in personality has revealed five personality trait dimensions—the five-factor model of personality. The "big five" refers to the view that the major dimensions of personality can be accounted for by just five factors, referred to as the *five-factor model* (FFM). Most of the well-known personality inventories, including Cattell's, Eysenck's, and the MMPI, can be reduced through factor analysis to five major factors or a subset of these factors. The "big five" personality dimensions are usually named for one end of the continuum they represent

1. *Extroverted*: gregarious, sociable, dominant, adventurous
2. *Agreeable*: affectionate, warm, kind, friendly
3. *Conscientious*: organized, planful, reliable
4. *Stable*: calm, worry free, stable
5. *Open*: original, insightful, inventive, wide-ranging interests

Five types of empirical evidence provide support for an evolutionary psychology of personality. First, comparative research has shown evidence for similar systems in animals that serve clear adaptive functions. Second, neurological research has shown evidence for a structural basis of these systems in the brain. Third, developmental research indicates the presence of recognizable precursors of the FFM personality traits as temperament dimensions in infancy. Fourth, extensive cross-cultural research has demonstrated the universality of the FFM. Finally, behavioral geneticists have demonstrated the heritability of FFM personality traits.

If personality systems have an evolutionary function, we would expect to find them also in animals. There is evidence for personality traits in wolves (shyness/boldness, social dominance; MacDonald, 1983), sunfish (shyness/boldness; D. S. Wilson, 1994), and chimpanzees (extraversion, neuroticism, agreeableness, conscientiousness; Figueredo & King, 1996; King & Figueredo, 1994). Reviewing the data for 12 quite different species, Gosling and John (1999) found evidence for extraversion, neuroticism, and agreeableness in most species: extraversion was found in 10 species (but not rats and hyenas); neuroticism (proneness to negative emotionality) was found in 9 species (but not in vervet monkeys, donkeys, and pigs); agreeableness was found in 10 species (but not in guppies and octopi). Conscientiousness was found only in humans and chimpanzees.

The data therefore indicate some differences in the systems that have evolved among different species. This is what one would expect if indeed personality systems mirror the ecology of the animal. It is not surprising, for example, that only humans and chimpanzees exhibit conscientiousness. As described below, conscientiousness involves focused effort in pursuit of long-term goals and evaluation. This activity requires a great deal of cognitive capacity, much of which is not present in most animals.

In humans, four of the five factors have been linked with temperament dimensions suggesting significant overlap between temperament and personality. Temperament research in early childhood yields a number of factors that map directly onto the FFM dimensions of extraversion, agreeableness, emotional stability, and conscientiousness. These results appear to be robust in the sense that though different temperament questionnaires yield different factors, they are consistently linked with the FFM dimensions (Rothbart & Bates, 1998).

As more studies are conducted using the FFM there is increasing evidence of the universality of the five factors across different cultures, though more data are required to make this assertion. The five-factor structure has now been replicated in many different linguistic groups using a variety of different instruments over the past 50 years (Rothbart & Bates, 1998; Rowe, 1994). The FFM dimensions appear regularly in cross-cultural research and among children and adults (Goldberg, 1990; Graziano & Ward, 1992; John, Caspi, Robins, Moffitt, & Sthouthamer-Loeber, 1994; Kohnstamm, Halverson, Mervielde, & Havill, 1998; Lamb, Chuang, Wells, Broberg, & Hwang, 2002; McCrae et al., 2002). Together, comparative evidence for similar systems in animals that serve clear adaptive functions, the early appearance of infant temperamental traits linked to the FFM, the structural basis of these systems in the brain, and their apparent universality across many different cultures suggest an evolutionary basis for individual variation in temperament and personality.

Heritability of Personality

The final and most crucial requirement for an evolutionary psychology of individual differences in personality concerns the genetic transmission of such traits. From this perspective, individual variation in personality traits must be shown to be heritable to some extent or the argument of a biological basis falls apart. Once again twin studies provide the critical test.

The most informative research design would contain a sample of monozygotic twins reared together (MZT), unrelated individuals reared together (URT), and monozygotic twins reared apart (MZA). Of course, the latter group is hard to find in sufficient numbers and as a result, relevant data can be obtained by just a few research centers specializing in twin studies.

Any similarity between identical twins reared apart (MZA) is considered to be genetic in origin, with no contribution attributed to environmental influence. Similar logic applies to unrelated individuals reared together (URT), though it is the inverse of the MZA design. These correlations represent the influence of shared environmental factors with no contribution of heritability. Finally, in the MZT design, the correlation confounds genetic and environmental influences. This means that the difference between the MZT and MZA correlations provides another estimate for the shared environmental influence.

In practice, most behavior genetic studies rely on model-fitting research designs that use equations outlining the expected correlations of different kinship groups in order that relatives of different types can be combined in a single analysis. The discrepancies between the expected and observed correlations provide a basis for testing the model's goodness of fit. The inclusion of many different types of kinship groups allows for more rigorous model fitting to the many different correlations that are observed. This type of analysis yields estimates of heritability and shared environmental effects.

In the Minnesota Study of Twins Reared Apart (MISTRA) a large sample of identical and fraternal twins was recruited as each twin pair came to light in the English-speaking world (Bouchard, Lykken, McGue, Segal, & Tellegen, 1990). The MISTRA researchers have demonstrated that the similarities observed between these twins on a wide array of measures including personality cannot be explained by factors like age of separation, amount of contact, or measurable characteristics of the families. In the MISTRA study the mean broad heritability coefficient for personality was found to be .41.

Similarly, an extensive analysis of different types of kinships gathered from the entire world literature by Loehlin and colleagues provide equally compelling evidence for genetic influences on personality (Loehlin & Rowe, 1992). Their analysis included a diverse range of behavioral genetics

TABLE 3.5 Parameter Estimates for Big Five Personality Dimensions

Dimension	Unshared Environment	Broad Sense h^2	Narrow Sense h^2	Siblings' Shared Environment
I. Extraversion	.49	.49	.32	.02
II. Agreeableness	.52	.39	.29	.09
III. Conscientiousness	.55	.40	.22	.05
IV. Emotional stability	.52	.41	.27	.07
V. Intellectual openness	.49	.45	.43	.06
Mean	.51	.43	.31	.06

Source: Adapted from Loehlin and Rowe (1992). ©1992 by Harvester Wheatsheaf.

research designs including MZ and DZ twins reared apart and together, and adoptive and biological parent-child and sibling resemblances. The advantages of such an extensive data set can be illustrated by comparing the following correlations for the FFM trait of extraversion: MZ twins reared together (.55), MZ twins reared apart (.38), biological siblings (.20), and unrelated siblings (-.06). Such a pattern is interpreted by behavioral geneticists as indicating that individuals who share genes are alike in extraversion regardless of rearing environment, while unrelated individuals reared together show virtually no similarity in the trait (Rowe, 1994). The results of Loehlin and Rowe's analysis indicate a mean broad heritability coefficient for personality is .43. Their results for all five of the FFM personality traits is shown in Table 3.5.

Best fitting models indicated that two major sources accounted for much of the individual variation in personality across traits: unshared environment and broad heritability. In contrast, the shared environment of siblings accounted for only 2% to 9% of the total variation. Finally, the least amount of influence on personality was the parent-child environmental influence, which was negligible. These findings (and others) should alert social scientists that the "social mold" model of personality development of the 1950s, in which the child's personality was seen as molded by parental behavior, is no longer tenable in scientific discourse (Rowe, 1994). Clearly, correlations between child-rearing styles and child personality traits in biological families do not constitute unequivocal evidence for socialization effects, as is often presumed. By themselves correlations can never provide a convincing argument for cause and effect, and in some cases they may be very misleading.

Environmental Influences on Personality

The idea that personality systems are brain structures designed by natural selection to solve certain problems does not imply that the systems can't be influenced by the environment. Research in behavioral genetics shows that about half the variation in personality results from people having different genes, and that the other half comes from people experiencing different environments.

Within an evolutionary systems perspective, environmental influences may be thought of as specific types of stimulation influencing specific systems. That is, an environmental influence that affects the conscientiousness system would be specific to that system and would not necessarily have an effect on other systems. For example, inhibited children placed in daycare within the first 2 years were more likely to change to a noninhibited pattern (Fox et al., 2001). This suggests that greater experience with nonfamily members during the early years results in a decrease in fear responses to new people. The environmental influence is specific to the fear system.

In general, environmental influences on personality are found by behavioral geneticists to be not shared within families. That is, families do not appear to have a consistent effect on all their children. For example, we have seen that inhibited children placed in daycare within the first 2 years become less inhibited. This effect would not usually be shared within families because it involves influences that occur outside the family. Moreover, if the child's inborn traits and dispositions are responded to differently by different mothers, this would lead to underestimating true shared environmental effects because behavioral genetics analyses would average across and thus nullify these effects of parents. For example, several studies have shown that some mothers may choose to withdraw from difficult infants while others increase their care giving (Peters-Martin & Wachs, 1984). If, on the other hand, the infant's genetic traits evoked consistent responses from different parents, this evocative gene–environment interaction would be subsumed under "genetic effects," as would passive gene–environment effects. However, in some cases, parenting styles can have dramatic effects on child outcomes.

For example, in the case of nurturance/love, it makes sense that the primary source of environmental influences would be adult caretakers—typically family members. The environmental stimulation most relevant to nurturance/love are the sorts of things we label warm and affectionate, and this type of stimulation is unlikely to come from outside the family, at least during infancy and early childhood. It is thus not surprising that traits related to nurturance/love do show evidence of shared environmental influence (Bouchard, 1996; Tellegen, Lykken, Bouchard, & Wilcox, 1988).

Shared environmental influence has also been found for security of attachment (Bokhorst et al., 2000). Again, it makes sense that influences on attachment security would be shared within families. All things being equal, a warm, affectionate, and responsive mother would be likely to treat all of her children in a similar manner and have a similar effect on all of them. Of course, things are not always equal. Some children are more affectionate than others and respond more positively to maternal affection than others.

In the end the causal chain between genes and phenotypes is a long one, with genetics (G) and environment (E) interwoven at every step. The distal effects of genes often depend on environmental triggers or enabling conditions, and the effects of different environments depend on the genetic characteristics of the individuals encountering an environment. But $G \times E$ covariances and their interactions are subsumed under genetic effects if one adopts the additive assumption of the behavioral genetics model. Because of these problematic assumptions of the additive model underlying behavioral genetic research, there can be no satisfying substitute for directly studying how the environment affects the child.

☐ Chapter Summary

All plants and animals share the same basic building blocks of eukaryotic cells. This shared characteristic is homologous, meaning that all of these multicellular organisms derived this structure from a common ancestor as life forms began to evolve and speciate over the past 4000 million years.

All of these living organisms contain the molecule deoxyribose nucleic acid, or DNA, which provides the essential mechanism for heredity. However, mitochondrial DNA (mtDNA) is passed on only from the mother; thus mitochondria are clones. Because its mutation rate may be more easily estimated than DNA, mtDNA can be used as a kind of "molecular clock" to estimate the degree of relatedness between different populations and to reconstruct patterns of evolution.

The vast majority of the cell's DNA is located within the cell's nucleus in structures called chromosomes that are large enough to be seen through a light microscope. Preliminary estimates from the Human Genome Project indicate that the 46 human chromosomes contain approximately 30,000 genes.

The development of the organism from the genotype is an epigenetic process that serves to specify methods of construction rather than a finished product. Genes work in combination rather than in isolation from one another, and make use of the same master instructions over and over again, allowing genes to be expressed to different extents in different locations.

Virtually every aspect of an organism's phenotype is the joint product of its genes and its environment. Three types of genotype–environment effects are thought to influence the development of personality: passive, active, and evocative. A passive effect refers to the rearing environment provided by genetically related parents. An active effect refers to the child's own choices to selectively attend to a specific aspect of the general environment. Evocative effects refer to the various responses by a child's parents, teachers, peers, and others that are elicited by the child because of some aspect of his or her genotype.

Genetic and early experience factors often interact in dramatic fashion. For example, a specific polymorphism in the serotonin transporter gene of rhesus monkeys is associated with deficits in serotonin metabolism, extreme aggression, and excessive alcohol consumption among monkeys who experienced insecure early attachment relationships, but not in monkeys who developed secure attachment relationships with their mothers during infancy. Early experiences in attachment quality provide a possible nongenetic mechanism for transmitting these patterns to subsequent generations.

Behavioral geneticists are interested in the extent to which individual differences between people in a given environment can be accounted for by differences in their genes. The quantitative evidence for genetic effects on behavior (heritability) derives from two principal sources, twin studies and adoption studies. Twin studies support three broad patterns regarding the heritability of infant temperament. First, there is moderate heritability of temperament shown when parental reports are used but only minimal evidence for heritability when using observational measures of temperament. Second, heritability estimates are consistently higher for indices of negative emotionality (defined variously as behavioral inhibition, shyness, fear, or distress) than positive mood. Third, heritability estimates in one developmental period do not necessarily generalize to other ages.

Personality systems may be thought of as evolved systems designed to deal with life's dangers and opportunities. Research in personality has revealed five personality trait dimensions—the five factor model of personality (FFM). The "big five" personality dimensions are usually named for one end of the continuum they represent:

1. Extroverted: gregarious, sociable, dominant, adventurous
2. Agreeable: affectionate, warm, kind, friendly
3. Conscientious: organized, planful, reliable
4. Stable: calm, worry free, stable
5. Open: original, insightful, inventive, wide-ranging interests

Five types of empirical evidence provide support for an evolutionary psychology of personality. First, comparative research has shown evidence for similar systems in animals that serve clear adaptive functions. Second, neurological research has shown evidence for a structural basis of these systems in the brain. Third, developmental research indicates the presence of recognizable precursors of the FFM personality traits as temperament dimensions in infancy. Fourth, extensive cross-cultural research has demonstrated the universality of the FFM. Finally, behavioral geneticists have demonstrated the heritability of FFM personality traits. Research in behavioral genetics shows that about half the variation in personality results from people having different genes, and that the other half comes from people experiencing different environments.

☐ For Further Inquiry

Lederberg J. (2001). The meaning of epigenetics. *The Scientist 15*(18), 6.

Rutter, M. (2006). *Genes and behavior: Nature-nurture interplay explained.* Oxford, UK: Blackwell.

Watters, E. (2006). DNA is not destiny: The new science of epigenetics rewrites the rules of disease, heredity, and identity. Discover Magazine http://discovermagazine.com /2006/nov/cover

Weaver, I. C. G. (2007). Epigenetic programming by maternal behavior and pharmacological intervention nature versus nurture: Let's call the whole thing off. *Epigenetics, 2*(1), 22–28.

Human Origins

This chapter serves as an introduction to physical anthropology and archeology, two of the subfields of paleoanthropology concerned with the study of human origins and human evolution. The scope of this subject is very broad, spanning over ten million years and covering prehistoric developments around the globe.

The first section addresses the nature of becoming human—what it means to be human and how the biological and behavioral characteristics of modern humans emerged over the past several million years. Evidence of the physical and cultural remains of our earliest hominid ancestors will be presented as well as modern genetic analyses of their fossil record where it has been possible to obtain DNA samples.

The second section addresses controversies regarding the origin of modern Homo sapiens. Proponents of the single-origin hypothesis claims that *H. sapiens* evolved in eastern Africa between 100,000 and 150,000 years ago and, some time afterwards, began recolonizing the rest of the world. It is currently the most widely accepted of the two current theories regarding the origin of anatomically modern humans. However, opponents of a single-origin hypothesis argue that the characteristics of modern humans are the result of genetic contributions from several earlier lineages that evolved on different continents of the Old World, each of which evolved into modern Homo sapiens with significant interbreeding between populations.

☐ Hominid Evolution

Down From the Trees

As primates, humans share many phylogenetic adaptations with other members of this order that have evolved over the past 60 million years. Compared with other mammals, primates have evolved large brains and relatively flat faces that permit excellent stereoscopic vision and depth perception. This was certainly advantageous for arboreal life, as was the development of relatively opposable thumbs useful in grasping while leaping from branch to branch (Ridley, 2004).

But before hands could evolve specialized dexterity compared to feet, something must have first compelled our ancestors to walk upright. This story begins with geological activity in east Africa over five MYA that set in motion a chain of events that would eventually lead to the evolution of Homo sapiens. The dense forest of east Africa began a gradual drying phase that broke up the forest into scattered trees surrounded by savannah grasslands. This ecological change created the selection pressures that led to a constellation of changes in a group of primates that would form the hominid line. First and foremost among these changes was a shift to bipedalism that occurred before other human attributes evolved. It is difficult to pinpoint the specific impetus that led to the evolution of bipedal locomotion. It may have served multiple functions, permitting a rapid and efficient means of travel over long distances and an increased ability to detect predators or prey over greater distances. Whatever the impetus, one important consequence was freeing the hands. Though there are many obvious physical differences between modern humans and apes, such as naked skin, lack of a tail, smaller leaner build, smaller teeth and face, and larger brain, the oldest and most critical difference is our manner of upright, bipedal locomotion.

The Australopiths

According to DNA analysis and the fossil record, the common ancestor of humans and chimpanzees lived in east Africa more than 5 MYA. Noble and Davidson (1996) and Rossano (2003) conclude from their reviews that it was partly arboreal, living on the edge of forests nesting in trees, and was moderately sized and small-brained, similar in size to modern chimpanzees. More hunted than hunter, it lived in small social groups in proximity to the trees, with a diet composed largely of fruit, leaves, and bugs, but very little meat. It had good vision, grasping hands, and was able to shift between quadripedal and bipedal locomotion. Like modern nonhuman primates its communication was primarily nonvocal with only limited vocalizations and no symbolic communication. Males were sometimes solitary and minimally involved in rearing offspring, while females and infants formed loose associations.

Martin (1989) estimates the common ancestor would have been small-brained at approximately 210 cc, and relatively small in stature, weighing only 42 pounds (19 kg), with marked sexual dimorphism in body size. The high degree of sexual dimorphism leads most scientists to conclude that early hominids were polygynous with extensive male–male competition for mates.

Using a phylogenetic approach, Harvard anthropologist Richard Wrangham compared the behavioral traits of humans and our three most closely related living species, common and bonobo chimpanzees, and gorillas. The goal of a phylogenetic comparison is to identify trends and common characteristics across a group of closely related species in order to discern the probable characteristics of their common ancestor.

According to Wrangham (1987) the following eight characteristics of the ape-hominid ancestor are most probable:

1. Closed social networks (i.e., in-group members were readily distinguished from out-of-group members).
2. Males dominated in-group relations.
3. Males occasionally existed singly away from the group.
4. Intergroup relations were generally antagonistic.
5. Males sometimes engaged in preemptive stalk-and-attack encounters with males of other groups.
6. Females left their natal groups for reproduction (exogamy).
7. Social bonds among females were weak but usually tolerant.
8. Males practiced polygyny.

The oldest identified hominid distinct from the common ancestor was first seen in the fossil record about 5 to 4.4 MYA. Almost nothing is known about this hominid, called *Ardipthecus ramidus*. Similarly, only fragmentary evidence exists for *Australopithecus anamensis* whose fossil remains were discovered in northern Kenya in 1995 and date back to about 4.2 to 3.9 MYA. It has been presumed to be an ancestor, the oldest hominid species for which a substantial fossil record exists.

While exploring the floor of a dry riverbed near Laetoli, Tanzania, a team of researchers led by Mary Leakey discovered footprints that had been formed approximately 3.6 MYA. The footprints were made by a pair of ancient hominids walking together stride for stride. Attributed to *Australopithecus afarensis*, the prints clearly reveal a human-like upright gait with the heel landing first, followed by a rocking through the ball of the foot and finishing by pushing off with the big toe. Smaller, slighter footprints appear to be tracking in the larger prints suggesting the possibility of a small family of hominids traveling across a soft layer of volcanic ash.

Shortly after this discovery, a remarkably intact skeleton of an early female *Australopithecus afarensis* was discovered in the Hadar region of Ethiopia in the 1970s, along with many other specimens by Johanson and Edey (1981). The species was highly sexually dimorphic, with females averaging about two-thirds the size of males. The skeleton, known as Lucy, was only about 3.5 feet tall, with a small, ape-like skull indicating a brain size of only 400 cc. However, *A. afarensis* walked upright and is considered to be an early ancestor of the Homo genus.

Lucy and her kin lived between 3.9 and 3 MYA and gave rise to several other *Australopithecus* species over the course of several million years, including *A. africanus* and *A. garhi*. As the ecology of east Africa underwent a prolonged cooling and drying, we see in the fossil record a number of Australopith species that inhabited a wide range of habitats from dense forests to a mixed habitat of savannah woodland, eventually spreading throughout Africa. Klein (1999) recognizes seven or eight species of Australopiths, though probably more than a dozen species once existed. The Australopiths proved to be extremely well adapted to these different environments as evidenced from their two million year existence on the African plains. Because of the continuous alteration of the fossil record with new and important finds, we may never be certain of the exact relationships between the various Australopith species and which species were ancestral to which others. Still, it is certain that one of the Australopith species was the direct ancestor of Homo habilis, the earliest documented species in the Homo genus.

Homo Habilis and Homo Erectus

After years of excavation at the Olduvai Gorge in northern Tanzania, Louis and Mary Leakey identified fossil remains of *Australopithecus*, but also uncovered the remains of a perplexing hominid that appeared to be older than some of the fossils remains, but was also less robust, with smaller teeth and a larger brain. Eventually Louis Leakey became convinced that this larger brained hominid was the real toolmaker of Olduvai and named him Homo habilis. For Leakey, H. habilis marked the origin of a new genus distinct from that of *Australopithecus* because of its larger brain (640 to 750 cc vs. 450 to 500 cc), more gracile form, and smaller molars and premolars.

Homo habilis makes its first appearance in the fossil record about 2.5 MYA. Although carbon dating techniques allow for a reliable estimate of the age range of fossil remains, the fossil record is still too fragmentary to determine the lineage or direct line of descent of Homo habilis.

Paleoanthropologists continue to debate how many different hominid species existed because of philosophical differences between "lumpers" and "splitters." One thing for certain is that there have been many species of hominids, some of which existed contemporaneously with Homo sapiens. We now have the rare, and somewhat dubious, distinction of being the only surviving member of our genus.

Without question, several related archaic Homo species form a connecting bridge between the Australopiths and the later emerging Homo erectus. Although views on the details differ, a general consensus exists that at least two species of archaic Homo coexisted in Africa with at least two species of later Australopiths approximately 2 to 2.5 MYA. Eventually, a new species called Homo erectus evolved in Africa and soon after migrated into the Middle East, Europe, and Asia, reaching China and Java 1.8 MYA (Tattersall, 2000) Great regional variation in the fossil records suggests that some speciation occurred as the result of entering these different environments. Overall, there was an evolutionary trend of increasing brain size (750 cc to 1250 cc) and decreasing sexual dimorphism (females increased from 62% to 83% of the size of males) from early to late Homo erectus. This new species of Homo adapted to a wide geographic range over a long period of time from 1.8 MYA to 250,000 years ago, though some evidence suggests that they continued to exist in isolated locations in Asia as recently as 26,000 years ago (Swisher et al., 1996).

Because of controversies regarding the number of distinct species of Homo (including *H. rudolfensis*, *H. ergaster*, *H. heidelbergensis*, etc.) that are beyond the scope of this introduction to research on human origins, I will hereafter refer to these two major groups of fossils as Homo habilis and Homo erectus. The physical features of H. erectus are more similar to modern humans than those of H. habilis, including body and brain size, teeth structure, and degree of sexual dimorphism. H. erectus also exhibits the first evidence we see of widespread migration beyond Africa, cooperative hunting, the use of fire for cooking and warmth, and significant advances in the manufacture and use of tools and weapons.

Freeing the Hands

An important direct consequence of bipedalism is the freeing of the hands from the task of locomotion. This allowed for the evolution of the fingers and thumb to support grasping and the fine manipulation of objects. Relatively recent adaptations, like a fully opposable thumb that permits a better grip on objects, may be shared by a small circle of primates that includes only the great apes. Still more recent adaptations like a pincer grip between thumb and forefinger that permits a more precise grip on objects is unique to the human species.

This aspect of human evolution has been clarified by recently identifying a gene enhancer that is expressed in the development of the human hand and concentrated on the forefinger. The enhancer, named HACNS1, exhibits stronger recurrent selection on the human lineage than any other conserved enhancer sequence. By testing combinations of human and chimpanzee HACNS1 sequences, Prabhakar et al. (2008) narrowed down the relevant functional mutations to an 81-base pair region containing 13 substitutions that arose during human evolution. This concentration of substitutions is highly unusual with respect to the genome as a whole, implying positive selection on this region during human origins (Wray & Babbitt, 2008). The functional explanation pertains to the unique evolution of human manual dexterity at a period when hominid tool making was on the rise. The flexibility and coordination of the human hand is distinctly superior to all other primates and evolutionary advances in structure provided ancient hominids with the ability to make stone tools over two MYA.

The Oldowan toolmakers produced the oldest known stone tools that date from approximately 2.6 to 1.5 MYA. These tools were used by the earliest hominds for cutting, slicing, and chopping. Oldowan tools did not require a high level of intelligence, but they did require the ability to plan a sequence of precise manipulations that shaped the stones into sharp cores and flakes. At this stage of human evolution the hand was on its way to becoming an instrument of tool manufacture that would eventually dwarf that of all other animals. Although other animals make primitive tools like shaping a twig to stick into a termite mound, nothing in such behavior would predict the astonishing capacity that humans possess to transform their world.

Another human trait that is unique, or at least unique in terms of degree, is handedness. Although some evidence exists to suggest that chimpanzees may show moderate preference for the right hand in laboratory tasks (Hopkins, 1996) their ratio of a 2:1 preference for the right hand is much less than the 8:1 preference found in humans. This human preference extends back at least half a million years (Keeley, 1977) and possibly as far back as the tool making at Oldowan (Walker and Leakey, 1993).

A related difference between chimpanzee and human behavior involves the throwing of objects. Chimpanzees will occasionally throw objects wildly as part of a threat display, but rarely throw at something for purposes of hunting and seem to never take aim. For example, Goodall (1986) reports less than 7% accuracy when chimpanzees throw at large objects only 6 feet away, making it very unlikely that a chimpanzee will ever be drafted as a major league quarterback or baseball pitcher! In contrast, human abilities in throwing can be honed to exquisite degrees of accuracy and strength.

Research has consistently revealed a pronounced sex difference in throwing accuracy when controlling for factors such as differences in strength or physique, previous sport experience, or gender identity, although sex differences have not been found in other primates. In humans, sex differences in throwing distance and velocity are present as early as 2 years of age, and are the most sexually dimorphic physical skill ever documented. In his systematic review of sex differences, Geary (1998) reports little overlap in throwing distance between preschool girls and boys; more than 9 out of 10 boys can throw farther than the average girl at this age. Such pronounced sex differences at an early age make it implausible that they are the result of differential socialization, though socialization practices probably magnify the differences. Geary (1998) attributes the difference, in part, to differences in the structure of the skeletal system that supports throwing. It is likely that over the course of hominid evolution there were selection pressures on males to develop throwing abilities for the purposes of hunting and defense. Calvin (1983) has argued persuasively that throwing took on increased evolutionary significance beginning with the advent of bipedalism. This is supported by large quantities of ancient spears and other projectile weapons that indicate the importance of throwing for hominids throughout the Paleolithic period. Because of the extensive division of labor between the sexes that relegated hunting and defense to males, selection pressures for females were not present (Westergaard, Liv, Haynie, & Suomi, 2000.)

Brain Expansion

Thus far we have noted a cascade of basic changes that together mark the emergence of a line of hominids that would eventually lead to the evolution of modern humans. Beginning with climate changes that brought about habitat changes for arboreal apes in east Africa, we see the gradual emergence of a group of archaic apes, the Australopiths, who began to favor an upright mode of locomotion. This change afforded the Australopiths a rapid and efficient means of travel over long distances, and an increased ability to detect predators or prey over greater distances. The Australopiths proved to be extremely well adapted to the African savannah, as evidenced by their two million year existence and gradual expansion throughout Africa into different habitats, which furthered the process of speciation. Walking on two feet also freed the forelimbs from the task of locomotion and allowed for the evolution of a more specialized hand. With this new dexterity archaic members of the emerging genus Homo pioneered the fabrication of primitive stone tools used to butcher animal carcasses for meat as early as 2.5 MYA.

Homo habilis was designated a new genus because of its larger brain, leaner more gracile form, and smaller molars and premolars. The substantial changes in the overall facial structure of H. habilis due to the decreased size of cheek and tooth areas may have enabled an increase in the size of the brain. This first sign of significant brain expansion in the hominid line had to be more the consequence, rather than the cause, of bipedal locomotion. The eventual increase in manual dexterity, tool making, and cooperative hunting, as well as the increased meat in the diet were all linked to the first signs of significant brain expansion. Meat as a source of protein is necessary to support increases in brain size because of the increased metabolic demands of a large brain. In this sense, the manufacture of tools and weapons and the evolution of cooperative hunting of large game rely upon greater cognitive capacities, but they also helped to create the biological conditions required to further the expansion of the brain. In any case, the fossil record clearly reveals a trend of relatively rapid brain expansion from the appearance of Homo habilus at 2.5 MYA to the emergence of an even more large-brained species, Homo erectus about 1.8 MYA (see Figure 4.1).

The evolution of hominid brain size illustrates the phenomenon of "punctuated equilibrium" rather than the model of evolution as a process of slow, continual change. From the arrival of the Australopiths at 4 MYA to the arrival of Homo habilus 2.5 million years later, relatively slight changes in brain size are seen from the fossil record. Another period of long-term stasis was evident from about 1.8 MYA to 500,000 years ago. Then this period was followed by the most rapid increase in brain size that began about 500,000 years ago and lasted until about 30,000 years

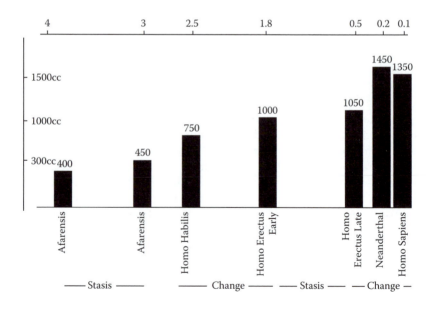

FIGURE 4.1   Two periods of brain expansion in the hominid line.

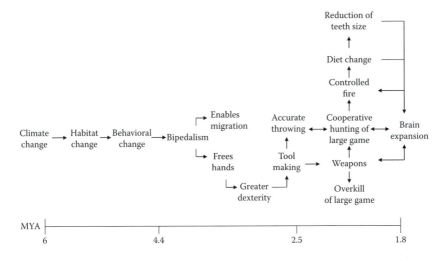

FIGURE 4.2   First major brain expansion.

ago. This fluctuation between long periods of equilibrium with relatively little change, punctuated by periods of rapid change, must correspond to prevailing selection pressures for increased brain size and cognitive capacity. What were these ecological conditions?

It is likely that the first period of significant hominid brain expansion (2.5 to 1.8 MYA) was driven by selection pressures arising from demands of the physical ecology of early Homo (Figure 4.2). Once successful adaptation was achieved in terms of mastering techniques of hunting, foraging, defense from predators, and shelter from the elements, this set of selection pressures would gradually diminish. Speciation would inevitably begin as hominid groups expanded into more diverse habitats (with distinct selection pressures) that were geographically separated from one another. While scientists interpret the fossil record somewhat differently, and new fossil finds occur regularly, the prevailing consensus is that there might have been as many as six to eight subspecies of Homo prior to the first major migration out of Africa.

Evidence suggests that the second period of brain expansion in the hominid line was driven by entirely different selection pressures (Figure 4.3). This period began about 500,000 years ago after Homo erectus migrated out of Africa and expanded its range across Asia and Europe. At the time of this expansion, challenges calling for greater intelligence likely arose from the social ecology, as has been argued by many scholars over the past 30 years (Humprey, 1976; Whiten & Byrne, 1988). Although much has been written about this social function of intellect, the gist of the argument is fairly simple. After achieving some degree of dominance and control of physical resources necessary for survival and reproduction within a given

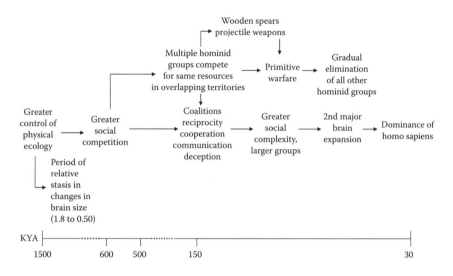

FIGURE 4.3 Second major brain expansion.

territory, new selection pressures arose from social competition within and between hominid groups for these vital resources. In this scenario, often referred to as the Machiavellian hypothesis (Whiten & Byrne, 1988), an evolutionary arms race propelled the evolution of social intelligence to new heights as individuals attempted to outmaneuver one another in a kind of chess match over access to key resources. In summary, throughout the course of human evolution selection pressures arising from demands and opportunities from the physical ecology (predators, prey, physical resources, shelter) led to the first significant brain expansion. One million years later the challenges arising from the complex social ecology (negotiation, coalitions, communication, cooperation, deception) of more advanced and ecologically dominant hominids led to the second major period of brain expansion (Alexander, 1989; Geary, 2005).

Homo Neanderthalensis

The term *Neanderthal Man* was coined in 1863 after the Neander valley or *thal* where the controversial skull was discovered. When several leading paleontologists and medical pathologists in Germany became aware of the fossils, a disagreement developed about who the Neanderthal Man might have been. It was suggested that he had been an old Roman, a Dutchman, or even a central Asian soldier in the service of the Russian czar during the Napoleonic Wars of the early 19th century. The reality that these bones were from an earlier variety or species of human was inconceivable to most of the scientific world prior to the publication of Darwin's *The Origin of Species* in 1859.

Today the remains of over 400 Neanderthals have been found, far more than any other ancient human species. This extensive fossil record seems to confirm that these ancient Europeans played an important role in modern human origins; however, just what exactly that role was is still under debate. No other ancient people have aroused more controversy and confusion than have the Neanderthals. Paleoanthropologists have long debated about whether Neanderthals should be classified as a separate Homo species or as a subspecies of Homo sapiens. Recent evidence from mitochondrial DNA studies has been interpreted as evidence that Neanderthals were not a subspecies of H. sapiens. Other scientists argue that fossil evidence suggests that the two species may have occasionally interbred, and hence were the same biological species. We shall revisit this controversy later in this chapter.

The Neanderthals inhabited Europe and Asia from about 230,000 to 28,000 years ago, during the Middle Paleolithic period (Wade, 2006). Recently scientists confirmed that fossil remains from a Siberian specimen were Neanderthal, extending the known range 1200 miles east of their European origins. By all accounts they were a physically diverse people, with regional differences apparent. The European groups were adapted to the cold climate of the Pleistocene or Ice Age, as indicated by their large braincases, heavy, muscular builds, large noses, and greater lung capacity, traits observed in Native American sub-arctic populations. On average, Neanderthal males stood about 5 feet 6 inches and weighed about 185 pounds. The relatively large heads and massive but short bodies of Neanderthals very likely were more efficient in cold climates since they would produce more body heat relative to the amount that is lost. They probably stood as erect as we do and were fully bipedal. They were not only strong but apparently quite athletic. The thickness and density of their leg bones suggests that they did a great deal of walking and running. The fact that adult Neanderthal skeletons frequently have multiple healed bone fractures suggests that these people had rough lives. Some researchers believe that many of the broken bones were the result of hunting large game animals up close with jabbing spears—a dangerous enterprise. They may also have been caused by fighting with other groups.

Neanderthal heads were long (from front to back) and gave the Neanderthal face and head an appearance reminiscent of late Homo erectus. Their brain sizes have been estimated to range between 1300 and 1800 cc (average 1450 cc) or somewhat larger than modern humans (1000 to 1700 cc, average 1350). The theory that Neanderthals lacked complex language was generally accepted until 1983, when a Neanderthal hyoid bone was found at the Kebara Cave in Israel. The bone that was found is virtually identical to that of modern humans. The hyoid is a small bone that holds the root of the tongue in place, a requirement for human speech and, therefore, its presence seems to imply some ability to speak. Further evidence in support of language comes from the Max Planck Institute in Leipzig where scientists have identified a gene complex called FOXP2 in the DNA from two Neanderthals. This gene contributes to language by acting directly on the brain and the nerves that control facial muscles. However, language itself leaves no fossils and it is debatable whether Neanderthals actually had language, or merely had the physical ability to produce a wide enough range of sounds to support linguistic development. Neanderthal archeological sites show both a smaller and a less flexible toolkit than in the Upper Paleolithic sites, occupied by the modern humans that replaced them. Their bone industry was relatively simple though they routinely constructed a wide range of sophisticated stone implements, including flakes, hand axes, and lances. Many of these tools were very sharp. Also, although they had weapons, none have as yet been found that were used as projectile weapons. However, a number of 400,000-year-old wooden projectile spears were found at Schöningen in northern Germany. These are thought to have been made by the Neanderthal's ancestors, Homo erectus (*heildelbergensis*). Generally, projectile weapons are more commonly associated with H. sapiens.

Neanderthals performed a sophisticated set of tasks normally associated with humans alone. For example, they constructed complex shelters, controlled fire, and skinned animals. Particularly intriguing is a hollowed-out bear femur with four holes spaced like four holes in the diatonic scale claimed by many to have been deliberately bored into it. This flute was found in western Slovenia in 1995 near a Mousterian Era fireplace used by Neanderthals, but its significance is still a matter of dispute. Although much has been made of the Neanderthal's burial of their dead, their burial rituals, if any, were less elaborate than those of anatomically modern humans.

One Species or Two?

Today we are still left with the question of whether Neanderthals were direct ancestors of our species or a separate species with whom we share a distant common ancestor. Two conflicting sources of evidence have shed light on this issue. This evidence is in the form of bones and genes.

In 2004, researchers from the Max Planck Institute for Evolutionary Anthropology in Germany completed tests for the presence of intact mitochondrial DNA in skeletal material from 24 Neanderthals and 40 early modern Homo sapiens. They found it in four of the Neanderthals and five of the early modern humans. These individuals lived 60,000 to 30,000 years ago in Central and Western Europe. The nucleotide sequences that were analyzed indicated that early modern humans were significantly different genetically from Neanderthals. It was estimated that only about 25% of the Neanderthal sequences were shared with their early modern human contemporaries. In an earlier study of mitochondrial DNA extracted from a Neanderthal skeleton discovered in Germany, it was established that there were 27 amino acid differences between this sample and random samples from modern living humans and chimpanzees. Based on these data, geneticists estimate that our common ancestor with Neanderthals lived about 690,000 to 500,000 years ago. All of this genetic evidence supports the view that the Neanderthals were not a subspecies of Homo sapiens and that they were not our direct ancestors. However, critics have pointed out that these differences between Neanderthals and modern humans could be accounted for by genetic drift causing rapid changes in gene pool frequencies and that Homo sapiens living at their time might not have been very different from them genetically.

The size of the total Neanderthal population appears to have diminished steadily from an estimated peak of about 15,000 individual beginning around 35,000 years ago. The last verifiable date for a Neanderthal site was about 28,000 years ago. What happened to them is not clear. However, their relatively abrupt disappearance roughly coincides with both the peak of the glacial expanse of the last Ice Age and the arrival and growth in population size of modern humans (Cro Magnon) in Europe (Figure 4.4). It is most likely that Neanderthals could not compete effectively with the technologically and linguistically more advanced and numerically larger Homo sapiens population.

New and controversial evidence regarding the question of one species or two arose as a result of the 1999 discovery of a 4-year-old child's skeleton in Portugal dating to 24,500 years ago (Duarte et al., 1999). The Iberian peninsula is an area where there was a significant overlap in time and place between Neanderthal and modern humans, and the two groups could have coexisted for as long as 10,000 years. The child appeared to have had a mixture of Neanderthal and modern human anatomical characteristics suggesting that he had been a hybrid. This was several thousand years after the last known Neanderthal. The implication is that some of the Neanderthals interbred with modern humans resulting in gene flow between the populations. If that is true, then the genetic difference between us and them must not have been as great as would be expected between two distinct species. In other words, this would suggest that the Neanderthals were an ancestor of Homo sapiens rather than a distinct species and that at least some people from Europe and possibly southwest Asia may share some Neanderthal genes. We shall revisit this controversy later in this chapter.

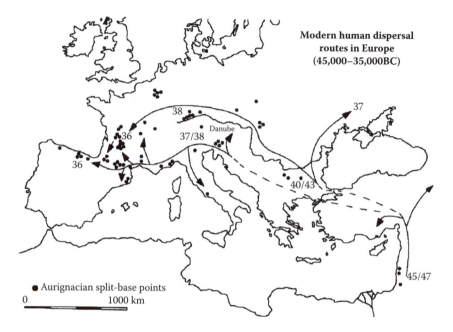

FIGURE 4.4 The arrival of modern humans in Europe and fall of the Neanderthals (From Wade, N. [2006]. *Before the dawn: Recovering the lost history of our ancestors.* New York, NY: Penguin. With permission.)

Regardless of how they are classified or what happened to them, we can assert that the Neanderthals were the first humans to live successfully in the Northern Hemisphere during the last Ice Age, which began in Europe over 75,000 years ago. Prior to 2004 all textbooks on human evolution claimed that Neanderthal was the last surviving species of our genus distinct from Homo sapiens. However, recent archaeological finds have completely altered the picture.

Homo Floresiensis

By far the most spectacular archeological find of recent times was the discovery of a very small human-like skull and other bones from the same individual on the island of Flores in 2003 (P. Brown et al., 2004; Morwood et al., 2004). An Australian–Indonesian team of scientists sifting through artifacts and skeletal remains in a damp cave on a remote Indonesian island have concluded that the bones are from human ancestors who stood 3 feet tall and lived between 18,000 and 12,000 years ago. Also uncovered are bone fragments from at least seven other diminutive individuals spanning about 80,000 years. Found throughout the cave with these remains were sophisticated stone tools at horizons from 95,000 to 13,000 years mingled with the charred bones of *Stegodon*, a dwarf elephant, presumably the prey of *Homo floresiensis*. Three characteristics of this new discovery stand out: (1) the relative recency of the find, (2) the exceptionally small body, and (3) the tiny brain (Argue, Donlon, Groves, & Wright, 2006; Martin, Maclarnon, Phillips, & Dobyns, 2006; P. Brown et al., 2004).

The research team had traveled to Flores to look for evidence of the original human migration of H. sapiens from Asia into Australia, but nobody expected to find a new species. A remarkable aspect of the find is that this species is thought to have survived on Flores until at least as recently as 12,000 years ago. This makes it the longest-lasting nonmodern human, surviving long past the Neanderthals (*H. neanderthalensis*) who went extinct about 28,000 years ago. The discovery suggests we shared the planet with this other species of humanity until quite recently in evolutionary terms. *Homo floresiensis* certainly coexisted for a long time with modern humans, who arrived in the region 35,000 to 55,000 years ago, but it is unknown if they may have interacted.

Flores has been described as "a kind of lost world," where archaic animals, elsewhere long extinct, had evolved into giant and dwarf forms through allopatric speciation. The island had dwarf elephants (a species of *Stegodon*, a prehistoric elephant) and giant monitor lizards akin to the Komodo dragon, as well as *H. floresiensis*. Local geology suggests that a volcanic eruption on Flores was responsible for the demise of *H. floresiensis* in the part of the island under study at approximately 12,000 years ago, along with other local fauna, including the dwarf elephant *Stegodon*. The discoverers suspect, however, that this species may have survived longer in other parts of Flores. In the mythology of the island, there were common references to small, hairy, language-poor cave dwellers called *Ebu Gogo* believed to have been present at the time of the Dutch arrival during the 16th century.

Small Bodies

H. floresiensis appears to be the most "extreme" member of the extended human family and are certainly the shortest and smallest. The type specimen of *H. floresiensis* has been estimated to be 1 meter in height, weighing about 25 kg (55 lbs.). The Morwood team suggests that they were the products of "island dwarfing": the tendency of large creatures living on isolated islands with few predators to gradually become smaller to adapt to limited resources, while small animals become larger to be able to compete (Morwood et al., 2004). Thus, the most probable evolutionary scenario is that *Homo floresiensis* was a reduced-size adaptation of Homo erectus, an early human ancestor that arrived on Flores about 800,000 years ago.

Because Homo erectus was approximately the same size as modern humans, this scenario would entail a drastic reduction in size. Indeed, the skull from *H. floresiensis* is even somewhat smaller than the much earlier ancestor australopithecines, for whom no fossil remains have been found outside of Africa, and none there later than 1.4 MYA. In sum, there appears to be no credible alternative theory to the H. erectus ancestor at present.

A single sequence of mtDNA from one of the specimens would be very informative about this scenario. The oldest fossil human DNA is from Europe, dating to as early as 40,000 years. The prospect seems unlikely because in tropical islands, DNA can degrade in as little as a few dozen years.

Small Brains

Paleontologists generally agree that no Homo erectus ever made the tools uncovered from the Liang Bua cave on the island of Flores. Indeed, no known hominid species apart from modern Homo sapiens was thought capable of making the blade tools and points found with the *Homo floresiensis* remains.

Thus, the diminutive size of the brain is puzzling. When the first skull was found, it was assumed to be that of a child. When it turned out to be a grown individual (closed fontanelles and worn teeth), it was thought to be microcephalic, but that theory has also been discredited. Comparisons with modern human dwarfs are flawed, because these people are not generally proportionally smaller than other humans, only short-limbed.

The brain is reduced considerably relative to the brain of this species' plausible immediate ancestor H. erectus, which is estimated at 980 cm. The brain size of the type specimen, at 380 cm, is at the lower range of chimpanzees or the ancient australopithecines. However, the brain to body mass ratio of *H. floresiensis* is comparable to that of Homo erectus.

The overall shape of the skull of *H. floresiensis* resembles that of *H. erectus*, although other morphological features indicate a more advanced brain than H. erectus, including enlarged frontal and temporal lobes. The frontal lobes of modern humans are associated with anticipatory planning and problem solving, and temporal lobes are thought to play a role in memory. One other indicator of intelligence is the size of region 10 of the dorsomedial prefrontal cortex, which is associated with self-awareness. This was estimated at about the same size as that of modern humans, despite the much smaller overall size of the brain.

The discoverers have associated *H. floresiensis* with more advanced behaviors than *H. erectus*. There is evidence of the use of fire for cooking. The species has also been associated with stone tools of the sophisticated Upper Paleolithic tradition typically associated with modern humans, who have nearly quadruple (1310 to 1475 cm) the brain volume of *H. floresiensis* (with body mass increased by a factor of 2.6). Some of these tools were apparently used in the cooperative hunting of local dwarf *Stegodon* by this small human species.

Recent Ancestry

Moreover, the discoverers of *H. floresiensis* conclude that the species or its ancestors could only have reached the isolated island by water transport, perhaps arriving in bamboo rafts around 100,000 (or if as *H. erectus*, then as early as 800,000) years ago. This perceived evidence of advanced technology and cooperation on a modern human level has prompted the discoverers to hypothesize that *H. floresiensis* almost certainly had language. These suggestions have proved the most controversial of the discoverers' findings, despite the probable high intelligence of *H. floresiensis*.

In conclusion, the discovery of these human remains is widely considered the most important of its kind in recent history and came as a complete surprise to the scientific community. The new species challenges many current ideas about human evolution. *Homo floresiensis* is so different in form from other members of genus Homo, *and so recent to us in time,* that it forces the recognition of a new, undreamt-of variability in the genus, and provides evidence against a simple model of linear evolution. The existence of *Homo neanderthalensis*, the late full-sized Homo erectus, and now *Homo floresiensis* as contemporaries of modern Homo sapiens tends to refute any "serial development theory" on its face, and imply something of a more "parallel" development scenario.

☐ Two Alternative Models of Modern Human Evolution

Given the relative scarcity of fossils and the discovery of important new finds like that of *Homo floresiensis*, researchers disagree about the details and course of modern human evolutionary history. Because of its time-scale and interdisciplinary nature, debates on modern human origins require an understanding of biological processes like speciation, and the details and fallibilities of research techniques in archeology and molecular genetics. Although scientists have revised this history several times over the last decades, they currently agree that the oldest named species of the genus Homo, Homo habilis, evolved in Africa around two MYA, and that members of the genus migrated out of Africa somewhat later. The descendants of these ancient migrants, including various subspecies of Homo erectus, have become known through fossils uncovered far from Africa, and are the key to understanding current controversies.

The Single-Origin Hypothesis

Charles Darwin was among the first to suggest that all humans had a single common ancestor who originally lived in Africa. In the *Descent of Man,* he wrote:

> In each great region of the world the living mammals are closely related to the extinct species of the same region. It is, therefore, probable that Africa was formerly inhabited by extinct apes closely allied to the gorilla and chimpanzee; and as these two species are now man's nearest allies, it is somewhat more probable that our early progenitors lived on the African continent than elsewhere. (1896, p. 155)

Darwin's analysis was prescient because in 1871 there were hardly any human fossils of ancient hominids available. Fifty years later Darwin was vindicated, as anthropologists began finding numerous fossils of ancient hominids all over Africa. Today all theories of early hominid evolution recognize Africa as the ancient homeland; however, controversies remain over modern human origins.

The *single-origin hypothesis* (or *recent Africa origins model*) initially proposed by Stringer and Andrews (1988) is one of two current theories regarding the origin of anatomically modern humans. According to this model, H. sapiens evolved from a single ancestral hominid population, whose descendants ultimately replaced all other species of hominids without interbreeding. H. sapiens are thought to have evolved in eastern Africa between 100,000 and 200,000 years ago and, some time afterwards, began recolonizing the rest of the world. These more recent migrants did not interbreed with the scattered descendants of earlier exoduses. For this reason, the model is sometimes called the "replacement scenario" as every species of the genus except Homo sapiens was driven extinct with no significant gene flow from archaic human populations into the present human population.

Evidence in support of this hypothesis is drawn from both fossil and DNA analysis, in particular from mitochondrial and Y chromosome DNA sequences. Most DNA is located in the cell's nucleus; however, a much smaller amount of genetic material, mitochondrial DNA (mtDNA) is located in mitochondria, which are assumed to have evolved separately. Because mitochondrial DNA is typically passed on only from the mother, the mitochondria are clones. This means that the only source of change in the mtDNA from generation to generation is mutation, unlike nuclear DNA which changes by 50% each generation because of the recombination of sexual reproduction. Because its mutation rate may be more easily estimated than that of DNA, mtDNA is used as a "molecular clock." This is accomplished in humans by sequencing about 440 base pairs of the mtDNA, out of a total of 16,568 base pairs located on 37 genes. These 440 base pairs are then compared with those of other individuals to determine maternal lineage. Similarly, the Y chromosomal DNA that is paternally inherited may also be used to trace lineage. Molecular geneticists use both techniques to estimate the degree of relatedness between different populations and to reconstruct patterns of evolution.

Based on these techniques, geneticists have concluded that genetic diversity among living human beings is relatively small compared with other species (e.g., 10% that of chimpanzees) and this variability is greatest in Africa. There are 15 surviving mtDNA lineages dating before 80,000 years ago in Africa, and only one for the rest of the world. This clearly suggests an early radiation of anatomically modern humans within Africa, before they migrated out of Africa. Based upon mutations on mtDNA and the Y chromosome, the oldest changes in the human genome took place in Africa about 150,000 years ago. Archeological sites of the oldest anatomically modern human remains in Ethiopia appear to confirm this.

The Multiregional Hypothesis

The opponents of a single-origin hypothesis argue that interbreeding indeed occurred and that the characteristics of modern humans are the result of genetic contributions from several earlier lineages that evolved on different continents of the Old World. This *multiregional origin hypothesis* holds that genetic variation between contemporary human races is partly attributable to genetic inheritance from either Homo sapiens subspecies, or other hominid species, that were dispersed geographically throughout Asia, and possibly Europe, prior to the evolution of modern Homo sapiens.

According to one of its main proponents, Milford Wolpoff, the multiregional origin hypothesis must be distinguished from earlier, discredited models involving polygenism or the theory that human races have had very ancient and isolated evolutionary histories (Wolpoff & Caspari, 1996). Wolpoff and colleagues claim that a direct test using the fossil record disconfirms the single-origin hypothesis and that the basic assumptions of molecular geneticists are untenable. Let us examine each of these claims separately.

The multiregional hypothesis was originally developed on the basis of fossil evidence. The logic of the researchers derives from the accepted migration routes of humans out of Africa through the Middle East into Indonesia and finally Australia. If the replacement scenario of the single-origin hypothesis is correct, then relatively recent (less than 30,000 years old) human skulls from Australia should be more similar to somewhat older (less than 100,000 years old) skulls of anatomically modern humans from the Middle East or Africa than to the archaic (more than

200,000 years old) skulls of Homo erectus from Indonesia. However, the data indicate that the Australian aboriginal skull is more similar to the hominid skull from Indonesia than the more recent human skull from the Middle East, in direct contradiction of the expected outcome derived from the single-origin hypothesis (Wolpoff, Hawks, Frayer, & Huntley, 2001).

Instead, these findings support the idea that the first exodus of archaic hominids from Africa gradually dispersed into different regions, and each evolved into modern humans. According to this multiregional scenario, the new selection pressures that resulted from the different ecologies propelled evolutionary changes in regional groups, that were in turn spread throughout the entire human population through interbreeding. Despite significant differentiation between groups, speciation was checked by gene flow. Thus, multiregional human evolution relies on gene flow to explain the paradox of shared genetic history with continuity for different anatomical features in different regions over long periods of time (Hawks & Wolpoff, 2003).

The second claim regarding the validity of several assumptions of molecular genetics with respect to testing evolutionary hypotheses relies upon several assertions. Multiregionalists question two key assumptions regarding the use of mtDNA to date prehistoric events, that (1) mtDNA mutation rates are constant over time, and (2) mtDNA has not been affected by natural selection. At the very least confidence intervals should be used whenever specifying a date based on a "molecular clock," since these quantitative estimates are several steps removed from factual information, and have often been dramatically revised as new methods of dating emerge. Regarding this general problem anthropologists like Hawks (2005) conclude that

> the problem is likely serious, and its full extent is not yet known. A basic cautionary attitude would indicate that it is no longer tenable to assert that the history of the mtDNA of a population is the same as the history of the population. There are just too many unaccounted variables to believe that methods that assume complete neutrality for mtDNA are giving accurate dates for population movements, expansions, or other events.

Recent events and new findings in genomics and archeology confirm this cautionary attitude. New archeological finds indicate that early humans may have roamed Europe as much as 1.2 MYA, far earlier than previously estimated. Spanish researchers excavated a jaw bone, teeth, and simple tools in a cave near the city of Burgos dated 400,000 years older than the previously oldest known remains found at a nearby site a decade earlier. The remains have been accurately dated using three techniques and now constitute the oldest known human remains in Europe.

Because they are similar to fossils that are 800,000 years old found at the same site in 1994 they seem to indicate a continuous human presence in Western Europe. The recent find supports the theory that early humans spread from Africa via the Middle East, not across the Straits of Gibraltar separating Africa from Europe, because the jaw was a similar shape to one unearthed in central Asia that was dated at 1.8 MYA. The investigators (Eudald et al., 2008) believe that the new discovery suggests that H. erectus settled in the Caucasus and eventually populated Europe not 800,000 years ago, but at least 1.3 MYA, a conclusion that most scientists would have rejected as recently as 2003. Such a discovery demonstrates the critical role that fossil evidence plays in the reconstruction of hominid movements. Up until this find archaeologists had only found evidence of human activity in Spain, France, and Italy around 1 MYA but no human remains, only animal bones and stone tools.

Recent findings from genetic analyses also fail to confirm a simple model of recent African origins. In the early 1990s evidence from genetics gave strong support to the "recent Africa origin," but subsequent data from the nuclear genome do not support any simple model of human demographic history (Eswaran, Harpending, & Rogers, 2005); other data are compatible with either theory (Relethford, 1998) and still other genetic evidence may actually favor a multiregional theory (Marth et al., 2003). Eswaran et al. (2005) propose a new model in which early humans originate in Africa and then advance across the world by local demic diffusion, hybridization, and natural selection. The Eswaran et al. model does not postulate any particular process of migration, but rather the spread of a modern gene complex that first evolved in Africa. This complex, consisting of a few co-adapted genes, conferred a selective advantage, and gradually spread via gene flow from its original source, a process known as introgression. Their simulations of this process replicate many of the seemingly contradictory features of the genetic data and suggest that as much as 80% of nuclear loci have assimilated genetic material from non-African archaic humans (i.e., 80% of loci may have some archaic admixture, not that the human genome is 80% archaic). Such a model would explain the contradictory stories of different genetic loci; some loci were part of the selective sweep that originated in Africa, and hence show a pattern of radiation from Africa, whereas other loci show no such pattern and represent the persistence of much older genomic ancestry. The idea that highly adaptive alleles may have introgressed from archaic populations into modern humans is speculative, but not far-fetched. When an introgressed archaic allele has a selective advantage, even rare interbreeding can lead to its spread or fixation in later human populations. Several genetic loci are candidates for such introgression, including microcephalin, a gene influencing brain development (Hawks, Cochran, Harpending,

& Lahn, 2008), and the FOXP2 gene complex related to language (Coop, Bullaughey, Luca, & Przeworski (2008). Coop and colleagues suggest that this beneficial human allele spread into Neanderthals (or vice versa) by introgression. Thus, it seems probable that Neanderthals either got the language gene from us, or we got it from them, long after many other genes in the two populations diverged. Hawks suggests that the evolution of human cognition may thus have depended in part on the genetic legacy of archaic hominids such as the Neanderthals.

I believe that at this point no reasonable scholar would attempt to draw firm conclusions about the timing of the origins and early population movements of the human species from the shifting sands of evidence from the young science of genomics and the continuously unfolding evidence and surprises from archeology. There is no doubt that the debate over the origins of modern humans will continue as new fossil evidence comes to light and better methods and models emerge.

☐ Chapter Summary

Modern human origins may be traced back to million years beginning with geological activity in east Africa that set in motion a chain of events that would eventually lead to the evolution of Homo sapiens. The drying of the rain forest and creation of a savannah grassland created the selection pressures that led to a constellation of changes in a group of primates that would form the hominid line. Chief among these changes was a gradual shift to bipedalism.

According to DNA analysis and the fossil record, the common ancestor of humans and chimpanzees lived in east Africa more than 5 MYA. This common ancestor was partly arboreal, living on the edge of forests nesting in trees, and was moderately sized and small-brained, similar in size to modern chimpanzees.

Eight characteristics of the ape-hominid ancestor are most probable:

1. Closed social networks (i.e., in-group members were readily distinguished from out-of-group members).
2. Males dominated in-group relations.
3. Males occasionally existed singly away from the group.
4. Intergroup relations were generally antagonistic.
5. Males sometimes engaged in preemptive stalk-and-attack encounters with males of other groups.
6. Females left their natal groups for reproduction (exogamy).
7. Social bonds among females were weak but usually tolerant.
8. Males practiced polygyny.

The oldest identified hominid distinct from the common ancestor was first seen in the fossil record about 5 to 4.4 MYA but little is known about this early ancestor. The more well-known *Australopithecus afarensis* lived between 3.9 and 3 MYA and gave rise to several other *Australopithecus* species over the course of several million years. Several related early Homo species form a connecting bridge between the Australopiths and the later emerging species. A consensus exists that several species of early Homo coexisted in Africa with at least two species of later Australopiths approximately 2 MYA.

Homo habilis makes its first appearance in the fossil record about 1.9 MYA. H. habilis marked the origin of a new genus distinct from that of *Australopithecus* because of its larger brain (640 to 750 cc vs. 450 to 500 cc), more gracile form, and smaller molars and premolars. Eventually, a new species called Homo erectus evolved in Africa and soon after migrated into Europe, the Middle East, and Asia. Overall, there was an evolutionary trend of increasing brain size (750 cc to 1250 cc) and decreasing sexual dimorphism (females increased from 62% to 83% of the size of males) from early to late Homo erectus. This new species of Homo adapted to a wide geographic range over a long period of time from 1.8 MYA to 250,000 years ago, though some evidence suggests that they continued to exist in isolated locations in Asia as recently as 26,000 years ago.

The physical features of H. erectus are more similar to modern humans than those of H. habilis, including body and brain size, teeth structure, and degree of sexual dimorphism. H. erectus also exhibits the first evidence we see of widespread migration, cooperative hunting, the use of fire for cooking and warmth, and significant advances in the manufacture and use of tools. An important direct consequence of bipedalism is the freeing of the hands from locomotion. This allowed for the evolution of the fingers and thumb to support grasping and the fine manipulation of objects. The flexibility and coordination of the human hand is distinctly superior to all other primates, and the changes in structure provided ancient hominids with the ability to make stone tools about 2 MYA. The Oldowan toolmakers produced the oldest known stone tools that date from approximately 2.6 to 1.5 MYA. These tools were used by the earliest hominids for cutting, slicing, and chopping.

It is likely that the first period of significant hominid brain expansion (2.5 to 1.8 MYA) was driven by selection pressures arising from demands of the physical ecology of early Homo. Once successful adaptation was achieved in terms of mastering techniques of hunting, foraging, defense from predators, and shelter from the elements, this set of selection pressures would gradually diminish. One million years later the second period of brain expansion in the hominid line may have been driven by entirely different selection pressures. This period began about 500,000 years ago after Homo erectus migrated out of Africa and expanded its range across Asia and Europe. At the time of this expansion, challenges calling for greater intelligence likely arose from the social ecology. The new demands of negotiation, coalitions, communication, cooperation, and detecting deception within groups of more advanced and ecologically dominant hominids led to the second major period of brain expansion.

The term *Neanderthal Man* was coined in 1863 after the Neander valley or *thal*, where the controversial skull was discovered in 1856. The Neanderthals inhabited Europe and parts of western Asia from about 230,000 to 28,000 years ago, during the Middle Paleolithic period. They were physically diverse, with regional differences apparent. The European groups were adapted to the cold climate of the Pleistocene or Ice Age, as indicated by their large braincases, short but robust builds, and large noses, traits observed in Native American sub-arctic populations. The Neanderthals were the first humans to live successfully in the northern hemisphere during the last Ice Age which began in Europe over 75,000 years ago.

By far the most spectacular archeological find of recent times was the discovery of a very small human-like skull and other bones on the island of Flores in 2003, indicating that hominids who stood 3 feet tall lived there as recently as 18,000 to 12,000 years ago. Found throughout the cave with these remains were sophisticated stone tools at horizons from 95,000 to 13,000 years mingled with the charred bones of *Stegodon*, a dwarf elephant, presumably the prey of *Homo floresiensis*. Three characteristics of this new discovery stand out: (1) the relative recency of the find, (2) the exceptionally small body, and (3) the tiny brain.

The discovery of these human remains is widely considered the most important of its kind in recent history, and came as a complete surprise to the scientific community. The new species challenges many current ideas about human evolution. The existence of *Homo neanderthalensis*, late full-sized Homo erectus, and now *Homo floresiensis* as contemporaries of modern Homo sapiens tends to refute any serial development theory on its face, and imply something of a more parallel development scenario.

Proponents of the single-origin hypothesis claim that H. sapiens evolved in eastern Africa between 100,000 and 200,000 years ago and, some time afterwards, began recolonizing the rest of the world. It is currently the most widely accepted of the two current theories regarding the origin of anatomically modern humans. However, proponents of the multiregional origin hypothesis hold that genetic variation between contemporary human races is partly attributable to genetic inheritance between several earlier lineages that evolved on different continents of the Old World, each of which evolved into modern Homo sapiens with significant interbreeding between populations. It is difficult to draw firm conclusions about the timing of the origins and early population movements of the human species from the shifting sands of evidence from the young science of genomics and the continuously unfolding evidence and surprises from archeology. There is no doubt that the debate over the origins of modern humans will continue as new fossil evidence comes to light and better methods and models emerge.

☐ For Further Inquiry

Argue, D., Donlon, D., Groves, C., & Wright, R. (2006). *Homo floresiensis*: Microcephalic, pygmoid, Australopithecus, or Homo? *Journal of Human Evolution, 51*(4), 360–374.

Eswaran, V., Harpending, H., & Rogers, A. R. (2005). Genomics refutes an exclusively African origin of humans. *Journal of Human Evolution, 49*(1), 1–18.

Flinn, M. V., Geary, D. C., & Ward, C. V. (2005). Ecological dominance, social competition, and coalitionary arms races: Why humans evolved extraordinary intelligence. *Evolution and Human Behavior, 26*, 10–46.

van Oosterzee, P., & Morwood, M. (2007). *A new human: The startling discovery and strange story of the "hobbits" of Flores, Indonesia*. London, UK: Collins.

Wade, N. (2006). *Before the dawn: Recovering the lost history of our ancestors*. New York, NY: Penguin.

http://johnhawks.net/weblog/hawks/hawks.html

5

Brain Evolution and Development

Investigating how nearly 100 billion neurons of the human central nervous system function is one of the outstanding achievements in all of 20th-century science. This chapter introduces research on the central nervous system, composed of the brain and spinal cord, and the peripheral nervous system, which extends the operation of the brain throughout the entire body. Together these two systems provide interactive feedback loops that are ultimately responsible for the behavior of the organism in relation to sensory inputs from the environment.

☐ History and Methodological Advances

Darwin's theory of evolution provided 19th-century neuroscientists like John Hughlings-Jackson and Paul Broca with a strong reason for expecting structural and functional continuity in the basic brain structures of various animals, including humans. We now know that there is a great deal of structural similarity among various vertebrate brains, which is due to the essentially conservative nature of the evolutionary process.

A useful metaphor for thinking about brain evolution is the pioneer homestead. Before the first winter sets in, the goal may be the construction of a basic house made of sod. The following year a wooden construction may be built with more rooms and the original dwelling converted to a storage shed. Eventually more rooms may be added and even a porch for sitting and looking at the sunset. In this metaphor, nothing is wasted or thrown away once it is built, and the order of the construction is not random, but guided by functional concerns. The first constructions may be crude, but are effective in promoting survival. As time passes, more refined structures serving a broader range of more specialized functions are added to the whole. When we state that brain evolution is essentially conservative we mean that the most basic systems in the brain responsible for controlling behavior that promote survival are phylogenetically ancient, having been preserved throughout vertebrates notwithstanding many important evolutionary advances.

Anatomical studies of vertebrate brains are consistent with this view. Brain anatomists organize the brain into three basic units: *hindbrain, midbrain*, and *forebrain*. The forebrain, which contains the cerebral cortex, is the region where most of the higher processes such as memory, logical thought, consciousness, and reasoning are carried out. The cerebral cortex and cerebrum are divided into right and left hemispheres. These hemispheres, which are separated by a band of nerve fibers called the corpus callosum, have their own level of specialization. The midbrain contains important switching centers and metabolic regulatory centers like the hypothalamus and pituitary gland. The hindbrain, which is separated from the forebrain by the midbrain, is located at the junction of the spinal cord and cerebrum. This region contains the most archaic structures of the brain from an evolutionary standpoint, but they function to regulate some of the most vital processes in the body. Breathing, heart rate, and muscle coordination are controlled here and sensory impulses are filtered and routed at this point.

From shrews to whales, mammalian brains vary over 10,000-fold in volume. Over this wide range are found regularities that suggest that brain structure may be subject to universal design constraints. For example, large brains are more folded than small brains. Across these different sized brains one can identify all of the major structures and neural pathways that are common to a wide range of vertebrates, as well as patterns of evolutionary advances. One such pattern involves the forebrain or cerebrum, which is progressively larger as one compares fish to reptiles to mammals, culminating in the human brain. Not only is this portion larger in the human brain than all other animals, it is also more differentiated, containing elements not found in other animal brains. Despite the more recently evolved specializations of the human neocortex, the brain systems that regulate emotional behavior have been preserved throughout many phylogenetic levels. The evidence in support of this view begins with an understanding of brain anatomy.

As early as 1878, the French neuroanatomist Paul Broca demonstrated that the area of the limbic lobe immediately surrounding the brain stem is common to the brains of all mammals. As can be seen in Figure 5.1, the limbic lobe (the lighter area) remains a common element, but it accounts for progressively less of the total cortical mass in the cat or monkey compared to the rabbit. This progression across these mammals reflects the growth of the neocortex, which reaches its zenith in the human brain, where it accounts for more than 90% of the total cortical mass. Nevertheless, the

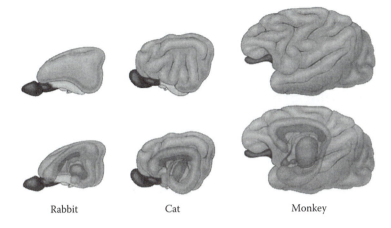

Rabbit   Cat   Monkey

FIGURE 5.1 The neocortex in mammalian evolution. Lateral (top) and medial (bottom) views of the limbic lobe (darker) and the neocortex (white) reveal a progression in the total mass of the neocortex that reaches its zenith in the human brain. (Adapted from MacLean, P. D. (1993). Cerebral evolution of emotion. In M. Lewis & J. M. Haviland (Eds.), *Handbook of emotions* (pp. 67-86). Reprinted with permission of Guilford Press.)

older central core retains its original functions, as later studies have shown. As neuroscientists began to develop the necessary research tools the comparative description of brain structure led to systematic research on the function of the different structures of the brain.

Brain Pathology

An early tool for understanding how the different components of the human brain work together was the study of the mental and emotional sequelae of brain trauma caused by accidents that affect brain functioning. Since the famous case of Phineas Gage, who in 1848 was involved in an explosion that drove an iron spike through his forebrain, brain scientists have attempted to understand the function of specific areas of the brain by recording the results of such trauma. Prior to his accident, Gage had been one of the railroad's best liked and responsible foremen, described by family and friends as amiable in character. However, after the injury to his brain he became capricious and subject to sudden fits of ill temper. His physician commented that the "balance, so to speak, between his intellectual faculties and his animal propensities seems to have been destroyed" (J. M. Harlow, 1868, p. 277). If it was possible to gain insight into the function of different areas of the brain by describing the effects of accidental lesions, which are essentially uncontrolled experiments of nature, it might be possible to build a science of the brain by conducting more controlled experiments involving systematic brain lesions.

Experimental Brain Lesions

Philip Bard (1928), who worked in Cannon's Laboratory, was a pioneer in developing the strategy of conducting systematic lesions to gather information about the localization of function in the brain. His initial experiments involved the surgical removal of the entire cerebral cortex of cats. These decorticate cats were observed to exhibit species-typical emotional arousal linked to the behavioral system of aggression. When provoked these cats would respond with a display called "sham rage," which involved crouching down, arching their backs, pulling back their ears, and unsheathing their claws, while hissing, snarling, and biting any object nearby. In addition, they also displayed clear signs of autonomic nervous system (ANS) arousal, such as pupil dilation and elevated heart rate and blood pressure. These observations led Bard and Cannon to suspect that the *hypothalamus* was the emotional center of the brain, while the *neocortex* functioned to check or inhibit unrestrained emotional expressions. Guided by this hypothesis, Bard made progressively larger lesions, starting with the cortex and moving downwards until he was able to eliminate the display of "sham rage." After removing the hypothalamus the emotional reactions were essentially eliminated, and the cats exhibited only sporadic fragments of the display that lacked the coordination of the more integrated behavioral system.

Another influential approach to understanding how the brain assigns emotional significance to incoming stimuli involved surgical lesions to study the emotional behavior of monkeys. Following the surgical removal of the temporal lobe, Kluver and Bucy (1937) reported that the animals lose their fear of stimuli to which they previously reacted with fear. They also attempt indiscriminant sexual and feeding behaviors that are maladaptive, such as eating rocks. The loss of coordinated function in these basic systems as a result of damage to the temporal lobe came to be known as the Kluver–Bucy syndrome. Later studies determined that lesions confined to the *amygdala*, an almond-shaped structure located in the temporal lobe, but sparing surrounding structures, were sufficient to produce the emotional components of the syndrome (Weiskrantz, 1956).

An important experimental technique that complements studies involving brain lesions is electrical stimulation. This technique, pioneered by the Swiss scientist Hess in the 1920s, involves sending small amounts of electric current through an electrode attached to the skull and inserted into a specific area of the brain. This artificial stimulation can reproduce the chain of events that occurs due to natural stimulation. If a particular set of *neurons*, or nerve cells, in the brain are stimulated in this manner, and a certain type of behavior follows, then neuroscientists assume that those neurons are the part of the brain that controls that behavior.

We know that the brain communicates on the basis of chemical and electrical signals transmitted from neurons in one area of the brain to another. For example, certain areas of the frontal cortex can be electrically stimulated to produce corresponding movements of certainly bodily parts. This happens because the motor cortex is connected to the spinal cord that in turn sends messages to control the movement of limbs. If the same area of the motor cortex is surgically removed, corresponding deficits in motor movements will occur. The combination of surgical lesions and electrical stimulation in animal research is referred to by LeDoux (1996) as the yin and yang of brain science methodology. Along with the imaging and tracing techniques introduced below, activating specific areas of the brain through artificial stimulation or deactivating areas by surgical lesions remain the key tools for understanding brain function.

Researchers are sometimes able to combine experimental techniques with more naturalistic methods. For example, Delgado (1969) implanted electrodes in the brains of macaque monkeys, which could be stimulated telemetrically while the animal is interacting with cage-mates. Using this technique, Delgado found that stimulating a particular brain site elicited threat expressions when the animal was placed with a group of subordinates, but submissive behavior if the same animal was placed with more dominant monkeys. Thus, even when using techniques of artificial electrical stimulation, the behavior that is elicited is open to influences from the social context.

The discovery of the brain's chemical messengers was made by the German scientist, Otto Loewi, in his research on electrical stimulation of the vagus nerve in frogs (Loewi, 1960). This discovery opened a whole new area of research on the brain, and Loewi was awarded the Nobel Prize in physiology in 1936 in recognition of this breakthrough. Loewi observed that he could slow the frog's heartbeat by electrical stimulation, but he went one step further in his inquiry. He decided to transfer the fluid surrounding a frog's heart that had been slowed by stimulation to a second frog's heart. When the heartbeat of the second frog slowed down as a result, he deduced that some chemical agent must have been released from the nerve endings of the first frog. After many thousands of more sophisticated experiments we now know that almost all neuronal communication depends upon chemical messengers. They are generally classified into three types, neurotransmitters, neurohormones, and hormones, according to their function.

The electrical stimulation artificially induced by Loewi instigated the brain's natural communication flow. When sufficiently stimulated a

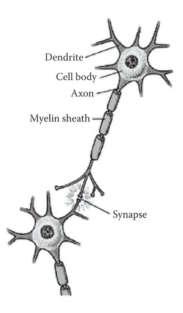

Dendrite

Cell body

Axon

Myelin sheath

Synapse

FIGURE 5.2 Neurons are composed of a cell body, axon, and dendrites. When stimulated by enough inputs at the same time, a neuron will emit an electrical charge that travels along its axon spreading through the cell's dendrites. When the electrical charges reach the axon terminal it causes a neurotransmitter to be released. This chemical messenger diffuses across synapses to the dendrites of adjacent cells. In this manner electrical and chemical processes sustain communication between neurons in the brain. (From LeDoux, J. E. (1996). *The emotional brain: The mysterious underpinnings of emotional life*. New York, NY: Simon & Schuster. With permission.)

neuron will release a wave of electrical charge, or *action potential*, down the output *axon* where it branches off into many axon terminals, as shown in Figure 5.2. When the action potential reaches a terminal it causes a chemical, called a *neurotransmitter* to be released. The neurotransmitter flows across the *synapse* (the space between the axon terminal of one neuron and the *dendrites* of its neighbor) to the dendrites of surrounding neurons where it contributes to the release of electrical energy, and so on throughout an area of the brain. In this manner both electrical and chemical stimulation form the basis for communication between nerve cells. Serotonin is an example of an evolved neurotransmitter. Antidepressants are designed to relieve depressive mood by making certain transmitter substances, such as serotonin, more available for use at synapses.

Another group of neurochemicals that is quite distinct from neurotransmitters are *hormones*. Hormonal systems like the hypothalamic–pituitary–

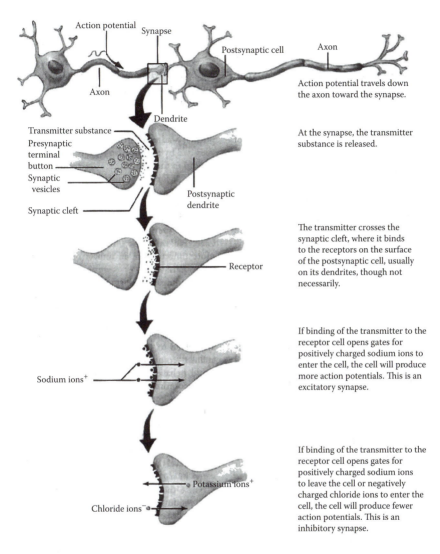

Action potential

Synapse

Postsynaptic cell

Axon

Axon

Action potential travels down
the axon toward the synapse.

Dendrite

Transmitter substance

Presynaptic
terminal
button

Synaptic
vesicles

Synaptic cleft

Postsynaptic
dendrite

At the synapse, the transmitter
substance is released.

Receptor

The transmitter crosses the
synaptic cleft, where it binds
to the receptors on the surface
of the postsynaptic cell, usually
on its dendrites, though not
necessarily.

Sodium ions$^+$

If binding of the transmitter to the
receptor cell opens gates for
positively charged sodium ions to
enter the cell, the cell will produce
more action potentials. This is an
excitatory synapse.

Potassium ions$^+$

Chloride ions$^-$

If binding of the transmitter to the
receptor cell opens gates for
positively charged sodium ions
to leave the cell or negatively
charged chloride ions to enter the
cell, the cell will produce fewer
action potentials. This is an
inhibitory synapse.

FIGURE 5.2   (continued).

adrenal system are activated by the *pituitary gland* or other glands located
in the body, which are controlled by outputs from the hypothalamus. Once
activated, the pituitary gland secretes stress hormones that stimulate the
production and release of adrenaline or cortisol that circulate in the blood
stream to reach the specific organs that respond to their presence. For
this reason hormones usually require more time to have an impact on the
body than neurotransmitters. Hormonal processes and chemical agents
are discussed in more detail in the next chapter.

A number of diseases may also be used to shed light on brain function, including rabies, psychomotor epilepsy, and Huntington's chorea. To illustrate this methodology, consider the early research on psychomotor epilepsy. Gibbs, Gibbs, and Fuster (1948) published an article in which they described this condition in which the patient experiences emotional feelings followed by amnesia and automatisms, rather than the convulsions more commonly associated with other epileptic seizures. This report was followed up by Penfield and associates in Montreal and yielded a dramatic experimental demonstration of the integration between limbic and neocortical functions. Penfield and Jasper (1954) found that it was possible to electrically stimulate precise sites in the limbic area of the brain to reproduce the subjective emotional states, subsequent automatism, and associated amnesia characteristic of an epileptic seizure. They also observed that the electrical discharges that occur in psychomotor epilepsy do not spread outside the limbic system. This finding, confirmed by animal research, was considered to be evidence for the physiological distinctness of the limbic system. The procedures developed by Penfield and associates provided a means to literally pinpoint those limbic structures involved in the generation of emotional feelings during the course of therapeutic neurosurgery. These striking results have led neuroscientists like MacLean (1993) to view psychomotor epilepsy as the key to understanding the cerebral evolution of emotion.

In psychomotor epilepsy there is generally an aura at the onset of an epileptic attack that is accompanied by feelings that can range from ecstasy to extreme terror. MacLean (1993) lists six general affective states: feelings of desire, fear, anger, dejection, affection, and gratulance. The latter may include profound feelings of discovery or revelation similar to drug-induced feelings of euphoria or enhanced reality. All these emotional feelings are, according to MacLean, detached from any particular emotion elicitor and instead perceived as free-floating affects.

As the nerve impulse associated with the seizure discharge spreads further into the limbic system, the patient exhibits automatic behavior that can range from simple to complex automatisms. These automatisms often correspond to the particular feeling experienced during the aura. MacLean (1993, p. 79) provides the following examples:

> Following a horrifying feeling of fear or terror, for example, a patient may run screaming to someone for protection. Or after a feeling of anger, there may be angry vocalization and pugilistic behavior, with the arms flailing somewhat like those of a fighting chimpanzee. Or there may be a gorilla-like hooting and striking of the chest. An opposite sort of behavior is that of a woman who would walk around the room showing marked affection for anyone present, or

that of a 20-year-old woman in whom "each slight seizure was followed by a paroxysm of kissing" (Gowers, 1881).

Functional Brain Imaging

Over the past decade there has been an explosive growth in the use of brain imaging techniques such as positron emission topography (PET scan), magnetic resonance imaging (MRI), and magnetoencephalography (MEG). These techniques give neuroscientists the opportunity to study the human brain at work by identifying those brain structures that are activated while subjects perform various tasks that call on specific abilities. PET scans provide a color image of the brain displayed on the screen of a computer monitor. The test consists of injecting a small quantity of glucose that is tagged with a radioactive substance, which can be used to trace where the glucose is consumed in the brain. For example, on the basis of PET scans we know that certain areas of the right hemisphere are activated when a person is asked to identify different faces (Sergent, Ohta, & MacDonald, 1992).

MRI uses magnetic detectors to measure the amounts of hemoglobin, with and without oxygen. This allows physicians and scientists to study the living brain by viewing it at different depths as if in slices. Brain areas that have been highly active can be identified because they have used up the oxygen bound to hemoglobin.

Finally, MEG also provides a color image of the brain at work that is based on electromagnetic fields that are created as electrochemical information passes between neurons. During a MEG test, a patient may be told to move the right index finger and an instant readout of the brain's activity is provided in the form of concentric colored rings that pinpoint the signals in the brain even prior to moving the finger! Currently, these techniques provide a noninvasive methodology that is beginning to bridge the gap between animal and human studies.

☐ MacLean's Triune Brain Theory

A number of contemporary investigators such as MacLean (1993) and LeDoux (1996) trace the development of their brain models back to an influential paper by Papez (1937). For the first time Papez proposed a model of the brain as a circuit and moved beyond the search for a single brain structure and proposed instead that emotion was mediated by several cortical structures. From this point on, all neurophysiological theories of emotion have generally agreed that multiple brain structures are involved in emotion. Papez proposed a circuit theory of emotion that implicated several distinct brain structures that were serially connected and operated together as a system. The structures he identified were the hypothalamus, anterior thalamus, cingulate gyrus, and the hippocampus. The loop connecting these structures came to be known as the Papez circuit. Papez speculated that sensory impulses travel to the thalamus, which then reroutes them into three pathways each responsible for a different dimension of the total emotional response. Thus the impulse traveling to the striatal region instigates movement, that to the neocortex thought, and that to the hypothalamus gives rise to the feeling and expressive components that make up emotion. This tripartite structure of the emotional brain was the immediate conceptual ancestor of the next important advance.

The next major step in the development of a neural model of emotion was taken by MacLean who renamed the structures of the Papez circuit, together with the amygdala, septal nuclei, orbito-frontal cortex, and the basal ganglia, the *limbic system* (see Figure 5.3).

In 1949, MacLean initially chose the term "visceral brain" to convey the difference between what we feel (strong inward feelings) and what we know (verbally mediated logic). MacLean argued that the visceral brain gives sensory impulses their emotional tone, and unlike information processed in the neocortex it "eludes the grasp of the intellect because its animalistic and primitive structure makes it impossible to communicate in verbal terms." Because of the ambiguity and misinterpretations arising from the use of the term *viscera*, MacLean eventually borrowed Broca's descriptive term *limbique* and introduced *limbic system* to refer to the limbic cortex and its primary brainstem connections (MacLean, 1952). These extensions to the Papez circuit, particularly the amygdala, have proved to be of enduring value to modern structural/functional analyses of the emotional brain.

A key idea that was emphasized by MacLean was the concept that the brain, as a product of a long evolutionary history, was modular in its design, composed of a hierarchy of three major developments. These three steps in the evolution of the human brain correspond to phylogenetic adaptations common to reptiles, early mammals, and late mammals, as shown in Figure 5.4. According to MacLean,

> there results a remarkable linkage of three cerebrotypes which are radically different in chemistry and function and which in an evolutionary sense are eons apart. There exists, so to speak, a hierarchy of three-brains-in-one or what I call for short, a triune brain. (From LeDoux, 1996, p. 98)

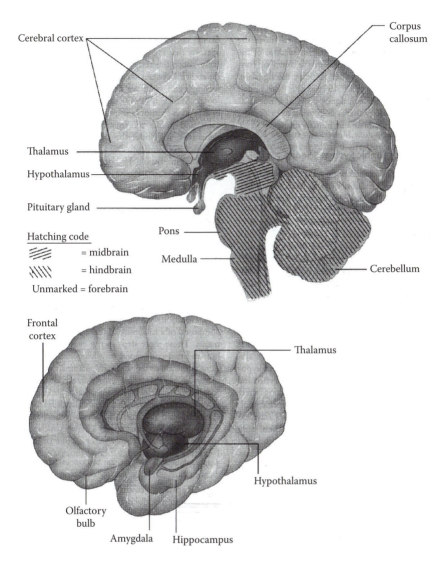

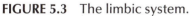

FIGURE 5.3 The limbic system.

The Reptilian Brain

In order to reach an understanding of the brain-behavior connections and the contribution of each of the three components of the triune brain to the experience of emotion, MacLean needed to integrate information from evolutionary biology and ethology with neurophysiology. He began this task by a careful examination of the fossil record detailing the evolution

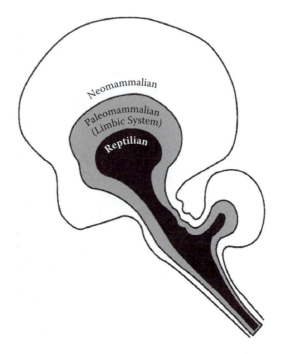

FIGURE 5.4   MacLean's triune brain. This evolutionary model of the brain is composed of three major divisions: the reptilian brain includes the striatal region, the paleomammalian brain includes the limbic system, and the neomammalian brain includes the neocortex. Each part is named for the era in which it is thought to have originated. (From MacLean, P. D. (1990). *The triune brain in evolution: Role in paleo-cerebral functions*. New York, NY: Plenum Press. With permission.)

of reptiles. Unlike fish and amphibians, reptiles evolved a mode of reproduction involving the amniote egg that permitted them to adapt to life on land. This fundamental change permitted an adaptive radiation into a new terrestrial environment, which eventually led to an evolutionary line of mammal-like reptiles called therapsids. The fossil remains of these mammal-like reptiles have been uncovered on every continent, indicating a very successful adaptation from the mid-Permian period, about 250 MYA to the mid-Triassic period, about 200 MYA. During this long period an evolutionary line emerged from the therapsids that is considered to be the prototype of the mammalian class. The critical changes of this period involved the acquisition of a mammalian posture, 5-digit fingers and toes, mammalian-like jaws and teeth, the mammalian ear, and the gradual transition from a cold-blooded to a warm-blooded organism (MacLean, 1990).

In order to understand the behavioral repertoire of these primitive mammal-like reptiles, MacLean chose to focus his behavioral analysis on lizards because they are the closest living relative of these ancient reptiles. Turning to ethology, he identified about 25 forms of behavior that constitute the ethogram, or general profile, of species-typical behavior patterns. The ethogram includes a wide variety of animal behaviors that have evolved within a species (or group of species) in order to promote the organism's adaptation to its ecological niche and to assure its survival and reproduction. For lizards, the ethogram includes basic behaviors such as nesting, foraging, territorial behavior, hunting, hoarding, greeting, grooming, flocking, migration, and mating. In addition to these basic behaviors four rudimentary displays are used in social communication, involving (1) signature or identification of the individual, (2) dominance or challenge, (3) submission or appeasement, and (4) courtship. Because these groups of behavior programs are very old, phylogenetically speaking, they are also expressed in various species-typical forms in more recently evolved animals, such as birds and mammals. As with development, earlier forms of behavior are not discarded with further evolution, but rather they are integrated within more recently evolved structures.

In order to test the hypothesis that the reptilian brain remains functional in higher animals, MacLean chose to study the distinctive species-typical greeting display in squirrel monkeys. This display, which is exhibited when a new monkey comes into view, involves elements of signature, dominance, and courtship displays associated in lizards with the striatal region of the brain. In one type of squirrel monkey (gothic type) this display is readily elicited by presenting the monkey with its mirror image, thus facilitating experimental work. In a series of experiments performed on 120 gothic-type squirrel monkeys, MacLean found that only the removal of portions of the striatal region eliminated the display behavior, whereas removal of limbic or neocortical systems did not result in an elimination of the display. Analagous experiments on lizards showed the same overall pattern of results, thus demonstrating continuity of structure and function in the oldest portion of the brain in animals as diverse as reptiles and primates.

The idea that the striatal region of the brain functions to schedule species-typical behavior patterns in order to promote the adaptation of the organism has also been supported by clinical observations of patients suffering from a genetic disease known as Huntington's chorea. This hereditary disease does not have known effects in childhood, but later in life patients become incapable of organizing and planning even simple daily routines. They can be engaged in these activities if directed to do so by others, but appear to lack the self-organizing capacity for such actions. Without external direction, they appear to be listless and apathetic, but this striking passivity is simply a lack of initiative, due to the damage caused by the disease to the striatal region of the brain responsible for organizing daily routines and motivating the individual.

The Paleomammalian Brain

A similar comparative analysis underlies MacLean's assertion that the limbic system has evolved as the common denominator in the paleomammalian brain. Again the first step in the analysis involved the comparative analysis of mammalian behavior in relation to the evolutionary advances already present in the reptilian ethogram. Such a comparison yields only three broad classes of behavior that are universally present in mammals, but completely absent in reptiles: vocal signal systems, attachment systems, and juvenile play. At first glance this may not appear to be such a monumental leap forward, but let us consider the implications of the addition of these three behavioral systems to the lives of mammals, as distinct from reptiles. Together these changes provided a major impetus for the evolution of social life and with it a primary role for emotions in regulating social interaction.

From a comparative perspective, the major unifying component of the mammalian order is the universality of maternal nursing and care giving. In contrast to the reptilian order, mammals invest heavily in the care and protection of their offspring. Early separation from the parent inevitably results in the death of the offspring, and this intensive selective pressure led to the evolution of behavioral systems "designed" to maintain proximity between parent and offspring. MacLean speculates that the earliest vocalizations in the evolution of mammals were the infant's cries of separation distress in order to restore the vital contact with the parent. In contrast, reptiles like lizards and turtles are mute. Unlike mammals, the only investment reptile parents provide to their offspring is the fertilized egg. Unlike birds, the eggs are laid and left to hatch on their own. Not only are lizards "remiss" in the care and protection of their offspring, the young must actually hide from their parents and other adult lizards to avoid being eaten by them! Considering the behavioral and social ecology of lizards, it should be clear that selection pressures in this line led away from infant vocalization, parental care, and the evolution of family cohesion and group living, all vital characteristics of mammals in general, and primates in particular.

The physical structure in the brain thought by MacLean to be responsible for regulating the evolving behavioral programs related to maternal care, infant attachment, vocal signaling, and play was the limbic system. He argues with the emergence of these new behavioral systems, the limbic system evolved in mammals as the brain's primary emotional and motivational system. This portion of the brain, referred to in Figure 5.4 as the paleomammalian brain, is closely connected with the hypothalamus that in turn controls the ANS. The term limbic system was inspired by Broca's term *limbique*, derived from the Latin word *limbus* or rim, which he used to describe the oval-shaped rim of the medial cortex. Based on both organizational structure and clinical findings, MacLean asserts that these two phylogenetically older modules (the striatal region and limbic system) lack any capacity for verbal communication with those areas of the human brain that are responsible for speech. This is the physiological substrate for MacLean's insight that much of what is processed in these areas cannot be easily processed in verbal reasoning. This idea concerning the duality of the heart and mind is a perennial theme in literature and was elegantly captured by the famous phrase, "The heart has reasons of which reason knows nothing," attributed to the French author Blaise Pascal.

The Neomammalian Brain

The third major division in MacLean's evolutionary model of the human brain is the neomammalian brain. This outer layer or cortex is considered to be the most recently evolved portion of the brain and for this reason is often referred to as the neocortex. As can be seen in Figure 5.4, it is more substantial in higher mammals, particularly primates. Within the primate order, this portion of the brain is much larger in humans than our closest relatives, the chimpanzee. The anterior cortical region has shown the most dramatic expansion in size over the course of phylogeny, and the large frontal lobes appear to be the most distinctive feature of the human brain.

The coordinated processes of duplication and divergence have continually shaped the evolution of the neocortex. Marcus (2004) identifies the process of gene *duplication* as a key catalyst for evolutionary innovation. A second copy of an existing gene, perhaps one that is already optimized to a vital function, can diverge at some future point without any loss in the original function, thereby providing the tinkering, blind hand of evolution with an opportunity to come up with a new function. Such an apparently minor process can give rise to wonderfully complex products, such as color vision, which appears to have been constructed via two such duplications. Mental modules might be disguised in the ragtag world of recycled and elaborated neocortex, rather than evident to the anatomist's eye like the discretely packaged and organized structures of the limbic system.

The greatly expanded neocortex plays an important role in many distinctive human behaviors such as reasoning and language, and metacognitive abilities, such as planning and anticipating events. The anterior cortical areas are also critically implicated in emotional behavior and experience (Davidson, Ekman, Saron, Senulis, & Friesen, 1990; Davidson &

Fox, 1982). The frontal cortex adds a dimension of emotional life to humans that may not be present in most primates. This dimension may be thought of as the interface of the cognitive and emotional functions that produces more complex human emotional states. Some human emotions are linked to the ability to anticipate outcomes of future events which are unknown or uncontrollable, but important to the individual. For example, emotions like anxiety, concern, and empathy often involve anticipating consequences that have not yet been realized, and the frontal cortex has been identified as a neural substrate for these characteristically human feelings.

☐ LeDoux's Amygdala Theory

Like MacLean, Joseph LeDoux considers evolutionary theory as critical in leading scientists to understand the origins of emotion in the brain. However, unlike MacLean who viewed emotion as a unitary faculty of mind mediated by a single unified system within the brain, LeDoux believes that different emotions may involve different brain systems. Instead of a universal emotion system in the brain, LeDoux believes that it is more plausible to assume that different emotions are mediated by different brain systems and that evolution acted upon each of these basic survival systems somewhat independently.

Historically, cognition was considered to be part of a trilogy of mind that also included emotion and motivation as equally important processes. The tendency of cognitive scientists to reduce these processes of the human mind to general cognitive information processing is reductionistic and inconsistent with recent formulations in the neurosciences regarding the relative autonomy of emotional processes. The analogy of the human brain to the information processing of a computer is certainly useful, but to understand human emotions it may be more useful to remember that it is only an analogy.

Rather than viewing the emotional brain as a general computer, LeDoux (1996), Panksepp (1993), Plutchik (1980), and others believe that during the long course of its evolution the brain evolved multiple behavioral-emotional systems, each with its own distinct structural and functional properties. From this perspective, because different emotions are involved in different adaptive tasks, seeking protection from the caregiver, defending against danger, securing a mate, etc., each emotional system may be linked to specific brain systems that evolved for each specific purpose. This idea leads LeDoux to propose that scientists investigate one emotional system at a time, without assuming, for example, that the emotional network responsible for activating the organism's response to fear is the same system that activates one's romantic attachments.

The key to understanding this point of view is the idea that natural selection often leads to functional equivalence in evolved systems across diverse species that must successfully solve common problems if they are to survive. As a result systems have been designed by natural selection for fear, anger, attachment, play, and sexuality that share common ground across diverse species of primates and mammals. This idea is very similar to MacLean's description of the triune brain and consistent with MacLean's data that demonstrate functional equivalence across different species regarding the same behavioral display. LeDoux differs from MacLean in assuming that each basic emotional system is somewhat localized anatomically and mediated by separate neural systems. From a research standpoint, one would hypothesize that each system would respond differently to lesions and electrical and chemical stimulation.

Given the arsenal of techniques available to neuroscientists to understand how emotional functions are mediated by specific patterns of neural connections, the only other requirement for progress is selecting a well-defined, reliably measured emotion. Because many of the methods outlined in this chapter can only be employed with nonhuman subjects, the emotion selected should also be common to a diversity of species.

In his book, *The Emotional Brain*, LeDoux argues that the basic emotion of fear is an excellent candidate for neurological study:

> Fear conditioning is thus an excellent experimental technique for studying the control of fear or defense responses in the brain. It can be applied up and down the phyla. The stimuli involved can be specified and controlled, and the sensory system that processes the conditioned stimulus can be used as the starting point for tracing the pathways through the brain. The learning takes place very quickly and lasts indefinitely. Fear conditioning can be used to study how the brain processes the conditioned fear stimulus and controls defense responses that are coupled to them. It can also be used to examine the mechanisms through which emotional memories are established, stored, and retrieved, and, in humans, the mechanisms underlying conscious fear. (LeDoux, 1996, p. 148)

Using a research strategy that combines the classical lesion method with modern neuroanatomical tracing techniques, LeDoux has developed a process model of the brain that demonstrates how a cognitive appraisal becomes transformed into an emotional response, with all the heart-pounding, bodily sensations that psychologists since James ascribe to fear. The key to this transformation in the brain is the involvement of the amygdala, which LeDoux describes as the hub in the wheel of fear, as shown in Figure 5.5.

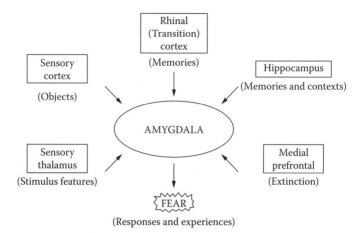

FIGURE 5.5   The amygdala plays a central role in the emotion process. Inputs from many sources with different levels of cognition may trigger an emotional response from the amygdala. Anatomical knowledge about which cortical areas project to the amygdala allow predictions about how those functions contribute to fear responses. (From LeDoux, J. E. (1996). *The emotional brain: The mysterious underpinnings of emotional life.* New York, NY: Simon & Schuster. With permission.)

To illustrate LeDoux's theory of the role of the amygdala in the processing of fearful stimuli, let us consider a hunter walking alone in the Maine woods who is suddenly deafened by the blast of a shotgun fired at close range. Previous models of how the brain responded to such inputs routed the incoming information from the sensory thalamus up to the sensory cortex where the sound was consciously perceived. The cortex then sent signals to subcortical areas of the limbic system (including the amygdala) responsible for appraisal. After evaluating the emotional significance of the sound as dangerous, the limbic system sent a return message up to the cortex to activate the fear system in the ANS, which in turn produced the heart-pounding subjective feeling of fear.

Skillful application of the experimental techniques of lesions and tracing LeDoux's research reveals that the brain can process the same auditory information via a shorter, more direct route that bypasses the cortex altogether. From an evolutionary vantage point, the direct route evolved first and remains the only pathway available in the lower vertebrates. With the evolution of the cortex, the older, more primitive processing system continued to function alongside the more complex system for millions of years, plenty of time to atrophy if it was not useful. But the direct thalamic pathway to the amygdala is two to three times faster than the thalamo-cortico-amygdala pathway. However, the increase in speed is offset by

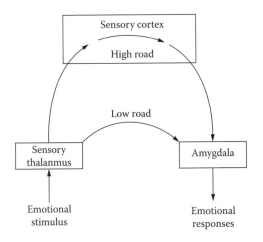

FIGURE 5.6 Two pathways to fear. LeDoux's research reveals a faster, subcortical path to the amygdala that has been retained in the human brain despite the evolution of the more cognitively sophisticated cortical route. The direct path allows for a rapid response to what appears to be a dangerous stimuli before we consciously process it. LeDoux believes that this direct path may control emotional reactions that we don't understand. (From LeDoux, J. E. (1996). *The emotional brain: The mysterious underpinnings of emotional life.* New York, NY: Simon & Schuster. With permission.)

reduced cognitive processing that could only be provided by the cortex. According to LeDoux, this gain in processing time must occasionally provide substantial benefits that more than offset the loss of information since both pathways remain functional in the human brain where they converge in the lateral nucleus of the amygdala.

Once the information arrives at the lateral nucleus of the amygdala via either route it can be quickly transmitted to the central nucleus which can release whatever level of defensive response the situation warrants. The response systems controlled by outputs from the amygdala central nucleus include ANS responses like blood pressure, endocrine responses that release stress hormones into the blood stream, reflexes, and other behaviors. This double pathway (Figure 5.6) may account for the common experience of sudden and extreme fright to a nondangerous stimulus that resembles a dangerous one, only to be followed seconds later by a second, slower, calmer response once the stimuli has been more fully evaluated. As shown in Figure 5.7, the frame-by-frame analysis captured by Eibl-Eibesfeldt's films dramatically illustrates this double reaction in a younger German girl and in a Yanomamo adult male when confronted with a stimulus that "fools" the amygdala but not the cortex. Of course, as

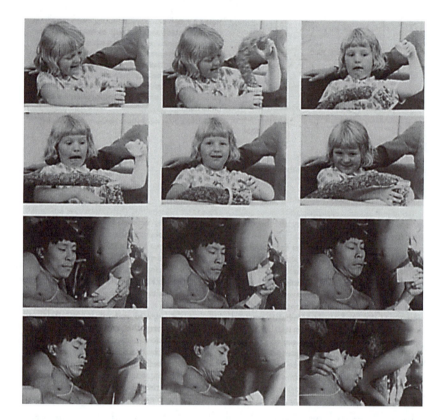

FIGURE 5.7 Fear reactions in a young German girl and adult Yanomamo male. Filming at 48 frames per second, Eibl-Eibesfeldt captures a double response to an unexpected event. Both subjects were given a box from which a cloth snake or cloth mouse jumped out when it was opened. The sequence of expressive reactions is nearly identical in these two subjects of different ages, gender, and cultural backgrounds. The first response is a classic fear reaction (notice the eye and mouth regions and the pulling back of the head) followed by a bemused expression mixed with smiling and embarrassment (for the German girl) when the slower cortical pathway allows them to complete their cognitive appraisal of the stimulus. (Photos courtesy of I. Eibl-Eibesfeldt.)

LeDoux argues, the retention of the double pathway in the human brain implies a functional significance to the faster processing system in our EEA. According to this logic, the price of false alarms (being startled into an aroused state when no real danger is present) was more than offset by the benefit of reacting quickly to real danger.

    Converging evidence in cognitive psychology and neuroscience supports the existence of these two quite different types of cognitive processing,

TABLE 5.1 Characteristics of Implicit and Explicit Processing

Implicit	Explicit
Unconscious	Conscious
Automatic	Controllable
Fast	Relatively slow
Evolved early	Evolved Late
Effortless	Effortful
Biological adaptation	Cultural adaptation

generally referred to as implicit and explicit processing (MacDonald, 2008). Implicit and explicit mechanisms may be contrasted on a number of dimensions. Implicit processing evolved first and is automatic, effortless, relatively fast, and responds automatically to large amounts of domain-relevant information. Explicit processing evolved much later and is open to modification by learning and socialization. In contrast to implicit processing (as shown in Table 5.1), it is conscious, controllable, effortful, relatively slow, and involves processing of relatively small amounts of information.

When the environment presents long-standing problems and recurrent cues relevant to solving them, the best solution is to evolve specialized modules that function via implicit processing (Geary, 2005; Tooby & Cosmides, 1992). For example, the visual system of monkeys and humans contains numerous areas specialized for different aspects of vision. Areas specialized for color and for motion are sensitive to different aspects of visual stimulation; processing in these different areas occurs in parallel and results in a unitary image. Other modules proposed include modules for social exchange (Cosmides, 1989), theory of mind (Baron-Cohen, 1995), fear (LaFreniere, 2000, 2005; LeDoux, 1996, 2000), folk physics (Povinelli, 2000), and grammar acquisition (Pinker, 1994).

☐ Sex Differences in Brain Function

As any evolutionary perspective would predict, sex differences in structure, neurochemistry, and function exist in every brain lobe, including regions centrally implicated in emotional and cognitive processes such as the hippocampus, amygdala, and neocortex (Cahill, 2006). Such differences are not just produced by circulating hormones, but also by the organizing effects of hormone release during prenatal development and direct genetic effects that are not mediated by hormones. Because selection pressures can operate on females and males in both similar and quite different ways, we should expect a priori that brain organization and function should be both highly similar in some basic processes and markedly different in others. This is precisely the pattern of empirical results that is now accumulating at an increasingly rapid rate due to emerging technical and methodological advances.

Recent imaging studies reveal anatomical sex differences in various regions throughout the human brain. In women, parts of the frontal cortex and limbic cortex are denser and the hippocampus is larger, while in men, parts of the parietal cortex and amygdala are larger than in women. Differences in the size or density of brain structures are generally thought to reflect their relative complexity and functional importance. In addition to size differences in discrete structures of the brain, researchers are also documenting anatomical sex differences at the cellular level. Such anatomical diversity may be caused in large part by the organizing activity of sex hormones during prenatal development. These steroids help to direct the organization and wiring of the brain during development and influence the structure and neuronal density of various regions. Positive correlations between brain region size in adults and sex steroid action in utero suggest that at least some sex differences are already present at birth.

In several important ways, sex differences in the brain's chemistry and construction influence how males and females respond to the environment, including reacting to stressful events and remembering such events. Once again sexual dimorphism is evident in structure, function, and neurochemistry. PET scans reveal that the brains of males produce serotonin, which enhances mood, at a faster rate than those of females. Serotonin is a neurotransmitter, or signal-carrying molecule, that is a key for mediating emotional behavior. A PET scan study at the National Institute of Mental Health showed that serotonin production was a remarkable 52% higher on average in men than in women (Nishizawa et al., 1997). Results such as these might help clarify why women are twice as likely as men to experience mood disorders that involve serotonin dysfunction, and which are commonly treated with drugs that boost the concentration of serotonin. Serotonin is the main depression-relieving neurotransmitter. Adequate brain levels of serotonin are directly associated with emotional stability, an inner sense of well-being, relaxation, and promote restful sleep, whereas low levels of serotonin are associated with many symptoms of anxiety and depression.

Besides anatomical differences in the hippocampus and amygdala, functional differences can sometimes involve opposing effects for males and females. For example, a brief exposure to stressful learning conditions produces an increase in neural interconnections in the hippocampal region in males, but a decrease in females (Shors, 2002), a result that has now been replicated in humans using Pavlovian conditioning (Jackson, Payne, Nadel, & Jacobs, 2005). Another example of opposing effects by gender involves the amygdala. In a recent experiment with rodents, male and female pups were temporarily separated from their mothers. Maternal vocalizations produced an increase in the serotonin receptors of the amygdala in male pups, but a decrease in female pups (Ziabreva, Poeggel, Schnabel, & Braun, 2003).

Other studies now document sex differences in amygdala function beyond the well-established finding that the amygdala is larger in men than in women (correcting for total brain size). Recall that the amygdala is located within the limbic system and has been reliably associated with aggression, fear, sexual motivation, and memory. In rats, the neurons in this region make more numerous interconnections in males than in females. Such anatomical dimorphism would be expected to produce differences in the way that males and females react to stress. Extensive research in rodents and humans has shown that the amygdala functions to modulate memory storage of emotionally arousing events through interaction with endogenous stress hormones (Cahill, 2006; McGaugh, 2004). This provides the organism with an evolutionary adaptation by creating memory strength proportional to the importance of the event.

As impressive as recent advances in the neuroscience of anxiety and stress are, we are still in a state of partial understanding of these complex systems. Among other complicating factors are a number of recent studies showing sex–hemisphere interactions in brain structures like the amygdala in response to emotional stimuli. Despite these complications, it is no longer tenable for scientists in any discipline to presume that sex differences in cognitive, affective, and behavioral functioning are unrelated to longstanding evolutionary pressures and the myriad of mechanisms in the brain and endocrine system designed by natural and sexual selection to enhance the adaptation of the organism.

☐ Brain Development and Plasticity

In humans, brain development is best viewed as an epigenetic process that serves to specify the methods of construction rather than a finished product. A brain that is built up and wired by individual cells following self-regulating recipes has a greater capacity to adapt itself to different environmental demands. "Wiring the mind" is a demanding and specialized task and genes have evolved to read internal as well as external signals indiscriminately to guide the process. By guiding the development of the brain using both genetic and environmental signals, which are relative rather than absolute, plasticity emerges as an inherent feature of the human brain.

From the moment the human brain begins its prenatal growth (about 25 days after conception) it increases at the rate of a million neurons every 4 minutes. Almost all of the 100 billion neurons that a human will ever have are already present at birth. After birth, the cortex continues to develop, but not by substantially increasing the number of neurons. Instead, neurons increase in size and become more complex in structure. Unlike the brain stem and limbic system, neurons produced for cortical regions actively migrate until they reach their final destinations. Once they arrive at their precise location neurons grow branching axons that form connections to other neurons. The number of connections (synapses) increases, peaking at different ages in different parts of the brain. Connections with other brain areas proliferate and then are pruned. The amount and type of stimulation influences the structure of the cortex, in the number of neuronal connections and the pruning of the connections in the cortex.

As noted by Nobel Prize–winning neurobiologist Gerald Edelman, this process is structurally similar to natural selection since the brain overproduces neurons and connections followed by selective retention of those that are most responsive to the developing individual's environment. Neurons with the strongest patterns of innervation retain their connections and the other cells die off. Two types of innervation are relevant: (1) endogenous neural firings and (2) exogenous neural firings produced by sensory inputs.

This "open program" of the developing brain is known as neural plasticity. To illustrate, imagine that one eye is kept closed during the development of the visual system. This would result in the individual's becoming functionally blind in that eye. Even though cells projecting from the retina produce normal outputs, the area in the cortex to which they feed will not respond appropriately to visual inputs.

We do not yet know everything about the brain, but one thing we do know is that it is not constructed from a genetic blueprint. Rather, the specialized information-processing centers of the neocortex are constructed by additive processes that are genetically controlled and subtractive processes that are highly sensitive to environmental input during ontogeny. The columnar structures containing approximately 3000 neurons each that make up the neocortex are very similar from one brain region to another and from one mammalian species to another. Although evolutionary psychology may provide useful hypotheses regarding modular brain systems, demonstrating their existence in credible neuroscientific research remains elusive (Panksepp & Panksepp, 2000).

Evolutionary and developmental processes work together to solve problems of adaptation. Once a developmental perspective fully informs an evolutionary vision, there will be less talk of "Stone Age minds." Notwithstanding the conservative nature of the evolution of the vertebrate brain, development in the 21st century ensures a 21st-century mind. If biological evolution proceeds at a snail's pace, cultural evolution is lightning fast. Children growing up in our interconnected global ecology absorb its new language and norms using longstanding domain-general cognitive mechanisms and think in both new and old ways as a consequence.

☐ Chapter Summary

Neuroscientists use a variety of techniques to identify the brain mechanisms by which we selectively attend, process, and evaluate sensory stimulation, and assign to it emotional significance. Historically, laboratory work with animals was important in this area because of the functional similarities of vertebrate brains and because artificial stimulation can reproduce the chain of events that occurs due to natural stimulation. Based on laboratory research we know that the brain communicates on the basis of chemical and electrical signals transmitted from neurons in one area of the brain to another.

When sufficiently stimulated a neuron will release a wave of electrical charge, or action potential, down the output axon where it branches off into many axon terminals. When the action potential reaches a terminal it causes a chemical called a neurotransmitter to be released. The neurotransmitter flows across the synapse (the space between the axon terminal of one neuron and the dendrites of its neighbor) to the dendrites of surrounding neurons where it contributes to the release of electrical energy, and so on throughout an area of the brain. If a particular set of neurons in the brain are stimulated and a certain type of behavior follows, scientists assume that those neurons are the part of the brain that controls that behavior.

In recent years there has been an explosive growth in the use of brain imaging techniques such as positron emission topography (PET scan), magnetic resonance imaging (MRI), and magnetoencephalography (MEG). These techniques give neuroscientists the opportunity to study the human brain at work by identifying those brain structures that are activated while subjects perform various tasks that call on specific abilities. Viewing computer images of the living brain at work, activating specific areas of the brain through artificial stimulation, and deactivating areas by surgical lesions remain the key tools for understanding brain function.

As a product of a long evolutionary history, the brain appears to be modular in its adaptive design, composed of a hierarchy of three major developments which are radically different in chemistry and function and which, in an evolutionary sense, are eons apart. The result is a complex system that MacLean views as three-brains-in-one or a triune brain. The three steps in the evolution of the human brain correspond to phylogenetic adaptations common to reptiles, early mammals, and late mammals.

The paleomammalian brain or limbic system is responsible for regulating the mammalian behavioral programs of maternal care, infant attachment, vocal signaling, and play. The limbic system evolved in early mammals as the brain's primary emotional and motivational system. This portion of the brain is closely connected with the hypothalamus which in turn controls the ANS. Based on both organizational structure and clinical findings, MacLean asserts that the triune brain's two phylogenetically older modules, the striatal region and limbic system, lack any capacity for verbal communication with those areas of the neocortex. The greatly expanded neocortex plays an important role in many distinctive human behaviors such as reasoning and language, and metacognitive abilities, such as planning and anticipating events.

Skillful application of the experimental techniques of lesions and tracing LeDoux's research reveals that the brain can process incoming sensory information via two routes, the thalamo-cortico-amygdala pathway, and a shorter, more direct route that bypasses the cortex altogether and is 2 or 3 times faster. From an evolutionary vantage point, the direct route evolved first and remains the only pathway available in the lower vertebrates. With the evolution of the cortex, the older, implicit processing system continues to function alongside the more complex explicit processing system. Implicit processing evolved first and is automatic, effortless, relatively fast, and responds automatically to large amounts of domain-relevant information. Explicit processing evolved much later and is open to modification by learning and socialization. In contrast to implicit processing it is conscious, controllable, effortful, relatively slow, and involves processing of relatively small amounts of information.

In humans, brain development is an epigenetic process that serves to specify the methods of construction rather than a finished product. From the moment the human brain begins its prenatal growth it increases at the rate of a million neurons every 4 minutes. Almost all of the neurons are present at birth that a human will ever have, about 100 billion. After birth, the cortex continues to develop. Neurons increase in size and become more complex in structure. Unlike the brain stem and limbic system, neurons produced for cortical regions actively migrate until they reach their final destinations. Once they arrive at their precise location neurons grow branching axons that form connections to other neurons. The number of connections (synapses) increases, peaking at different ages in different parts of the brain. Connections with other brain areas proliferate and then are pruned. Neurons with the strongest patterns of innervation retain their connections and the other cells die off. Two types of innervation are relevant: (1) endogenous neural firings and (2) exogenous neural firings produced by sensory inputs.

This "open program" of the developing brain is known as *neural plasticity*. The specialized information-processing centers of the neocortex are constructed by additive processes that are genetically controlled and subtractive processes that are highly sensitive to environmental input during ontogeny. Thus, evolutionary and developmental processes work together to solve problems of adaptation.

☐ For Further Inquiry

Cahill, L. (2006). Why sex matters for neuroscience. *Nature Reviews: Neuroscience, AOP.*

LeDoux, J. (1996). *The emotional brain.* New York, NY: Simon & Schuster.

Marcus, G. (2004). *The birth of the mind: How a tiny number of genes creates the complexities of human thought.* New York, NY: Basic Books.

Hormones and Behavior*

Hormones represent a group of neurochemicals that is quite distinct from the neurotransmitters discussed in the preceding chapter. Hormones are produced by the endocrine system which interacts with the nervous system mainly through connections between the hypothalamus and the pituitary just beneath it. The hypothalamus produces some hormones, such as oxytocin, and sends them via its axons as neurotransmitters to the pituitary for storage and release into the bloodstream where they can act on their target tissues. The hypothalamus also produces *releasing hormones* that reach the pituitary through special arteries and that stimulate the pituitary to produce various other hormones of its own (see Figure 6.1).

Most of these pituitary hormones act on other endocrine glands to stimulate them to produce hormones that act on final target tissues. An example is the HPA (hypothalamus-pituitary-adrenal cortex) system. The hypothalamus produces the releasing hormone CRF, which stimulates the pituitary to produce ACTH, which in turn stimulates production of the adrenal corticosteroid hormones, such as cortisol, which cause adjustments to stressful situations. Because they travel via the bloodstream, hormones usually require more time to have an impact on the body than neurotransmitters whose impact on the generation of an action potential in the neuron's axon occurs in nanoseconds.

---

* This chapter coauthored with Dr. Glenn Weisfeld.

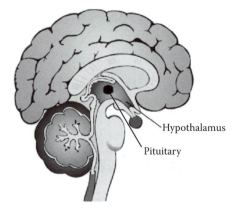

FIGURE 6.1   Many hormones are produced by the hypothalamus and the pituitary.

☐ Evolution of Hormones

In comparing hormones and neurotransmitters, it is useful to understand their evolution. The current evolutionary model (Snyder, 1985) is presented in Figure 6.2. The first and most basic form of chemical communication (model a) evolved to provide a primitive form of intercellular communication so that the organism could behave as a unit rather than a collection of uncoordinated cells. As organisms evolved into more complex forms, two lines of chemical communication evolved from this simple system. Neurotransmitters evolved to equip the organism with the ability for rapid and specific behavioral adjustments. As shown in model b, they travel an extremely short distance (measured in nanometers, or billionths of a meter) to produce their effects. The second line of evolution produced hormones that must travel much longer distances in the circulatory system, and thus provide for much slower and more generalized behavioral adjustments, as shown in model d. Another important difference between hormones and neurotransmitters is that the effects of hormones can be felt over the lifespan of the organism and some effects are irreversible and occur before birth. We shall distinguish between the organizing influence of hormones during prenatal development and their activating influence during biological events such as puberty.

Although quite different in terms of their functions in general, sometimes the same biochemical can serve as both a neurotransmitter and a

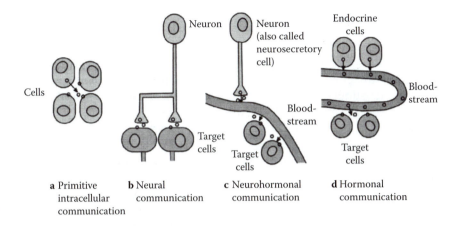

FIGURE 6.2 Evolution of chemical communication between cells. From a common ancestor (a) three distinct modes of chemical communication have evolved. In neural communication (b) chemicals diffuse across a short synapse to other cells. In neurohormonal communication (c) chemicals travel a longer route via the bloodstream to reach target cells, and in hormonal communication (d) endocrine glands release chemicals that reach target cells via the bloodstream. (Adapted from Gray, 1999, originally from Snyder, 1985.)

hormone, as in the case of oxytocin, above. Another example is noradrenalin, which is the neurotransmitter of sympathetic division neurons but also is produced by the adrenal medulla and, released in the bloodstream, acts as a hormone. Regardless of which route it uses to reach its target tissues, norepinephrine has the same effects, such as increasing the strength of heart contractions.

Other evidence of a commonality between neurotransmitters and hormones comes from the discovery of a special class of chemical messengers that fall midway between these two types. Known as neurohormones (model c), they are produced from neurons and released from axon terminals (like neurotransmitters), but are absorbed into the bloodstream (like hormones). This group includes peptides that appear to modulate synaptic transmission in a wider diffusion than neurotransmitters. It also includes natural opiates that, like artificial drugs, can modulate pain or other emotional systems. Research on neurohormones is still in its infancy, and much remains to be learned about their role in influencing emotional moods and other states of consciousness. In this chapter we shall focus on the role of hormones in influencing emotions, behavior, and development.

☐ The Endocrine System

Hormones are biochemicals that are produced by endocrine glands and selectively affect certain target tissues. Hormones reach their target tissues by traveling in the bloodstream or by diffusing into neighboring cells. By contrast, exocrine glands release their products outside of tissues through ducts. Exocrine glands include the salivary glands, sweat glands, and digestive glands.

Hormones affect cellular processes such as cell multiplication and differentiation, the production of other hormones, and various other metabolic processes. They do so by activating or deactivating genes within the target cells. Hormones either enter the cell nucleus to do this, usually acting through an intermediate chemical in the nucleus, or else activate receptors within the cell membrane, leading indirectly to influences on cellular processes (Mendelson, 2004). The latter process can occur within seconds or minutes, whereas the former can take hours or days.

Chemically, most hormones are either steroids, amino acids, peptides, or proteins (the latter two being strings of amino acids). The steroid hormones are the androgens, estrogens, progesterone, and adrenal corticosteroids. Because they are chemically related and share the same metabolic pathways, the steroid hormones are all produced by the same endocrine glands, although in different ratios. These steroid-producing glands are the testis, ovary, adrenal cortex, and placenta. Because of their chemical similarity, these hormones, especially androgens and estrogens, can have either the same or opposite effects on a receptor.

The endocrine system is very complicated; it constitutes an entire bodily system. Moreover, the endocrine and nervous systems have many interconnections and in fact are not completely distinct from each other. Dozens of hormones have been identified. We shall focus here on several hormones that are involved in sex differentiation and brain development before birth, growth and maturation throughout life, puberty, emergency response systems, and other developmental and behavioral processes. We organize this discussion in developmental sequence whenever possible, beginning with two critical events that occur before birth.

☐ Prenatal Development

Sex Differentiation

A gene on the Y chromosome produces a protein that converts the undifferentiated gonad into a testis early in fetal life. The testis then secretes androgens, which masculinize the internal and external genitals, resulting in the appearance of the penis, scrotum, prostate, etc. Another testicular hormone, *Mullerian inhibiting substance* (MIS), suppresses development of the incipient female internal genitalia (Mullerian duct system): the uterus, oviducts, and proximal vagina.

In girls who lack this testis-determining factor, development proceeds in the female direction. The external genitals become the labia and clitoris, and the internal genitals are free to develop. The male internal genitals, the Wolffian duct system, do not develop in the absence of testosterone.

Later in prenatal development, during the second trimester, a second surge in testosterone occurs in males. This causes masculinization of behavior in childhood. Girls who are exposed to high levels of androgens before birth can develop masculinized external genitals and masculine behavior. Such girls are often regarded as tomboys since they prefer rough play and show little interest in babies (Meyer-Balburg et al., 2004). The elevated levels of androgens can come either from a tumor of androgen producing cells of the adrenal cortex, a condition called congenital adrenal hyperplasia (CAH), or from steroid hormone therapy formerly prescribed in cases of threatened miscarriage.

Some sex differentiating (organizational) hormonal effects before birth set the stage for sex differences that occur under the influence of (activational) pubertal hormones. For example, prenatal events set the hypothalamus of girls to cycle at puberty.

Newborn boys experience a surge in testosterone levels that may function to enhance testicular development, since experimental suppression of this surge in a monkey resulted in impaired testicular function at puberty (Griffin & Ojeda, 2004). In general, however, gonadal hormone levels are low in both sexes throughout childhood.

Sex Differences in Behavior

Only one generation ago neuroscientists were taught that sex differences in the brain were limited to the hypothalamus, a small structure at the base of the brain involved in regulating hormone production and controlling basic behaviors such as eating, drinking, and sex. However, contemporary research using imaging techniques such as positron-emission tomography (PET) and functional magnetic resonance imaging (fMRI), demonstrates sex differences in many areas of cognition and behavior, including memory, emotion, vision, hearing, the processing of faces, and responses to stress. In their 2001 report on sex differences in human health, the National Academy of Sciences concluded "sex matters. Sex, that is, being male or female, is an important basic human variable that should be considered when designing and analyzing studies in all areas and at all levels of biomedical and health-related research." (Wizeman & Pardue, 2001, p. 30)

Hormones are major regulators of sex differences in prenatal brain development. They affect neural development directly by influencing neuronal growth, and indirectly, by modifying peripheral structures, like muscles, that in turn directly affect neurons. These various effects can occur during all stages of neural development. Ongoing research on sex differences in neuroanatomy seeks to (1) describe the location and extent of these sex differences; and (2) demonstrate their hormonal basis by experimental manipulation of the steroid environment during early development.

As discussed in the previous chapter, many recent imaging studies reveal anatomical sex differences in various regions throughout the human brain. In women, parts of the frontal cortex and limbic cortex are denser, while in men, parts of the parietal cortex and amygdala are larger than in women. Differences in the size or density of brain structures are generally thought to reflect their relative complexity. Humans, as primates, rely more on vision than olfaction, but for Fido, the family dog, the opposite is true. While his human servant is taking in the scenery, the morning walk for Fido is really an extensive sniffing expedition. Thus, human brains have evolved proportionately larger regions devoted to vision, while dogs devote more space to olfaction.

Several behavioral studies add to the evidence that sex differences in the brain can arise before birth. Based on a wide array of experimental evidence, sex differences in play in mammals have been shown to be influenced by hormones, social rearing, and contextual factors (Panksepp, 1998). Clear evidence for a direct influence of sex hormones on animal play may be found in experimental research on rats and rhesus macaques. Prenatal exposure to higher levels of androgen in females is related to increased rough-and-tumble play, regardless of rearing environment (Geary, 1998).

Many researchers over the years have demonstrated that girls and boys show sex-typed preferences when selecting toys. Boys more often choose balls or toy cars, whereas girls more typically reach for a doll. In the past it was difficult to say whether those preferences were shaped by culture or by brain biology. Studies of vervet monkeys revealed that male monkeys also spent more time playing with "masculine" toys than their female counterparts did, and female monkeys spent more time interacting with the playthings typically preferred by girls (G. M. Alexander & Hines, 2002). In studies of human infants, Baron-Cohen (2005) found that one-year-old girls spend more time looking at their mothers than boys of the same age do. And when these babies are presented with a choice of films to watch, the girls look longer at a film of a face, whereas boys prefer a film featuring cars. To eliminate possible socialization effects, Baron-Cohen examined the preferences of babies that were only one day old. The infants saw either the friendly face of a live female student or a mobile that matched the color, size, and shape of the student's face and included a scrambled mix of her facial features. They found that girls spent more time looking at the student, whereas boys spent more time looking at the mechanical object. Taken together, these results imply that toy preferences and other sex differences in social interest in children stem *in part* from biological brain differences that are laid out during prenatal development.

Throughout early and middle childhood, the levels of circulating sex hormones do not differ much between the sexes, and as a result, biosocial theories predict fewer biologically based sex differences during this period than after puberty (Geary, 1998). An exception to this general principle is once again found in research on the direct influence of sex hormones on differences in two types of play between boys and girls in early childhood: allo-parenting and rough-and-tumble play (Collaer & Hines, 1995). Prenatal exposure to higher levels of androgen in girls is related to increased physical competition and rough play, and decreased interest in infants and doll play regardless of social and contextual factors. We shall discuss these and other sex differences in behavior and their functional significance in more detail in Chapter 11.

☐ Infancy and Childhood

Growth and Maturation

An animal grows to attain the optimal size and shape for its way of life. There are advantages and disadvantages of large and small size. For example, small animals can reach mature size quickly and begin to reproduce. Large animals, if they are predators, can eat smaller animals, and in turn are less likely to be eaten.

Animals need, not only to grow larger but also to mature, to change their form. As an animal gets older, it meets different selective pressures to which it must adjust. For example, a primate infant initially does not really need its legs because it is transported by its mother. A newborn baby's legs are literally too weak to support it. However, a primate infant needs rather advanced powers of learning, and so its brain is almost full-grown at birth.

Maturational changes occur largely through the action of *thyroid hormones*. For example, thyroid hormones cause metamorphosis in amphibians and the periodic shedding of feathers in birds. In human children, a shortage of thyroid hormones can cause incomplete maturation of the teeth, bones, brain, and other structures. The child retains childlike bodily proportions, rather than just being short of stature. Thyroid hormones also increase the metabolic rate throughout the life span. Thus, one symptom of hypothyroidism is lethargy.

Growth hormone (GH) works together with the two thyroid hormones, but its main effect is on growth of the whole body, including soft tissues. GH increases the production of somatomedins by the liver. It is these growth factors that actually cause body cells to multiply. GH sees to it that bodily parts remain in proper proportion to each other throughout development, so that no organ is too large or too small. A small organ would be insufficient to provide its specialized services to the others, and a large organ would be wasteful. Normal bodily proportionality is called *allometry*. Many factors affect GH production. For example, GH production is stepped up during deep sleep. An excess of GH during childhood can result in abnormally great height or, after the long bones have stopped growing, a thickening of the bones of the jaw, hands, and feet.

Of course, nutrition must be adequate for normal growth to occur. If the organism is deprived of adequate nutrition, once normal nutrition is restored, growth greatly accelerates, even supernormally. This catch-up growth may completely compensate for the period of growth retardation, but permanent stunting can occur if the nutritional deficiency was bad enough. Psychological stress can also retard growth, as discussed in a later section.

Regulation of Body Weight

Body weight is tightly regulated by a large number of factors, including the hormone *leptin*. Leptin is produced by the body's fat cells, distributed mainly under the skin and in the abdominal cavity. Leptin informs the hypothalamus about the body's fat reserves. Fat is the most efficient form in which the body stores energy. A gram of fat contains about twice the calories of a gram of protein or carbohydrate.

When a person has not eaten for a while, the low level of blood glucose stimulates the hypothalamus to register hunger and initiate food seeking. Meanwhile, energy is drawn from bodily reserves. The first reservoir tapped after blood glucose is glycogen, which is stored in the liver and skeletal muscles. Glycogen is a complex carbohydrate, essentially a string of sugar molecules. Glycogen is broken down into glucose by the pancreatic hormone glucagon. Glucose enters the bloodstream and is utilized by the various tissues. When this limited store is depleted, the body draws on its fat reserves. When these are exhausted, protein in muscles is broken down. (Carbohydrates and nonessential fats can be converted into each other, but they cannot be converted into protein—which can be converted into glucose.)

When a person eats and the food is broken down by digestion, blood glucose rises, as do blood levels of fatty acids (digested fat) and amino acids (digested protein). Blood glucose enters the muscles and liver and is converted into glycogen by the pancreatic hormone *insulin*. Insulin also converts fatty acids into fat for storage in fat cells. Cells can use either glucose or fatty acids for energy—but the brain cannot use fatty acids.

As eating proceeds, the hypothalamus receives feedback about food intake via various hormones and sensory nerves. The presence of food is registered by the mouth, stomach, small intestine, and large intestine. Most food is digested by the duodenum, the first 12 inches of the small intestine. Digested food passes first to the liver, which can neutralize any toxins and which also registers food intake. The liver then passes the digested food into the general circulation. Thus, the body possesses multiple feedback mechanisms to track food intake. Some mechanisms provide "quick and dirty" feedback, whereas others are slower but provide more detailed and accurate information.

The body needs not just a certain number of calories but also adequate amounts of 9 essential amino acids (10 for infants), 3 essential fatty acids, some carbohydrate (sugars and starch), and numerous vitamins and minerals. Levels of these nutrients are all monitored, so that hunger for specific foods develops when their levels are low. Even weaned infants will eat a balanced diet if offered a range of nutritious foods to select.

Animals must keep their weight within narrow limits. Most mature animals and people maintain almost the same weight from year to year. They must maintain adequate reserves of energy, but must also be agile enough to escape predators or to catch prey. The only animals that are stout are domesticated animals that are provisioned and protected by humans, who sometimes intentionally breed livestock for the flavor of abundant fat. Also, women need extra fat to provide energy for the fetus and for lactation. Other selective factors are cold and food shortage. Animals and people that live in cold or barren climates tend to have abundant, insulating subcutaneous fat and rounded bodies to conserve heat. For example, the noses of Asians tend to be short; most Asians originated in the cold climate of central Asia.

Obesity

Why are more and more Americans, including children and adolescents, obese? In order to understand the cause of some phenomenon, we need to identify its distribution, to know who is affected and who is not. In 1991, only four states had obesity rates of 15% or more (Strumpf, 2004). By 2007, only one state had a prevalence of obesity less than 20%. Thirty states had a prevalence of 25% or more; three of these states had a prevalence of obesity of 30% or more. Currently, 66% of American adults are overweight or obese. Minority and low-socioeconomic-status groups are disproportionately affected at all ages (Wang & Beydoun, 2007).

According to the Centers for Disease Control and Prevention (2004), 16% of children and adolescents are overweight (over 9 million)—a number that has tripled since 1980. Overweight adolescents have a 70% chance of becoming overweight or obese adults. This increases to 80% if one or more parent is overweight or obese (United States Department of Health and Human Services, 2008).

Because the current epidemic of obesity in the United States began around 1980 and has been increasing ever since, we must ask what has changed over this period? Although genes play some role in body weight, with heritability around .66 (Plomin, DeFries, & McClearn, 1990), the genetic makeup of Americans has not changed significantly since 1980. Thus purely genetic causes of this epidemic can be confidently ruled out.

Research reveals that fat consumption is up somewhat, but not nearly as much as carbohydrate consumption—considered by most experts to be the main cause of the epidemic. Americans consume a lot of carbohydrates, and many of these calories are stored as fat. There is now general agreement about carbohydrate consumption being the culprit. What remains unclear is why Americans now eat so many carbohydrates.

Again, we want to know what is different now from conditions a couple of decades ago. One likely factor is the omnipresence of junk food. The danger posed by junk food is not its caloric content. All food has somewhere between 4 and 9 kilocalories of energy per gram. What makes junk food "junk" is its low nutritional content. It has few vitamins. Now, the body needs a minimum level of each essential vitamin. If the diet is low in vitamin concentrations, the only solution is to eat more. The carbohydrates that today's Americans consume are much lower in vitamins and desirable minerals than were the carbohydrates that hunter-gatherers consumed (Eaton, Eaton, & Konner, 1999). The latter ate plenty of carbohydrates, but they derived from fresh fruits and other plants.

But this explanation begs another question: Why are Americans drawn to food that is so low in nutrients? Aren't our evolved mechanisms for seeking vitamins operating? Here we encounter some other factors that, like junk food, were not present when hominids were evolving and against which we have little evolved protection. Junk food is cheap to produce, being mainly corn syrup. Therefore junk foods are highly profitable, and therefore heavily advertised. Also, junk food is made artificially tasty by adding salt and sugar—good flavors to seek in the wild where they signal nutritious fruit and the essential mineral sodium chloride, but false promises in the case of junk food. Much junk food is fruit flavored, fruit being the original main food of primates. Junk food is also convenient, being packaged in ready-to-eat or fast-food form. Junk food is cheap partly because it has a long shelf life. It is laced with preservatives that keep the food from spoiling but do not retard degradation of vitamins. The rise of junk food is exemplified by the beverages sold in high school cafeterias. Whereas in past decades milk ("Nature's most perfect food") was featured prominently, nowadays soda pop predominates. Americans consume soda pop in enormous quantities and it is pure dissolved sugar. Another influence is the food lobby, which has pressured the U.S. government to recommend consumption of large amounts of carbohydrates—the base of the food pyramid (Eaton et al., 1999). As junk foods have been introduced into other countries, increases in obesity have followed in its wake—even in countries where people exercise more than Americans.

Obesity carries distinct health risks, especially diabetes, cancer, and heart disease. It also causes lethargy, which carries additional health risks. To understand this increase in lethargy due to obesity, we need to consider experiments on food-deprived rats. These rats lose weight, but also become sluggish. They adopt an evolved strategy of conserving calories by minimizing exertion in the face of starvation. They also eat a great deal when abundant food becomes available, especially nutritious or calorie-rich (fatty) food. Similarly, starved people, or those who are dieting and hence are below their set point, are often binge eaters who nevertheless are finicky. They tend to be lethargic and to have low metabolic rates—and so they often do not eat excessively, since their sluggishness conserves calories. Thus, these metabolic and behavioral adjustments constitute an evolved adaptive strategy to enhance survival under conditions of food scarcity. Another part of the strategy is the rebound weight gain that often occurs in human dieters and starved rats once they can eat at will. In both species, body weight often comes to exceed that before caloric reduction. The body anticipates, in effect, another bout of food shortage and lays in surplus fat.

According to the *developmental-origins hypothesis* (Barker, 1992, 1997) reduced fetal growth is strongly associated with a number of chronic conditions (obesity, coronary heart disease, stroke, diabetes, and hypertension) later in life. This increased susceptibility results from adaptations made by the fetus in an environment limited in its supply of nutrients. The most widely accepted mechanisms thought to underlie these relationships are those of fetal programming by nutritional stimuli or excess fetal glucocorticoid exposure. It appears that the fetus makes physiological adaptations in response to changes in its environment to prepare itself for postnatal life. This means that in poor nutritional conditions, a pregnant female can modify the development of her unborn child such as to prepare for survival in an environment in short supply of resources, resulting in a thrifty phenotype (Hales & Barker, 1992). Individuals with a thrifty phenotype will have "a smaller body size, a lowered metabolic rate and a reduced level of behavioural activity ... adaptations to an environment that is chronically short of food" (Bateson & Martin, 1999, pp. 110–111). The fetus appears to adapt to an adverse intrauterine milieu by optimizing the use of a reduced nutrient supply to ensure survival. However, individuals with a thrifty phenotype who actually develop in an affluent environment may be more prone to obesity and type II diabetes in later life.

Based on this generally accepted analysis, what is to be done? Dieting is seldom successful, despite claims by interested parties to the contrary (Wooley & Garner, 1991). Controlled studies reveal that few patients lose weight, and those that do almost always gain it back within a couple of years, and often experience rebound weight gain. Dieters almost always go off their diet—because they are unhappy in a food-deprived state.

Similarly, exercise programs would succeed in principle, but people seldom stick to their exercise regimen—especially the obese, whose lethargy militates against exercise (Logue, 1991). Also, when the body draws down its fat reserves through exercise, work, or shivering, leptin production declines and eating increases. People "work up an appetite," usually making up for the caloric expenditure within two days (Rodin, 1977). If this were not so, then normal-weight individuals who undertook some exercise program would wither away. Furthermore, the body is very efficient in conserving calories, so one would need to exercise a great deal to lose much weight even if one did not increase food consumption.

This is not to say that some people do not lose weight permanently. In one study that recruited successful weight losers, 77% of the subjects had experienced some new motivating factor, such as a health scare or humiliation (Klem, Wing, McGuire, Seagle, & Hill, 1997). Most of these people limited intake of certain foods, and exercised faithfully. But these successful dieters were not representative of any treatment program. Most weight loss programs achieve a success rate of only a few percent, and any such therapy would not normally be recommended—were it not for the great profits to be gained from diet books, exercise gyms, and the like.

Gastrointestinal surgery has been employed in cases of extreme obesity, but the side effects and surgical dangers are usually considered prohibitive. Similarly, drug treatment is seldom safe and effective. Remember that the body has multiple and back-up mechanisms to keep body weight stable, so changing one mechanism will still leave others to restore the status quo. Weight control is very complex. Few obese people, for example, have reduced leptin production, thus some drug introduced to "correct" a nonexistent deficiency is unlikely to be of much benefit.

Psychological factors can be important, but do not seem to be important as a cause of recent trends. Remember that people had psychological problems before the obesity epidemic began. Also, some people overeat when unhappy, but others overeat when happy. Obese people are often unhappy because they are disparaged by others. Obese patients who lose weight often experience a rise in self-esteem—suggesting that the obesity caused low self-esteem, rather than the reverse (Rodin, 1977). Psychotherapy for obesity is generally unsuccessful.

Another obstacle to effective treatment is that obesity tends to be permanent. A fat child is very likely to become a fat adult. Part of the reason seems to be that by adolescence the body establishes its total number of fat cells, and then these fat cells tend to remain filled with fat (Spalding et al., 2008). Early overfeeding results in numerous fat cells, and then this number does not change very much subsequently. Thus, a parent who overfeeds her young child because of a population history of starvation may predispose him to obesity under conditions of abundance.

An evolutionary perspective does suggest some effective preventive measures. Breastfeeding significantly reduces the risk of subsequent obesity, as well as dozens of other diseases in the child and the mother. Bottle-feeding constitutes a radical departure from nature's design; cow's milk is designed for calves, not babies. Cow's milk contains more protein, for growth, than mother's milk, and different concentrations of other nutrients. Its low glucose and fat content, compared with mother's milk, is inappropriate for the rapidly growing primate brain, and may help explain the lower IQ of bottle-fed babies. Moreover, any formula will lack the growth factors, hormones, and antibodies of mother's milk. The infant's immune system is immature. The infant was not exposed to antigens in the womb and so has not yet developed antibodies and must rely heavily on the mother's antibodies and white blood cells, passed through the milk, to fight infection.

A natural diet is probably desirable after weaning also. What would our prehistoric ancestors have eaten? Certainly not cookies, soda pop, and potato chips. The most nutritious foods are those that one would find in the wild—fresh fruit, roots, legumes, seafood, lean meat, eggs. Our prehistoric ancestors are thought to have eaten a diet high in protein but low in fat, and one similar to ours in carbohydrate, but with many fresh fruits and vegetables and, consequently, a lot of fiber (Eaton et al., 1999). Fruit is especially healthy; the plant wants its fruit to be eaten and its seeds transported, and does not want to poison vectors of its seeds. Nuts are also healthy, because the plant relies mainly on the shell to prevent the nut from being eaten, rather than on toxins in, say, a leafy plant. Milk, for those who can digest it (i.e., people descended from populations that practiced dairying), contains the entire range of essential nutrients. Admittedly, whole milk has cholesterol, associated with heart disease in some people. Contemporary hunter-gatherers consume lots of cholesterol, but their consumption of abundant nutrients seems to result in low cholesterol levels. It is not necessary to avoid fatty foods. In fact, some fats are essential, and some vitamins are fat-soluble and so are absent from skim milk. The body can count calories, and so fatty foods are more filling than others. Meat is richer in amino acids than plant food, and is well digested by our species. Plant foods should be eaten raw or else steamed, to reduce vitamin loss.

Claims about what foods are best and worst seem to change every week. A more durable guide may be to eat a diet similar to that which our hominid ancestors ate. Research indicates that such a diet is associated with much higher amounts of essential nutrients and much lower rates of heart disease and cancer than the foods we commonly consume (Eaton et al., 1999).

The development of body weight is an interesting developmental phenomenon. Genes and parental practices, reflecting starvation pressure on the person's ancestors, play a major but not overwhelming role, leaving room for adjustments to current environmental conditions. The individual's past experience greatly influences subsequent eating behavior, because an episode of life-threatening starvation must serve as a cautionary tale. Food-deprived children, like starved rats, often hoard food when it becomes available. The organism samples its early experience and sets its developmental course accordingly.

☐ Adolescence

Adaptive Significance of Puberty

Birth and puberty are the major developmental transitions in our species. At puberty the individual goes from still being somewhat dependent on parents to being full-grown, independent, and capable of attracting mates, reproducing, and caring for one's children. Puberty is the time of greatest sex differentiation, preparing boys and girls for their respective reproductive roles. Because of this challenge of independence, many measures of bodily and behavioral competence, such as body size and abstract reasoning ability, peak in adolescence. Analogously, in all traditional societies adolescents undergo a period of intense instruction in the responsibilities of men and women in that culture, culminating in formal graduation into adulthood—puberty rites (Weisfeld, 1997). This is a good example of collaboration between biology and culture.

Paralleling the psychological growth spurt provided by puberty rites and cognitive maturation, both sexes undergo a physical growth spurt. To understand the growth spurt functionally, we need to consider its distribution in the animal kingdom. Most animals undergo rapid growth after birth. Subsequently the velocity of growth tapers off. This allows the organism to attain its ideal, mature size rapidly.

The Primate Growth Pattern

Old World primates are an exception to this general pattern of growth in animals. They undergo rapid growth at first, but then enter a period of relatively slow juvenile growth. This is followed by a spurt in body weight—the adolescent growth spurt. So we need to explain this growth spurt in terms of the primate way of life.

The leading explanation for the primate growth spurt at adolescence is this (see Janson & van Schaik, 1993). Primates follow a K-selected developmental strategy. They produce few young, usually only singletons rather than litters, and the young receive extensive and prolonged maternal care. The long period of immaturity and protection gives them time to learn how to survive. In particular, they devote much time and energy during the juvenile phase to play, which gives them practice in locomotion and social skills in particular. Primates need lots of time to learn to locomote in trees, unlike other mammals. Primate behavior is very flexible, so they need to learn how and when to execute a large variety of behaviors. Many primates are also highly social and must develop skill at dominance fighting or maternal behavior. This is why primates have large brains, and brains that grow quickly early on, even while the rest of their bodies grow slowly. The long period of immaturity gives them time for this protracted learning, and the slow rate of growth frees up calories for the vigor of play. Primates also have little need for large size as protection against predation, because they are relatively safe up in the trees. Living in warm climates, most primates have little need for large size to retain heat, and many are warmed by their mothers at night. Also, their mothers and others often protect young primates on the ground. Lastly, small size confers an advantage to an arboreal species, since it allows the animal to venture onto thin branches in search of food and to avoid predators. Having grown slowly, the adolescent primate must grow quickly in order to make up for lost time—hence the growth spurt.

A few qualifications of this model are necessary. Small primates do not seem to need a growth spurt—because they never become very big. Slow but prolonged growth during the juvenile phase is sufficient. Thus, the generally smaller New World primates do not undergo an adolescent growth spurt, nor do the smallest ("lesser") apes, the gibbons and siamang. Also, whereas only a few other primates undergo a spurt in body length (Shea, 1985; Tanner, Wilson, & Rudman, 1990), human adolescents gain sharply in height as well as weight, for reasons that are not well understood.

In about half (9 of 21, in one review) of Old World primate species the females do not undergo a growth spurt (Leigh, 1996), apparently because, unlike males, they have little need for large size in dominance fighting. In most primate species, the males take longer than the females to reach adult size; they require more time to grow and also to practice fighting.

The growth spurt of girls is thought to function to provide size enough for efficient bearing of our rather large fetuses; the human newborn is 88% larger than the chimpanzee newborn (Harvey & Clutton-Brock, 1985). The human female growth spurt is comparatively brief, so that growth does not usually compete with the fetus' need for calories. Infants born to women who are still growing are prone to low birth weight (Frisancho, Matos, Leonard, & Yaroch, 1985).

In general, then, the human growth pattern follows the principles of primate growth quite closely (Leigh, 2001), despite contrary claims of a fundamental departure from the simian pattern (e.g., Bogin, 1999). The most distinctive feature of human growth is the slow rate of maturation. Humans take longer than any other mammal to mature.

Physiology of Puberty

Due to the activating effects of hormones, at puberty dramatic morphological changes occur. These changes include the growth spurt (timed earlier for girls, but more extensive in boys), the emergence of primary and secondary sex characteristics, and a general increase in *sexual dimorphism*. It is well known that puberty accentuates sex differences through the influence of testosterone in men and estrogen in women. However, the changes in morphology and behavior that are produced through the action of sex hormones are almost never discussed by developmental psychologists in functional terms. As Weisfeld and Billings (1988, p. 207) noted,

> Textbooks on adolescent development have, through the years, faithfully detailed these morphological changes, but without acknowledging that these biological phenomena must necessarily possess identifiable adaptive functions ... even the suggestion that some of the behavioral changes of adolescence might have an evolved basis virtually never appears in textbooks. Reading these accounts, one almost gets the impression that the sex drive itself appears because of television and "peer pressure" (other people's teenagers).

Before puberty the adrenal cortex produces an increase in adrenal androgens, at around age 6 or 7 (De Peretti & Forest, 1976; Tanner, 1990; unless otherwise noted, all ages in this section refer to well-fed, modern populations). This increase probably occurs because of a rise in ACTH and helps launch the growth spurt and the appearance of pubic and axillary (armpit) hair. In humans, as in other animals, the adrenal glands produce a sex hormone that is the same for both sexes called

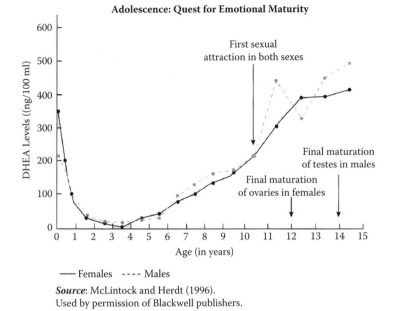

Adolescence: Quest for Emotional Maturity

—— Females   ---- Males

Source: McLintock and Herdt (1996).
Used by permission of Blackwell publishers.

FIGURE 6.3   Blood levels of adrenal androgen DHEA in girls and boys as a function of age. (From McLintock, M. K., & Herdt, G. [1996]. *Current Directions in Psychological Science, 6,* 178–183. With permission.)

dihydroepiandrosterone (DHEA). As shown in Figure 6.3, the amount of DHEA secreted by the adrenal glands peaks during the early teens.

This hormonal event, *adrenarche*, is suspected of contributing to the romantic attraction of some children to a child of the opposite sex—schoolboy crushes (McClintock & Herdt, 1996). Beginning at around seven years of age, children often seek out a single attractive child of the opposite sex, want to be near him or her and to hug and kiss him or her, offer gifts, and are jealous of rivals. However, true sexual desire is absent at this age (Jersild, 1968). With puberty comes maturation of sexual desire. Whereas a child can fall in love, the genital sex drive, or libido, is not yet present. The adolescent, by contrast, tends to be sexually attracted to the object of amorous attraction—although sexual attraction can occur in the absence of amorousness felt toward that person.

Evidence in support of this later stage of sexual development comes from research in human ethology that has documented that attraction to members of the opposite sex is based on a biologically programmed perceptual bias (Eibl-Eibesfeldt, 1995). Given the choice between line drawings of female and male body contours, prepubertal children of both sexes prefer same-sex drawings. But beginning at about the age of 12 in both

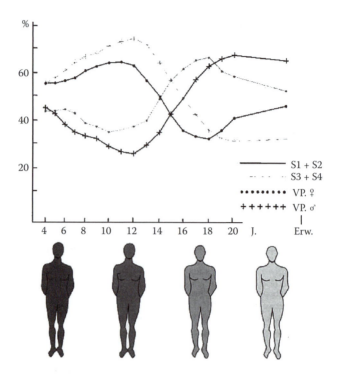

FIGURE 6.4 Masculine and feminine model choice by boys and girls as a function of age. The transition between preference for same-sex body contour and opposite-sex preference occurs between 12 and 18 years for both sexes. (Adapted from Eibl-Eibesfeldt, 1995).

sexes, a dramatic reversal takes place, as shown in Figure 6.4, with female and male adolescents showing a clear preference for opposite-sex body profiles.

The pubertal growth spurt begins, at 10 to 11 years in girls and 12 to 13 in boys, on average, when an increase in adrenal androgens in both sexes triggers a rise in nighttime secretion of GH (Ganong, 1997). The growth spurt then ensues through a synergism of gonadal hormones, growth hormone, and thyroid hormones. Androgens in boys and estrogens in girls mold the skeleton into its appropriate sex-specific configuration. These gonadal hormones eventually bring about fusion of the growth plates near the end of long bones, terminating growth.

Reproductive maturation begins at around age 9 in girls and 10 in boys with sleep-associated increases in LH. Various stressors such as poor nutrition can cause the hypothalamus to delay this increase until more auspicious conditions occur. Also, puberty proceeds slowly and less completely under stressful conditions. For example, children with many siblings tend to be shorter than children with fewer. A healthy, low-stress childhood tends to result in early and complete maturation, followed by healthy adulthood (Martorell, 1995). Thus, early maturing boys and girls tend to be more sex differentiated and physically attractive than late maturers, and to have fewer psychological problems. The alleged psychological problems of early maturing girls are only temporary (Faust, 1960) and are found mainly in U.S. girls, who are prone to obesity, especially if they are early maturers (Hayward et al., 1977; Simmons, Blyth, & McKinney, 1983). They also live in a society with conservative attitudes toward sex and where teasing of early maturing girls is common; the deleterious effect of early maturity in girls is not seen in Germany, for example (Silbereisen et al., 1989). Cross-culturally, early maturing girls marry younger and have more children, so they certainly do not suffer in fitness terms (Borgerhoff-Mulder, 1989).

Although most stressors delay puberty, family problems tend to accelerate it in girls. For example, father absence speeds menarche (Ellis & Garber, 2000). The current evolutionary explanation is that a girl who is not benefiting from living at home may be better off leaving home and beginning to reproduce. Early maturing girls everywhere tend to begin their sex lives early and to begin to bear children early. This is a good example of the genetically based plasticity that developmental mechanisms can exhibit.

Sex differentiation at puberty in boys occurs through the action of androgens. Testosterone is converted into dihydrotestosterone, which is chiefly responsible for growth of the penis and prostate before birth and at puberty, and of body hair. Testosterone itself causes increases in muscle mass and appearance of libido. Some pubertal changes, such as lowering of the voice, are irreversible, but other changes, as in muscle mass, are at least partially reversed if androgen production falls. Fertility in boys is attained rather early in puberty. Presumably this allows a boy who manages to secure sexual opportunities a chance to reproduce. Later in puberty he will become larger, stronger, and more intimidating, and therefore better at attracting females. The growth of body hair and other masculine features such as large mandible and brow ridges serve, as in other species, to intimidate rival males and attract females.

In girls, feminization of the body occurs because of an increase in estrogens. However, normal girls also experience some masculinizing changes at puberty, such as growth of body hair, lowering of the voice, and appearance of libido. These changes are caused by adrenal androgens and are less marked than in boys, who possess testes to provide much higher levels of androgens. In girls, unlike boys, fertility is attained late in puberty. A girl must grow almost to full size in order to deliver a fetus. However, signs of pubertal development such as breasts and other sexual lures appear years before the onset of fertility and lactation—why? In most traditional cultures adolescents are seldom effectively restricted from engaging in sex (Broude & Greene, 1976). This allows them practice in sexual relationships, and sometimes girls can receive gifts for sex. Pregnancy seldom results from these liaisons because fertility does not begin until around age 17 in these traditional societies, and marriages are usually arranged by then. Youth in a bride is desirable everywhere, because a young wife maximizes the man's reproductive chances with her, while his chances of being cuckolded are minimal since his wife is only coming into fertility. In boys and girls, fertility gradually rises and is highest for a woman when she is in her 20s.

☐ Adulthood

Reproduction

The production of gonadal hormones occurs as follows. A hypothalamic releasing hormone, *GnRH* (gonadotropin releasing hormone), causes the pituitary gland to produce the two gonadotropins, *FSH* (follicle stimulating hormone) and *LH* (luteinizing hormone). At puberty, FSH and LH cause the germ cells—sperm and ova—to mature, and cause the gonads to produce gonadal hormones. The levels of FSH, LH, and gonadal hormones fluctuate over the menstrual cycle via complex feedback mechanisms. Production of gonadal hormones in men—androgens and other steroids— is fairly steady, although peaks occur in the morning and in the summer.

In women estrogen levels rise gradually before ovulation. FSH and LH spike shortly before ovulation and are thought to trigger it. After ovulation, the ovarian follicle that held the now-released ovum reduces its hormone production and then resumes it. But now, changed in appearance and called the corpus luteum, this structure produces progesterone as well as estrogens. Levels of these hormones rise during the second half of the menstrual cycle. Then, if fertilization does not occur, these levels fall as the corpus luteum degenerates.

If fertilization occurs, in the oviduct where sperm meets egg, secretion of estrogens and progesterone continues to increase. When the placenta forms, it eventually takes over their production, and adds several other hormones. These hormones contribute to the changes of pregnancy. Many of them also promote maternal behavior. One of these is *oxytocin*, which plays a role, but not the only hormonal role, in delivery of the baby (parturition), shrinking down of the uterus after delivery, and release of the milk.

Another hormone that rises through pregnancy is *prolactin*, which promotes milk production after the placenta is passed at birth. Prolactin increases parental behavior also. In mammalian species in which the males provide some parental care, during a pregnancy the male's as well as his mate's prolactin level rises. This happens in our species too, and men who experience large rises in prolactin tend to be more disturbed by hearing the recorded cry of a distressed infant than do those with small increases (Storey et al., 2000).

This research provides a reminder that many human social behaviors, such as sex, aggression, parental behavior, and social bonding, have hormonal bases. Androgens increase aggressiveness and self-confidence, and they rise in response to competitive situations in male mammals. For example, young men in violent neighborhoods where one must be prepared to fight tend to have high testosterone levels (Mazur & Booth, 1998). And single and divorced men, who must compete for mates more than married men, tend to have higher testosterone levels than married men. In a threatening situation, then, male testosterone levels rise, apparently to bolster the man's self-confidence and aggressiveness as he faces a challenger. Cortisol and sympathetic division activity also increase, to mobilize the male for exertion.

In such a situation, however, women often experience another hormonal reaction: a rise in oxytocin. This bonding hormone induces a "tend and befriend" response—to protect one's children or to seek protection from others (Taylor, 2006). In mammals, oxytocin has been shown to increase affiliation, maternal behavior, grooming, and bonding to conspecifics present when the oxytocin was administered. Oxytocin seems to reduce stress—to lower cortisol and sympathetic division activity in animals and people, such as breastfeeding women, women who receive frequent hugs from partners, and men given exogenous oxytocin. Thus, oxytocin seems to reduce the physiological mobilization of stress, to provide an alternative behavioral strategy to fighting or fleeing. The effects of oxytocin seem to be greater in women than in men. Consistent with this sex difference, estrogen potentiates the action of oxytocin.

The development of primate parental behavior, and not just the attachment that sets the stage for parental behavior, is a topic much in need of study. For example, at first a rhesus mother does not let her infant wander away; she retrieves him immediately. Later she will accompany him on his forays. Later still she will let him venture out alone but will retrieve him periodically. How does she know what to do when? Some research suggests that a primate mother separated from and then reunited with her offspring treats him as though he is younger than he actually is, so primates may possess some internal timetable about offspring development. However, age-appropriate parental behavior may also be regulated by the hormone-dependent changing appearance of the developing offspring. The parent has to decrease her parental care, to allow the offspring more independence, as it develops.

For example, pubertal maturity seems to cause hormonally based changes in parent-adolescent relations in our species. When the adolescent's growth peaks, so does friction between parent and adolescent. This may be caused by the adolescent's hormonal changes but it might also result from the adolescent's changing appearance. Later in adolescence, contentiousness declines (Steinberg & Hill, 1978). Interestingly, boys tend to then win most of the arguments with their mother but not their father, whereas daughters continue to defer to both parents. The same thing happens in chimpanzees, but daughters typically never overtake either parent.

Emergency and Stress Response Systems

The body is designed to "gear up" in an emergency. The brain registers some form of distress, such as pain, cold, heat, fear, effort, defeat, anger, and even boredom and loneliness, and activates two parallel systems for coping with the adversity.

One system is called the *general adaptation syndrome* and was studied by Hans Selye in Montreal. The hypothalamus, where virtually all emotional affects are represented, produces a hormone that travels down special blood vessels to the pituitary gland beneath it. The pituitary in turn produces ACTH, a hormone that stimulates the adrenal cortex to produce its hormones, notably cortisol and other corticosteroids, or "stress hormones." These corticosteroids cause various adjustments to a metabolic challenge, such as increased blood glucose for fuel, and increased blood volume to protect against blood loss from wounding. Less urgent bodily processes, notably growth, reproductive maturation and function, wound healing, and immune system function, are suppressed. These bodily adjustments take similar form in response to different stressors, hence the terms "general" and "syndrome."

The other system is called the *emergency reaction* or flight-or-fight response. It was studied mainly by Walter Cannon in the United States. Again, under the influence of the hypothalamus, negative emotions trigger a more or less standard cascade of physiological adjustments. In this case, the hypothalamus signals the medulla oblongata, in the base of the brain, to make certain adjustments in the activity of the viscera. These adjustments are mediated by the sympathetic division of the autonomic nervous system, including the adrenal medulla, which releases the hormones adrenalin and noradrenalin (epinephrine and norepinephrine) into the bloodstream. Through these hormones and through nerves that innervate various viscera, the sympathetic division increases the heart rate, respiratory rate, blood pressure, and blood supply to the brain and muscles for quick, vigorous, and sustained action. Blood clotting is enhanced, to protect against hemorrhage in the case of a wound or injury. Red blood cells are released by the spleen, to provide a transfusion. Sweating increases to cool the active body. Some of these adjustments are apparent to observers and thus constitute emotional expressions. For example, we may observe someone who is anxious or angry to be tense because of heightened activation of the muscles. As with the general adaptation syndrome, less urgent bodily processes are suppressed, such as digestion, sexual function, labor contractions, and excretion.

From a functional standpoint, one might ask, why doesn't the body maintain a high level of mobilization all the time? The answer seems to be that suppression of maintenance functions such as digestion and wound healing take their toll eventually. Prolonged stress can cause stunting of growth, delayed sexual maturation, poor reproductive function in adulthood, memory impairment, and increased susceptibility to infections and cancer. The body has only so much metabolic energy, and it must allocate this energy adaptively to its various systems. The *law of economy* explains why animals tend to rest when they can and why movements become more economical with practice.

Recently mice have been raised with low-calorie diets and they live a long time. However, they do so by lowering their metabolic rate, not growing to normal size, and seldom reproducing. Energy is diverted from these latter processes in order to keep the animal alive. Similarly, men who are castrated, especially before puberty, live a long time because they have little muscle, which is energetically costly, to maintain. This is also the main proximate explanation for the fact that female birds and mammals generally outlive the males. The main reason is not sex-linked disease, because in birds it is the females that have the short sex chromosome but they still live longer than the males.

Postreproduction

In the elderly, fertility declines along with gonadal hormone production. This results in a decrease in sexual differentiation in body and behavior. Pronounced sex differentiation is no longer needed for reproduction, so the organism returns to its prepubertal state of comparatively little sex differentiation. In effect, metabolic energy and bodily form are again being devoted maximally to survival rather than reproduction.

Post-reproductive survival occurs rarely in animals and apparently mainly when the senescent individual can aid its kin after it ceases to reproduce. For example, poisonous butterflies survive after their reproductive span because their self-sacrifice can bring down or deter predators on their young. However, this does not occur in butterflies that are mimics of poisonous species. If these parents were to be eaten by a predator, the predator would only survive to eat the young. Post-reproductive humans tend to provide tangible help to their children and grandchildren, rather than imposing burdens on them. Menopause occurs because natural selection has favored investment in kin over continued reproduction with its risks of genetic anomalies. It occurs mechanistically because of a decline in gonadal hormone production and not because of a shortage of ova (Leidy, 1999). Hunter-gatherer women only ovulate around 160 times, since they are pregnant or lactating much of the time, leaving them with hundreds of eggs, yet they reach menopause around age 47 (Eaton & Eaton, 1999).

☐ Chapter Summary

Hormones are produced by the endocrine system which interacts with the nervous system through connections between the hypothalamus and the pituitary. Most pituitary hormones act on other endocrine glands to stimulate them to produce hormones that act on final target tissues. Hormones reach their target tissues by traveling in the bloodstream and usually require more time to have an impact on the body than neurotransmitters. Chemically, most hormones are either steroids, amino acids, peptides, or proteins. The steroid hormones are the androgens, estrogens, progesterone, and adrenal corticosteroids. Because they are chemically related and share the same metabolic pathways, the steroid hormones are all produced by the same endocrine glands.

Besides their critical role in determining the sex of the developing organism, hormones are major regulators of sex differences in prenatal brain and behavioral development. They directly influence neuronal growth, and exert indirect effects by modifying peripheral structures, like muscles, that in turn directly affect neurons. These various effects can occur during all stages of neural development. Contemporary research using imaging techniques demonstrates sex differences in many areas of cognition and behavior, including memory, emotion, vision, hearing, the processing of faces, and responses to stress.

During the second trimester a second surge in testosterone occurs in males, causing masculinization of behavior in early childhood. Girls who are exposed to high levels of androgens before birth can develop masculinized external genitals and masculine behavior. Prenatal exposure to higher levels of androgen in girls is related to increased physical competition and rough play and decreased interest in infants and doll play regardless of social and contextual factors.

Later maturational changes occur largely through the action of thyroid hormones. In children, a shortage of thyroid hormones can cause incomplete maturation of the teeth, bones, brain, and other structures. Thyroid hormones also increase the metabolic rate throughout the life span. Growth hormone (GH) works together with the two thyroid hormones, but its main effect is on growth of the whole body, including soft tissues. In most primate species, the males take longer than the females to reach adult size. In general, the human growth pattern follows the general principles of primate growth quite closely. The most distinctive feature is the slow rate of maturation. Humans take longer than any other mammal to mature.

Body weight is tightly regulated by a large number of factors, including the hormone leptin. Leptin is produced by the body's fat cells, distributed mainly under the skin and in the abdominal cavity. Leptin informs the hypothalamus about the body's fat reserves. Most mature animals and people maintain almost the same weight from year to year. They must maintain adequate reserves of energy, but must also be agile enough to escape predators or to catch prey. The carbohydrates that today's Americans consume are much lower in vitamins and desirable minerals than were the carbohydrates that hunter-gatherers consumed from fresh fruits and other plants. A diet high in vitamin-poor carbohydrates is an important cause of the current epidemic of obesity in children and adults in the United States.

Due to the activating effects of hormones, at puberty dramatic morphological changes occur. These changes include the growth spurt, the emergence of primary and secondary sex characteristics, and a general increase in sexual dimorphism. Sex differentiation at puberty in boys occurs through the action of androgens. Testosterone causes increases in muscle mass and appearance of libido. Some pubertal changes, such as lowering of the voice, are irreversible, but other changes, as in muscle mass, are at least partially reversed if androgen production falls. In girls, feminization of the body occurs because of an increase in estrogens. However, girls also experience some masculinizing changes at puberty, such as growth of body hair, lowering of the voice, and appearance of libido. These changes are caused by adrenal androgens and are less marked than in boys, who possess testes to provide much higher levels of androgens. Upon fertilization, secretion of estrogens and progesterone continues to increase. When the placenta forms, it eventually takes over their production, and adds several other hormones. These hormones contribute to the changes of pregnancy. Many of them also promote maternal behavior. One of these is oxytocin, which plays a role—but not the only hormonal role—in delivery of the baby (parturition), shrinking down of the uterus after delivery, and release of milk.

Another hormone that rises through pregnancy is prolactin, which promotes milk production after the placenta is passed at birth. Prolactin increases parental behavior also. In mammalian species in which the males provide some parental care, during a pregnancy the male's as well as his mate's prolactin level rises. This happens in our species too, and men who experience large rises in prolactin tend to be more disturbed by hearing the recorded cry of a distressed infant than do those with small increases.

This research provides a reminder that many human social behaviors, such as sex, aggression, parental behavior, and social bonding, have hormonal bases. Androgens increase aggressiveness and self-confidence and rise in response to competitive situations in male mammals. In such a situation, however, women often experience another hormonal reaction: a rise in oxytocin. This bonding hormone induces a "tend and befriend" response—to protect one's children or to seek protection from others. In animals, oxytocin has been shown to increase affiliation, maternal behavior, grooming, and bonding to conspecifics.

The emergency reaction, or flight-or-fight response, involves a cascade of physiological adjustments triggered by negative emotions via the operation of the hypothalamus. Through the release of the hormones adrenalin and noradrenalin (epinephrine and norepinephrine) into the bloodstream and through nerves that innervate various viscera, the sympathetic division increases the heart rate, respiratory rate, blood pressure, and blood supply to the brain and muscles for quick, vigorous, and sustained action. Blood clotting is enhanced, to protect against hemorrhage in the case of a wound or injury. Sweating increases to cool the active body.

In the elderly, fertility declines along with gonadal hormone production, resulting in a decrease in sexual differentiation in body and behavior. Pronounced sex differentiation is no longer needed for reproduction, so the organism returns to its prepubertal state of comparatively little sex differentiation. In effect, metabolic energy and bodily form are again being devoted maximally to survival rather than reproduction.

☐ For Further Inquiry

Guillemin R. (2005). Hypothalamic hormones a.k.a. hypothalamic releasing factors. *Journal of Endocrinology, 184*, 11–28.

Kushiro, T., Nambara, E., & McCourt, P. (2003). Hormone evolution: The key to signaling. *Nature, 422*, 122.

Weisfeld, G. E. (1999). *Evolutionary principles of human adolescence*. New York, NY: Basic Books.

Facial Expressions and Basic Emotions in Infancy

☐ How Signals Evolve

Communication is ubiquitous in the animal world and is often striking and elaborate. Ethologists studying animal behavior in the field have long been intrigued about the origin and function of the displays they observe. Classic signal theory was based upon Darwin's principles (1872) and later elaborated by Tinbergen (1951, 1963), Marler (1984), Huxley (1966), and other ethologists who refined the Darwinian notion that signals evolved from incidental and involuntary expressions of internal states like emotions, a process known as *ritualization*. If an incidental result of emotional arousal and autonomic state activity involved an observable effect (i.e., a facial or vocal expression or erection of hair or feathers), through ritualization this movement could evolve into an effective signal that carries important information. Each signal is rigidly linked to a specific function, hence the term "fixed" signal. The information conveyed by the signal was thought to pertain to the animal's internal state, rather than some external condition of the environment, hence Darwin's title *The Expression of the Emotions in Man and Animals*.

One difficulty of the classical explanation of the evolution of signal systems is its assumption of mutual benefits of increasingly accurate information transfer from sender to receiver. This view is summarized by Tinbergen (1964, p. 206), "One party—the actor—emits a signal, to which the other party—the reactor—responds in such a way that the welfare of the species is promoted." However, the assumption of mutual benefit of truthful signals is deeply problematic from the standpoint of contemporary views of natural selection emphasizing individual (Williams, 1966) or gene selection (Dawkins, 1976) rather than "the welfare of the species." From this latter perspective, signals that accurately convey one animal's intentions could be used by the receiver to gain a strategic advantage over the sender, especially in situations involving assessment, competition, or conflict. If by sending a clear signal, the sender stands to lose ground in the Darwinian struggle to survive and reproduce, how did signal systems evolve?

One answer to this puzzle involves rethinking signal function. Today many ethologists believe that signals evolved towards greater persuasiveness rather than towards increasingly accurate read-outs of inner states and intentions. This position proposes that expressions that exaggerate or minimize internal emotional states may be strategically advantageous to their sender on some occasions, particularly if they are likely to be accepted as true (Dawkins & Krebs, 1978). The individual's adaptation within the social group may depend upon its ability to manage its own signals and assess the veracity of signals directed to them. Owings and Morton (1998) argue that the tension between management and assessment issues drives the evolution of communicative systems to new heights by fostering successive adjustments in both the subtlety of displays and in the ability to interpret them. This "evolutionary arms race" is thought to have supported the evolution of primate social intelligence.

☐ Evolution of Nonhuman Primate Facial Expressions

Little is known about the genetic basis of primate facial displays, though careful study of the patterns of variation between species and among members of the same species strongly suggest a genetic basis, in that a peculiar variation from a common general form may be found in just one species, but is present in all of its adult members (Chevalier-Skolnikoff, 1973). Ethologists have long assumed that closely related species have more similar patterns of facial expressions than more distantly related species. Indeed, the similarities and differences in the expressive displays of different species, breeds, phyla, and classes noted by Whitman and Heinroth gave rise to the idea that behavioral patterns could be used as reliably as morphological features to indicate genetic relatedness (Lorenz, 1973).

One of Darwin's most enduring contributions to the study of facial expressions was his exacting description of the precise movements that contributed to the overall expression and his emphasis on its underlying muscular anatomy. Over a century later, Darwin's work is still considered to be the most encompassing on the subject because of his insight regarding the relationship between the form and function of the muscles involved in the evolution and production of facial expressions. The details of this analysis are beyond the scope of this text, but the ideas will be summarized because they are central to his hypothesis that human facial expressions evolved from our primate heritage.

The general trend in the evolution of facial displays from the most primitive primates, the prosimians, to monkeys, apes, and humans involves an increase in the number of muscles in the midface and the diversity of expressions that they permit. Because they are generally nocturnal, prosimians rely primarily on smell, sound, and touch rather than vision for vital information about their environment. Moreover, they do not share the general primate characteristic of group living and instead lead relatively solitary lives. Consistent with these ecological conditions, they make only a few facial expressions, and their facial muscles function mainly for movements associated with eating and biting.

In contrast, the Old World monkeys have adapted to a very different environment, one that is diurnal, arboreal, and highly social. Keen vision is essential to their adaptation and they have evolved somewhat different facial muscles. There is a reduction of the muscles involved in smelling and hearing, and an increase in the size and number of midface muscles that allows a greater range of movement in the lip and cheek. Compared to prosimians, Old World monkeys are much more expressive, although the two groups share some expressions that are similar in form and function, primarily expressions of fear, threat (anger), and affection. Rhesus monkeys and Hamadryas baboons, shown in Figures 7.1 and 7.2, are among the Old World monkeys.

As depicted in Figure 7.3, the ancestral line leading to humans and the great apes split off from that leading to Old World monkeys about 20 to 25 MYA. The great apes (chimpanzees, bonobos, orangutans, and gorillas) show a continuation of the trend towards an increase in midfacial musculature and decrease in ear, scalp, and forehead musculature. In particular, the size and number of muscles in the area around the mouth and lip show an increase. Primatologists consider the chimpanzee to be more expressive than any other nonhuman primate. However, many of the expressions of the great apes are also found in similar form among the Old World monkeys, and appear to be clearly homologous (Chevalier-Skolnikoff, 1973). Indeed, an experienced observer of macaque expressions would be capable of recognizing many of the chimpanzee expressions and vice versa.

An example of a homologous expression is the universal human display of smiling and laughing. These expressions are thought to have evolved

FIGURE 7.1 Cuddly features of a rhesus infant. The term *Kindchenschema* was coined by Lorenz to refer to the relatively large head, large eyes, and soft, rounded features of the typical infant's face, that are thought to help elicit an emotionally based care-giving response from the adult. (Photo courtesy of Frans de Waal.)

from two originally independent primate displays that have become closely related in Homo sapiens. The bared-teeth display and the relaxed open-mouth display occur in existing primate species like monkeys (e.g., rhesus and crab-eating macaques) and chimpanzees. The silent bared-teeth display is the probable evolutionary precursor of human smiling, and the relaxed open-mouth display is the precursor of laughing. This speculation is supported by a cluster analysis of chimpanzee behavior conducted by van Hooff (1972). According to van Hoof, the open silent bared-teeth display was observed in affiliative or friendly social interactions, while a slight variation of the same was observed in submissive contexts involving appeasement. The relaxed open-mouth display was predominantly observed during social play.

FIGURE 7.2   Birth of a baboon. The interest and sensitivity of adult apes to the arrival of the newborn is evident in this photo. The attribution of so called "human" emotions to the Great Apes was once considered anthropomorphic, but this taboo is breaking down, especially among ethologists like Goodall, de Waal, and others who work closely with these primates. (Photo courtesy of Frans de Waal.)

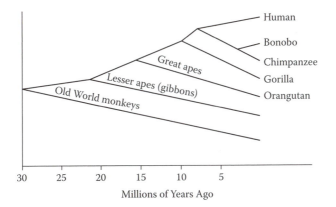

FIGURE 7.3   Hominoid evolution. This diagram represents the ancestral line of primates that eventually led to hominoid evolution, including African apes (gorillas, chimpanzees, and bonobos) and humans. Recent DNA analyses indicate that the hominid line diverged from that of the African apes more recently than was previously believed.

Because chimpanzees are more closely related to humans than they are to gorillas, sharing between 98% and 99% of our genes, they have received a great deal of scientific attention. Those primatologists (Fouts, 1997; Goodall, 1986) who have adopted the Lorenzian approach of actually living and communicating with the animals that they are studying seem to have the most insight into the emotional behavior of chimpanzees. They all agree that chimpanzees express their emotions in ways that are so similar to us that no specialized translation of their emotional behavior is required. Roger Fouts, who trained Washoe, the first chimpanzee to master sign language, comments on understanding her facial expressions:

> When it comes to non-human primates, much of their facial repertoire is similar to our own. Apes flash their eyebrows just as we do. When Washoe was unhappy she wrinkled up her face, pulled back the corners of her mouth, and curled her lips outward—which made her look like she was crying. When she was happy she drew back her lips and exposed her bottom teeth in a big smile. When she was really happy to see me she pursed her lips and gave me a small kiss. ... When I used to tickle Washoe, she made an open-mouth "play face" and a sound like the wheezing laughter of a human child. ... When Washoe was frustrated she would throw a tantrum by screaming. Before opening her birthday presents she would start panting and hooting in anticipation. Neither one of us needed sign language to figure out the other's moods. (Fouts, 1997, pp. 67–69)

Because of the extensive fieldwork of Goodall (1971, 1986) and others, we can assert that all of these behaviors are typical of the wild chimpanzee. Of course, these species-typical emotional displays involve more than just facial expressions. They include body movements, gestures, and vocalizations as well. Consider the resemblance between a toddler's full blown tantrum and that of a young chimp. The chimp will throw itself to the ground, screaming, and flailing about, and may pound the ground or throw objects for added emphasis. Goodall (1986) notes a number of typical chimpanzee emotions and the contexts in which they occur, including anger and fear in the context of aggression, wariness in response to a stranger, distress when lost, irritation when bothered by a juvenile, social excitement, sexual arousal, tenderness during reconciliation, sadness during mourning, and many others.

Although it was once considered *anthropomorphic* to attribute such human-like emotions to animals, even closely related primates, most primatologists today consider this view to be outmoded, if not downright antiscientific. The Dutch ethologist Frans de Waal considers the anthropomorphic critique to be one-sided as well. While it is perfectly acceptable, and quite common in practice, to describe aggressive, competitive, and deceitful behavior in nonhuman primates in anthropomorphic terms (e.g., the Machiavellian hypothesis), it becomes unacceptable when applied to affectionate, loving, or peaceful behaviors. According to this double-standard, if two chimpanzees come together after a fight and seal their desire for reconciliation with a kiss, it must be described scientifically as "a postconflict interaction involving mouth-to-mouth contact." De Waal defends the more user friendly description by noting that,

> Animals, particularly those close to us, show an enormous spectrum of emotions and different kinds of relationships. It is only fair to reflect this in a broad array of terms. If animals can have enemies they can have friends; if they can cheat they can be honest, and if they can be spiteful they can also be kind and altruistic. Semantic distinctions between animal and human behavior often obscure fundamental similarities (de Waal, 1996, p. 19).

This point of view has gained ascendancy among those scientists who are not only studying the great apes, but also engaged in a desperate attempt to safeguard their continued existence in their native habitats. According to Fouts, "drawing an all-or-nothing line between species is completely futile. Nature is a great continuum. With every passing year we discover more evidence to support Darwin's revolutionary hypothesis that the cognitive and emotional lives of animals differ only by degree, from the fishes to the birds to monkeys to humans" (Fouts, 1997, p. 372). Or as the early ethologist Heinroth put it a century ago, "animals are emotional persons with very little understanding."

☐ Human Facial Expressions

Based on recent DNA analyses, the line leading to Homo sapiens diverged from that of chimpanzees and bonobos about 5 or 6 MYA. In humans, the trend towards an increase in midfacial musculature and decrease in ear and scalp musculature continued, with one exception. Rather than increasing in size and number, the midface muscles increased in number but decreased in size. The jaw bones and teeth are smaller as well, probably as a result of hominid tool use and less reliance on strength of jaws, teeth, and lips than in the great apes (Washburn, 1960).

The complex muscular anatomy of the human face supports a vast number of possible expressions, though the number of expressions that are considered to be homologous to chimpanzees is limited to 6 or 8 basic expressions. Ethologists like Chevalier-Skolnikov (1973), Eibl-Eibesfeldt

(1972, 1989), and van Hooff (1972) have attempted to develop models of the evolution of distinctive human social signals such as the smile, laugh, and the eyebrow flash. The initial behavior pattern has a species-typical form and is assumed to be reliably associated with a specific emotional state. Among primates, there has been selection for facial markings, in the form of hair patterns and skin color, in order to enhance the signal. A good example of this enhancement is the distinct line of hair above the eye, that allows for a social signal that may be observed pan-culturally in humans, the eyebrow flash. This signal may be observed during distal greetings between familiar partners in many cultures and has been extensively studied and filmed by Eibl-Eibesfeldt during greetings in cultures as diverse as Western Europe, Bali, Papua New Guinea, Kalahari, South American Indian, etc. According to Eibl-Eibesfeldt (1972), when greeting friends and acquaintances over a distance, people all over the world raise their eyebrows rapidly for about one-sixth second, as shown in Figure 7.4. Though they may not be fully conscious of this behavior, people respond strongly to the signal by smiling recognition and responding with the same signal in return. Eibl-Eibesfeldt notes that the basic behavior pattern is overlaid with cultural prescriptions, which in some cases may suppress its use, as in Japan, where it is used by adults only when greeting children. Alternatively, among Samoans it is used by nearly everyone. In most cultures, it is used along with a smile to signal a positive attitude associated with recognition and approach.

Eibl-Eibesfeldt speculates that this signal evolved from the raising and opening of the eye during the experience of surprise. This represents the initial-state starting point of a process of ritualization leading to several distinct signals involving the eyebrow lift. Two distinct forms can now be observed in humans. In the first, the eyebrow flash evolved from friendly surprise to requesting or approving social contact, where it is often accompanied by nodding and smiling. It may be displayed in a variety of contexts, such as flirting, seeking attention or confirmation during conversation, and thanking or expressing approval. In the second instance, the raised eyebrow may be held in place and accompanied by a continuous stare, signifying disapproval or indignation, and eventual withdrawal or rejection. Notice the many differences in form and context that serve to differentiate the two displays so that it would be quite unlikely that they would be confused. While heuristic in terms of research on human nonverbal communication, Eibl-Eibesfeldt's evolutionary model remains somewhat speculative and difficult to substantiate with comparative evidence. It does appear to be the case that the eyebrow flash in nonhuman primates is associated with alertness (Hinde, 1974), and, at least in chimpanzees, with greeting behavior (Fouts, 1997).

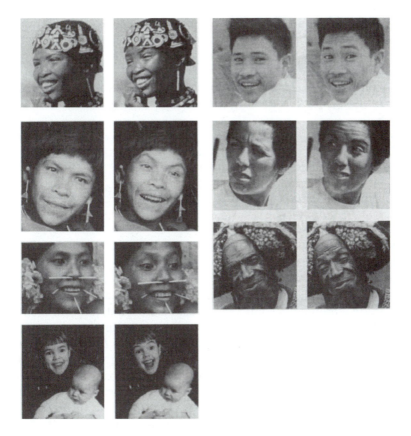

FIGURE 7.4   The eyebrow flash is used as a distal greeting between friends in many diverse cultures. (Photos courtesy of I. Eibl-Eibesfeldt.)

☐ Basic Emotions

Eight emotional systems have received a great deal of attention by researchers since Darwin's seminal contribution (1872). Positive emotions like joy, surprise, and interest have been investigated in thousands of studies, as have negative emotions like anger, sadness, distress, disgust, and fear. The criteria for inclusion on this short list of basic emotions may vary somewhat among modern researchers. Some contemporary investigators differentiate two lines of emotional development, a nonverbal affect system and a verbal-conceptual system that are localized in separate hemispheres in the brain (Gazzaniga, 1985; Krystal, 1978). Evidence is now available that indicates that the right hemisphere mediates arousal due to pleasure and pain and certain biologically primitive emotions associated with these sensations (Semenza, Pasini, Zettin, Tonin, & Portolan, 1986; Schore, 1994).

According to a leading proponent of the concept of *basic emotions*, Ekman (1992), nine criteria must be met:

1. Universal expression
2. Quick onset
3. Comparable expressions in other animals
4. An emotion-specific physiology
5. Universal antecedent events
6. Coherence in response systems
7. Brief duration
8. Automatic appraisal mechanism
9. Unbidden occurrence

These few emotions are presumed to be basic to all humans because they share a number of common characteristics. First, they are rooted in our ancient evolutionary heritage, make their appearance early in infancy, and arise quickly and automatically in the course of interaction with the environment. Second, they are characterized by universal facial expressions, which are remarkably constant and recognized across different cultures as indicating the presence of a particular emotion. Third, these expressions are considered to be prewired into the neural circuitry linking the brain to the facial muscular system, are correlated with distinct autonomic system activity, and may show subcortical conditioning. While learning will eventually play a critical role in how, when, and where the individual displays a basic emotion, no social learning appears to be necessary to their initial production or reception in early infancy (Figure 7.5).

Biosocial theorists view the compliment of infant reflexes as a kind of storehouse of phylogenetic behavioral adaptations that have been retained because they provided some advantage or function for the infant's survival during our evolutionary past. They provide a starting point for the individual's emotional development by giving direction to the process and providing something for development and learning to act upon. Thus, the smile, startle, cry, or expression of disgust that researchers commonly report in newborns represent the physiological prototypes necessary for the emergence of the primary affective systems in infancy. For an evolutionist the task is to determine how these basic emotions are related to adaptive biological, motivational, and social processes that have functional significance for the organism. For a developmentalist the task is to describe how each affective system emerges from earlier precursors

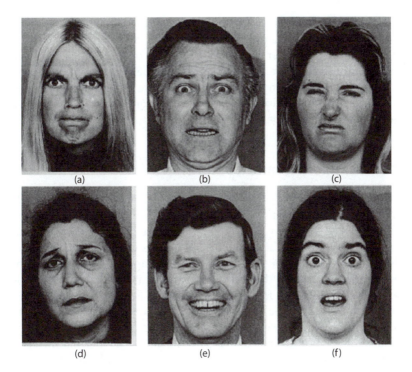

FIGURE 7.5   Posed Facial Expressions of Six Basic Emotions: (a) Anger: Brows drawn together and downward, eyes fixed, mouth squarish; (b) Fear: Brows level, drawn in and up, eyelids lifted, mouth retracted; (c) Disgust: Nose wrinkled, upper lip raised, tongue pushed outward; (d) Sadness: Brows' inner corners raised, mouth drawn out and down; (e) Joy: Mouth forms smile, cheeks lifted, twinkle in eyes; and (f) Surprise: Brows raised, eyes widened, mouth rounded in oval shape.

and the process by which it is transformed and reorganized over the life course. We begin this discussion with the development of emotional capacities in the first 6 months of life.

☐ The Newborn's Preadaptations for Emotional Communication

A modern developmental perspective recognizes the inherent capacities of the newborn to engage the social world, to respond to it, and to learn from experiences with it. This view that the infant is preadapted to begin life with a caregiver is based upon a wide array of evidence, including the inborn capacities and preferences human infants exhibit in visual and auditory perception, their capacity for reflexive or automatic responses to various stimuli, and their ability to learn from their experience and accommodate to their environment. In this section we focus on the visual system and the infant's abilities to recognize faces and discriminate between different facial expressions.

Visual Capacities and Preferences

Infants are born with a visual system that is still in the process of developing. At 2 weeks, an infant's visual acuity is still rudimentary, and has been estimated to be the equivalent of an adult with 20/300 vision. Although, even after 6 months, the visual acuity of infants is moving closer to adult vision, it is still only about 20/100 (Banks & Salapetek, 1983). By 2 months of age, infants' eyes have the ability to focus distant objects as well as close objects; but they do not focus very accurately. Focusing is when special muscles change the shape of the lens of the eye to form a clear image of the world on the back of the eye (the retina). Young infants sometimes focus too close (in front of the object) and sometimes too far (behind the object). As they practice this ability to focus their eyes visual acuity improves. Because the images on the back of our eyes are flat and two dimensional, our brain combines information from the separate images of the two eyes to create a three-dimensional view of the world. Visual experience along with development in the brain neurons responsible for combining images from the two eyes leads to the emergence of binocular depth perception around 3 to 5 months of age.

Research on infant visual perception, using duration of visual attention, systematic recording of eye-movements, electrical activity in the brain in response to visual stimuli, and other techniques, has demonstrated a number of significant capacities and preferences. From very early in life infants orient to movement, to curved rather than straight lines, to light/dark contrasts, and to a moderate degree of complexity, all features possessed by a human face (Banks & Salapetek, 1983). Caregivers who lean over their baby smiling, nodding, and cooing to capture and hold the infant's attention provide quite naturally just the sort of visual stimulation that attracts infants.

Because of an innate tracking reflex, even newborn infants will follow an object with their eyes if the object is large enough, has enough contrast, and is moving slowly. However, their eyes will follow the object with "jerky" motions, unlike adults who track very smoothly. Newborns will not always track, especially if they are in a room with lots of activity, noise, and other things to look at. Again this system improves rapidly with practice and by 3 months most infants are able to follow an object quite smoothly, as long as it is not moving too fast.

Since newborns are unable to detect fine-grained patterns in complex stimuli they prefer stimuli with bolder, sharper contrasts that present detectable patterns. As infants begin to resolve finer details they also shift their preference to the more detailed pattern, a principle known as contrast sensitivity (Banks & Salapetek, 1981). Development of contrast sensitivity is primarily determined by maturation in the neurons of the eye and to a lesser extent neurons in the brain. Visual pattern recognition requires greater processing in the visual cortex and, as a result, develops more gradually.

Consistent with their increasing ability to perceive details and patterns, infants begin to develop more complex scanning patterns in the first few months. For example, when presented with drawings of the human face, 1-month-olds do not look as long as 2-month-old babies. They also do not look at the face in the same manner. Although they have enough detail vision to be able to see most of the features of your face from arm's length, they tend to be attracted to the borders of objects, especially high-contrast borders. Thus, when looking at a human face, newborns are more likely to concentrate their gaze on a single element, such as the hairline or beard, and limit their exploration to the outer edges of the face. As contrast sensitivity and scanning ability improve, older infants explore internal features by moving their eyes around the figure, pausing to look at each element, and especially moving elements like the eyes and mouth (Maurer & Salapetek, 1976). By 2 months of age they naturally develop a preference to attend to those features of the face that have the greatest signal value (Figure 7.6).

Infants' general tendency to scan all the elements in a pattern is directly applied to their perception of human faces. Young infants study complex stimuli longer than simpler ones, and by 2 to 3 months infants show a preference for a facial pattern over the same elements scrambled in another configuration. In a study comparing 3-month-old and 6-week-old infants, the older infants looked longer at a face than at the same pattern reversed, but showed no such preference when shown an abstract pattern and its negative (Dannemiller & Stephens, 1988).

Recognizing Faces

These capacities and preferences lead to a remarkable development at 3 months. At this stage the infant is beginning to organize the various elements into a distinct pattern or schema for the human face that may be recognized. At this age infants can recognize their mother's face in a photograph and they prefer to look at her rather than a stranger (Barrera & Maurer, 1981a). If the mother's face as a schema is not assimilated, because

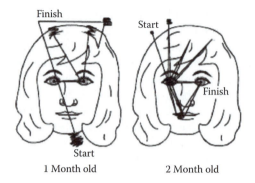

FIGURE 7.6 The infant's visual exploration of the face. At 1 month infants scan the outer edges of the face, but by 2 months they seem to have discovered the eyes as the window of the soul. 2-month-olds look at the face longer and concentrate their gaze on the internal features, particularly the eyes. (From Maurer, D., & Salapetek, P. (1976). *Child Development, 47*, 523–527. With permission.)

the mother's bearded brother has taken her place at the crib, the infant may become quite distressed.

Soon after 3 months, infants can remember and distinguish between faces of different strangers and prefer more attractive faces (Langlois et al., 1987). A preference for physically attractive faces was once presumed to be a learned cultural stereotype, although these data have led to a reexamination of this position. Although it is clear that infants show preferences for the same kind of faces adults find attractive long before socialization practices could have produced a culturally specific standard, it is unclear what specific characteristics influence infants' choices. It may be that infants prefer attractive faces because they contain more of the individual features that infants prefer, such as high contrast, contours, curves, and vertical symmetry. Or it could be that babies are attracted to faces that approach an innate prototype face and look longest at stimuli that come closest to the prototype. Whatever the explanation, babies are clearly predisposed to attend to human faces because of the important functional significance of face-to-face interaction for later socio-affective development.

Recognizing Facial Expressions

As infants' visual acuity improves and they gain experience with human faces in social interaction they begin to make finer and finer discriminations of facial affect. A number of convergent findings from experimental work suggest that infants develop the capacity to discriminate between different facial expressions at about 3 months (Haviland & Lelwica, 1987; Nelson & de Haan, 1997). At this age, infants can discriminate happy and sad faces from surprised faces (Younge-Browne, Rosenfeld, & Horowitz, 1977), smiles from frowns (Barrera & Maurer, 1981b), and smiling faces that vary in intensity (Kuchuk, Vibbert, & Bornstein, 1986). By 4 months infants are capable of discriminating joyful faces from angry or neutral faces (LaBarbera, Izard, Vietze, & Parisi, 1976) and by 5 months they are beginning to make discriminations among negative expressions like sad, fearful, and angry expressions (Schwartz, Izard, & Ansul, 1985).

By the second half of the first year, infants are able to perceive emotional expressions as organized wholes. They can distinguish mild and intense expressions of different emotions (Ludemann & Nelson, 1988), and they respond to happy or surprised expressions differently than sad or fearful faces, even if these emotions are expressed in slightly varying ways by different people (Ludemann, 1991). Infants also begin to rely upon their caregiver's facial expressions as an important indicator of how to respond emotionally to an uncertain situation or event. This *social referencing* is one of the first clear examples of emotion regulation. Like other examples throughout the first year, it occurs in a dyadic context. As early as 10 weeks, infants begin to respond meaningfully to their mother's facial expressions (Haviland & Lelwica, 1987) and by 10 months, infants rely on these emotional cues to decide how to respond to a wide variety of events for which they lack experience. For example, 10-month-olds can more readily overcome their typical wariness of an intruding stranger, if their mothers show positive behavior towards the stranger.

Similarly, maternal facial expressions serve to regulate the coping behavior of infants to other interesting, but frightening, objects. Klinnert and coworkers (1983) exposed 12- to 18-month-olds to three unfamiliar toys—a model of a human head, a dinosaur, and a remote-controlled spider, instructing the mothers to look alternately from the toy to the infant while expressing joy, fear, or a neutral attitude. Infants guided their behavior according to their mother's expression, retreating towards her when she showed fear, but approaching the toy when she was happy. In a modification of the visual cliff experiment, all 1-year-olds avoided the deeper side when their mothers posed a fearful expression, but 74% of the infants crossed the cliff when their mothers expressed happiness (Sorce, Emde, Campos, & Klinnert, 1985). Because the face carries the most information, by 14 months infants use it more than any other cue (Walden & Ogan, 1988). Clearly these advances in the recognition and understanding of facial expressions play a central role in the development of early relationships. Just consider how your social life would be affected if you could not recognize faces of familiar people or interpret the meaning of different facial expressions!

The primate infant by virtue of its extended period of care and protection can learn to regulate its behavior by observing others, particularly the caregiver. For example, attachment researchers have studied how the presence of the caregiver provides a secure base for the infant's confident exploration of the environment. If something threatening should occur, the infant's attention will be directed to the caregiver's face. Should the caregiver express fear in relation to an event, a fear response can be classically conditioned to that event after a single trial. Evolution is better served by constructing an organism capable of evaluation and observational learning than by constructing hundreds of specific reflexes for the myriad potentially dangerous events facing a primate (LaFreniere, 2000).

This ability of social referencing illustrates the superiority of an open program over a closed program for promoting flexible adaptation to a wide range of environmental stimulation (Mayr, 1982). According to Mayr, a closed program is based on a genotype that does not allow appreciable modifications during the process of development, whereas an open program allows for additional input and modification based on learning and experience throughout the lifespan. A closed program can be highly adaptive in short-lived species facing relatively constant life challenges, but an open program is more adaptive in long-lived species facing diverse and variable life challenges. The altricial status of primates, including humans, provides an extended period that enables each generation to learn the many variable characteristics of life-relevant stimuli required for successful adaptation.

Without question the widely successful adaptation of humans to a diversity of environments is due to our ability to solve variable and novel problems. However, not all human challenges involve novelty. In the social environment, an important constant in human adaptation are the facial displays and signals of other humans. These may be sufficiently small in number, stereotyped, and important to allow for evolution to construct recognitory programs that are relatively closed. Thus, while emotion expression and regulation may eventually incorporate a high degree of learned behavior, basic emotions, such as fear, also regulate behavior through closed, prewired, genetic programs that control their production and reception. A great deal of evidence now supports the classic Darwinian viewpoint that such processes are innate. As Campos and Barrett (1984) have stated, "no social learning appears necessary either for the *reception* of facial and gestural signals or for the *production* of such" (p. 229). Having considered infants' ability to receive facial signals, let us now focus on their ability to produce such signals with a discussion of smiling and crying.

Reflexes

In addition to the infant's built-in capacities for sensing and orienting to social stimulation, the infant possesses a wide range of *reflexes*. Reflexes are congenitally organized stimulus-response connections, which are automatically released when the infant encounters the appropriate stimulation. Ethologists speak of "releasing" a behavior because the behaviors themselves are, in a sense, already present. When the sign stimulus appears the behaviors are emitted without the benefit of prior learning, although learning will play an important role in shaping reflexes into adaptive, cognitively mediated responses.

Human reflexes represent a storehouse of *phylogenetic adaptations* that have been retained because they provided some advantage or function for the infant's survival during our evolutionary past. They are the starting point of behavioral development in that they give direction to the process and provide something for development and learning to act upon. There is an automatic, involuntary quality to reflexive behavior, in much the same sense as a "knee jerk response." Many of the reflexes that are critical for infant care and socialization will be transformed during the first months of life into voluntary behavior guided by the infant's motivation and cognition. For example, two especially important reflexes for establishing social communication, smiling and crying, provide a biological foundation for the development of several discrete emotions.

Smiling

The infant smile is a very influential social signal even when no communication is intended by the sender. The earliest smiles to appear in the neonate have been labeled *endogenous smiles* (Spitz, Emde, & Metcalf, 1970; Wolff, 1963) because these smiles are spontaneous or reflexive and seem to depend on the infant's internal state and typically occur during REM (rapid eye movement) sleep. These first smiles, which involve simply turning up the corners of the mouth, do not occur when the infant is awake and alert, but only when the infant is asleep, most often in periods characterized by low levels of cortical activity. The endogenous smile occurs more frequently in premature infants, and among all infants declines in frequency over the first 3 months (Emde, McCartney, & Harmon, 1971; Spitz et al., 1970). This decline is associated with the development and functioning of the cortex, which does not appear to be implicated in the production of endogenous smiles, since they have been observed in a microcephalic infant without a functioning cortex (Harmon & Emde, 1972).

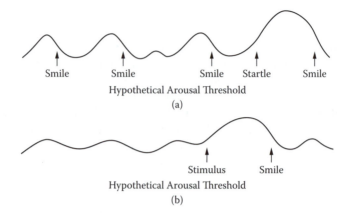

FIGURE 7.7 Hypothetical threshold of arousal. The newborn's smiles during sleep are related to fluctuations in CNS activity. Smiles may occur spontaneously (a) when the infant's depth of sleep changes. Following a startle it takes some time before the excitation falls below the arousal threshold (straight line) and the smile recurs. As shown in (b), sleep smiles may also occur in response to mild stimulation such as shaking a rattle. (From Sroufe, L. A. (1996). *Emotional development: The organization of emotional life in the early years.* New York, NY: Cambridge University Press. Reprinted with permission.)

According to Sroufe (1996), endogenous smiles are due to fluctuations in central nervous system (CNS) arousal, with the smile occurring during the drop below a hypothetical threshold of arousal as the infant relaxes following a momentary excitation of the CNS (see Figure 7.7).

Light stimulation of the newborn during sleep, but not when awake, will produce a smile 5 to 8 seconds after the stimulation. Shaking a rattle or gently shaking the sleeping infant will tend to produce a series of little smiles. If startled, causing arousal levels to spike, sleep smiles will not occur for some time. These findings are interpreted by Sroufe as indicating that the endogenous smile is produced during the relaxation phase of excitation-relaxation cycles as the infant's arousal drops below a threshold.

The first waking smiles of the infant appear to be very similar to endogenous smiles. They are produced by the same type of mild stimulation, and they still involve the action of a single muscle. At about 1 month, infants move to the phase of exogenous smiles, in which smiling occurs in response to a wide range of external stimulation while the infant is awake and alert. Alert smiles involve the action of multiple muscles and include the crinkling of the eyes as the mouth is pulled into a grin. Known as *Duchenne smiles* after the French scientist who first described them, these broad smiles are readily identified by adults as expressions of happiness (Emde, Izard, Huebner, Sorce, & Klinnert, 1985).

Infants may smile in response to a wide variety of stimulation, including vigorous tactile stimulation, interesting sights, and social stimuli such as faces and high pitched voices. Gradually these smiles become less dependent on organismic state with less of a latency following stimulation. Spitz et al. (1970) showed that the emergence of smiling to a still face at about 2 months points to a new organization in which the infant's expression is less reflexive and more responsive. This is accompanied by decreases in endogenous smiles and important developments in the cortex as indexed by EEG and sleep patterns. Sroufe (1979, 1996) views this stage to be a midpoint between the reflexive, physiological prototype of the endogenous smile and the first true social smiles which clearly indicate immediate joy at the arrival of the caregiver. They are intermediate because they no longer depend entirely on external stimulation, but may also occur as a function of the infant's active engagement of the stimulus. *Recognitory assimilation* (Kagan, 1971; Piaget, 1952) reflects an emerging cognitive component that is fundamentally different than the earlier excitation-relaxation cycle produced by stimulation. According to Piaget (1952, 1962), recognitory assimilation involves both an affective and a cognitive component. When the infant is presented with a stimulus such as the stationary face there is strong effort leading to assimilation of the schema, followed by tension release and smiling. If there is no successful assimilation the infant may turn away or cry.

The evidence supporting the involvement of cognition in infant smiling at about 2 to 3 months is extensive. Infants who show delayed cognitive development, such as institutionalized infants (Gewirtz, 1965) and infants with Down syndrome (Cicchetti & Sroufe, 1976) also show delays of several weeks in their responsiveness to a stationary face. In addition, there is a dynamic quality to effective stimuli suggesting the importance of novelty or challenge involved in recognitory assimilation. Since effortful assimilation is central, stimuli that are effective at an early age lose this potency over time. For example, a stationary face no longer reliably elicits a smile after age 3 to 5 months (Gewirtz, 1965; Spitz et al., 1970). The cognitive involvement of the infant may also be shown in a repeated measures experiment, in which infants smile at the stimulus for several trials but return to neutral looking after a series of presentations. With these repeated exposures there is no longer any effort required to assimilate the schema. However, if a novel or discrepant aspect, such as a masked face is introduced, there is renewed smiling followed again by a decline with repetition (Kagan, 1971; Sroufe & Wunsch, 1972). Finally, older infants smile more readily to the same novel stimulus than younger infants, indicating more rapid accommodation (Zelazo & Komer, 1971). In summary, smiles produced by recognitory assimilation represent a new phase of active, cognitive engagement of the infant that is not present earlier.

With the emergence of cognitive factors in infant smiling, the first truly social smiles appear. As the infant becomes increasingly involved in rudimentary social interaction, the content and meaning of an event become a more reliable clue to the emotional reaction than the amount of external stimulation. This is illustrated by changes in the infant's response to social stimuli during the first year. As we have seen, the schema of a human face evokes a broad grin from infants between 6 and 8 weeks. By 3 months infants begin to show a preference for familiar faces and by 4 or 5 months infants smile in response to their caregiver's voice or face. At this point the smile is no longer elicited by a stranger regardless of context, and the silent stranger's face will begin to elicit a wary look from the infant. The appraisal process has led to a very different emotional response than that of the 2-month-old infant. That affect and cognition are intimately linked is perhaps best illustrated by the widespread use of affective responses to demonstrate advances in infant cognition (Charlesworth, 1969; Cicchetti & Hesse, 1983; Piaget, 1952; Sroufe & Wunsch, 1972; Zelazo & Komer, 1971).

As the smile becomes firmly embedded in the infant's behavioral repertoire, its functional significance becomes clearer. Even before the smile becomes a truly social act, its presence has a special significance for the caregiver, who is likely to interpret it as a sign of affection and joy. The infant's smile to the face suggests recognition of the caregiver and enhances the parent's interest in and affection for the child. Mothers report feeling good when shown photographs of an infant's positive expressions and they stated that they would talk, play, and interact more with the infant as a result (Huebner & Izard, 1988). At 2 months smiles are easily elicited by a variety of social stimulation, providing reinforcement of care giving to parents. By 3 months infants begin to smile selectively to their caregivers, further shaping their behavior (Camras et al., 1993), and infants smile more in response to the smiles and vocalizations of their mothers than equally responsive, but unfamiliar, female adults (Wahler, 1967). As the infant enters the phase of attachment in the making, their smile is used to greet the arrival of the mother and to engage her in play (Ainsworth, 1977). The most important social functions of the smile include eliciting approaches and positive responses from others and in promoting positive social interaction. The smile also functions to promote mastery by shaping social partners to provide novel stimulation. Smiling during effortful play releases tension and allows the infant to stay engaged as well as encourages caregivers to continue the stimulation (Sroufe, 1996). Finally, the smile is one of the infant's expressive behaviors, along with gaze aversion, that mediates the intensity of face-to-face interaction, essential to the development of reciprocity (Field & Fogel, 1982; Tronick, 1989).

Crying

So-called negative emotions like fear and anger are often experienced as disruptive and unpleasant, but these emotions clearly serve adaptive functions within a biodevelopmental model. This functionalist approach to emotion is illustrated in the research of Caroll Izard. In a longitudinal study on infant emotion, Izard and colleagues videotaped 25 infants at 2, 4, 6, and 18 months of age during a series of routine medical injections required for the diphtheria–pertussis–tetanus immunization (Izard, Hembree, & Huebner, 1987). At 2 months and throughout the first 6 months, all the infants responded with physical distress signal including facial expressions of pain-distress and strident crying. The strength of this response would appear to channel all the infant's energies into a cry for help. During the period from 2 to 7 months, 90% of the infants showed a clear, full-faced anger expression following the pain-distress expression. The anger expression was fleeting and secondary to the pain-distress. One year later, as 19-month-olds, these same infants responded to the fourth and last inoculation with anger. In contrast to their response in early infancy, these toddlers showed short-lived physical distress and 100% showed an anger expression that was dominant for a relatively long period of time. Izard (1991) interprets these developmental changes in the following manner:

> The young infant is incapable of defending himself against such stimulation, so the baby channels all his energy into the physical distress expression, an all-out plea for help. This is the most natural and adaptive thing for the relatively helpless and defenseless young infant to do. However, as the child becomes capable of warding off painful stimulation or participating in his own defense, channeling all of his energies into a plea for help would not be maximally adaptive. Our study showed that as the baby matures, his expressive behavior changes. The all consuming physical distress expression gives way to the anger expression. The anger expression is more adaptive in the face of unanticipated painful stimulation because anger mobilizes energy that can be used for protection and defense … eventually the child has to learn not only how to regulate or inhibit anger but how to harness anger-mobilized energy in instrumental acts of self-defense when situations call for it. (Izard, 1991, p. 246)

Many infancy researchers view the initial starting point for the development of the negative affects as a state of undifferentiated distress (Bridges, 1932; Camras, 1992; Matias & Cohn, 1991; Oster, Hegley, & Nagel, 1992; Sroufe, 1979, 1996). In an interesting contemporary counterpart to

Darwin's observational study of his infant son, Linda Camras observed and videotaped her daughter Justine's emotional expressions during the first 3 months of life. She observed considerable overlap in the elicitors of these four negative emotions, as well as alternating patterns of sad, angry, and pain-distress expressions during single episodes of crying. From detailed observations of Justine's emotional expression in context, Camras provides a number of examples of elicitors that appear to be mismatched with expression. For example, Justine showed a fear expression when she was protesting being fed, distress-pain in response to the removal of her pacifier, and sadness in response to a distasteful vitamin. In Camras's view, Izard was correct in his identification of basic and universal human emotions, but wrong in assuming that facial expressions in infants are necessarily "automatic read-outs of emotion." Instead, she proposes that expressions of sadness may first appear as muted, less intense expressions of distress, with pain and anger reflecting more intense levels of the same general state.

The Emergence of Infant Emotions

Anger

Sroufe (1979, 1996) views anger as an *emergent* system in the same sense that we saw earlier in his description of the development of joy. According to this model, physiological prototypes of the mature emotion exist at birth in the form of reflexes. The initial stage in the development of anger, defined as an "immediate, negative reaction directed at an obstacle to an intended act," may be seen in the first days of life in the reflexive flailing of the infant in response to restraining the head. Sroufe views this as the physiological prototype of anger, not anger itself. Following the newborn period, precursor emotions emerge that are no longer purely physiological, but are beginning to incorporate psychological components related to evaluating the content and meaning of a specific event. The precursor is not yet the equivalent of the mature emotion. Rather than an immediate response, it is expressed only after a gradual building up of tension. It is also a more diffuse reaction than later responses, often involving the whole body, and it is based on a general rather than specific evaluation of the content and meaning of the elicitor.

At about 2 months Brazelton (1969) has observed a precursor of anger in the infant's response to the failure to execute a well-established motor pattern. He offers the following description:

> The force behind this integration can be aroused in a baby of this age by leaving him with a toy that he cannot pull into him. He is left

with vision and fingers. He will play happily this way for a period. Then, his frustration builds up as he strains to get his mouth on it. He ends up by screaming furiously when he cannot examine it all over with his mouth and hands, as well as his eyes. (p. 131)

Also at 2 months, Lewis, Alessandri, and Sullivan (1990) have reported displays of anger and fussiness in response to the extinction of a learned contingency. Infants learned to pull on a string attached to their arm to turn on a short period of music. Infants as young as 2 months learned the contingency and expressed pleasure as a result of their mastery of it. However, when the contingency was removed, the infants expressed anger as a result of the violation of expectancy and loss of control of the situation. This would be a common elicitor of anger at any age. For example, if you learned to routinely save your thesis text onto your hard drive, but in following the same procedure as always, lost it, you can imagine your own emotional response to this violation of expectancy and loss of control.

An angry response, as opposed to a sad response, may be adaptive, if it promotes instrumental goals. In the paradigm above, infants who responded to extinction of the contingency with anger were also more likely to relearn the contingency. In contrast, infants who displayed just sadness, showed the least interest and joy during the relearning phase of the experiment. In this example, it appears that anger can energize and prepare the organism for sustained and persistent effort. Lewis et al. (1990) suggest that these early individual differences may be precursors of mastery and learned helplessness orientations.

Cross-sectional studies of infant's responses to physical restraint or removal of an object reveal developmental changes in facial expressions. Stenberg & Campos (1990) have observed negative facial and vocal expressions in 1-month-olds and found them to be delayed, gradual, and undifferentiated responses, in much the same manner as Sroufe's concept of a precursor. However, in 4- and 7-month-olds, the expressions are clearer, more immediate, and directed toward the elicitor, meeting the criteria of a mature angry response.

Since Aristotle and Darwin, anger has been associated with the cognitive capacity of means-end thinking. Defined by many theorists as an emotional response to enable the organism to overcome an obstacle, it implies that the organism has some knowledge of the necessary means to achieve a goal. While anger may be seen as maladaptive, it can also be seen as serving a variety of adaptive functions. First and foremost, anger supplies the organism with a surplus of energy necessary for sustained goal-directed activity. This may be illustrated in the infant's response to a violation of a learned contingency as in the Lewis et al. (1990) study cited above. A more dramatic example would be the response to unprovoked aggression or victimization. Anger, as opposed to sadness, would be the emotion best suited to mobilize and sustain a long and difficult course of action. However, dysregulated anger could also lead to maladaptive responses, so we can see that adaptation or competence is not inherent in the emotion itself, but rather in the coordination of emotion, cognition, and behavior. Ultimately, only the behavior of the organism can promote or undermine its adaptation and thoughts and feelings that do not lead to expressive or instrumental behavior do not count in the biological game of adaptation.

Fear

Infants become distressed for a variety of reasons besides pain and cry as a response to separation from the caregiver, hunger, and other unpleasant experiences. John Bowlby (1969) considered that infant fears are caused by a combination of biology and experience and that infants would more readily respond with fear to events or situations that provided the infant with "natural clues to danger." Bowlby listed only four such cues: pain, being left alone, sudden changes in stimulation, and rapid approach. Gray (1987) has expanded the list of the potential stimuli that might have an evolutionary basis to include fear of strangers, separation anxiety, and fear of being alone, fear of open places, heights, falling or loss of support, fear of the dark, and fear of snakes or spiders. We shall discuss an infant fear response that has received much attention from researchers and has implications for later social development: separation anxiety.

The infant's response to separation has received considerable scrutiny by researchers following the publication of John Bowlby's landmark trilogy on attachment, separation, and loss (1969, 1973, 1980). Accumulating data from primate (including human) studies indicate that separation from the mother is associated with changes in the infant's level of activity, heart rate, play, and affective expression. Ethologists view these infant responses as functionally significant in terms of their signal value as well as the regulation of internal state. Facial, vocal, and other nonverbal displays often elicit care giving from others. The protest and crying of infants to separation typically results in their caregiver's return, followed by soothing and attention, and the communicative function of these displays is self-evident.

Depressed activity and withdrawal may also serve an adaptive function if protest has been unsuccessful in bringing about the caregiver's return. A primate infant in the wild that is separated from its mother and alone is extremely vulnerable. The depressed activity level and withdrawal may allow the infant to recover from agitation that is costly in terms of energy depletion. Another cost of continued crying may result from drawing unwanted attention from potential threats in the environment that would be increased as a result of continued activity and exploration. It may be that natural selection has equipped the infant with a conditional strategy that first calls for a vigorous attempt to reestablish the care and protection of the parent or another member of the social unit. Should this fail, a second strategy is enacted, calling for depressed levels of activity and withdrawal that serves to reduce energy depletion and the probability of harm until help is forthcoming.

Separation anxiety emerges according to a developmental timetable during the second half year in human infants (see Figure 7.8). By 8 or 10 months infants become increasingly active in their relationship with the caregiver as well as increasingly mobile. With this new mobility the infant expands the capacity for eager exploration of the outer world, returning to the caregiver as a "secure base" (Ainsworth, 1967; Sander, 1975). At just this time separation anxiety begins to peak, possibly as a result of the infant's new preoccupation with the presence and location of the caregiver. Research on infants from cultures as diverse as Kalahari bushmen, Israeli kibbutzim, and Guatemalan Indian indicate that infants display quite similar patterns in their response to maternal separation, which peaks at the end of the first year and remains elevated for variable lengths of time (Kagan, Keasley, & Zelazo, 1978). Cultural practices would also appear to have an impact on separation anxiety. Infants who remain in constant contact with their mothers may show an earlier onset of separation anxiety (Ainsworth, 1967), and possibly more intense and longer periods of reactivity. For example, Japanese infants who are tested in Ainsworth's Strange-Situation show more intense reactions to the separation, presumably as a result of cultural norms prescribing constant contact

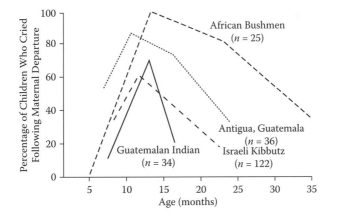

FIGURE 7.8   Infant separation anxiety in different cultures. These graphs show the percentage of infants in different cultures who cried during a brief separation from their mothers. This distress response appears to peak in human infants at about one year. (From Kagan et al., 1978).

between mother and infant for the first several years of life (Paquette & LaFreniere, 1994).

Finally, although the onset of stranger anxiety is precisely timed, it is less clear when this behavior disappears. For example, it is not unusual for toddlers and preschoolers to show intense separation anxiety when they are dropped off at daycare, especially during the first week or two. Their distress may actually be a mixture of separation anxiety and stranger anxiety. Typically, children will gradually accept the new situation and though they may show intense distress when the parent leaves, they tend to settle eventually and become engaged in the many interesting people and activities that surround them.

The study of fear requires a balanced treatment of the role of hereditary and environmental factors in promoting the adaptation of the organism. In everyday life many fears can be acquired without direct negative experience through observational learning. As Charlesworth (1982) has argued, an important constant in human adaptation are the facial displays and signals of other humans. These may be sufficiently small in number, sufficiently stereotyped, and sufficiently important to allow for evolution to construct recognitory programs that are relatively closed. Thus, while emotion expression and regulation may eventually incorporate a high degree of learned behavior, basic emotions, such as fear, regulate behavior through closed, prewired, genetic programs that control their production and reception.

Mineka's studies of observational learning in the development of fear of snakes in rhesus monkeys serve to illustrate the interaction of innate and learned components in the production of adaptive fear responses. In the wild, monkeys show a strong fear of snakes that generalizes to objects that even resemble snakes. Better to err on the side of caution. This fear is so strong and so universal in the wild that early observers, such as Hebb, were inclined to believe that it was innate. This question was reopened 40 years later when Mineka and colleagues compared wild-reared and lab-reared rhesus monkeys and found that the lab-reared monkeys did not show fear of snakes (Mineka & Cook, 1988). It is interesting to note that the wild-reared monkeys had been captured and imported from India 24 years prior to the study. Yet they all maintained a strong fear of snakes, despite having had no experience with them for nearly a quarter of a century! This too could have led the investigators to conclude that this was an innate fear. Instead, Mineka and colleagues paired a wild-reared monkey with a lab reared-monkey in order to demonstrate how quickly and permanently fear of snakes could be conditioned. In the test situation, lab-reared monkeys showed no differences in their responses to a live boa constrictor, snake-like objects, or neutral objects that were placed in a Plexiglas box and moved toward them. But when the lab-reared monkeys were exposed to the fearful reactions of the wild-reared monkeys, they quickly learned to fear the snake and snake-like objects. From the standpoint of classical conditioning, it may be that the expression of fear was the unconditioned stimulus and the snake was the conditioned stimulus.

In summary, the role of learning is interwoven in subtle and complex ways with genetic predispositions to provide for the safety of the primate infant. Clearly, for an organism to adapt to a complex environment of opportunities and dangers a dynamic balance must be struck between its intrepid exploration of the novel and a measured response to threat ranging from cautious wariness to terror and rapid flight. Moreover, these responses cannot be acquired over long periods of time through trial-and-error or gradual shaping. The individual who cannot escape the predator or who falls off a real cliff will be eliminated from the breeding population. One evolutionary solution to this *adaptive problem* is to provide the infant offspring with reflexes that quickly mature into adaptive responses and to hardwire into the neural circuitry of the organism certain innate fears. Fear of being alone, heights, and impending collisions would appear to fit this category.

Another functional solution is to equip the young with the capacity to acquire a fear response to a given stimuli on a single trial and with no direct experience of it. Clearly, one experience with a poisonous snake or spider, or an aggressive conspecific, will also eliminate the individual. Natural selection would strongly favor individuals capable of using the parent as a source of information from which to quickly learn what to approach and what to avoid. This solution provides for rapid acquisition of the fear response, as well as the capacity for flexible modulation or regulation of the emotion, and the behavioral response, according to contextual cues. The use of the parent as a secure base from which to explore the novel or unfamiliar is clearly a hallmark of primate socialization and will be taken up in the next chapter.

□ Chapter Summary

Among Darwin's most enduring contributions to the study of facial expressions was his exacting description of the precise movements that contributed to the overall expression and his emphasis on its underlying muscular anatomy. Ethologists have long assumed that closely related species have more similar patterns of facial expressions than more distantly related species. Abundant evidence supports the view that the primate face has been the site of intensive selective pressure for tens of millions of years. This selection pressure has produced an intricate set of facial muscles responsible for controlling the facial expressions of the great apes and humans. In particular, the social ecology of primates, with its challenging flux of coalitions and alliances, has led to finely tuned abilities to produce and conceal subtle expressions, and to detect such subtleties in the course of social interaction (de Waal, 1986, 1996). Neurobiological studies reveal that the primate brain has evolved specialized collections of neurons responsible for processing sensory information sensitive to faces, including the recognition of familiar faces and emotional expressions (Hauser, 1997). These evolutionary achievements suggest that the expression and recognition of emotional cues is of central importance for primate adaptation.

Classical ethologists like Tinbergen and Lorenz believed that signals evolve from incidental and involuntary expressions of emotions, a process known as *ritualization*. Today most ethologists believe that signals evolve towards greater persuasiveness rather than towards increasingly accurate read-outs of inner emotional states and intentions. From this more recent perspective, signals that accurately convey one animal's intentions could be used by the receiver to gain a strategic advantage over the sender, especially in situations involving assessment, competition, or conflict. The tension between management and assessment issues drives the evolution of communicative systems to new heights by fostering successive adjustments in both the subtlety of displays and in the ability to interpret them. This "evolutionary arms race" is thought to have supported the evolution of primate social and emotional intelligence.

The complex muscular anatomy of the human face supports a great number of possible expressions, though the number of expressions that are considered to be homologous to chimpanzees is quite limited. According to Ekman, nine criteria must be met for an emotion to be considered "basic": (1) universal expression, (2) quick onset, (3) comparable expressions in other animals, (4) an emotion-specific physiology, (5) universal antecedent events, (6) coherence in response systems, (7) brief duration, (8) automatic appraisal mechanism, and (9) unbidden occurrence.

Six *basic emotions* are joy/happiness, surprise/interest, anger, sadness/distress, disgust, and fear. These six emotions are presumed to be species-typical because they are shared by humans everywhere and because they exhibit a number of common characteristics. They are rooted in our primate evolutionary heritage and make their appearance early in infancy, arising automatically in the course of interaction with the environment. Moreover, they are characterized by universal facial expressions that are remarkably constant and recognized across different cultures as indicating the presence of a particular emotion. Finally, these expressions are considered to be hardwired into the neural circuitry linking the brain to the facial muscular system, are correlated with distinct autonomic system activity, and may show subcortical conditioning.

Research in infancy demonstrates a remarkable set of inborn competencies, including (1) the newborn's capacities and preferences in visual and auditory perception, (2) their capacity for reflexive responses to various stimuli, and (3) their ability to learn from their experience and accommodate to their environment. Together this extensive evidence leads contemporary developmental theorists to believe that newborns are preadapted for communication with their caregivers.

Infants begin to discriminate between different facial expressions at about 3 months and by 5 months they make discriminations among negative expressions like sad, fearful, and angry expressions. By the second half of the first year, infants are able to perceive emotional expressions as organized wholes. They can distinguish mild and intense expressions of different emotions and they respond to happy or surprised expressions differently than sad or fearful faces, even if these emotions are expressed in slightly varying ways by different people.

Infants also begin to rely upon facial expressions as an important indicator of how to respond emotionally to an uncertain situation or event. *Social referencing* is one of the first clear examples of emotion regulation. Like other examples throughout the first year, it occurs in a dyadic context. As early as 10 months infants rely on these emotional cues to decide how to respond to a wide variety of events for which they lack experience.

Biosocial theorists view the compliment of human reflexes as a kind of storehouse of phylogenetic behavioral adaptations that have been retained because they provided some advantage or function for the infant's survival during our evolutionary past. Reflexes provide a starting point for the individual's emotional development by giving direction to the process and providing something for development and learning to act upon. Thus, the smile, startle, cry, or expression of disgust that researchers commonly report in newborns represent the physiological prototypes necessary for the emergence of the primary affective systems in infancy.

Throughout the chapter, the related themes of development and adaptation were emphasized in relation to basic emotional systems. The development of basic emotion systems from earlier physiological prototypes and the process by which they are transformed and reorganized during infancy was discussed. Understanding emotional development in infancy requires an appreciation of the unity of development, particularly the reciprocal influence of cognition and affect. Finally, evidence was reviewed in support of the view that basic emotions are related to adaptive biological, motivational, and social processes that have functional significance for the organism.

☐ For Further Inquiry

Ekman, P., & Friesen, W. V. (2003). *Unmasking the face*. Cambridge, MA: Malor Books.

Facial Recognition homepage: http://www.face-rec.org/

Keltner, D. (2007). *Evolutionary approaches to emotion*. Berkeley, CA: University of California Press.

Reading the mind in the eyes test: http://www.glennrowe.net/BaronCohen/Faces/EyesTest.aspx

CHAPTER

Attachment in Infancy

The study of mother-infant attachment came of age during the 1970s and has now broadened its influence in psychology well beyond the period of infancy. British clinician John Bowlby set the stage for this advance with an ethological model of attachment incorporating ideas from ethology, primatology, object relations theory, and systems theory. His theoretical synthesis was complemented by methodological and empirical advances by Mary Ainsworth, Alan Sroufe, Everett Waters, Mary Main, Jay Belsky, and many others. In this chapter, research during infancy based upon Ainsworth's original strange situation paradigm is described as well as contemporary longitudinal research that examines the developmental significance of early attachment over the life course. Finally, attachment patterns are interpreted from a life history perspective as resource-dependent reproductive strategies that are set in motion in infancy.

☐ Early Theory and Research

Bowlby's Ethological Attachment Theory

Drawing upon dynamic systems theory and classic ethology, British clinician John Bowlby developed a model of attachment as a dyadic, behavioral system distinct from earlier models. He framed his model using the technical language of *cybernetics*, the scientific study of systems of control and communication common to organisms and certain machines, like computers. Bowlby initiated a discussion of mother-infant attachment modeled after a control system that operates in terms of set goals, feedback loops, goal correction, and function. An easy way to think about such a system is the familiar thermostat connected to a heating unit. A thermometer records the temperature in the room as it falls below a set point. The thermostat activates the furnace at that point and monitors the rising temperature until it reaches the upper threshold when it is deactivated, thus maintaining room temperature at a comfortable level between a lower and upper boundary. As a cybernetic system, attachment is activated when the infant's dynamic threshold for threat in the environment is surpassed and remains operative until proximity with the caregiver is reestablished. Bowlby defined the set goal of the attachment system as proximity to the caregiver. As an evolved system, attachment was viewed as a product of natural selection, selected for its effect on the individual's survival and ultimate reproductive success in the environment of evolutionary adaptedness.

As a developmental system, the infant's repertoire of attachment behaviors arises naturally in the context of interaction with the caregiver according to a relatively fixed timetable. The primate infant is preadapted to engage the caregiver with innate behaviors such as looking, smiling, crying, and clinging. In time, other behaviors such as following and more complex signaling emerge with the same set goal of maintaining proximity to the caregiver. The interactive presence of the caregiver alone provides a sufficient context for the species-typical attachment behaviors to emerge and to become organized into a dynamic system. With time social learning impacts the system's organization and shapes individual differences in the specific qualities of the system.

Prior to the general acceptance of Bowlby's ethological attachment theory, psychologists of both psychoanalytic and behaviorist schools viewed attachment as a secondary drive, derived from primary drives like hunger. According to these theories, the infant eventually became attached to the mother because she supplied food, and thus became the object of the infant's attachment through association with feeding and the reduction of other primary needs. In contrast, Bowlby argued that the attachment process is a primary behavioral system that evolved in primates through natural selection in order to insure the survival of the helpless offspring.

Abundant evidence now supports this view, while traditional learning theory models of attachment as drive reduction were refuted in a classic series of studies by Harry Harlow and colleagues during the 1950s and 1960s (Harlow & Harlow, 1966). Using an ingenious paradigm involving surrogate "mothers," Harlow was the first to put the notion that attachment to the mother forms as a result of feeding to an empirical test. In one study, Harlow separated infant rhesus monkeys from their mothers at birth, then reared them with two surrogate mothers, one made of stiff wire equipped with a bottle for feeding, the other covered with soft terry cloth, but without the bottle. If an infant monkey became attached by associating the mother with food, we would expect to see attachment behaviors exhibited toward the wire surrogate with the bottle. Instead

FIGURE 8.1 Harlow's experiments with surrogate monkey mothers established that feeding was not the primary cause of mother-infant attachment. Photos courtesy of Harlow Primate Lab, University of Wisconsin.

the infant monkeys all showed a clear preference for the soft, cuddly surrogate without the bottle, spending most of their time (when not feeding) clinging to it and leaping into its "lap" when frightened or distressed. Although feeding may be an important context for the development of the mother-child bond in nature, contact comfort is clearly more central than feeding per se (Figure 8.1).

Ainsworth's Strange-Situation Paradigm

The first and most important test for Bowlby's theory of attachment was conducted by Mary Ainsworth in a series of naturalistic and laboratory studies (Ainsworth, 1967, 1977). Ainsworth became involved in attachment research at London's Tavistock Clinic under the direction of John Bowlby. Her subsequent experience of observing 28 Ugandan mothers

FIGURE 8.1   (continued).

and their infants in their everyday environment convinced her of the essential validity of Bowlby's ethological model. She observed that the typical Ugandan infant formed a specific attachment to the mother, used her to explore the surrounding environment, and protested separation by crying or attempting to follow her.

Taking Bowlby's cue that differences in attachment security reflected differences in quality of care giving, Ainsworth conducted extensive exploratory analyses on the factors associated with security of attachment, but came away from this initial study convinced that more formal research would be needed to draw firm conclusions regarding this important question. Then, in 1962, Ainsworth returned to this task in her now classic Baltimore longitudinal study of mother-infant attachment. Again she relied upon extensive naturalistic observation of relatively few subjects. Regular 4-hour home visits were made to observe 26 families beginning a few weeks after delivery and continued at 3-week intervals until about 54 weeks. Consistent with the traditions of ethological fieldwork, Ainsworth believed that only extensive naturalistic observation could provide a broad enough and fine enough net to capture the details of the

---

TABLE 8.1 Ainsworth's (1967) List of Attachment Behaviors

---

1. Differential crying (i.e., with mother as compared with others)
2. Differential smiling
3. Differential vocalizations
4. Crying when the mother leaves
5. Following the mother
6. Visual motor orientation toward the mother
7. Greeting through smiling, crowing, and general excitement
8. Lifting arms in greeting the mother
9. Clapping hands in greeting the mother
10. Scrambling over the mother
11. Burying face in the mother's lap
12. Approach to the mother through locomotion
13. Embracing, hugging, kissing the mother (not seen in Ugandan infants but observed frequently in infants in Western societies)
14. Exploration away from the mother as a secure base
15. Flight to the mother as a haven of safety
16. Clinging to the mother

---

attachment process as it was played out in each unique setting. From this inductive approach involving about 72 hours of observation in each home, together with the cross-cultural observations in Uganda, Ainsworth was able to document an ethogram of the typical attachment behaviors shown by the Ugandan and American infants (see Table 8.1).

With this descriptive base, Ainsworth was now in a position to develop a laboratory procedure to assess attachment patterns. The impetus for developing such a procedure was provided in part by her failure to observe the secure base phenomenon in the American babies, as she did with the Ugandan babies. Ainsworth reasoned that the American infants were comfortable with the familiar routines of the mother coming and going inside the home and that she would need to place the infant and mother in a less familiar environment in order to elicit the secure base behavior. The breakthrough came during a half-hour flash of inspiration during which Ainsworth worked out the essential details of what has become known as the *strange situation* (Karen, 1994). The goal of the procedure was to provide a novel environment that would stimulate the infant's motivation to explore while at the same arouse a certain degree of security seeking. Separation in such an unfamiliar setting would also be likely to activate the attachment system and allow for a direct test of its functioning. The strange-situation paradigm consists of eight episodes that can be construed as involving mild, but cumulative, stress for the 1-year-old American infant.

TABLE 8.2 Episodes in the Strange Situation

1. Experimenter introduces parents and baby to playroom, then leaves.	
2. Parent is seated while baby plays with toys.	Parent as a secure base.
3. Stranger enters, is seated, and talks to parent.	Reaction to an unfamiliar adult.
4. Parent leaves room. Stranger responds to baby and offers comfort if upset.	Separation anxiety.
5. Parent returns, greets baby, and if necessary offers comfort. Stranger leaves room.	Reaction to reunion.
6. Parent leaves room.	Separation anxiety.
7. Stranger enters room and offers comfort.	Ability to be soothed by stranger.
8. Parent returns, greets baby, if necessary offers comfort and tries to reinterest baby in toys.	Reaction to reunion.

Source: Ainsworth, M. D. S. et al. (1978). *Patterns of attachment.* Hillsdale, NJ: Lawrence Erlbaum Associates. With permission.

Note: Episode 1 lasts about 30 seconds; the remaining episodes each last about 3 minutes. Separation episodes are cut short if the baby becomes very upset. Reunion episodes are extended if the baby needs more time to calm down and return to play.

No single behavior can be used to assess the quality of the infant's attachment to the caregiver. By itself, crying in response to separation merely shows that the attachment system has been activated. Infants could differ in the amount and intensity of crying as a function of many factors including age, temperament, and transitory contextual factors like illness. In her second book, *Patterns of Attachment, a Psychological Study of the Strange Situation* (Ainsworth, Blehar, Waters, & Wall, 1978), Ainsworth and colleagues describe the behavior-in-context criteria for scoring attachment in the strange situation. The key to assessing the quality of attachment lies in detecting the organization or pattern of the infant's responses to the changing context, particularly the infant's response to the caregiver upon reunion. See Table 8.2 for an abstraction of the criteria adapted from this source.

Ainsworth's strange-situation paradigm provided the impetus for several decades of international research efforts involving thousands of empirical studies, and during this period attachment research took center stage in developmental research. It is ironic that Ainsworth has been criticized for relying on an artificial laboratory procedure to assess the quality of the infant's attachment to the mother. No one, before Ainsworth, and no one since, has ever invested anything like the 72 hours of home observation per infant-mother pair, to say nothing of the earlier years invested in observing attachment patterns in the everyday life of Ugandan mothers and children. Looking back at the phenomenal interest the scientific community has accorded her labo-ratory procedure, Ainsworth commented, "The fact that the Strange Situation was not in the home environment, that it was in the lab, really helped ... I only did it as an adjunct to my naturalistic research, but it was the thing that everyone could accept somehow. It was so *demonstrable*" (Karen, 1994, p. 163).

Patterns of Attachment

Using the strange-situation procedure, three basic patterns of attachment were described by Ainsworth, and a fourth type has recently been added by one of her most influential students, Mary Main (Main & Solomon, 1990). Using Ainsworth's original taxonomy, researchers in the United States and elsewhere have observed a securely attached pattern in approx-imately 65% of all infants. Two distinct types of anxious patterns were originally described by Ainsworth, resistant attachment (about 15% to 20%) and avoidant attachment (about 10% to 15%), though these percent-ages vary in different cultures. Finally, a fourth type, disorganized attach-ment, has been observed by some investigators, though it is observed in less than 10% of all infants.

Secure attachment. These infants show an optimal balance between exploration and play and the desire to remain near their caregiver in the unfamiliar laboratory context. They typically separate read-ily from the caregiver but remain friendly towards her and to the stranger as well. They may be upset during the separation episodes, but their contact with the caregiver upon reunion provides effec-tive relief from this distress. Upon settling they once again become engaged in play. Infants who show little distress during separation show that they are pleased by greeting their mothers upon their return and engaging them in social interaction by smiling and shar-ing discoveries with her.

Resistant attachment. This pattern is characterized by emotional ambiv-alence and physical resistance to the mother. The infant is typically reluctant to separate from the mother and quick to show anxiety and distress in the unfamiliar setting. Their general wary attitude extends to the stranger and they become highly distressed by the separation, which is not surprising given their need for contact prior to it. The key behavioral criterion is the difficulty these infants have settling in the reunion episodes with the mother. The classification is also referred to as anxious-ambivalent because of the anger expressed by these infants towards their mother at the same moment that they are expressing their need for contact and comforting. They often mix contact seeking with active resistance, squirming, fussing, and even striking out at their mothers when they are upset.

Avoidant attachment. As its label suggests, the key behavioral criterion in this pattern is the active avoidance of the mother when the infant is upset. These infants readily separate from their mothers to explore and may be more friendly towards the stranger than their own mother. Unlike securely attached infants they show little preference for the caregiver and little affective sharing when playing. Their emotional distance from the caregiver becomes more evident following separation. Some infants may begin to seek proximity upon reunion, then suddenly break off the intended movement and turn away. The avoidance of the mother is typically more pronounced following the second separation. These approach-avoidance conflicts sometimes result in displaced behaviors, behaviors that appear out of sequence and have no apparent function. For example, an infant may tearfully toddle towards the caregiver, then just before contact, turn and examine the leg of an adjacent table. Ethologists interpret displaced behavior as resulting from the simultaneous activation of two conflicting motivational systems, in this case, the infant's emotional dependency and fear of rejection.

Disorganized attachment. The fourth category reflects a variety of confused and contradictory behaviors on the part of the infant. For example, during reunion with the parent, the infant might look away while being held by the mother or approach her with a blank or even depressed look. Many of these babies convey a dazed or disoriented facial expression. Others may exhibit confusing patterns such as crying unexpectedly after having settled or displaying odd, frozen postures.

Determinants of Attachment Security

Bowlby theorized that the interactive history between the infant and the caregiver is the major determinant of the quality of attachment observed at one year. In his view, the infant will come to form an expectation concerning the availability and responsiveness of the caregiver based on the repeated cycles of distress signals and responses throughout the first year of life. Bowlby referred to these cognitive representations of the self and other that infants construct from their interactions with their caregiver as an *internal working model*. The infant's internal working model of their relationship is thought to be revealed in the infant's behavior towards the caregiver in the strange situation.

Ainsworth was the first to provide empirical support for Bowlby's ideas. Ainsworth's method uses systematic changes of salient aspects of the immediate mother-child context to study transactional patterns in a situation of increasing stress for the infant. From this perspective, active avoidance of the caregiver, or a mixture of approach and resistant behaviors by the infant while under stress, interferes with the contact and comfort typically afforded by attachment figures. Apparently dysfunctional behaviors like actively resisting the caregiver's efforts to comfort or lashing out in anger at the caregiver are interpreted as a response formulated by the child that reflects a history of inconsistent, chaotic care. Similarly, the infant's active avoidance of the caregiver while stressed reflects an internal working model of the caregiver as someone who is often emotionally unavailable. It is the observation that infants are particularly avoidant when they are in distress that led attachment researchers to view this behavior pattern as a defensive response by the infant to a difficult situation, rather than a precocious sign of independence. In this sense, the history and quality of the relationship itself may be discerned from a careful analysis of infant behavior in relation to changes in context, particularly the separation and reunion episodes with the caregiver.

Ainsworth rated maternal sensitivity towards the infant at several points over the first year and found that when caregivers had been rated high on sensitivity their attachment relationship with their infants were more likely to be classified as secure. In contrast, caregivers who were rejecting of their infants' desire for contact and comfort were more likely to have anxious attachments with their infants (Ainsworth et al., 1978; Blehar, Lieberman, & Ainsworth, 1977). Ainsworth's basic findings relating quality of care to quality of attachment have been widely replicated (Bates, Maslin, & Frankel, 1985; Belsky & Isabella, 1988; Egeland & Farber, 1984; Isabella & Belsky, 1991). In each study, Ainsworth's sensitivity scale was related to attachment assessments at one year. The link between caregiver rejection and avoidant attachment has also been replicated in several studies (Grossman, Grossman, Spranger, Suess, & Unzer, 1985; Isabella, 1993).

Various studies have generally shown that emotional availability and other aspects of emotional communication are related to security of attachment (Tronick, 1989). For example, infants whose mothers are depressed are often found to be insecurely attached (Egeland & Sroufe, 1981) and may be depressed themselves (Lyons-Ruth et al., 1990), though not all infants of depressed parents will develop insecure attachments. It is the quality of care giving, not the depression per se, that is predictive of attachment.

As would be expected, when care giving is extremely insensitive, as in the case of child abuse and neglect, major disruptions to the infant-caregiver attachment are observed. Among maltreated infants, the rates of all three patterns of insecure attachment are high, and as many as 90% of maltreated infants form insecure attachments (Lyons-Ruth et al., 1991) especially the disorganized pattern.

Temperament and Attachment

Attachment researchers generally agree that the infant's temperamental traits are visible during the strange situation. For example, babies with difficult temperaments are predictably more upset by the separation from the caregiver. Using both parental reports as well as measures of cortisol reactivity to stress, researchers have found that temperament predicts the amount of crying during separation but not reunion episodes (Gunnar, Mangelsdorf, Larson, & Herstgaard, 1989; Vaughn, Lefever, Seifer, & Barglow, 1989). In his analysis of the alternating sequences of separations and reunions in the strange situation, Thompson (1990) noted that temperament seems to determine what infants require from their caregivers upon reunion. Similarly, an infant who has been recently ill or atypically stressed may require more contact on reunion before settling. However, being upset by separation from the caregiver is not the same as being insecurely attached. Most attachment researchers have consistently argued that attachment status and temperament are largely independent. According to Sroufe (1996, p. 188) there are two main reasons for this:

> First, they represent different levels of analysis. Assessments of attachment are at the level of the organization of behavior. Thus, it is not how much an infant cries and squirms, but in what context and sequenced with what other behavior and in what manner that are critical. (Infants who cry a great deal during separation, even early in reunions, and who squirm mightily with the stranger are still judged to be securely attached if they are comforted by caregiver contact and return to play.) Second, ... securely attached infants (and anxiously attached infants) show great differences of behavioral style, from slow to arouse and noncuddly (B1) to slow to warm up and easily aroused (B4).

These conceptual distinctions regarding temperament and attachment constructs are supported by behavioral genetics findings that show considerable heritability for basic temperament traits, but negligible heritability for attachment quality (Bokhoost et al., 2000; O'Connor & Croft, 2001). Although temperament traits are clearly related to some behaviors observed in the strange situation, they are not expected to be related to attachment quality, *unless difficult temperament is combined with unresponsive care giving*. Longitudinal studies that provide repeated measurements of infant temperament, maternal care giving, and infant attachment status are most relevant to this important debate. The empirical literature extensively documents that the quality of maternal care giving, not the infant's inborn temperamental dispositions, consistently predicts the quality of infant-mother attachment (Ainsworth et al., 1978; Bates, Maslin, & Frankel,

1985; Belsky, Rovine, & Taylor, 1984; Blehar, Lieberman, & Ainsworth, 1977; Egeland & Farber, 1984; Vaughn et al., 1989).

If parental ratings of temperament are not directly related to attachment security, infant characteristics nevertheless exert an important indirect influence whenever they affect the quality of care giving the infant receives. For example, newborns with neurological problems were not more likely to be classified as insecurely attached, except when this factor was combined with low levels of social and emotional support for caregivers (Crockenberg, 1981). Similarly, infant proneness to distress was not predictive of anxious attachment, except in combination with high levels of maternal controlling-ness (Mangelsdorf, Gunnar, Kestenbaum, Lang, & Andreas, 1990). Because of the complex nature of the relationship between neonatal irritability, care giving responsiveness, and eventual attachment status in midinfancy, researchers are likely to persist in their efforts to clarify the transactional nature of this important milestone in emotional development.

In their longitudinal study, van den Boom (1991, 1994) and colleagues have taken a closer look at the early emotional development of infants who are at risk for developing insecure attachment (highly irritable infants born to mothers having low socioeconomic status). Dutch infants who were assessed as highly irritable at 10 and 15 days using Brazelton's Neonatal Behavioral Assessment Scale (NBAS) were more likely to be classified as insecurely attached (especially avoidant) to their mothers at one year than nonirritable infants drawn from the same low SES sample. These irritable infants were also judged by their mothers as more difficult at 6 and 12 months using traditional parental ratings of temperament. These same mothers were found to be minimally responsive to the relatively few positive expressions of their infants. Mothers of future resistant babies were inconsistent in their responses, showing a mixture of effective soothing and ineffective attempts at distraction that often increased the infant's distress. Mothers of future avoidant infants tended to ignore infant crying for relatively long periods and were more distant in their soothing attempts. Both findings are consistent with Ainsworth's previous work and can be viewed in terms of child effects on maternal behavior (prolonged infant irritability suppresses maternal sensitivity) and maternal care-giving effects on type of attachment classification.

Recent evolutionary formulations about the nature and function of infant cries reveals that prolonged crying bouts are virtually absent in traditional small-scale societies. The widespread prevalence of colic appear to be a direct consequence of care-giving practices of Western societies that are very recent and radically different from those to which infants adapted during the long expanse of human evolution. For example, !Kung San mothers are much more responsive to infant crying (92% of the time within 10 seconds) than are Western mothers, who deliberately refrain from responding 40% of the time (Barr, Konner, Bakeman, & Adamson,

1991). Barr (1999) proposes that positive immediate and long-term outcomes are more likely when crying bouts are frequent and short, while long crying bouts predispose towards negative consequences in a manner similar to van den Boom's findings. Finally, comparative data with respect to several species of monkeys and free-ranging chimpanzees show a similar adaptation involving high levels of mother-infant contact and contingent responsivity to infant signals as the !Kung San. Barr concludes that the normative behavior of frequent, short crying bouts that receive contingent responses from the mother (i.e., feeding, soothing, cooing, etc.) may contribute to the infant's survival via both nutritional and secure attachment pathways.

Hunziker and Barr (1986) hypothesized that infant crying could be reduced by supplemental carrying, that is, increased carrying throughout the day in addition to that which occurs during feeding and in response to crying. In a randomized controlled trial, 99 mother-infant pairs were assigned to an increased carrying or control group. At the time of peak crying (6 weeks of age), infants who received supplemental carrying cried and fussed 43% less overall and 51% less during the evening hours. This decrease in crying and fussing was associated with increased contentment and feeding frequency. The authors conclude that relative lack of infant carrying in our society may predispose to crying and colic in normal infants. In this instance, this practical advice to parents was inspired by evolutionary theory and descriptive anthropology, and then verified by clinical trial.

Research has also shown that some mothers choose to withdraw from difficult infants while others increase their care giving. It may be that the lower levels of support and higher levels of life stress that characterize mothers living in isolation or poverty provide the key for understanding such transactional dynamics. Certainly inborn traits and dispositions may be responded to quite differently by different mothers making main effects of genetic characteristics unlikely as development proceeds. Summarizing the data on temperament effects on attachment, temperament experts Rothbart and Bates (1998) conclude that research has *not* demonstrated that inherited temperament can have a direct effect on attachment security without the mediation of care giving. Conversely, demonstrating associations between a biological parent's child-rearing style and childhood outcomes like attachment status does not rule out a genetic contribution to the association, particularly via gene–environment interaction effects.

Behavioral genetics research demonstrates that shared environmental influence is substantial for security of attachment. These results make sense because a warm, affectionate mother would be likely to treat all of her children in a similar manner and have a similar effect on all of them. However, most shared environmental effects on child outcomes are reported to be close to zero. There are at least three possible reasons for consistently underestimating shared environmental effects. First, if children's inborn traits are responded to differently by different mothers, this would lead to underestimating true shared environmental effects because behavioral genetics analyses would average across and thus nullify these effects of parents. For example, several studies have shown that some mothers withdraw from difficult infants while others increase their care giving. Second, if the infant's genetic traits evoke consistent responses from different parents, this evocative gene–environment interaction would be subsumed under "genetic effects." Third, if parents' genes cause them to create a particular quality of environment for their child, any passive gene–environment effect stemming from this would also be subsumed under genetic effects in the behavioral genetics model. Warm, empathic parents have children with a high genetic potential for empathy and warmth, but they also provide optimal environments for the facilitation of the development of their children's empathy. Children would be expected to benefit differentially from the environments provided by high-investment parents and the result would be a substantial passive gene–environment interaction.

Parents and their children are a coevolving system in which genotype–environment correlations are likely to be of great importance. The causal chain between genes and phenotypes is a long one, with genes (G) and environment (E) interwoven at every step. The distal effects of genes often depend on environmental triggers or enabling conditions, and the effects of different environments depend on the genetic characteristics of the individuals encountering an environment. But G × E covariances and their interactions are subsumed under genetic effects if one adopts the additive assumption of the behavioral genetics model. Because of the problematic assumptions of the additive model underlying behavioral genetics research, there can be no satisfying substitute for directly studying how the environment affects the child.

What can more direct studies tell us about gene–environment interaction? We know that genetic and early experience factors often interact in dramatic fashion. For example, in rhesus monkeys that experienced insecure attachment relationships, a specific polymorphism in the serotonin transporter gene is associated with extreme aggression and excessive alcohol consumption. However, these genetic effects were not observed in monkeys that developed secure attachment relationships with their mothers during infancy. The quality of their early experience appears to buffer these monkeys against the deleterious effects of the gene (Suomi, 2003). According to Suomi, daughters tend to develop the same type of attachment relationships with their own offspring that they experienced with their mothers early in life. He concludes that early experiences in attachment quality provide a possible nongenetic mechanism for transmitting these patterns to subsequent generations.

To the extent that attachment security is not fixed by the infant's biology, but rather shaped by the care-giving environment, researchers should be able to demonstrate that (1) attachment security can change during infancy, (2) these changes are meaningfully related to corresponding changes in the care-giving environment, (3) interventions that are successful in improving caregiver sensitivity and responsiveness also increase infant-caregiver attachment security, 4) quality of attachment may vary depending upon whether the infant is assessed with mother or father, and (5) infants showing identical patterns of attachment can have different temperaments. All five of these predictions have been supported by empirical evidence.

Several studies reveal how malleable early infant-mother attachment is under changing life circumstances. Researchers found that when mothers experienced changes in their level of stress that influence the quality of their care giving, the quality of their attachment to their infant was also observed to change. Such changes reflect coherence in the attachment relationship, which may improve if life circumstances for the caregiver improve or worsen under conditions of increasing stress for the caregiver (Thompson & Lamb, 1984; Vaughn, Egeland, Waters & Sroufe, 1979). Logically, these environmental influences form the theoretical basis for early intervention. An analysis of 12 attachment-based interventions by van IJzendoorn, Juffer, and Duyvesteyn (1995) demonstrates that behaviorally oriented, short-term interventions are consistently effective in increasing parental sensitivity and, to a lesser extent, in improving children's attachment security.

Infant characteristics such as temperament do interact with care-giving abilities and other environmental factors to increase or decrease the risk of insecure attachment. However, this is quite different than asserting that infant temperament determines attachment or that care giving and temperament play an equal role in determining attachment. Further insight regarding this issue may be gained by comparing the attachment status of infants in relation to both their mothers and fathers. If the infant's temperament determines attachment status, researchers should find the same basic pattern of attachment regardless of which parent is present during the strange situation. In contrast, if temperament does not determine the quality of attachment, then infants could show differences in their attachment to their mother and father, if they differ in their sensitivity of care.

A number of studies have established that infants do show a different pattern of attachment with their mothers and fathers (Fox, Kimmerly, & Schafer, 1991). In one study that examined this question, Main & Weston (1981) found that about half the infants they studied formed a different pattern of attachment with each parent. In order to determine the father's contribution to the infant's social development they compared the social responsiveness of infants who were securely attached to one parent only, with infants who were securely attached to both or insecurely attached to both. Not surprisingly, infants who were securely attached to both parents were the most socially responsive. Importantly, infants who were securely attached to one parent only (whether father or mother) were more social than infants without a secure attachment relationship. The same care-giving qualities that promote secure mother-infant bonds apply equally well to fathers. If the father engages in sensitive care giving and becomes the object of his baby's affection, he too will begin to serve as a secure base for his infant (Hwang, 1986).

In American families fathers tend to become increasingly involved with their infants over the first year of life; however, they may not be doing the same things with their infant as mothers do. Typically, mothers devote more time to physical care, holding, soothing, and feeding their baby, whereas fathers are more likely to engage their baby in playful physical stimulation (Lamb, 1997; MacDonald & Parke, 1986). Considering these different styles, it is not surprising that most infants seek out their mothers when distressed and look to their fathers for stimulation and play.

Attachment and Culture

Attachment theorists propose that infant attachment behavior and complementary care-giving behavior have a species-characteristic genetic basis (Bowlby, 1969). As a result, one expects evidence for a certain degree of universality in attachment processes across diverse human societies. However, because any particular attachment relationship is always embedded in a larger family or cultural system, one also expects variation in attachment relations to arise owing to differences in care giving both within and across different cultures. The earliest empirical work from this theoretical perspective (Ainsworth, 1977) provides a two-point cultural comparison between Baltimore and Ugandan samples and reveals much similarity between these groups in the development of infant attachment behavior, in the distinction between secure and anxious patterns of attachment, and in relations between maternal attitudes and behavior and attachment patterns. However, cross-cultural differences were also found for several important aspects of infant behavior relating to separation anxiety, fear of strangers, and the use of the mother as a secure base from which to explore.

A summary of attachment research using the strange situation in different cultures shown in Table 8.3 indicates that the distribution of attachment types in U.S. samples ($N = 1230$) and samples from other countries

TABLE 8.3 Distribution of Attachment Types (Percentages) Across Various Samples

	Attachment Type (%)		
Samples	A	B	C
Germany (FRG) (3 samples, N = 136)	35	57	8
Great Britain (1 sample, N = 72)	22	75	3
Netherlands (4 samples, N = 251)	26	67	6
Sweden (1 sample, N = 51)	22	74	4
Israel (2 samples, N =118)	7	64	29
Japan (2 samples, N = 96)	5	68	27
China (1 sample, N = 36)	25	50	25
USA (18 samples, N = 1230)	21	65	14
Total (32 samples, N = 1990)	21	65	14

Source: Van IJzendoorn & Kroonenberg (1988). Reprinted by permission of SRCD.

(N = 760) are identical (van Ijzendoorn & Kroonenberg, 1988). But this general comparison may mask important divergences. For example, anxious patterns of attachment in German, Japanese, and Israeli samples appear to be substantially different from American norms, though the sample sizes in these countries are far too limited to serve as a basis for national norms. Such differences in attachment classification could arise from sampling error, a lack of conceptual equivalence in the assessment procedure, or from genuine cultural differences in early child-rearing patterns. The assumption of conceptual equivalence would be violated if infants and/or mothers from other cultures experience the strange situation differently from their American counterparts, despite the most stringent attempts to standardize the procedure.

In their study of Japanese mother–infant dyads, Miyake, Chen, and Campos (1985) reported that 37% of all subjects were classified as anxious/resistant in the strange situation while none were classified as anxious/avoidant, a marked difference from American norms. In some respects the behavior of this group of infants was quite similar to resistant infants in American samples; they cried a great deal at separation and were unable to settle upon reunion. However, when interpreted within the cultural context of traditional Japanese society where mothers rarely leave their infants alone for even a few minutes during the first year, and never in a strange setting, this result becomes more comprehensible. Moreover, Sroufe (1985) comments that the Japanese investigators, in their zeal to duplicate precisely Ainsworth's procedure, allowed very stressful separations to continue for the required 3-minute interval, rather than cutting them short, as is the practice among American investigators. As a result of these cultural differences in care giving and procedural differences in the test situation, it is doubtful that the average level of stress that was experienced by the Japanese infants was comparable to that experienced by American infants.

Interpreting infant behavior within a cultural context does not require postulating difficult Japanese temperaments. Indeed, such an interpretation counters previous characterizations of Asian infants as more placid and composed than American infants (Freedman, 1974). This issue is partly resolved by a study of a group of Japanese mothers who exhibit child-rearing styles similar to American norms, confirming the primacy of child-rearing practices as the principal source of variation in the classification of infants in the strange situation (Durett, Otaki, & Richards, 1985).

Another instructive example from the cross-cultural literature is provided by a series of studies in Germany. Grossman, Grossman, Huber, and Wartner (1981) reported a markedly higher incidence of avoidant patterns of attachment in a North German sample, while data from a South German sample were congruent with American norms. Rather than implicating North German temperament, the Grossmans suggest that culture-specific child-rearing attitudes and practices were responsible for a higher proportion of avoidant patterns of attachment in the North German sample. These mothers emphasize training towards obedience and independence before the end of the first year, in advance of the middle-class South German and American norms. In behavioral terms, mothers in the North German sample tended to respond to attachment behaviors such as crying by diverting or scolding their infants, rather than offering solace and close bodily contact. As a result, mean levels of sensitivity at 10 months were lower and less variable than corresponding measures at 2 or 6 months. Moreover, only the earlier measures of sensitivity predicted quality of attachment at 12 months. Viewed as a natural experiment, these results support Bowlby and Ainsworth's central hypothesis that quality of attachment is dependent upon maternal sensitivity. Cross-cultural research on this human universal will help us distinguish what is species-specific from what is culture-specific in attachment relations in infancy and their role in subsequent development.

Attachment and Social Competence

Attachment theorists have proposed that patterns of coregulation established within early social relationships provide an *internal working model* (IWM) for later social relations (Bowlby, 1980, 1988; Sroufe, 1983, 1996). Most developmental psychologists view the infant's primary attachment relationship(s) as a foundation for subsequent relationships because the attitudes, expectations, and interpersonal skills that the child acquires are carried forward and reintegrated into emerging developmental contexts (LaFreniere & Sroufe, 1985). Competence in one developmental period tends to promote adaptation within that period, while preparing the way for the formation of competence in the next (Sroufe & Rutter, 1984). Because homeostatic mechanisms are inherent to both the family system and the attachment subsystem, family environment and quality of attachment tend toward stability, though early deviations are likely to result in greater disturbances later in life. The child who shows persistent deviations may be assumed to be involved in a continuous maladaptive process. A transactional model implies that a stable manifestation of maladaptation depends on environmental support, while the child's characteristics, reciprocally, partially determine the nature of the environment. Central questions for developmental psychopathology have to do with where such stability resides and how positive change may be realized.

Attachment theorists believe that the child's representational model of the attachment figure is closely interwoven with the child's emerging self-concept and the child's representation of relationships. For example, Bretherton argues that "if an attachment figure frequently rejects or ridicules the child's bids for comfort in stressful situations, the child may come to develop not only an internal working model of the parent as rejecting but also one of himself as not worthy of comfort or help" (Bretherton, 1985, p. 12). Alternatively, if a child experiences the attachment figure as trustworthy, loving, and sensitive, the child is likely to form a related model of the self as lovable and worthy of help and comfort from others. These inner representations or IWMs are thought to guide the processing of social information, as well as the child's beliefs, attitudes, and feelings about the self and expectations regarding relationships. Although IWMs remain open to new input as the child encounters new people, they nevertheless tend towards stability because the child actively selects partners and forms new relationships that fit the existing model. According to Bowlby, an IWM will be resistant to change once it is initially constructed, since it tends to operate outside the child's conscious awareness and because new information is assimilated to the existing model (Bowlby, 1980). In a new social milieu the child actively elicits confirmation of the IWM, while often ignoring or discounting counter evidence. Such "self-fulfilling" prophecies may bias a child's socio-emotional development positively or negatively by creating developmental pathways that originate with the caregiver's behavior towards the child.

Developmental theorists such as Ainsworth (Ainsworth, Bell, & Stayton, 1974), Erikson (1963), Kopp (1982), and Sroufe (1996) view the toddler period as critical for the development of an autonomous self-system, capable of independence and initiative, as well as responsiveness and conformity to rules and expectations of others. Human evolution is rooted in the basic primate patterns of group living involving elements of both cooperation and competition, and the socialization of children in all cultures changes dramatically at this age by presenting the child with a wider variety of social partners than during infancy. Fathers, who are often much less involved with infant care than mothers, become more central to the socialization of toddlers. They typically provide a somewhat different style of interaction, often involving the child in vigorous physical play, creating new challenges while at the same time providing emotional support (Lamb, 1981; Parke & Stearns, 1993). In many societies, siblings take on added responsibilities in the care of a younger brother or sister, as well as the role of a sometimes challenging playmate (Dunn & Kendrick, 1982; Tronick et al., 1992). In Western societies, rudimentary peer interaction also begins during this period, with much of the interaction centered around the interesting objects that attract the toddlers' attention in a typical daycare center. Other adults besides the parents become more involved, including grandparents and other relatives, daycare staff, baby-sitters, and other members of the adult community (Whiting and Edwards, 1988). Despite this increased diversity of social partners, central developmental tasks for this period still involve changes in the ongoing relationship with the primary caregivers.

Attachment theorists believe that the child's capacity for *emotion regulation* is shaped within the child's closest relationships. Sroufe (1996) employs the term *guided self-regulation* to capture the intermediate position of the toddler, between the earlier stage when the *dyadic-regulation* provided mostly by the caregiver predominates, and the later stage when the preschooler achieves *true self-regulation*. In this intermediate stage, toddlers are learning how to regulate their own emotions and behavior within the limits and guidelines provided by their caregivers. Two important influences on the dynamics of this learning process have been clarified by research: (1) the overall quality of the parents' approach to discipline during the toddler period is more important than any specific child-rearing practice, and (2) attachment history has an impact on the transition towards more autonomous functioning. Substantial evidence demonstrates a link between parenting styles involving warmth and control and later child outcomes (Arend, Gove, & Sroufe, 1979; Baumrind, 1967; Crockenberg & Litman, 1990; Maccoby & Martin, 1983) though genetic factors and gene–environment correlations may underlie these associations.

In this research variables are often formulated to index qualitative dimensions of parenting that operate across a wide range of different contexts. For example, Sroufe and colleagues view emotional support and quality of assistance as key aspects of parental competence (Matas, Arend, & Sroufe, 1978). Their approach, widely used by others (Bates, Maslin, & Frankel, 1985), involves a series of different problem-solving situations, each presenting the parent-toddler dyad with a unique challenge. The first situation involving free play is minimally challenging, particularly with respect to the issue of autonomy. The next situation, in which the parent was instructed to interrupt the child's play at a prearranged signal and get him or her to put the toys away, is designed to test how smoothly the pair could accommodate a potential conflict of wills. The third situation involved a graded series of physical problems presented from the simplest to the most difficult to assure that at some point all children would be taxed beyond their capabilities to solve the problem. This procedure is designed to assess the flexibility of the parent–child dyad, including parental support and guidance, and the child's emotion regulation and motivation.

Toddlers with a history of secure attachment with their mothers were found to be more enthusiastic in this context, expressing more positive affect and less frustration, and were more successful, by virtue of their greater persistence, flexibility, and cooperation. Toddlers with a history of anxious attachment showed different patterns of maladaptation. An earlier pattern of anxious-resistant attachment was associated with poor emotional regulation. These toddlers were often clingy, and easily prone to emotional dysregulation, becoming frustrated and/or oppositional in the cleanup and problem-solving situations. Toddlers with an anxious-avoidant history were somewhat disengaged with the tasks, showing little pleasure or enthusiasm, and often ignoring their mothers' attempts to involve them. Historically, this research was important for demonstrating continuity in both the patterns of the child's emotional competence and maternal sensitivity across different developmental periods, at a time when researchers were questioning such continuities.

A number of studies provide convergent evidence for these results and the link between attachment in infancy and the quality of the parent-toddler relationship. In particular, toddlers who were earlier assessed as anxious-avoidant were more prone to enter into conflict with their mothers. Reciprocally, their mothers were more restrictive and controlling. As with the attachment assessment, these studies reveal disturbances in the parent-child relationship, rather than problems that reside exclusively within the child. During the toddler years, however, the tensions and problems experienced with the primary attachment figure may be carried forward into other adult-child relationships, and several studies have shown this to be the case (Londerville & Main, 1981; Thompson & Lamb, 1983). It appears that the capacity for regulating affectively arousing stimulation is central to positive adaptation in both the family and peer system. For example, Easterbrooks and Lamb (1979) and Lieberman (1977) found secure attachment to be associated with positive, reciprocal exchanges with age mates at 18 months and 3 years, respectively.

During the preschool years, basic patterns of attachment are transformed reflecting developments in language and cognition, as well as shifting issues in psychosocial adjustment. For the child experiencing a secure relationship, there is a new partnership with the caregiver that reflects these advances and allows for increased autonomy and initiative within and beyond the dyad (Erikson, 1963; Sroufe, 1983). Within the parent-child relationship, the secure strategy incorporates perspective-taking, mutual communication of affect and desires, and joint planning; however, a number of deviations from this pattern are possible (Crittendon, 1992; Sroufe, 1989). A transactional model casts the child as an active agent rather than a passive recipient of environmental input or a direct product of genetic determinism. A new social milieu, such as the preschool, may be constructed differently by different children according to their attachment history. This provides a possible response to the question posed at the beginning of this chapter, by suggesting that a child actively seeks out or avoids various resources and opportunities within the new niche according to expectations derived from genetic propensities, past experiences, and previous relationships.

Considerable evidence has established a direct link between an infant's primary attachment relationship and the quality of a child's peer relations. Using a variety of sources and measures, researchers report that compared to insecurely attached preschoolers, securely attached preschoolers behave more positively towards their peers and receive more positive behavior from them, are better liked by peers, enjoy more positive and synchronous friendships, and are more highly regarded by their teachers as helpful, cooperative, empathic, and socially competent (Belsky & Cassidy, 1994; Erickson, Egeland, & Sroufe, 1985; Jacobson & Willie, 1986; LaFreniere & Sroufe, 1985; Youngblade & Belsky, 1992).

A recent study from the National Institute of Child Health and Human Development (NICHD Early Child Care Research Network, 2006), suggests that there may be continuing effects of early secure attachment that can be observed even when parental conditions change. Declining parenting quality was not associated with increased classroom externalizing problems for children with early secure attachments with their mothers as it was for children with insecure attachments at 15 months of age. Securely attached children appeared to be protected against declining maternal parenting, suggesting that early attachment may have served as a protective factor against declines in optimal parenting. The internalized working models may enable securely attachment children to approach social situations with positive expectations from others. Children with secure attachment histories remember positive events (presented in a puppet show) more than negative events, whereas the reverse is true of children with insecure attachment histories (Belsky, Spritz, & Crnic, 1996).

The quality of parental care across the early childhood years exerts its own effects on child outcomes independent of earlier patterns of mother-infant attachment. In one study, Belsky and Fearon (2002) found that the effects of early attachment organization on children's 3-year functioning were dependent on the quality of mothering experienced by the children at 24 months of age. More positive child outcomes were observed when an insecure attachment was followed by high maternal sensitivity than when a secure attachment was followed by low maternal sensitivity.

Attachment history has also been related to emerging behavioral problems in preschoolers. In the Minnesota Longitudinal Study, attachment assessments in the strange situation at 12 and 18 months were related to behavior in the preschool classroom (Erickson, Egeland, & Sroufe, 1985). Results indicated that for this high-risk, inner-city sample behavioral problems were evident (as assessed by teacher ratings) for 85% of infants with stable insecure attachments, 60% with unstable attachments (secure at one time, insecure at the other), and 29% with stable secure attachments. The investigators then examined other risk factors in the home in order to discover why some securely attached infants showed later behavioral problems and other insecurely attached infants did not. Compared to securely attached infants without later problems, the secure infants that did show problems had mothers who were less emotionally supportive and not as clear or consistent in their guidance and limit setting during the toddler and early preschool years. Other evidence suggested that these mothers experienced more confusion and disorganized mood states during this period and were less involved with their child than mothers of secure infants without behavior problems.

The comparison between insecure infants with and without behavior problems revealed that those without problems had mothers who were warmer, more supportive, and more appropriate in their limit setting at 42 months. Reciprocally, these children were more affectionate and compliant with their mothers in this latter assessment. These results are important in demonstrating continuity of child adaptation in stable environments and coherence in child adaptation in unstable environments. That is, when children with an earlier history of secure attachment were subsequently exposed to less than adequate maternal care and support, they were more likely to manifest behavior problems than secure infants in stable care-giving environments. Similarly, anxiously attached infants could become well-functioning preschoolers if their caregivers responded adequately to their needs during later developmental stages (Sroufe, Egeland, Carlson, & Collins, 2005).

The pattern of anxious-resistant attachment to the primary caregiver in infancy has been identified in longitudinal research as a risk factor for internalizing behavior problems, including anxiety, high dependency on adults, social withdrawal, passivity, and submissiveness with peers (Erikson, Egeland, & Sroufe, 1985; LaFreniere & Sroufe, 1985; Sroufe, Fox, & Pancake, 1983). As infants and toddlers they were observed to be wary, easily upset, and difficult to settle. They were also characterized by a poverty of exploration and at times they showed explicitly angry, tantruming behavior, all presumably based on a history of inconsistent or chaotic care (Ainsworth et al., 1978). In the Minnesota Longitudinal Study (LaFreniere & Sroufe, 1985; Sroufe, 1983) infants who were classified as anxious-resistant at 12 and 18 months were found to become low-status, peripheral members of their preschool peer group 3 years later. Some of these children exhibited extreme passivity and an infantile dependence on adults, while others were more forward with their peers, but became easily overaroused and disorganized in the face of minor frustrations.

Children with a history of anxious-avoidant attachment have been shown to have a different pattern of strengths and weaknesses in their social adaptation and emotional adjustment to the preschool classroom. Their adoption of an avoidant behavioral style in order to cope with chronic insensitivity and rejection by their primary caregiver may lay the foundation for a defensive personality characterized by hostility and negative expectations of others. In a naturalistic observational study that directly compared the emotional expression of preschoolers with different attachment histories, those with anxious-attachment histories were found to express more hostility and negative affect towards their peers, and were more rejected by them than securely attached children (LaFreniere & Sroufe, 1985).

More recent studies have replicated these findings. For example, McElwain, Cox, Burchinal, and Macfie (2003) reported that a history of avoidant attachment was related to instrumental aggression during child–friend interactions; a history of anxious-resistant attachment was related to less self-assertion among friends. Following a sample of children of adolescent mothers from 12 months to 9 years of age, Munson, McMahon, and Spieker (2001) found that children with histories of either avoidant or disorganized attachments showed higher levels of externalizing problems at age 9 compared with children with secure attachment histories. Lyons-Ruth, Easterbrooks, and Cibelli (1997) found that infants with either avoidant or disorganized histories were rated high on both internalizing and externalizing symptoms at age 7 compared with children with secure attachment histories. Finally, in a recent NICHD study involving over 1000 U.S. children, infants with avoidant classifications were clearly the group most associated with both parenting and demographic risk as well as problematic outcomes in later years (NICHD Early Child Care Research Network, 2006).

Relations between early attachment organization and child outcomes in the child's first 3 years have been systematically examined with these NICHD data, often replicating results found in the earlier Minnesota Longitudinal Study. Consistent with previous data, McElwain et al. (2003) found that avoidant attachment history was related to more instrumental aggression during child–friend interaction, and resistant attachment history was associated with less self-control and assertion among friends even when maternal sensitivity and concurrent attachment were controlled.

A consistent finding across many studies indicates that preschoolers with a history of avoidant attachment are at risk for externalizing problems that may be expressed in relational aggression. For example, Troy & Sroufe (1987) observed the development of peer relationships in pairs of preschoolers during a series of free play sessions. They found that a high percentage of children with avoidant histories took advantage of and mistreated their play partner. In all cases of victimization the "exploiter" had an avoidant history, while the victim was often a child with a resistant history. In addition, preschool teachers often have distinct emotional reactions to children with different attachment histories. Several studies have shown that they often nurtured and protected children with resistant histories, but sometimes reacted with anger to the open defiance and bullying of children with avoidant histories. These distinct emotional responses on the part of new caregivers underscore the transactional nature of these early emotional disorders.

Finally, children with disorganized patterns (D) of early attachment, about whom less is known, show no coherent attachment strategy in infancy and respond to their mothers in the strange situation with a variety of contradictory behavior patterns, odd or mistimed movements, or disorientation (Cassidy & Mohr, 2001). Other evidence has linked the disorganized attachment pattern to specific forms of behavioral and emotional problems in preschoolers. Main and Solomon (1990) believe that these children respond to internal conflict by displaying contradictory or incomplete behavior patterns formed in response to chronic abusive or frightening parental behavior. As preschoolers, they appear to be inflexible and controlling, possibly as an attempt to bring some semblance of order to an otherwise chaotic network of close relationships. This pattern may also involve a role reversal between parent and child in care giving and punishment. Such behaviors are believed to be mediated by deviant patterns of emotional regulation and communication in the parent–child relationship (Lyons-Ruth, Repacholi, Mcleod, & Silva, 1991). Consistent with this deficit in emotion regulation, researchers have identified greater incidence of aggression, externalizing disorders, and oppositional defiant disorder in these children (Lyons-Ruth & Jacobvitz, 1999; van IJzendoorn, Schuengel, & Bakermans-Kranenburg, 1999).

A Life History Perspective

Several evolutionary psychologists have attempted an integration of the existing body of research and theory on attachment described above with a life history perspective. Life history theory is an analytical framework widely used in biology and evolutionary psychology that postulates species-typical characteristics that have evolved to guide somatic and reproductive efforts over the life course.

According to life history theory because individuals have a finite amount of time, energy, and resources, basic decisions must be made regarding the allocation of these resources with respect to different life goals (Levins, 1968). Goals directly related to reproductive success such as survival, growth, mating efforts, parenting efforts, etc., may at times be in direct conflict, necessitating strategic trade-offs. Time, effort, and energy used for one purpose diminish the time, effort, and energy available for another. For example, resources spent pursuing multiple mates cannot be spent in investing in current offspring.

These trade-offs and strategies can be compared between species. Two of the most well-known trade-offs involve number of offspring (few or many) and timing of reproduction (accelerated maturation and reproduction versus delayed, allowing for larger size and more complex social supports). The extremes at the species level of these fundamental dimensions are traditionally termed r/K selection theory. An r-selection strategy (e.g., most species of fish) is the production of a large number of offspring (of whom only a minority may survive) as early in life as possible. The K-selection strategy (e.g., lions, wolves, elephants, humans) is to produce and invest heavily in a smaller number of offspring with much higher survival chances.

Examples of species typical life history characteristics include

Age at weaning
Age of sexual maturity or puberty
Adult body size
Age-specific mortality schedules
Time to first sexual activity or mating
Time to first reproduction
Duration of gestation
Litter size
Interbirth interval

Besides its utility in comparing differences between species, life history theory has provided new perspectives in understanding many aspects of human reproductive behavior, including parental investment and attachment. According to life history theory the individuals of a species are able to make limited shifts in reproductive strategies in response to prevailing circumstances. Depending on resource availability, individuals shift their reproductive strategy in one direction or the other to take advantage of available resources or to compensate for resource shortage or uncertainty.

Any individual reproductive strategy involves a coordinated response to the organism's environment resulting from the need to optimally partition mating and parenting effort. For example, in environments with relatively stable, predictable resources characteristics such as intimate pair bonding between parents, high-investment parenting, relatively low fertility, and delayed maturation of the young are likely to be adaptive (MacDonald, 1997). Research using the Adult Attachment Interview provides some supportive evidence for this reproductive strategy. The relationships of secure spouses are more supportive and longer lasting than those of insecure people (Hazen & Shaver, 1987).

In an early application of life history theory to developmental outcomes associated with low paternal investment (father-absent households), Draper and Harpending (1982) found that girls in father-absent homes showed a more precocious interest in sex than girls in two-parent families. They interpreted this finding as an adaptive response to conditions of economic disadvantage and uncertainty by producing offspring early and at a high rate. This trade-off between maximizing current reproduction at the expense of future reproduction by increasing fertility but decreasing future parental investments makes adaptive sense when resources are limited and unpredictable. Theorists such as Belsky and Chisholm view different attachment styles as reflecting similar allocation trade-offs.

In their review of the human data, Belsky, Steinberg, and Draper (1991) report large intercorrelations among spousal harmony, parent–child relationship quality, children's interpersonal style, timing of puberty, sexual behavior, and level of parental investment. Both Belsky (1997) and Chisholm (1996) argue that alternate reproductive strategies may be seen as a response to the presence or absence of environmental stress and high or low resource availability. In their view, a low-investment reproductive strategy may be an adaptive response to environmental stress from the vantage point of inclusive fitness. The developmental pathway in an ecology with low or uncertain resource availability begins with spousal disharmony or paternal disengagement and insensitive, unresponsive parenting styles. This in turn leads to insecure attachment and an opportunistic interpersonal style among offspring. Empirical studies have found that insecure-avoidant individuals are more sexually precocious, promiscuous, and prone to unstable pair bonds compared to secure individuals and, among girls, family conflict in childhood is predictive of earlier onset of puberty.

At a sociological level of analysis this idea of alternate reproductive strategies is also very much in evidence. Evolutionary scholars such as Bobbi Low (2000) view high resource availability as an environmental cue compelling parents to invest more heavily in fewer offspring in order that their children can effectively compete with others with similar backgrounds. Sociological evidence for this speculation is twofold: (1) birth rates are much lower in wealthy, technologically advanced societies than in developing countries; and (2) families in these wealthy societies invest 15 to 20 times more economic resources per child than families in the developing world (Low, 2000). The evolutionary principle of high investment in fewer offspring in competitive environments appears to be true whether analyzing data across species (r vs. K selection), across human societies, or within a given society containing economic disparity.

Thus, parental investment operates as an integrating force on development because it is intimately related to reproductive strategy and success with respect to inclusive fitness. All things being equal, individuals who invest highly in children must be able to maintain viable family relationships, and they must be able to inhibit attraction to short-term gains (e.g., low-investment sexual relationships) in favor of long-term benefits. Correspondingly, their children must be able to benefit from the added attention and care their parents are able to provide. As we have seen in attachment research, although human life history strategies are species-typical with heritable individual differences, they are also highly sensitive to environmental inputs.

□ Chapter Summary

Initiated by pioneers John Bowlby and Mary Ainsworth, attachment theory has broadened its influence in psychology well beyond the period of infancy. Bowlby developed an ethological model of attachment incorporating ideas from ethology, primatology, object relations theory, and systems theory. This theoretical synthesis was complimented by methodological and empirical advances by Ainsworth, Sroufe, Waters, Main, and others. In this chapter, research during infancy based on Ainsworth's original strange-situation paradigm was described as well as contemporary longitudinal research that examines the developmental significance of early patterns of attachment.

Using the strange-situation procedure, three basic patterns of attachment were described by Ainsworth, and a fourth type was subsequently added. Researchers have observed a securely attached pattern in approximately 65% of all infants. Two distinct types of anxious patterns were originally described by Ainsworth, resistant attachment (about 15% to 20%) and avoidant attachment (about 10% to 15%), though these percentages vary in different cultures. Finally, a fourth type, disorganized attachment, has been observed by some investigators, though it is observed in less than 10% of all infants.

Bowlby theorized that the interactive history between the infant and the caregiver is the major determinant of the quality of attachment observed at one year. In his view, the infant will come to form an expectation concerning the availability and responsiveness of the caregiver based on the repeated cycles of distress signals and responses throughout the first year of life. Bowlby referred to these cognitive representations of the self and other that infants construct from their interactions with their caregiver as an *internal working model*.

Various studies have generally shown that emotional availability and other aspects of emotional communication are related to security of attachment. For example, infants whose mothers are depressed are often found to be insecurely attached though not all infants of depressed parents will develop insecure attachments. It is the quality of care giving, not the depression per se, that is predictive of attachment. As would be expected, when care giving is extremely insensitive, as in the case of child abuse and neglect, major disruptions to the infant-caregiver attachment are observed. Among maltreated infants, the rates of all three patterns of insecure attachment are high, and as many as 90% of maltreated infants form insecure attachments.

Distinctions between temperament and attachment constructs are supported by behavioral genetics findings that show considerable heritability for basic temperament traits, but negligible heritability for attachment quality. Although temperament traits are clearly related to some behaviors observed in the strange situation, they are not expected to be related to attachment quality, *unless difficult temperament is combined with unresponsive care giving*.

A number of important findings have become established regarding distinctions between attachment and temperament. First, patterns of infant attachment to the mother have been shown to be stable in middle-class samples from 12 to 18 months, with the secure pattern the most prevalent. Second, a number of studies show that attachment quality at this age is related to maternal responsiveness and sensitivity, but not directly related to infant temperament. Third, infant characteristics like difficult temperament or neurological problems have been shown to indirectly influence attachment security if they affect the quality of care giving. These effects appear to be more likely in care-giving environments that are stressful with low levels of support. Fourth, changing patterns of attachment reflect coherence. If life circumstances for the caregiver improve or deteriorate, corresponding changes in attachment security may be observed. Fifth, the infant's attachment relationships may be different for fathers and mothers if care-giving sensitivity is different between the two parents. Sixth, cross-cultural research on attachment has begun to investigate how cultural influences modify this basic primate adaptation to fit the ecology in which the infant and caregiver are immersed.

Parents and their children are a coevolving system in which genotype–environment correlations are likely to be of great importance. The causal chain between genes and phenotypes is a long one. The distal effects of genes often depend on environmental triggers or enabling conditions and the effects of different environments depend on the genetic characteristics of the individuals encountering an environment. For example, in rhesus monkeys that experienced insecure attachment relationships, a specific polymorphism in the serotonin transporter gene is associated with extreme aggression and excessive alcohol consumption. However, these genetic effects were not observed in monkeys who developed secure attachment relationships with their mothers during infancy. The quality of their early experience appears to buffer these monkeys against the deleterious effects of the gene.

Longitudinal research in humans has consistently demonstrated links between the quality of the infant's attachment relationship with the primary caregiver and adaptation in other developmental periods and social contexts. Security of attachment in infancy has been linked with more prosocial, empathic behavior towards peers and greater acceptance and popularity in the peer group. Preschoolers with a history of secure attachment express more positive and less negative emotions when interacting with their peers. Preschoolers with avoidant attachment histories have been found to express more dependence towards teachers and greater hostility, negative affect, and aggression towards their peers. Preschoolers with anxious-resistant attachment histories have been found to be more anxious, withdrawn, passive, and immature with their peers. Preschoolers with disorganized attachment histories have been found to be inflexible and controlling, though more studies are needed to clarify the different patterns of psychosocial risks associated with specific anxious attachment histories.

Finally, findings from attachment research were interpreted from a life history perspective, noting how early patterns of attachment may represent alternate reproductive strategies that are set in motion in infancy. Depending on resource availability, individuals can shift their reproductive strategy in one direction or the other to take advantage of available resources or to compensate for resource shortage or uncertainty. In environments with relatively stable, predictable resources characteristics such as intimate pair bonding between parents, high-investment parenting, relatively low fertility, and delayed maturation of the young are likely to be adaptive.

☐ For Further Inquiry

Belsky, J. (1997). Attachment, mating, and parenting: An evolutionary interpretation. *Human Nature, 8*, 361–381.

NICHD Early Child Care Research Network. (2006). Infant–mother attachment classification: Risk and protection in relation to changing maternal caregiving quality. *Developmental Psychology, 42*, 38–58.

Sroufe, L. A., Egeland, B., Carlson, E. A., & Collins, W. A. (2005). *The development of the person: The Minnesota Study of risk and adaptation from birth to adulthood.* New York, NY: Guilford Press.

CHAPTER

Theory of Mind and Language

☐ Theory of Mind

In this chapter we explore potential discontinuities between animal and human cognition that stem from the unique features of the human brain. Recently evolved modules enable symbolic representation, language, and the understanding of internal states. The term "theory of mind" refers to an abstract causal system that allows one to explain and predict behavior through reference to unobservable mental states such as beliefs, intentions, desires, and emotions. The development of the child's theory about inner states underlies the increasing complexity of the child's social cognition and emotional experience.

In a landmark study in primatology that launched a new wave of research among developmental psychologists, David Premack and Guy Woodruff explored the question: Does the chimpanzee have a theory of mind? By this they meant, do apes attribute states of mind to others, and do they use these attributions to predict or explain other's behavior? Their ingenious experimental investigations of intentional communication in chimpanzees seemed to demonstrate that chimps were capable of clever deceptions that might be based upon their understanding of the desires, emotions, and intentions of their human trainers (Premack & Woodruff, 1978; Woodruff & Premack, 1979). They presented 3- to 4-year-old chimps with the following dilemma: the chimps knew the location of a hidden banana but couldn't reach it without the help of a trainer who could reach it, but did not know where it was hidden. During a number of trials, the chimps were exposed to two different trainers, a kind trainer who, when shown where the banana was hidden, would give it to them to eat, and a villainous trainer who, if shown the correct location, ate the banana himself. Faced with such duplicity, one of the chimps, Sarah, learned to direct honest communications to the kind trainer, but to deceive the villainous trainer by pretending not to know where the banana was hidden or even by pointing to the wrong container. Premack and Woodruff believed that Sarah consciously employed a deceptive strategy based upon her understanding of the intentions of the villainous trainer, though it remains difficult to distinguish such a strategy from other types of deception based on conditioning.

Intentionality is central to understanding communication because signals that communicate one's intentions may be used by another to gain a strategic advantage, especially in situations of competition or conflict. As a result false signals, or deception, could be advantageous to the sender on those occasions, if others respond to them as true signals. Thus, an evolutionary arms race ensues resulting in more subtle forms of deception on the one hand and more vigilance and subtle forms of detection on the other. This dynamic is seen as central to the evolution of human intelligence as a key mechanism for promoting the adaptation of the individual within a social group (Dawkins & Krebs, 1978; Humphrey, 1976; Whiten & Byrne, 1988).

Chimpanzee Social Cognition

Although chimpanzees appear to show some surprising abilities in deception, they make fewer attributions than humans, since they cannot attribute states of mind that they themselves do not possess. Naturalistic and experimental evidence suggests that apes make simple attributions of seeing, wanting, and expecting, rather than attributions about beliefs. Thus, they appear to possess only a limited theory of mind. In a similar sense, 3-year-old children may possess a theory of mind that is also limited by their cognitive development. The experimental primatologist David Premack has been comparing the cognitive abilities of chimpanzees and children for over 20 years. His rule of thumb is that if a child of 3.5 years cannot do it neither can the chimpanzee (Premack, 1988). This observation leads to an obvious question: what are the cognitive limitations shared by chimpanzees and young children?

Premack addressed this question by dividing states of mind into simple and complex states:

> Simple states are those produced by processes that are hard-wired, automatic or reflex-like, and encapsulated … perception is the prototypic simple state, we may add others: first, certain basic motivational states; and secondly, somewhat more controversially,

expectancy, a state that is produced by conditioning or simple learning. These three states—seeing, wanting, expecting—have in common a restricted and automatic production process that is independent of language both at the input level of the system and of internal representation …

Complex states, of which belief is the prototype, are of course everything that simple states are not. Belief is not automatic, encapsulated, or hard-wired; moreover it definitely depends on language, most certainly at the level of internal representation though often also at the level of input to the system. (Premack, 1988, p. 172)

Current research indicates that this division between simple and complex states may provide a rough estimate of the abilities that chimpanzees and other nonhuman primates do and do not possess. Chimpanzees know what others can and cannot see and they can use this information to compete more effectively for food (Call & Tomasello, 2008). However, it is less clear how far their visual perspective-taking skills go. Does this skill allow them to make correct inferences about what others know? Current evidence is still too fragmentary to make any strong claims about knowledge attribution. Although chimpanzees possess a basic capacity to follow the gaze direction of others using body orientation as a cue rather than eyes, they seem to lack the visual perspective-taking skills of 3-year-old children. Thus, chimpanzees do not appear to understand gaze as referential communication, and they clearly do not understand pointing as such (Povinelli, Bierschwale, & Cech, 1999). Nor do chimpanzees appear to discriminate between accidental and intentional behavior (Povinelli, Reaux, Bierschwale, Allain, & Simon, 1997), nor between a knowledgeable and naïve experimenter (Call & Tomasello, 2008). Chimpanzees have not been successful on nonverbal false belief tests. In general they appear to lack the human capacity for abstract causal reasoning or the ability to posit unobservable constructs to explain observable events, that is central to a mature theory of mind (Bering & Povinelli, 2003).

In a recent summary of 30 years of research (Call & Tomasello, 2008), growing consensus from experimental evidence seems to indicate that chimpanzees understand others in terms of a perception-goal psychology, but not in terms of a belief-desire psychology. Humans, of course, clearly do understand others in terms of their desires and beliefs, and they do so at an early age.

Belief-Desire Psychology

By 3 years, children show a rudimentary understanding that the mind has connections to the external world. On the input side of this relation (behavior-to-mind), they grasp the principle that seeing implies knowing. For example, they know about hiding places and if a toy is well hidden in a box, they know that only someone who has looked inside knows where the toy is hidden (Flavell, Shipstead, & Croft, 1978). Similarly, a typical 3-year-old knows that if someone has seen an event, then that individual knows something about that event (Pratt & Bryant, 1990).

On the output (mind-to-behavior) side, children appear to connect desires and emotions to action, prior to understanding the relation between beliefs and action. Henry Wellman (1990) proposes a developmental model of *belief–desire psychology*. In his developmental sequence, desire psychology emerges first and refers to the ability to explain and predict another person's behavior based on our assumptions about their emotions and desires. For example, most 3-year-olds can explain and predict action and emotional expressions based on desires. If a girl really wants a kitten for her birthday, 3-year-olds could tell you that she might ask her parents for one and that she would be happy if she opened her present and saw a kitten inside the box. But 3-year-olds appear to know less about how a person's beliefs might influence their behavior (Wellman & Wooley, 1990).

Because of advancing linguistic skills, children's (but not chimpanzees') understanding of the nature of the mind is revealed in their explanations about it, as well as their behavior. Preschoolers can inform us at an early age that thoughts cannot be seen or felt; that they happen inside your head. "How can you reach inside your head; besides it's not even there" (Wellman, 1990). Yet somehow the dividing line between imagination and reality is not altogether clear. During testing in our make-believe hide-a-bear task, one 3-year-old girl burst into tears at the thought of the hunter capturing her bear who was hiding and we needed to reassure her that she could take the bear home, that the hunter is really nice and not really a hunter, but just pretending, etc. (LaFreniere, 1988). Research indicates that even older preschoolers are not too certain that an imaginary creature could not just possibly bite their finger off! In exploring the views of children aged 4 to 6 years, Harris and colleagues found that they all asserted that an imaginary monster was not real. However, when asked to pretend that an empty box contained the imaginary monster, they generally preferred to poke their finger into an empty box that contained an imaginary puppy instead and studiously avoided the box with an imaginary monster. In addition, several 4-year-olds asked the experimenter not to leave them in the room with the empty box, even after verifying that it was empty. Although nearly everyone "knew" that the monster was only pretend and not real, only about half the children were convinced that it was not in the box! (Harris, Brown, Whittall, & Harmer, 1991).

A major step forward in thinking about the mind that is beyond the understanding of most 3-year-olds entails the ability to reflect on the representational process and understand that a belief is a representation of reality, not reality itself. Unlike a desire, a belief may be true or false, and the external world may be represented accurately or inaccurately. By the age of four or five, children, but not chimpanzees, generally pass verbal and nonverbal *false-belief tasks* as first demonstrated by Wimmer and Perner (1983) and others. In these tasks children may be told stories in which the protagonist is led to believe that an object was hidden in one place while they themselves knew it was actually hidden elsewhere. When asked where the protagonist would search, the 3-year-olds ignored the protagonist's false beliefs and predicted she would search the correct location, while 4- to 6-year-olds predicted she would search the incorrect location. A number of studies have now confirmed that 4-year-olds generally understand that another person may have beliefs that are different from their own; beliefs that may turn out to be incorrect. Of course false beliefs may be induced, not just about concrete things (like hidden objects), but also about more private phenomena, such as a person's internal state or feelings. We turn next to investigations of children's understanding of the distinction between appearances and reality.

Distinguishing Appearance and Reality

John Flavell and his colleagues developed a research program exploring how children come to learn that things are not always what they seem to be. They developed a series of *appearance-reality tasks* which required that children demonstrate their understanding that appearances could sometimes be misleading and not an accurate representation of reality. In these tasks they showed children objects that looked liked other objects, such as a sponge that looked like a rock, or objects viewed through tinted glass. They consistently found that children younger than 4 years tended to equate reality with appearances. For example, if a glass of white milk is wrapped in a green filter, 3-year-olds will say that the milk not only "looks" green, but "really and truly is" green (Flavell, Green, & Flavell, 1986). Like the false belief task, the appearance-reality distinction requires meta-representational skills or the ability to represent representations. And like the child's understanding of false beliefs, it is mostly absent in 3-year-olds and still quite fragile for children between 4 and 6 years of age.

Grasping the distinction between real and apparent emotion is similar from the standpoint of meta-representation, but even more difficult. For most 4-year-olds this distinction is not clear, and most emotional expressions are taken at face value, though they understand the distinction between real and pretend. In contrast, most 6-year-olds understand that other people can be misled by displaying facial expressions that are different from what one actually feels (Gross & Harris, 1988). For example, they understand that someone may fall and hurt themselves, but try not to show that they are frightened, scared, or hurt, if they think they might be teased as a result. Six-year-olds may have considerable difficulty deciding whether any given expression is real or apparent, but they understand the distinction and realize that they need not coincide.

Tactical Deception

How would children react to the type of problem Premack presented to his chimps? To find out, we investigated the developmental aspects of tactical deception within a game context in which the child must try to conceal a hidden object from an adult interrogator. Sixty children, from 3 to 8 years of age were filmed in the "hide-a-bear task" (LaFreniere, 1988). After hiding a toy bear in one of three hiding places, the child was instructed to try to "fool the hunter," an adult experimenter who questioned the child regarding the bear's location. With one exception, children younger than 4 years were always unsuccessful in their attempts to fool the adult, 5- and 6-year-olds were only occasionally successful, and 8-year-olds were successful significantly more often. Some 3-year-olds attempted to inhibit information by shrugging their shoulders and pretending that they did not know the location of the bear, but they were unable to fool the adult because they freely leaked information by glancing repeatedly at the location of the hidden object under questioning. Older children gained increasing control over nonverbal leaks and were more able (like Premack's Sarah) to withhold this information from the interrogator. But, nearly all the children under the age of 6 used a predictable hiding strategy in which the toy was hidden in each of the three locations for each of the three trials. Thus, by the third trial, they would give away the location of the bear. Only the 8-year-olds were able to correctly infer that such a regular hiding strategy would provide useful information to the adult interrogator; 80% of these older children employed an irregular hiding strategy.

In addition, only the 8-year-olds showed a significant increase in the use of the more effective strategy of intentionally misleading the interrogator when they were being questioned. This could take the form of quick glances at an incorrect location during questioning. Later they would state that they looked at a place where no bear was hidden because they thought that the adult would be fooled into thinking that the bear would be hidden there. In general, older children showed greater awareness of the effects of their own behavior on the experimenter's state of mind in the hide-a-bear task, demonstrating a recursive level of awareness of intentionality by providing misleading cues and by altering a regular hiding strategy so as not to provide inadvertently useful information to the experimenter. They were also the most successful in forestalling nonverbal leakage by successfully controlling their facial expression.

Subsequent research into the early development of children's deception has been lively, with numerous studies of verbal and nonverbal deception in situations that range from naturalistic (Josephs, 1993, 1994; Lewis, Stanger, & Sullivan, 1989) to highly contrived (Chandler, Fritz, & Hala, 1989; Hala, Chandler, & Fritz, 1991; Sodian, Taylor, Harris, & Perner, 1991). In general, this work demonstrates that the early forms of deception enacted by preschoolers younger than 4 years are unsophisticated and consist of attempts to withhold information by not confessing to transgressions (Lewis, Stanger, & Sullivan, 1989) or by removing incriminating evidence (Chandler, Fritz, & Hala, 1989). Most studies have shown that more sophisticated forms of deception that rely upon a more mature theory of mind (i.e., planting misleading evidence or adopting misleading expressive behavior), do not emerge until after 4 years. Not all acts of nonverbal deception rely upon the same cognitive capacities.

Sodian and Schneider (1990) used another version of a hiding game for children from 4 to 6 years inspired by Premack's work with chimpanzees. In this task, target pictures (e.g., a policeman) could be hidden in places of strong (police station) or weak association (sports arena) under two conditions: cooperative (a nice king who is looking for the policeman) or competitive (a burglar). Success at the task involved demonstrating an understanding of the relevance of the cognitive cues by hiding the policeman in the sports arena, rather than the police station in the competitive condition. Only a few 4-year-olds, half the 5-year-olds, and almost all the 6-year-olds chose the appropriate hiding place in relation to the cooperative/competitive condition.

Monitoring the social partner's face, especially the eyes, is a prominent means of seeking information with respect to the person's intentions. As discussed in Chapter 7, infants are preadapted to attend to facial expressions. From birth, children preferentially focus on the face, looking longer at open eyes than closed eyes (Bakti et al., 2000; Pellicano & Rhodes, 2003). By 3 months infants can discriminate facial and vocal expressions and are sensitive to adult gaze shift (Haviland & Lelwica, 1987; Hood, Willen, & Driver, 1998; Nelson, 1987). By 6 months they can follow adult gaze when it is paired with head orientation. From 12 to 18 months they respond with appropriate affect, show social referencing and can follow eye gaze alone. From 18 to 24 months they use eye gaze or pointing cues alone. At 2 to 3 years toddlers can use eye gaze to infer mental states such as desires and thinking. And, around 4 to 5 years they are sensitive to duration and frequency of eye gaze when attempting to make inferences about mental states (Freire, Eskritt, & Lee, 2004). In Figure 9.1, Simon Baron-Cohen

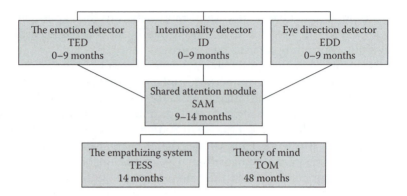

FIGURE 9.1 Early achievements leading to the initial establishment of a working theory of mind in young children. (Adapted from Simon Baron-Cohen, 1995.)

(1995) summarizes the early achievements leading to the initial establishment of a working theory of mind in young children.

In early infancy, Baron-Cohen's model proposes the emotion detector (i.e., discrimination of basic emotions), the intentionality detector (i.e., basic understanding that actions have goals), and an eye direction detector (i.e., understanding that things with eyes can see). At 9 months, these skills are coordinated and feed into a shared attention mechanism that allows for organized joint attention between the child and another. At 14 months, the empathizing system keys into detecting emotional states and allows for appropriate empathetic reactions to another's emotional state. And, finally, the TOM mechanism, as discussed earlier, is proposed to be evident at 4 years of age.

However, recent research that has examined how and when children make use of eye gaze to interpret behavior suggests a later timetable for the emergence of a mature theory of mind. Pellicano & Rhodes (2003) found that eye gaze did not enhance 3- and 4-year-olds performance of false-belief tasks. However, it appears that 5-year-olds are beginning to make use of such nonverbal cues. For example, Freire, Eskritt, and Lee (2004) found that in a deceptive task, 5-year-olds, but not 3-year-olds, were able to use eye gaze cues to infer intentions, despite contradictory verbal cues. The authors conclude "the detection of deception from such cues may emerge beyond the preschool years and develop well into adolescence" (Freire, Eskritt, & Lee, 2004).

Attention to nonverbal facial cues like smiling in game situations that could involve deception has been shown in previous research to develop well after age four. To investigate how well children could use expressive cues to detect ongoing deception in others, LaFreniere (1998) modified an experimental task previously used by Schultz and Cloghesy (1981) to explore children's recursive awareness of intentionality. In the original task, a card game was designed such that one player, after noting the color of the top card of the deck (lying face down) pointed to a red or black card (lying face up) as a cue to the other player, whose task it was to guess the color of the top card. The card game was modified so that the truthfulness of the cue was contingent on the facial expression of the experimenter providing the cue. For example, every time I sent a false signal I smiled slightly. Thus, the "contingency detection task" involves the detection of an expressive cue (smile) that is contingent upon the truthfulness of a social signal (pointing to a red or black card). Children from 4 to 8 years were instructed "to try to guess the color of the next card. I'm going to look at it first and then point to a red or black card to give you a hint about what color it might be. But be careful, because I might try to fool you sometimes." Children were tested in two age groups (preschoolers, first graders) under two conditions (smile = true, smile = false).

Preschoolers were rarely successful in solving the contingency detection task, with only 8% scoring significantly above chance levels across the 15 trials. Older children solved the contingency more often, with 50% scoring above chance. There was also a significant effect of condition in the older group. Three out of four of the older children solved the contingency task when the experimenter smiled while presenting a false cue (LaFreniere, 1998). In their own words they knew when the experimenter was trying to fool them because of the "sneaky grin" on his face. However, only one of four was able to solve the task when the experimenter smiled while being truthful and kept a poker face while presenting a false cue. Although they have learned to associate the smile with attempts at deception, their "mindreading" skills need additional tuning before they should sit in on high stakes poker games!

In a follow-up study testing children from ages four to eight, older children again demonstrated a greater ability to inhibit their nonverbal signals, use an irregular strategy when attempting to trick a partner, and use false or misleading nonverbal cues than younger children, all of which led to more success in the game (R. Smith & LaFreniere, 2008). These developments after age four in children's understanding and ability to manipulate their own nonverbal cues in order to influence the behavior of a partner are based upon their understanding of recursive awareness of intentionality. Successful manipulation of their own behavior demonstrates that they are not only aware of what cues their partner is using to detect intentions but that they also have developed the ability to inhibit true signals and fabricate convincing false ones. Together with previous research, these results demonstrate that the skills required to successfully complete these tasks are not present in the average preschooler but show significant development from six to eight years of age.

☐ Vocal Communication and Language

In both an ontogenetic and phylogenetic sense, language and thought are best viewed as reciprocally determined. Although human thought may be highly dependent on language, it is also clear that there are a number of critical prerequisites for human speech, in terms of both vocal and cognitive capacities. These foundational abilities must be supported by evolved brain mechanisms, which are in turn encoded in the DNA/RNA that serve as recipes for the various kinds of proteins that ultimately structure the organism. Because humans share over 98% of their mitochondrial DNA with chimpanzees, in this section we shall focus our attention on a direct comparison of the cognitive and communicative competencies of humans and chimpanzees with the goal of identifying the unique features of human communication systems.

Ethologists have long assumed that closely related species share more similar patterns of behavior than more distantly related species, embodying Darwin's vision of a gradual, stepwise progression in the evolution of various characteristics. But when we consider the special case of human language, and the culture and technology that it made possible, a sharp discontinuity between human and ape appears evident. Of course the apparent discontinuity between existing species of nonhuman primates and humans could still be consistent with a gradualist vision of the evolution of the hominid line in which many separate and closely related species once existed, but are now extinct. One can both overstate and understate the similarities between ourselves and our nearest genetic relatives, and a balanced perspective must be grounded in a variety of relevant disciplines. A seemingly simple question regarding human-ape differences is like tossing a stone into a quiet pond producing expanding ripples encompassing an ever widening knowledge base.

Vocal Communication in Nonhuman Primates

Nonhuman primates vocalize in a wide range of contexts, though in general, much of this vocalization is devoted to social interaction. However, the great apes, including gorillas, chimpanzees, and bonobos vocalize less frequently than many species of New World monkeys, and the social function of their vocal communications appears to be less developed (Snowden, 2004). It may be that visual signal systems evolved more readily in these terrestrial primates, while aboreal primates were more likely to favor vocal signals.

Natural selection has shaped a primate vocal tract that is capable of producing a broad range of acoustic variation (Hauser, 1996). For example, Amazonian monkeys like the pygmy marmoset have a vocal repertoire of at least 25 sounds, and the cotton-top tamarins use at least 35 different calls or call combinations (Snowden, 2004). Call variants are used in specific contexts such as mobbing, mild and severe alarm, approaching an attractive food source, eating it, encountering a strange group, etc. Speech perception is also well developed and many species of nonhuman primates can discriminate human speech sounds using the same categories as humans—a compelling argument that this perceptual ability has a long evolutionary history (Kluender, 1994). From the standpoint of both speech production and perception it would seem that many of the biological building blocks for human language exist in nonhuman primates, and yet nothing approaching the power and efficiency of human language exists in the animal world. This is especially true when we compare the vocalizations of wild chimpanzees and humans. But if chimpanzees were provided an optimal language learning environment by human caretakers, could they begin to bridge this gap?

Ape Language Research

Perhaps the strongest claims in favor of the gradualist view of the evolution of language come from animal language researchers. Although efforts have been made to train other apes in sign language, the chimpanzee has proved to be the species of choice for most systematic efforts at language training. Because of the fundamental differences in the vocal tracts of chimpanzees and humans, the Gardners decided to attempt to teach a 1-year-old female chimpanzee, Washoe, to communicate with humans using the hand gestures of American Sign Language (Gardner & Gardner, 1969). Washoe learned to make about 85 different signs, which she used to indicate things that she wanted. She occasionally combined these signs into simple strings, but fundamental questions and much skepticism remained as to just what these achievements signified. Most scientists concluded that there was no evidence that Washoe understood what these "words" meant or that anything beyond conditioning was involved in the learning process.

A somewhat different orientation was later used by Duane Rumbaugh (1977) involving the use of geometric symbols or lexigrams to train another female chimpanzee, Lana. From the beginning, researchers sought to train Lana to produce grammatically correct lexigram strings, analogous to the syntax a child uses in learning to speak in sentences. Once again, critics portrayed Lana's linguistic achievements as learned chain associations, rather than a communication system involving syntax. Nevertheless, the

Rumbaughs defended a number of important findings produced in the Lana Project:

> First, it showed that computerized keyboards facilitated research on apes' language learning skills … Second, the Lana Project showed that Lana was capable of learning and using numerous lexigrams. Third, it provided evidence that Lana was innovative in her communicative statements and requests, despite never having been trained to demonstrate such innovation … one of the most practical benefits of this research was a conversation board that proved to be fully functional and useful in promoting cross-species communication. (Rumbaugh, Beran, & Savage-Rumbaugh, 2004, pp. 404–405)

Moreover, Lana demonstrated long-term memory of the lexigram names for objects. More than 20 years after her training ceased, Lana was able to correctly identify a majority of the items on the first trial.

Lexigrams proved to be an excellent medium of communication as ape language research continued. In the 1980s, Savage-Rumbaugh (1986) used techniques of associative learning to train a pair of male chimpanzees, Sherman and Austin. She also introduced a new technique that emphasized the communicative aspect of symbols. As a result, Sherman and Austin began to use symbols to communicate information about objects that were not present and to indicate what they intended to do before they did it. Moreover, Sherman and Austin learned to correctly categorize familiar lexigrams into categories such as "food" or "tool" and remarkably demonstrated the ability to correctly categorize novel items and lexigrams into these same categories.

The next superstar to emerge in the Rumbaugh's ape language lab surpassed all previous achievements. Serendipity apparently played a role. Sue Savage-Rumbaugh began lexigram training with a mature female bonobo, Matata, who had a young son, Kanzi. Although the adult showed little aptitude for the lexigram board, her young son began to show remarkable abilities without formal training, and by two and a half years demonstrated an understanding of human speech and then lexigrams. Rather than formal training involving associative learning, Kanzi participated in daily routines with his human caretakers and experienced language in his environment in much the same way that human children do and was learning new words at a higher rate than common chimpanzees. Because his human caretakers not only spoke aloud, but also used a visual keyboard, Kanzi grew up participating in conversations about past, present, and future events and was soon announcing his own actions and intentions. The Rumbaughs concluded that Kanzi spontaneously used his keyboard to refer to things that were not present using sentences that possessed a primitive grammar and were not simply imitations of the human caretakers.

Using this technique of observational learning through immersion in a linguistic environment at a young age, the Rumbaughs began another study that involved the corearing of a female chimpanzee (Panzee) and a female bonobo (Panbisha) from their first weeks of life. Both apes came to demonstrate abilities similar to Kanzi, including the comprehension of human speech. The Rumbaughs concluded that although there may be slight differences in language ability favoring the bonobo, understanding symbols and speech in both apes was facilitated by a logically structured, language-rich environment.

The tradition of ape language research has systematically demonstrated that chimpanzees possess some of the capacities for language acquisition that were once considered unique in humans. In particular, research by the Rumbaughs provide a glimpse into the zone of proximal development by showing what chimpanzees can accomplish, not in the wild, but in the context of an educational milieu designed by human language specialists. Based on this approach the Rumbaughs assert that chimpanzees can achieve one of the keys to human language, the ability to make internal, symbolic representations, and to use these symbols to communicate information and to comprehend and respond to similar communications from their human caretakers (Rumbaugh, Beran, & Savage-Rumbaugh, 2004).

Comparative research makes equally clear that significant gaps remain between human and ape cognitive and linguistic abilities. First, speech production is severely limited in apes, which possess limited control of voluntary vocalizations. Second, key cognitive abilities that support the learning of more elaborate usages of language are either severely limited or completely absent. For example, though chimpanzees and many other species of nonhuman primates possess a basic capacity to follow the gaze direction of others, they seem to lack the visual perspective-taking skills of 3-year-old children and cannot comprehend the referential intent of pointing (Bering & Povinelli, 2003). Other studies have shown that chimpanzees do not have the capacity to represent the mental states of others, including beliefs, desires, and intentions, that we observe in 4-year-old children (Call & Tomasello, 2008). In general chimpanzees lack the human capacity for abstract causal reasoning, or the ability to posit unobservable constructs to explain observable events, which is central to a mature theory of mind.

From Animal Signals to Human Symbols

Despite the best efforts of scientists of many stripes, including linguists, biologists, and psychologists, over the past half century, no convincing account of the evolution of human language has yet emerged. This is not to say that such a theory is not in the process of being constructed. The story begins with an account of the defining features of language.

Unlike animal signals, human language derives its power and unique complexity from the fact that it is symbolic. Symbols allow humans, and only humans, to represent past, present, future, and even hypothetical events, as well as abstract concepts, principles, logic, and other essential ingredients of modern civilization. Language is intentional and implies elaborate cognitive foundations related to reasoning about hidden internal states such as emotions, desires, and beliefs. The conscious control of this symbol system relies upon the foundation of contextual freedom, whereby the pairing of sound and meaning is decoupled from the one-to-one correspondence we observe in fixed animal signals (Oller, 2004). In humans, the use of arbitrary and discrete sounds, known as phonemes, permit an almost infinite number of combinations and permutations of sound-meaning pairings. For example, the lexicon of the average college student is about 60,000 words, with comprehension of more than 100,000 words. Generativity implies that these sounds can be combined in grammatical utterances (sentences) to produce an endless number of communications about all sorts of things. This is made possible by syntax or the rule system a given language uses to construct these speech utterances. Without syntax, comprehension would drop precipitously.

How speech evolved in humans and the related question of why it did not evolve in the chimpanzee, or other nonhuman primates, remains a puzzle, though many ingenious hypotheses have been put forward over the years. But as linguists are fond of saying "language leaves no fossils." Indeed, to the extent that any new theory of language evolution is untestable and thus cannot be disconfirmed, we will simply accumulate more and more theories. Currently we have theories that posit that language evolved in humans as an incidental by-product of our big brains, or as a response to increases in group size and the need for vocal grooming, or to plan future coordinated events, or to engage in courtship and sexual display, or to engage in cooperative breeding, or to gossip. Other theorists view language as evolving from gestures and nonverbal communication, or from our ability to represent space, or from motor neurons designed to control muscle movement. We also have the aquatic ape hypothesis and as I write this sentence someone, somewhere is publishing a new theory on language evolution. While these creative explanations all have some merit, I believe that a compelling, empirically supported theory of how human language evolved is still a long way off. Future theories may be grounded in the steadily growing knowledge base in comparative neuroanatomy, neuroscience, and molecular genetics, though this will still be difficult because there is no likely one-to-one correspondence between genes and specific areas of the brain, nor between specific areas of the brain and complex cognitive functioning (Marcus, 2004).

Comparative analyses are promising if they reveal unique features of human anatomy that are clearly involved in speech production and perception and absent in our closest relatives. Several anatomically based explanations have been advanced, including the idea of a restricted range of vocalizations due to the position of the larynx in chimpanzees, which is much higher than in adult humans (Lieberman, 1975), or the absence of neural architecture in the chimpanzee brain that supports the cognitive control of vocalizations necessary to produce the richly elaborated intentional sounds of human speech (Jurgens, 1995). Hopefully future progress in cognitive neuroscience will delineate the precise nature of the neuroanatomical differences that may underlie the different levels of language ability in apes and humans.

Comparative analyses that do not imply descent from a common ancestor may also be fruitful sources of hypotheses regarding the ecological conditions that may have favored some foundational capacity for vocal communication found in human speech. This approach seems all the more useful given the relative paucity of vocal signals in the great apes relative to other animals, including some birds, monkeys, and marine mammals. For example, assuming that arboreal species of monkeys may rely more on vocalizations to communicate than terrestrial apes, one might look to cooperatively breeding arboreal monkeys for clues about environmental forces driving the evolution of human language. This type of comparative analysis seeks to understand *convergent evolution*, the process by which unrelated species have evolved similar adaptations (e.g., flight in dinosaurs, birds, bats, and insects) because of similar environmental demands. Such analyses cannot tell us how humans evolved language, but they may provide clues about the relevant ecological conditions that favor the evolution of vocal communication in general.

Another promising line of empirical research is the investigation of infant speech and language development from birth through childhood. Without assuming that "ontogeny recapitulates phylogeny," there is often a necessary and common logic to the progressive steps that need to be taken in both development and evolution from the most simple "protowords" to complex language with fully developed grammar and syntax. We will refer to this common logic as epigenetic logic (Sinha, 2004). Epigenetic logic may be involved in determining the process that governs the emergence of symbols from the more rudimentary "fixed" signals. According to Sinha, the following sequence may be common to both the development and evolution of language:

Intentionality, intersubjectivity, and reference
Conventionalization based on intersubjectivity
Structural elaboration yielding flexible construal

Each of the above processes of symbolic communication may be contrasted with its counterpart in signal-based communication. "Intentionality contrasts with stimulus dependence, conventionalization contrasts with (though perhaps emerges from) simple social coordination, and structural elaboration contrasts with code rigidity" (Sinha, 2004, p. 232). In Sinha's view, the social ecology of infancy may have played a crucial role in the evolution of human symbolic capacity. In this view, emergent hominid capacities for speech production were not appended to the endpoint of the nonhuman primate pathway, but woven into the human developmental pathway from birth forward.

Detailed longitudinal studies describing the universal features of infant language development support this idea and provide a useful check on creative speculation, guiding scientists toward plausible theories of how language could have evolved in progressive steps from earlier precursors. As a result of extensive research, the broad outline of vocal development in humans has become increasingly clear (Oller, 2000). With the achievement of well-formed syllables by 5 months of age, human infants surpass the vocal capabilities of all other nonhuman primates at any age (Hauser, 1996; Seyfarth & Cheney, 1997). Developmental research outlining the steps prior to this stage of "canonical babbling" suggests that the hominid departure from the great apes may have begun with an increased capacity for flexible vocalization that allowed for a decoupling of signal from function, and proceeded later to the uniquely human capacity of syllable production, the unique and essential foundation of human speech (Oller & Griebel, 2005). This research vindicates Chomsky's prescient view that humans possess some sort of evolved language module that distinguish them from the apes, without presupposing that this evolutionary step occurred by some massive biological leap forward (Chomsky, 1968, 1986), a view at odds with how we know evolution proceeds. Rather than vague leaps based on major mutations that magically created preformed structures that served radically new functions, evolution probably proceeded more in the manner of a tinkerer. From this perspective, the recombination of bits and pieces of old elements in new combinations eventually led to dramatically new functions—a view of progressive change that is consistent with the results of modern genetics and with what we observe in anatomical evolution in the fossil record, in developmental research, and in cultural evolution. For example, in cultural evolution, more and more complex looms were invented for weaving fabrics in the textile industry that, in turn, provided binary card-punching that led directly to the invention of the first computers. It just took a bit of creative tinkering.

☐ Chapter Summary

In this chapter we explored potential discontinuities between animal and human cognition that stem from the unique features of the human brain. We began our discussion with a review of research on chimpanzee and human understanding of internal states called theory of mind (TOM). A *theory* of mind refers to an abstract causal system that allows one to explain and predict behavior through reference to unobservable mental states such as beliefs, intentions, desires, and emotions. Research on TOM originated in experimental work on chimpanzee social intelligence. These experiments appeared to demonstrate that chimps were capable of clever deceptions that seemed to rely upon an understanding of the desires, emotions, and intentions of their human trainers. Subsequent research shows that chimpanzees may lack the human capacity for abstract causal reasoning or the ability to posit unobservable constructs to explain observable events. Chimpanzees make fewer attributions about complex mental states than humans since they cannot attribute states of mind that they themselves do not possess. Current evidence suggests that apes make simple attributions of seeing, wanting, and expecting, rather than attributions about beliefs.

Models of *belief–desire psychology* propose a two-step sequence of human development that begins with a simple desire psychology. At this stage, young children can explain and predict action and emotional expressions based on desires. The next major step forward in children's thinking about the mind permits reflection on the representational process and the understanding that a belief is a representation of reality, not reality itself. Unlike a desire, a belief can be true or false, and the external world can be represented accurately or inaccurately. Four-year-old children, but not chimpanzees, generally pass *false-belief tasks*, confirming their understanding that another person can hold beliefs that are different from their own; beliefs that could be incorrect, but which nevertheless determine their behavior.

Researchers have also been active in exploring how children come to learn that things are not always what they seem to be. These researchers employ *appearance-reality tasks* that require children to demonstrate their understanding that appearances can sometimes be misleading and not an accurate representation of reality. Like the false belief tasks, the appearance-reality distinction requires meta-representational skills or the ability to represent representations. This distinction is mostly absent in 3-year-olds and still quite fragile for children between 4 and 6 years of age. Six-year-olds may have considerable difficulty deciding whether any given expression is real or apparent, but they understand the distinction and realize that they need not coincide.

Research on tactical deception demonstrate that early forms of deception enacted by preschoolers younger than 4 years are unsophisticated and consist of attempts to withhold information by not confessing to transgressions or by removing incriminating evidence. Most studies have shown that more sophisticated forms of deception that rely upon a more mature theory of mind do not emerge until after 4 years. Research examining how and when children make use of eye gaze to interpret behavior also suggests a later timetable for the emergence of a mature theory of mind. Five-year-olds, but not three-year-olds, were able to use eye gaze cues to infer true intentions, when faced with contradictory verbal cues. Attention to nonverbal facial cues like smiling in game situations that could involve deception has also been shown to develop well after age four. The development after age four in children's understanding and ability to manipulate their own nonverbal cues in order to influence the behavior of a partner is based upon their understanding of recursive awareness of intentionality. Successful manipulation demonstrates that they are not only aware of what cues their partner is likely to use to detect intentions but that they also have developed the ability to inhibit true signals and fabricate convincing false ones.

As with TOM, language implies a number of evolutionary and developmental prerequisites, both in terms of vocal and cognitive capacities. These foundational abilities must be supported by evolved brain mechanisms, hence our attention to the cognitive and communicative competencies of primates, especially chimpanzees.

Nonhuman primates vocalize in a wide range of contexts, especially during social interaction. However, the great apes vocalize less frequently than New World monkeys, and the social function of their vocal communications appears to be less developed. Speech perception is well developed and primates can discriminate human speech sounds using the same categories as humans—a compelling argument that this perceptual ability has a long evolutionary history.

Research involving the use of geometric symbols or lexigrams shows that chimpanzees are capable of learning and using numerous lexigrams, they can be innovative in their communicative statements and they possess long-term memory of the lexigram names for objects. Chimps have also been shown to use symbols to communicate information about objects that were not present and to indicate what they intended to do before they did it. The Rumbaughs assert that chimpanzees can achieve one of the keys to human language, the ability to make internal, symbolic representations, and to use these symbols to communicate information and to comprehend and respond to similar communications from their human caretakers.

Comparative research makes equally clear that significant gaps remain between human and ape cognitive and linguistic abilities. First, speech production is severely limited in apes, which possess limited control of voluntary vocalizations. Second, key cognitive abilities that support the learning of more elaborate usages of language are either severely limited or completely absent. For example, though chimpanzees and many other species of nonhuman primates possess a basic capacity to follow the gaze direction of others, they seem to lack the visual perspective-taking skills of 3-year-old children and cannot comprehend the referential intent of pointing.

Unlike animal signals, human language derives its power and unique complexity from the fact that it is symbolic. Symbols allow humans to represent past, present, future, and even hypothetical events, as well as abstract concepts, principles, logic, and other essential ingredients of modern civilization.

Comparative analyses are promising if they reveal unique features of human anatomy that are clearly involved in speech production and perception and absent in our closest relatives. Several anatomically based explanations have been advanced, including the idea of a restricted range of vocalizations due to the position of the larynx in chimpanzees, which is much higher than in adult humans or the absence of neural architecture in the chimpanzee brain that supports the cognitive control of vocalizations necessary to produce the richly elaborated intentional sounds of human speech.

Another promising line of empirical research is the investigation of infant speech and language development from birth through childhood. With the achievement of well-formed syllables by 5 months of age, human infants surpass the vocal capabilities of all other nonhuman primates at any age. Developmental research outlining the steps prior to this stage of "canonical babbling" suggests that the hominid departure from the great apes may have begun with an increased capacity for flexible vocalization that allowed for a decoupling of signal from function, and proceeded later to the uniquely human capacity of syllable production, the unique and essential foundation of human speech.

☐ For Further Inquiry

Baron-Cohen, S. (2005). The empathizing system: A revision of the 1994 model of the mindreading system. In B. J. Ellis & D. F. Bjorklund (Eds.) *Origins of the social mind: Evolutionary psychology and child development* (pp. 468–492). New York, NY: Guilford Press.

Call, J., & Tomasello, M. (2008). Does the chimpanzee have a theory of mind? 30 years later. *Trends in Cognitive Science, 12,* 187–192.

Oller, D. K., & Griebel, U. (2008). *Evolution of communicative flexibility*. Cambridge, MA: MIT Press.

Povinelli, D. J. (2000). *Folk physics for apes: The chimpanzee's theory of how the world works*. New York, NY: Oxford University Press.

Premack, D. (1988). Does the chimpanzee have a theory of mind? Revisited in R. W. Byrne & A. Whiten (Eds.), *Machiavellian intelligence: Social expertise and the evolution of intelligence in monkeys, apes, and humans*. Oxford, UK: Oxford University Press.

Reading the mind in the eyes test: http://www.glennrowe.net/BaronCohen/Faces/EyesTest.aspx

Sex Differences

Evolutionary psychologists view pan-cultural gender differences in behavior and personality systems as evolved affective-motivational systems that represent alternative strategies for attaining the evolutionary goals of survival and reproduction. Two essential theoretical concepts provide the starting point for an evolutionary theory of sexual dimorphism: sexual selection and parental investment theory.

☐ Sexual Selection and Parental Investment Theory

Sexual selection was defined by Darwin in *The Descent of Man and Selection in Relation to Sex* (1871, p. 256) as a specific form of natural selection that arises "from the advantage that certain individuals have over other individuals of the same sex and species, in exclusive relation to reproduction." Darwin identified two basic types of sexual selection: (1) *intrasexual competition*, the process of competing for mates and (2) *intersexual selection*, the process of choosing mates. A century later an important theoretical contribution was made by Trivers (1972) based on Williams's (1966) recognition that there were widespread consequences of the differential investment made by each sex in reproduction. Trivers's *parental investment theory* is based on the observation that there is typically a difference in the degree of parental investment in offspring favoring females that results in a marked asymmetry in sex roles. Mating competition would be expected to be greater in the lower-investing sex, while mate choice would be expected to be greater in the higher-investing sex. The logic here is simple: if one sex provides a much greater parental investment they become an important reproductive resource for which the other sex will compete. Thus, almost all examples of sexual selection involve either male-male competition or female choice. Because these forces are thought to account for much of the observable sexual dimorphism across a wide variety of species, let us examine each of them in more detail.

Male–Male Competition

The particular dynamics of sexual selection for any given species are shaped by the reproductive efforts of the two sexes constrained by the physical and social ecology. *Reproductive effort* involves three different costs: (1) *mating* (including competing for mates); (2) *parenting* (including feeding, care, and protecting offspring); and (3) in some species, such as humans, *nepotism* (helping relatives to survive and reproduce more successfully). Because mammals are characterized by internal gestation and a high degree of postnatal maternal care, parental investment of females greatly exceeds that of males. Indeed, females in 95% of mammals provide all of the parental care (Clutton-Brock, 1991). Some of the few exceptions occur in different species of carnivores and primates, where males provide some paternal care for the offspring of the group. Because of these stark asymmetries in parental effort, the reproductive success of males can often be greatly enhanced by mating effort, chiefly by competing with other males for females. Besides direct competition, this type of mating effort is also reflected in the male's striving for status, political power, resources, or territories, again depending on the social and physical ecology of the species. These basic differences in parental investment in mammals lead to the widespread observation of greater size, physical strength, and higher levels of aggression in males than females.

Female Choice

If males are often actively competing with other males for females, females play an active role in the mating game by selecting males for mates, although it is often difficult to determine what male characteristics form the basis for female choice. In theory, an arbitrary female preference for any genetically linked male trait could result in selection for that trait. Fieldwork and experimental studies tend to support a "good genes" model for the sexual selection of secondary sexual characteristics in males that are honest signals of genetic and phenotypic quality. For example, a currently influential model of female choice in bird species views the bright plumage of males as an honest signal of health because it signifies that the bird is free of parasite infestation (Hamilton & Zuk, 1982). In other bird species, female choice is related to factors such as the male's willingness and ability to provide resources (Geary, 1998). Whatever trait is used, males who possess it will be more likely to pass their genes on to the next generation than males who do not, insuring that the trait will increase in frequency with each passing generation.

Sexual Dimorphism

In most species the effects of male-male competition (e.g., the male lion's greater size and strength) and female choice (e.g., the peacock's gaudy tail) readily account for the observed physical differences between the sexes or sexual dimorphism. Of the two types, the female type is usually more directly suited to the physical characteristics of the species' habitat. For example, the smaller size and weight of the adult lioness is ideally suited to the demands of cooperatively hunting the fleet gazelle on the open African savannah. Similarly, the peahen with her small tail and cryptic coloration is better suited to survival from predators than the peacock. These "less adaptive" features of the male are maintained in the population via sexual selection.

Of course, sexual selection produces a myriad of more subtle differences between the sexes as well. Besides the spectacular physical differences just noted, other sex differences may be found in the brain, endocrine system, physiology, emotion, cognition, personality, and behavior. Ethologists report different patterns of sex differences in different species, but the pattern of sex differences is by no means arbitrary. Ultimately, these differences between the sexes serve adaptive functions and are directly related to species-typical reproductive strategies and parental division of labor. Neurological, cognitive, affective, and behavioral propensities of the two sexes begin to develop during prenatal development due to the organizing influence of gonadal hormones. The fate of these divergences depends on further environmental support and the later activating influence of sex hormones at puberty before the mature adult behaviors and physical characteristics emerge (Daly & Wilson, 1978; Geary, 1998). As always, these complex systems evolve somewhat differently in different species depending on their ecology.

As a large group of species, primates vary considerably in their social and physical ecologies, reproductive strategies, and degree of sexual dimorphism. Even within a species, subspecies may differ as a function of regional ecological constraints and opportunities (Kummer, 1971). For example, Kummer reports that some subspecies of hamadryas baboons living in arid conditions with few resources are monogamous, while others living nearby in more fertile ecologies are polygynous. In hamadryas baboons, monogamy appears to have evolved to increase the chances of offspring survival under harsh conditions where two providers would be more successful than one. In general the life histories of females and males in any given species are quite different. With these points in mind, let us examine typical sex differences in one species that has received much scientific attention, rhesus monkeys.

☐ Sex Differences in Primates: Rhesus Macaques

Like humans, sex differences among rhesus monkeys are typically relative rather than absolute, with some overlap between the sexes. For example, compared to male peers, young females spend considerably more time in the presence of adult females, and at sexual maturity they remain with their mothers, sisters, aunts, and daughters for the rest of their lives. Female rhesus monkeys show considerably more interest in young infants and engage in alloparenting or play parenting throughout their juvenile years much more than males (Geary, 1998; Pryce, 1995). The functional significance of this type of play is apparent in primates, as research in five species shows that the chances of survival of the monkey's firstborn offspring is two to four times higher for mothers with previous experience in caring for infants (Pryce, 1993). Finally, daughters are socialized differently by their mothers. For example, female rhesus monkeys hold their daughters closer and show more concern if they should wander, compared to male offspring (Lindburg, 1971; Mitchell & Brandt, 1970).

In contrast, rhesus mothers will more often direct displays of anger toward a male offspring, and males are weaned at an earlier age. Young male rhesus monkeys spend more time in the company of peers, often without the mother close by, and engage in high-energy games of chasing and play fighting, and leave their natal troop at sexual maturity (Drickamer & Vessey, 1973). From an evolutionary standpoint, these aggressive displays are costly, since they involve a high expenditure of energy and risk of injury. Although females do not shun this rough and tumble play entirely, they participate rarely and with less energy. As adults, male rhesus monkeys engage in more aggression than females, who generally avoid aggression and direct competition (de Waal, 1996).

Based on a wide array of experimental evidence, rough-and-tumble play is influenced by hormones, social rearing, and contextual factors (Panksepp, Siviy, & Normansell, 1984). The clearest evidence for direct influence of sex hormones on behavior may be found in experimental research on sex differences in play in rhesus macaques. Prenatal exposure to higher levels of androgen in females is related to increased physical competition and high-energy physical play, regardless of social and contextual factors. (Geary, 1998; Wallen, 1996).

Monkey infants of both sexes begin to prefer the company of same-sex peers at an early age, and among juveniles, sex segregation is the rule (Rosenblum, Coe, & Bromley, 1975). While differential socialization of male and female monkeys certainly supports the divergence in behaviors between the sexes, longitudinal research of isolated rhesus monkeys also demonstrates sex differences in behavior that cannot be attributed to socialization (Harlow & Harlow, 1966; Sackett, 1966).

☐ Sex Differences in Children

If sex differences in behavior, reproductive strategy, and life history are pervasive in nonhuman primates, does that imply that human sex differences may also be found? To begin our discussion of human sex differences we first examine the nature of social play in childhood.

Play and Social Behavior

Play is so common in mammals that questions regarding the function of this high-energy activity must be addressed. Ethologists generally regard play as providing delayed benefits to the individual because adult skills critical to survival and reproduction are practiced. In our discussion of play as practice we focus on two types of play in which sex differences are widely observed in primates, including humans: alloparenting and rough-and-tumble play (Fagen, 1981, 1995).

First, experimental research reveals a direct causal influence of sex hormones on differences in both types of play between boys and girls in early childhood. Prenatal exposure to higher levels of androgen in girls is related to increased physical competition and rough play and decreased interest in infants and doll play regardless of other social and contextual factors (Collaer & Hines, 1995). As previously discussed, these same differences are found in many different species of nonhuman primates, confirming hypotheses derived from parental investment theory.

Second, a general pattern of results in both preindustrial and industrial societies also demonstrates consistent sex differences in rough-and-tumble play favoring boys and alloparenting favoring girls. For example, in an American sample of preschoolers, DiPietro (1981) found that boys engaged in rough-and-tumble play involving playful pushing, shoving, hitting, tripping, wrestling, etc., four to five times as often as girls. Cross-cultural research indicates that although the magnitude of these sex differences varies across cultures, the direction of the differences is constant (Eibl-Eibesfeldt, 1989; Maccoby, 1988; Whiting & Edwards, 1988). For example, Whiting and Edwards (1988) studied social development in Guatemala, India, Japan, Kenya, Liberia, Mexico, Peru, the Philippines, and the United States. They concluded that two sex differences were common across these diverse cultures: girls were found to be more nurturing than boys, and boys engaged in more dominance behavior than girls. More recently, a multinational study involving 10 cultures (Austria, Brazil, Canada, Chinese, France, Italy, Japan, Russia, Spain, and the United States) using the same methodology of teacher ratings found universal sex differences in empathy and social competence favoring girls and physical aggression and dominance favoring boys (LaFreniere et al., 2002).

In a cross-cultural analysis of children's social behavior in 93 societies, Low (1989) found that sex-differentiated patterns of child-rearing were systematically related to various dimensions of the social ecology in ways predictable from evolutionary theory. In polygynous nonstratified societies in which men can elevate their social status and achieve higher reproductive success by marrying more women, boys are socialized to be industrious, competitive, and aggressive. In these societies the larger the maximum number of wives, the more boys were socialized to be competitive. These results were not found in monogamous, stratified societies in which men's social status and reproductive success could not be advanced by competitive and aggressive behaviors, although socialization for industriousness was still evident.

Similarly, socialization for girls in societies where women could inherit wealth and hold political office tended to emphasize more aggressive behavior and achievement in girls, than in those societies in which men had near total control of economic and political power (Low, 1989). In cultures that exhibit relatively harsh parenting practices (as opposed to warm parenting styles), children are generally more competitive and aggressive, but relative differences between the sexes remain consistent with the universal pattern (MacDonald, 1992). In a multinational study of preschoolers' social behavior in 10 countries, girls were found to be consistently less aggressive than boys in each country studied, but relative levels of aggression were higher in countries with fewer resources and harsher socialization practices (LaFreniere et al., 2002). In summary, cross-cultural research demonstrates that parenting styles can influence childhood behavior in ways that align such behavior with the demands of a particular social ecology. At the same time, cross-cultural research consistently demonstrates universals in sex roles. In general, biological and cultural factors collaborate to produce adaptive behavior within any particular ecology.

Peer Socialization of Sex Differences

Many developmental psychologists believe that in addition to hormones, socialization factors are also a likely source for some of the many differences in behavior between girls and boys. We next examine peers as an important socialization agent throughout childhood and adolescence. The details of the behavioral ecologies of boys and girls are important to understand because of the role that peers play with respect to gender identity and sex roles.

Universally, children begin to sort themselves into sex-segregated enclaves beginning at about 3 years, which also marks the emergence of *gender identity*, or the recognition by the child of his or her own gender as an enduring quality of the self. *Prior* to establishing sex-segregated play groups, girls and boys begin to develop sex differences in toy preferences. Toddlers show distinct sex differences in toy choices before they have established a stable gender identity or can accurately label toys as "boy things" or "girl things" (Blakemore, LaRue, & Olejnik, 1979; Fagot, Leinbach, & Hagan, 1986). As early as 14 months girls are selecting dolls and soft toys while boys are choosing trucks and cars (Caldera, Huston, & O'Brien, 1989; Smith & Dalgliesh, 1977). Such differences between boys' and girls' toy preferences are thought by many to arise from socialization. However, Alexander and Hines (2002) have shown that vervet monkeys display sex differences in toy preferences similar to those in children. Contact time with toys typically preferred by boys (a car and a ball) was greater in male vervets than in female vervets, whereas the contact time with toys typically preferred by girls (a doll and a pot) was greater in female vervets than in male vervets. Their results suggest that sexually differentiated object preferences arose early in primate evolution and that these evolved object feature preferences may contribute to present-day sexual dimorphism in toy preferences in children.

To the extent that preferences for certain types of toys and activities are distinct between girls and boys, they may begin to associate more often with same-sex peers on the basis of these similarities. One study that addressed the origin of same-sex preferences found that by 2 years of age, girls are already beginning to prefer same sex peers while boys do not show a similar preference until age 3 (LaFreniere, Strayer, & Gauthier, 1984). These data, derived from extensive observations of peer play in 15 different children's groups, may actually reflect avoidance of boys by girls, rather than preference for same-sex peers. This reasoning is based on a wide array of observational and experimental evidence in the nature and quality of play in groups of girls and boys, as well as negative sociometric nominations of boys by girls. Whatever the underlying causes of gender segregation during the preschool years, as same-sex play becomes increasingly evident, a number of differences emerge between the sexes.

According to Hartup (1989), sex differences in social behavior and peer relationships in childhood should not be dismissed lightly, as male and female "cultures" appear to differ in many ways. Researchers have generally found that boys are more physically active, engage in more risk taking and rough-and-tumble play, and exhibit more anger and aggression towards peers than girls (DiPietro, 1981; Eaton & Yu, 1989; Ginsburg & Miller, 1982; Humpreys & Smith, 1987; Maccoby & Jacklin, 1974, 1980; Marcus, Maccoby, Jacklin, & Doehring, 1985; Money & Ehrhardt, 1972; Parke & Slaby, 1983; Strayer & Strayer, 1976). From the point of view of most young girls, these sex-typed behaviors are all good reasons to avoid groups of boys. In addition, boys tend to play in larger groups (Eder & Hallinan, 1978), occupy more space, control more resources (Charlesworth & LaFreniere, 1983), and are more likely to do all of the above away from adult supervision than are girls (Carpenter, Huston, & Holt, 1986). In contrast, girls engage in more dyadic play than boys (Benenson, 1993) and prefer the company of their mostly female preschool teachers more than do boys, although one study found that girl's preference to remain nearer to adults was evident only when boys were present (Greeno, 1989).

In laboratory studies with the adults absent, investigators have consistently found that boys are not very responsive to verbal prohibitions and requests that are directed to them by girls (or by other boys), and boys use these strategies to obtain resources much less than girls in both same- and mixed-sex groups. The picture that emerges from a combination of naturalistic and experimental studies is one of limited but systematic sexual dimorphism in social behavior and emotional expression that is well established by early childhood and increases thereafter. These sex differences in children's social and expressive behavior are apparent if one compares the behavior of girls and boys in mixed-sex groupings (Charlesworth & LaFreniere, 1983; Jacklin & Maccoby, 1978; LaFreniere & Charlesworth, 1987; Powlishta & Maccoby, 1990), or if one compares the behavior of groups of girls with groups of boys (Charlesworth & Dzur, 1987; Jacklin & Maccoby, 1978).

If early sex-segregated play reflects girls' avoidance of boys, by the end of the preschool years preference for same-sex peers is transformed into clear avoidance of crossing the gender divide for both boys and girls. Not only do preschoolers prefer to spend more time in the company of same-sex friends, they also express the belief that their own sex is better than the other (Kuhn, Nash, & Brucken, 1978). This belief is present as soon as gender identity is established and appears to increase throughout childhood (Serbin, Powlishta, & Gulko, 1993). Similarly, segregation between the sexes increases throughout early childhood. By age 4 the ratio of same-sex to opposite-sex peer play has increased to 3:1, and by age 6 it has climbed to more than 10:1 (Maccoby, 1988). The preference for same-sex peers is also reflected in children's affiliations and friendship choices. Several naturalistic studies of preschoolers' stable friendship relations have found that 90% to 95% of "strong associates" or close friendships are formed between same-sex peers (LaFreniere & Charlesworth, 1983; Hinde, Titmus, Easton, & Tamplin, 1985). Similarly, sociometric studies reveal that girls and boys rate members of their own sex as more liked in preschool and kindergarten and show increasing gender bias in their sociometric choices throughout middle childhood (Denham & McKinley, 1993; Hayden-Thomson, Rubin, & Hymel, 1987). As researchers attend to the details of activities of peers, particularly in naturalistic settings with little adult supervision, the types of play and the experiences associated with them appear to differ substantially between girls and boys, and peers themselves may be contributing substantially to the development and maintenance of these differences.

Parental Socialization of Sex Differences

In contrast to the belief held by most college students in the social sciences (and many of their instructors), research does not support the view that sex differences arise in boys and girls mainly because they are treated differently by their parents. In fact, a comprehensive review of 172 studies involving almost 28,000 participants using observational methods, parental reports, and child self-reports indicates almost no sex differences in the ways that parents socialize boys and girls (Lytton & Romney, 1991; Rowe, 1994) in the United States and other Western countries. In their meta-analysis, Lytton and Romney categorized parental socialization into eight areas as shown in Table 10.1.

TABLE 10.1 Gender "Treatment Quotients" by Major Socialization Area for North American Studies

Area	Boys' Mean	Girls' Mean	No. of Studies
Interaction	99.6	100	74
Encouragement of achievement	100.3	100	22
Warmth	99.0	100	63
Encouragement of dependency	98.5	100	16
Restrictiveness	101.2	100	40
Discipline	101.2	100	53
Encouragement of sex-typed activities	106.5	100[a]	30
Clarity/reasoning	99.3	100	13

Source: Data are from Lytton and Romney (1991).
Note: Conversion of standard scores to IQ-type metric assumes a female mean of 100 and a standard deviation of 15.
[a] Difference statistically significant.

The one exception to this generally egalitarian treatment of boys and girls by parents was their encouragement of sex-typed activities, particularly by fathers. This difference stems from paternal behavior toward their sons that indicates discouragement of female sex-typed play with dolls. There was no indication that fathers (or mothers) discouraged masculine sex-typed behavior in their daughters. This apparent double standard in the treatment of girls and boys may reflect broader values in our culture with respect to violations of gender norms. For example, the negative connotation of "sissy" is much stronger than for "tomboy." This double standard is also apparent in the behavior of boys towards other boys. This is so much in evidence in North American society that Maccoby observes "whereas girls are socialized to be nice, boys are socialized not to be girls" (personal communication).

Sex Differences in Personality

Parental investment theory and the rigors of intersexual competition leads to the prediction that males will generally pursue relatively high-risk strategies compared to females and will thus be higher in behaviors typical of *behavioral approach systems* (BAS; dominance/sensation seeking, risk taking, impulsivity, exhibitionism) and lower on *behavioral inhibition systems* (BIS; fear, wariness, caution, safety seeking; as shown in Table 10.2). Based on these predictions ethologists and evolutionary psychologists are interested in studying early gender differentiation in patterns of approach and avoidance behavior.

Developmental research in humans has produced a wealth of evidence that is generally consistent with predictions derived from parental investment theory. Research relevant to the BAS has consistently demonstrated that compared with girls, boys are more physically active from an early age (Eaton & Yu, 1989; Marcus, Maccoby, Jacklin, & Doehring, 1985; Money & Ehrhardt, 1972; Parke & Slaby, 1983), more assertive (Parke & Slaby, 1983), more aggressive, competitive, and dominant with peers (LaFreniere & Charleswood, 1983; LaFreniere, Dumas, Dubeau, & Capuano, 1992; Maccoby & Jacklin, 1974, 1980; Strayer & Strayer, 1976), and more oppositional with adults (LaFreniere et al., 1992). Boys are also more likely to take physical risks (Christophersen, 1989; Ginsburg & Miller, 1982), engage in more rough-and-tumble play (DiPietro, 1981; Humpreys & Smith, 1987), and more high-energy socio-dramatic play involving guns and superheroes (Paley, 1984; see Table 10.2).

In contrast, research on the BIS has shown that preschool girls are more compliant to parents and teachers and rated by them as more socially competent (Cowan & Avants, 1988; LaFreniere et al., 1992; Maccoby, 1988).

TABLE 10.2 Sex Differences in Behavioral Approach System (BAS) vs. Behavioral Inhibition System (BIS)

Compared with girls, boys show more behaviors characteristic of the BAS:
   Physically active
   Assertive
   Aggressive and competitive with peers
   Oppositional with adults
   Physical risk taking
   Rough-and-tumble play
   High-energy sociodramatic play involving guns and superheroes

Compared to boys, girls show more behaviors characteristic of the BIS:
   Compliant to parents and teachers
   Social competency
   Nurturance and empathy
   Responsive towards infants
   Fearful and timid
   Cautious in situations involving risks

Girls rate themselves as more fearful, timid, nurturant, and empathic than boys (Fabes, Eisenberg, & Miller, 1990; Maccoby, 1988), and girls tend to show more interest and are more responsive towards infants than are boys (Blakemore, Berenbaum, & Liben, 2008). Parental ratings indicate that when sex differences are found in fearfulness and timidity, parents rate girls as more fearful than boys (Buss & Plomin, 1975; Maccoby & Jacklin, 1974), and they are more cautious in situations involving risks as noted above. All data derived from indirect sources must be interpreted cautiously and wherever possible validated against direct observation since the gender biases of the raters (parents, teachers, or child) cannot be ruled out. For example, observational data do not show systematic sex differences in empathy and prosocial behavior, and in some situations boys or men are more likely to offer assistance than girls or women, particularly in situations involving significant risk (Eagly & Crowley, 1986; Fabes, Eisenberg, & Miller, 1990).

Many investigators conclude that these sex differences in early childhood are due to a constellation of environmental influences as well as the *organizing* effects of sex hormones during prenatal development. As discussed in Chapter 6, the *activating* effect of sex hormones is not present until the onset of puberty in early adolescence. Throughout childhood the levels of circulating sex hormones do not differ much between the sexes and, as a result, biosocial theories predict fewer biologically based sex differences during this period than after puberty (Geary, 1998).

Puberty and Adolescent Peer Relations

With the onset of puberty, biological, cognitive, and social factors lead to a peak in sexual dimorphism during adolescence. Adolescence is a period of dramatic changes in all aspects of development. With its origins in the latin word *adolescere*, meaning "to grow into adulthood," the period comes to a close with the full transition to adult status. As discussed in Chapter 6, due to the activating effects of hormones, at puberty dramatic changes occur, including growth spurts, the emergence of primary and secondary sex characteristics, and a general increase in sexual dimorphism. Sex differences in the timing, duration, and extent of the pubertal growth spurt follow the primate pattern (Leigh, 1996) and are associated with the relative intensity of physical male-male competition across different primate species (Mitani et al., 1996).

In traditional human societies this transition in males is marked by culturally specific rites of passage. This term was first used by the Belgian anthropologist Arnold van Gennep (1960) who noted that traditional societies practiced a three-part transitional ritual involving (1) an initial isolation phase, (2) a phase of intentional confusion in which the identity of the adolescent is broken down, and (3) a phase of reinstatement in which the adolescent is incorporated into the adult community. These rites of passage signal to the individual and all others in the group that the transition to adult status is completed. Besides this signal value, human ethologists also suggest that puberty rites function to provide instruction in adult sex roles and instill cultural loyalty (Weisfeld, 1997).

Different dynamics originating with the onset of puberty also influence changes in the structure and function of peer relationships. As noted earlier, preschool children begin to prefer and interact with same-sex peers at about 3 years, and this preference grows in magnitude throughout childhood. In preadolescence same sex cliques or close-knit groups of mutual friends who spend a great deal of time interacting together are the norm. The preadolescent clique may be as large as 10 or 12 members, but are typically composed of 5 or 6 same-age, same-sex peers.

In the United States, a junior high school cafeteria is an excellent setting for a participant observer to witness these unisex cliques in action. For example, one clique may be composed of a small group of girls who have lunch together every day, and who interact with each other after school and on weekends, and who would not dream of sitting at the boys' table a few feet away. These boys may all be members of the junior high football team, and spend practically all their free time together, practicing after school, watching sports on TV, hanging out on weekends, and discussing the girls at the table next to them during lunch hour. At this age gender boundaries typically prevail, though interest in members of the opposite sex is clearly evident as some individuals enter the early stages of puberty.

In an ethological study of same-sex peer relations in early adolescence, Savin-Williams (1987) reports findings that extend our discussion of the similarities and differences in the social interaction of same-sex cliques. This study was partially based on classic methods developed by Sherif and colleagues (1961) in their famous Robber's Cave Experiment investigating the social structures and group dynamics in cliques of boys during summer camp. Savin-Williams chose to study eight same-sex cliques of 12- to 16-year-old girls and boys during the course of a 5-week summer camp. It represents a blend of naturalistic and experimental methodologies and provides a counterpoint to the questionnaire studies and self-report methodologies common to most psychological research on adolescence.

Both groups of girls and groups of boys who shared the same cabin over the 5-week period established dominance hierarchies, traded insults, ridiculed low-status members, and competed for resources. However, they did all of these things in qualitatively different ways. For example, boys established highly stable status hierarchies on the day of their arrival at the cabin using very direct and overt strategies of physical dominance and verbal ridicule. In contrast, girls used physical assertion much less often and were more indirectly manipulative in their verbal directives and ridicule. One of the girls who gradually took control of a cabin did so by ostracizing a high-status peer and undermining her through gossip, directing middle-status peers with "suggestions," and subtly ridiculing a low-status peer with "assistance." For example, she would put down a low-status girl by embarrassing her in front of the others: "Dottie, pass Opal a napkin so she can wipe the jelly off her face" (Savin-Williams, 1987, p. 92).

Dominance in boys' cabins was often anything but subtle. Almost 90% of the 1600 recorded instances of dominance behavior in one cabin were overt rather than indirect. Quantitative analyses of all eight cabins reveal that the most overt female cabin (57%) was less overt than the least overt male cabin (67%). Dominance behavior was not only more overt among boys, it was also more frequent occurring 16.25 times per hour, compared to 6.34 times per hour in the female cabins. Boys were often involved in rough play which could occasionally escalate to real fighting. When this happened, strained relations were quickly patched up with assertions that it was all "in fun." Whereas boys ordered, teased, argued, and dominated through physical play, girls gossiped, ostracized, and provided unsolicited advice. In cabins of girls some conflicts were dealt with by giving the other the "silent treatment," which could last for days on end. Status in girls groups was also revealed in terms of the lower-status girl recognizing the higher-status girl by giving compliments, asking favors and advice, and by imitation much more often than in groups of boys (Savin-Williams, 1987).

In general, adolescent girls value intimacy in their relationships. Mutual disclosures, shared secrets, and talk about feelings characterize close friendships among adolescent girls more than boys. Girls often use their friends as a means of managing initially anxiety-arousing experiences, and can be on the phone for hours sorting out the events of the day (Douvan & Adelson, 1966; Hill, 1980). For example, Apter (1990) found that girls turn to their friends for advice on emotion management when they felt hurt or disappointed by friends or their dating partner. In addition, LeCroy (1988) found that girls not only report that they value emotional support from their friends, but they also turn to a smaller group of close friends or one best friend for emotional support.

Boys value friendships for quite different reasons in which social support may take on different meanings. Like girls, boys derive security and status from belonging to a close-knit clique or group of friends. However, unlike girls emotional support does not take the form of long intimate discussions of their feelings. Instead, emotional support might be provided by active assistance (e.g., helping a friend repair his car) or by coming to the aid of a friend in a physical conflict, or by being with the friend and enjoying high-spirited fun in a free and easy manner. Perhaps because of the group dynamics of adolescent males, the characteristic that boys value the most in their friendships is loyalty, and friendships between boys tend to remain stable. There is also much evidence that boys and girls differ in their communication styles. For example, in opposite-sex friendships and dating relationships, boys tend to use more active and girls more tentative speech. As boys and girls begin to develop heterosexual relationships after spending much of middle childhood apart, it is not surprising that they will have to adjust their behavior and learn the communication styles of the opposite sex.

With the onset of puberty the structure of the peer group is gradually transformed. Same-sex cliques give way to larger collectives or crowds. The *crowd* may be composed of several same-sex cliques, in which high-status members begin to interact more frequently with opposite-sex peers. Gradually, as other members begin to follow this example, same-sex cliques are transformed into heterosexual cliques. The crowd may be based more on reputation, style of dress, and stereotypes than actual behavior (Brown, 1990), or in some American cities the crowd may be organized by ethnic groups. The celebrated play *West Side Story* provides a dramatic illustration of a fully developed crowd in New York City, and portrays all the universal themes (identity, autonomy, intimacy) as well as the unique cultural elements that make late adolescence an exciting and sometimes dangerous period of development.

In urban Western societies adolescent male cliques may take more threatening forms as is evidenced by the widespread phenomenon of juvenile street gangs. These facts of urban life have led human ethologists Margo Wilson and Martin Daly (1985) to refer to the high levels of risk taking, violence, and aggression commonly observed among adolescent males as "the young-male syndrome." An examination of United States census bureau data confirms this asymmetry between the sexes. Male arrests for all categories of violent crimes consistently exceed female arrests. Not only do these statistics reveal a considerable gap between the sexes, with males exceeding females by margins that are typically as high as 10 to 1, but these rates are highest among younger rather than older males, and both findings are consistent in every year for which data is available (Uniform Crime Reports, 1997).

Wilson and Daly (1985) point out that many of the violent acts committed by young males are triggered by challenges to their status and other signs of disrespect. Acquiring status and respect is one of the foremost reasons for joining a street gang. Many violent acts are retaliations for perceived insults, they are more often performed when other young men are present, and young men who murder regularly choose to do so publicly as a means of proving their toughness and acquiring greater status (Figure 10.1).

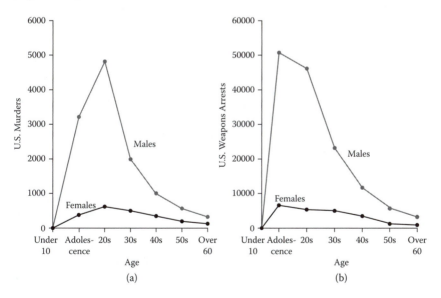

FIGURE 10.1   **(a)** 1998 Census Bureau Data on murders as a function of age and gender. **(b)** 1998 Census Bureau Data on weapons arrests as a function of age and gender.

We next examine sex roles in non-Western societies that clearly reveal the explanatory and predictive power of sexual selection and parental investment theory.

Sex Roles in Non-Western Societies

As in modern societies, gender identity and sex roles in traditional societies are firmly established by middle childhood when gender segregation and same-sex socialization reach their peak. As a dramatic illustration of gender norms, after 20 years of fieldwork in 30 remote tribal societies in Asia and Africa, Francisco Abati (2006, personal communication) has never seen a girl climb a tree. However, like boys who do so frequently, they are certainly capable of doing so. Why would traditional cultures evolve such social norms regulating the behavior of the sexes in such seemingly arbitrary fashion?

Evolutionary biologists invoke concepts such as sexual selection and parental investment to explain universal features of sexual division of labor, such as men hunting and women cooking and caring for infants. These universals are far from arbitrary and make clear sense when viewed from the standpoint of adaptive advantage. The manufacture and use of weapons for hunting and warfare is an exclusive domain of males in all traditional societies, with almost no exceptions (Daly & Wilson, 1978; Murdock, 1981).

This particular division of labor, assigning to males the role of protection and defense of the group, has a long evolutionary history that predates the arrival of Homo sapiens. Basic differences in parental investment in mammals lead to the widespread observation of greater size and physical strength in males for purposes of defense. Human males in traditional societies must frequently travel long distances for herding, hunting, or warfare that would be impractical for women with infants and children. Although both parents share responsibilities for children, mothers are clearly more involved in early childcare. Typically, mothers are more nurturant and empathic towards infants and more involved in emotional communication than fathers, who typically engage in more rough-and-tumble play with children, especially boys. The evolution of a culture's sex roles will thus be shaped by universal forces of sexual selection operating in a particular cultural context of ecological and historical factors. To illustrate, let us examine the sexual division of labor in two types of small-scale societies: pastoralists and agriculturalists.

The convergent demands of cattle herding make pastoralist societies like the Himba, Zemba, Datoga, and Masai of Africa very similar in structure and practices. The Himba represent a typical seminomadic pastoralist culture in Southern Angola. The men accompany the main herd of cattle into the fields, often roaming many miles from the camp to allow for optimal grazing. From an early age, male Himba children play an important role in tending livestock and learn this role by directly observing the adult same-sex models that surround them. At the start of a typical day women, assisted by their daughters, milk the cows and then prepare a type of yogurt which can be preserved throughout the heat of the day.

But not all the day is devoted to work. Given the high protein diet of their pastoralist life, Himba children have great reserves of energy to expend in play. The earliest roots of modern sport can be seen in games where Himba adolescent males use small wild melons as balls, exhibiting great athletic skill. Ethologists view such competitive play as functional in honing adult skills while regulating social status in the peer group. Social learning is evident as younger boys are keen imitators of their older brothers. Same-sex play of this sort is ubiquitous in both traditional and modern societies and contributes to the establishment of gender identity with a given culture.

The Masai of Tanzania are also seminomadic pastoralists. Cattle represent the most important resource and Masai men are recruited to defend them against natural predators and attacks by neighboring tribes. The Masai, like many tribes, practice polygyny. Wealthy males often have as many as four wives, though the first wife retains an elevated status. As is typical of small-scale polygynous societies, socialization practices tend to encourage play fighting and physical prowess in young boys, in line with their future adult role. The male rite of passage to the status of warrior or defender occurs every 7 years and is critical for the renewal of the traditional male role of protector of the herd, common to pastoralists in general. Among the Masai, gender roles are assumed by each successive generation in the tradition of their ancestors. Life transitions are marked by public rites of passage which serve to confer a new status and identity to the individual. A close-knit and relatively affluent society, the Masai provide a firm identity and social security to all members of the group.

In the Matig-Saluk, a slash-and-burn agricultural society, men and women also spend much of the day in gender-segregated activity. From the earliest age, members of the Matig-Saluk tribe experience life as part of the surrounding community. Throughout the day, girls and boys engage in gender-stereotyped play without adult prompting or supervision that they find highly enjoyable, but which also prepares them for their future roles in Matig-Saluk society.

Collaborative tasks involving the whole tribe, such as building a house or repairing it after a typhoon, demonstrate another universal aspect of the division of labor, with men assuming the higher-risk part of the task up on the roof, while women and children provide the necessary raw materials. Such a scene resembles a similar barn raising among the Amish, as depicted in the film *Witness*. In this film the men and older boys are directly involved in the construction, with the younger boys imitating their elders in pretend play with hammers and nails. At the same time the women and girls prepare a feast for all to enjoy.

An activity for all members of the tribe involves exploiting the natural resources of the forest to produce goods for market. Again men are engaged in the riskier task of slicing the wood with machetes while women and children work together to finish the job with smaller tools. In this and countless other ways, the Matig-Saluk culture embodies the ancient Chinese concept of Yin and Yang or balanced harmony between the sexes in which women and men play complementary roles for the well-being of all members of the community. Their traditional feminine multitasks in the home might combine basket weaving with cooking and simultaneously attending young children. These are predominantly, but not exclusively, female activities in traditional cultures around the world. Young girls often stay nearby and observe while caring for their younger siblings, learning skills that will serve them well in raising their own children. As in many traditional cultures, men typically take on tasks that require strenuous labor, often far from the village, while women excel in tasks that require fine dexterity typically in the house or village compound.

Gender segregation is so ubiquitous in indigenous peoples that sex-differentiated behavior occurs even for the same task. For example, all members of the Batak society enjoy fishing, although they do so in different ways and within peer groups based on age and gender. Older boys enjoy the sport of diving into cold waters to spear fish, an athletic skill that earns them status in the peer group. Men construct different types of traps to catch fish from the river depending on the flow of water. Women and girls enjoy familiar pole fishing with hook and line that allows them the possibility of carrying infants on their backs and tending to small children as they fish. Clearly these sex-differentiated activities are not prewired into their genes, but are mediated by complex processes in which biological and cultural factors are interwoven. In a different culture fathers may take their sons out fishing using a rod and reel that is more similar to the fishing style of the Batak women. What is not arbitrary is the fact of gender segregation and the biological constraints on the evolution of cultural practices. Thus, in none of the 30 cultures studied by Abati do women engage in activities that take them on extensive journeys away from home and hearth. It would simply not be practical given that in all these cultures they have primary responsibility for early childcare.

Of course things are different in a modern Western society. Certainly things can be different, they are allowed to be different, even encouraged to be different. Yet as I write this sentence 100% of the 20 students in the child study lab course involving participation in a university preschool are young women. It is an elective, not a required course for psychology majors. Over my 25-year teaching career, female student participation has ranged from 80% to a high of 100% in such classes, with an average female to male ratio of approximately 9:1. Similarly in 25 years of research using preschool teachers as informants we have collected data from more than a thousand teachers, more than 90% of whom were female. Television and film portrayals notwithstanding, North American patterns of real-life behavior are more sex-typed and gender segregated than the average college student believes. It is simply a matter of observing everyday behavior in the real world.

Sexual Selection and Male Aggression

Typically mean differences between girls and boys on some trait or behavior as measured by questionnaires is relatively slight and there is often more variation within gender than between gender groups. Paradoxically, when scientists examine the extreme tips of the normal distributions of the two sexes for behaviors that occur in the real world outside the lab, it is more often the case that extreme groups are heavily skewed by gender. For example, in the United States, 80% of all children diagnosed with conduct disorder are boys (Richman, Stevenson, & Graham, 1982; Rutter & Garmezy, 1983), 85% of all violent crimes by adolescents are perpetrated by boys, and over 90% of all murders are committed by men (FBI crime reports, 1997). Although homicide rates vary by culture, one way to correct for differences in rate is to compare the levels of male versus female same-sex homicides. In every culture that Daly & Wilson (1988) tested they found that men kill other men about 20 times more often than women kill women.

This preponderance of violent aggression by males is remarkably consistent not only across human cultures but also throughout history. A similar picture emerges across primate groups. In nonhuman primates, an increase in male aggressiveness during puberty is typical across many species, while female aggressiveness is largely unaffected by puberty and remains much lower than male levels. In humans, testosterone, a primarily male activating hormone, has been linked to gender differences in aggressive behavior (Geary, 1998), while estrogen, a primarily female activating hormone, has been linked to depression (e.g., Strober, 1985), though these relationships are not always found and are always mediated by developmental history and other contextual factors.

Prevalence rates of depression and aggression are quite different between adolescent males and females. Depression is uncommon in childhood and sex differences are negligible. However, adolescent girls and women are significantly more likely to report suffering from depression than adolescent boys and men (Kessler et al., 1993). Similarly, homicide is relatively rare in childhood but with the onset of adolescence there is a remarkable increase in male rates of homicide. Year after year, throughout the world, about 90% of all homicides are committed by men, mostly young men (excluding warfare, which is even more asymmetrical), and their victims are almost always (80%) men of the same age (Daly & Wilson, 1988).

In the past, many psychologists insisted that these sex differences stemmed from purely environmental forces shaping the behavior of boys and girls through modeling, reinforcement, and other forms of social learning. Biologists disagree with such a one-sided view of human sociality, particularly biologists who study different animal species showing the same persistent asymmetries between the sexes across many different species. From an evolutionary perspective the reproductive risks and rewards for competition and aggression are far greater for males than females in primates and mammals in general. This universal fact derives from simple logic: Unlike females, males can increase their reproductive success greatly through multiple matings (Daly & Wilson, 1978; Geary, 1998; Trivers, 1972).

Much greater variability among males in reproductive success was true for humans during the long formative period of our evolution, as supported by historical evidence and contemporary studies of preindustrial societies. For example, the anthropologist Napoleon Chagnon reports far higher variability in reproductive success among males than females among the Yanomamo. The most reproductively successful man had 43 children, and his father had over 400 great-great grandchildren (Chagnon, 1979). In contrast, other Yanomamo men had few or no children or grandchildren.

These are modest attainments compared to one of history's most reproductive kings, a Sharfian emperor of Morocco who had 888 direct descendants (Daly & Wilson, 1978). More remarkable still is the genetic imprint of a highly successful male on future generations. Zerjal et al. (2003) identified a Y-chromosomal lineage present in about 8% of the men in a large region of Asia. They estimate that this particular Y chromosome is present in about 16 million men living in the region of Asia that correspond to the extent of Genghis Khan's empire. The paper suggests that the pattern of variation within the lineage originated in Mongolia about 1000 years ago, was carried by the male-line descendants of Genghis Khan, who established the largest land empire in history and initiated a male dynasty that remained in ascendance from his death in 1227 to the mid-17th century.

To summarize, it is clear that the number of potential offspring is far greater in males than females and male variation in reproductive success is related to dominance status. Throughout human history, intermale competition and coalition-based aggression has been related to reproductive success. In her historical analysis of the first six great civilizations, Laura Betzig makes the following generalization: "powerful men mate with hundreds of women, pass their power on to a son by one legitimate wife, and take the lives of men who get in their way" (Betzig, 1993, p. 37). The motives for the high levels of intergroup conflict and violence among men in these societies included retaliation, economic gain, political power, territorial conquest, capture of women, and personal prestige, all of which could potentially enhance their reproductive success. A provocative question for students of evolutionary psychology is: to what extent are these forces still operating today? It may be that the introduction of guns into the dynamics of intertribal warfare has destabilized traditional cultures and eliminated the association between male violence and reproductive success, particularly when inclusive fitness spanning generations is considered. In modern Western societies the link may be even more tenuous, as life in prison or an early death from gang violence is hardly conducive to one's inclusive fitness. We will continue to explore this issue and other questions in the next chapter on mate selection and reproductive strategies.

☐ Chapter Summary

Two theoretical concepts provide the starting point for an evolutionary theory of sex differences: sexual selection and parental investment theory. Sexual selection was defined by Darwin (1871, p. 256) as a specific form of natural selection that arises "from the advantage that certain individuals have over other individuals of the same sex and species, in exclusive relation to reproduction." Darwin identified two basic types of sexual selection: (1) intrasexual competition, or competing for mates; and (2) intersexual selection, or choosing mates. Trivers' parental investment theory views the degree of parental investment in offspring favoring females as an evolutionary cause for a basic asymmetry in sex roles. Mating competition would be expected to be greater in the lower-investing sex, while mate choice would be expected to be greater in the higher-investing sex. Thus, most, but not all, examples of sexual selection involve either male-male competition or female choice.

The particular dynamics of sexual selection for any given species are shaped by the reproductive efforts of the two sexes constrained by the physical and social ecology. Reproductive effort involves three different costs: (1) *mating* (including competing for mates), (2) *parenting* (including feeding, care, and protecting offspring), and (3) in some species, such as humans, *nepotism* (helping relatives to survive and reproduce more successfully). Because mammals are characterized by internal gestation and a high degree of postnatal maternal care, parental investment of mammalian females vastly exceeds that of males. Hence the reproductive success of males can often be greatly enhanced by mating effort, chiefly by competing with other males for females. Besides direct competition, this type of mating effort is also reflected in the male's striving for status, political power, resources, or territories, again depending on the social and physical ecology of the species. Basic differences in parental investment in mammals lead to greater size and physical strength in males for purposes of competition and defense.

Females play an active role in the mating game by selecting males for mates. A current model of female choice in bird species views the bright plumage typical of males as an honest signal of health because it signifies that the bird is free of parasite infestation. In other bird species, female choice is related to factors such as the male's willingness and ability to provide resources. Whatever trait is used, males who possess it will be more likely to pass their genes on to the next generation than males who do not, insuring that the trait will increase in frequency with each passing generation.

Like humans, sex differences among rhesus monkeys are typically relative rather than absolute, with some overlap between the sexes. Compared to male peers, young females spend more time with adult females, show more interest in young infants and engage in play parenting. The functional significance of this type of play is apparent as the chances of survival of the monkey's firstborn offspring is two to four times higher for mothers with previous experience in caring for infants. Monkey infants of both sexes begin to prefer the company of same-sex peers at an early age, and among juveniles, sex segregation is the rule. Young male rhesus monkeys spend more time in the company of peers, often without the mother close by, and engage in high-energy games of chasing and play fighting, and leave their natal troop at sexual maturity. As adults, male rhesus monkeys engage in more aggression than females. Prenatal exposure to higher levels of androgen in females is related to increased physical competition and high-energy physical play.

The same pattern of results emerges showing sex differences in rough-and-tumble play favoring boys and allo-parenting favoring girls is found in humans, as are similar effects of prenatal androgen. American boys engage in rough-and-tumble play about 4 to 5 times as often as girls. The magnitude of these sex differences varies across cultures, but the direction of the differences is constant. Universally, children begin to sort themselves into sex-segregated play groups beginning at about 3 years. Male and female peer "cultures" differ in many ways. Researchers have found that boys are more physically active, engage in more risk taking and rough-and-tumble play, exhibit more anger, play in larger groups, occupy more space, control more resources, and are more likely to do all of the above away from adult supervision than are girls. In contrast, girls engage in more dyadic play than boys and prefer the company of their mostly female preschool teachers more than do boys, although one study found that girls' preference to remain nearer to adults was evident only when boys were present. Parental investment theory predicts that males will generally pursue relatively high-risk strategies compared to females and will thus be higher in behaviors typical of behavioral approach systems (BAS: dominance/sensation seeking, risk taking, impulsivity, exhibitionism) and lower on behavioral inhibition systems (BIS; fear, wariness, caution, safety seeking). Developmental research in humans has produced a wealth of evidence that is generally consistent with these predictions.

Observation of adolescent groups of girls and groups of boys reveals that peers establish dominance hierarchies, trade insults, ridicule low status members, and compete for resources. However, girls and boys do these things in qualitatively different ways, with dominance struggles more frequent and more overt in boys. Adolescent girls value intimacy in their relationships, while boys value loyalty.

In urban Western societies adolescent male cliques may take more threatening forms leading human ethologists Margo Wilson and Martin Daly (1985) to refer to the high levels of risk taking, violence, and aggression commonly observed among adolescent males as "the young-male syndrome." Male arrests for all categories of violent crimes consistently exceed female arrests by margins that are typically as high as 10 to 1.

Patterns of sex differences in traditional cultures reveal similar patterns, with men more involved in competition, aggression, and defense and women more involved in child-rearing and cooking. The manufacture and use of weapons for hunting and warfare is an exclusive domain of males in all traditional societies, with almost no exceptions. Men kill other men about 20 times more often than women kill women regardless of culture. This preponderance of violent aggression by males is remarkably consistent across human cultures and throughout history. A similar picture emerges across primate groups. In nonhuman primates, an increase in male aggressiveness during puberty is typical across many species, while female aggressiveness is largely unaffected by puberty and remains much lower than male levels. In humans, testosterone, a primarily male activating hormone, has been linked to gender differences in aggressive behavior, providing one mechanism for the universal finding of higher levels of male physical aggression. Throughout human history, intermale competition and coalition-based aggression has been related to reproductive success.

☐ For Further Inquiry

Geary, D. C. (1998). *Male, female: The evolution of human sex differences*. Washington, DC: American Psychological Association.

Geary, D. C. (2006a). Sex differences in social behavior and cognition: The utility of sexual selection for hypothesis generation. *Hormones and Behavior, 49,* 273–275.

Schmitt, D. P., Realo, A., Voracek, M., & Allik, J. (2008). Why can't a man be more like a woman? Sex differences in Big Five personality traits across 55 cultures. *Journal of Personality and Social Psychology, 94,* 168–182.

Mate Choice and Reproductive Strategies*

Of all the recurrent adaptive problems humans have faced throughout their evolution, none are more central to a biological perspective than issues surrounding sex and reproduction. It follows that current evolutionary psychologists would have a deep and abiding interest in these topics, and we have seen an explosion of recent research yield interesting results concerning the psychological, ecological, and evolutionary pressures that have shaped reproductive strategies of women and men in many cultures around the world. In this chapter, various mating systems and male and female reproductive strategies are described, as well as contemporary research that examines universals in human mate choice as well as variations by culture and gender.

One caveat that applies to all domains of evolutionary psychology, but especially to the evolution of reproductive strategies, is the fact that evolved tendencies are produced over deep time. Tendencies that are common to mammals have been produced by selection pressures operating over hundreds of millions of years, primate tendencies date back 50 million years, and features that are unique to humans have arisen during the time period after our split with our common ancestors over 5 MYA. It follows that evolved human tendencies do not respond to abrupt changes that occur in periods of thousands of years, much less changes like birth control that date back less than a century. Of course, we as humans respond to changes in our society almost overnight, and social, political, economic, and cultural changes can sweep the nation at the speed of the Internet. This means that with respect to human mate choice, a mix of ancient and modern influences operate on both conscious and unconscious levels. Keep in mind that in this chapter we focus our discussion on evolved

---

* This chapter is coauthored with Dr. Rochelle Smith.

tendencies that have operated throughout human history often below the radar of our conscious awareness.

☐ Mating Systems

Throughout the animal kingdom, mating systems vary from monogamy to polygamy (polygyny and polyandry), to a mixed strategy as is evident in humans. These various mating systems can be seen as reflecting the different reproductive strategies of males and females in a given species operating within a given ecology. Monogamy is the condition in which a male and a female exclusively combine their reproductive efforts and share the costs and energy of raising offspring. Monogamy can be subdivided into perennial and serial categories. Perennial monogamy involves mating with one other individual for life. Serial monogamy involves the exclusive pairing of two individuals for a shorter period of time, such as a mating season. The pair is faithful until the season ends and then the pair splits and during the next season a new exclusive partner is chosen. The phenomenon of serial marriages in Westernized cultures can be seen as an example of serial monogamy. Monogamy is the most highly prevalent mating system in birds, but very rare in mammals, where it is limited to some prosimians, New World monkeys, the lesser apes, and many human societies. Polygamy is a mating system in which an animal has more than one mate. It is subdivided into polygyny (a male having multiple female partners) and polyandry (a female having multiple male partners). Polygyny is by far the most prevalent mating system for most species, while polyandry is exceedingly rare. So the first question for an evolutionary scientist is *why* this is so.

To answer this question, let's go back to some basic facts regarding the birds and the bees. Biological sex is defined by the relative size of gametes or sex cells. By biological design, the female of the species, defined as the sex with the larger gametes, typically invests more in the process of reproduction than the male, who typically provides a smaller initial investment in the form of sperm. In all mammals, females not only invest more in the ovum, but also in the biological costs of internal fertilization and gestation, a prolonged pregnancy, and lactation. A female mammal must sustain her investment in her potential offspring over a great deal of time, and she is limited to relatively few offspring over the course of her lifetime compared to a male. Thus, her basic strategy involves a commitment to nurture relatively few offspring rather than to maximize the production and fertilization of gametes. Each of the evolutionary achievements that define a mammal results inevitably in a more concentrated

TABLE 11.1 Mating Systems

Mating Systems

Category	Description	Examples	Prevalence
Monogamy	Individuals mate with one partner at a time and share the raising of the young	Penguins Ravens Swans Humans	92% of bird species, rare in mammals
Polygyny	Males mate with more than one female	Elks Elephant seals Hamadryas baboons Red grouse Wild horses Humans	The most common mating system in vertebrates, prevalent in mammals
Polyandry	Females mate with more than one male	Jacanas Tasmanian hens	Rare, but found in some bird species and in certain environmental conditions

female investment in a decreasing number of offspring (Daly & Wilson, 1978). In contrast, male mammals provide a tiny initial investment in the offspring. Moreover, in 95% of the 4000 species of mammals males provide no parental care after birth (Clutton-Brock, 1991).

Notice in Table 11.1 that monogamy is by far the most common mating system in birds, but extremely rare in mammals, where polygyny is the most prevalent mating system. Again the question to be addressed is why this is so. The answer lies in the striking evolutionary contrast in parenting strategies between egg-laying birds and live-bearing mammals. From a strategic standpoint, female birds have externalized the tasks of parental care relatively early in the life cycle. This paves the way for the evolution of paternal care and monogamy (and even occasionally polyandry) in a manner and to a degree that is just not possible in mammals.

As outlined in the preceding chapter, Trivers' (1972) parental investment theory focuses on the amount of effort and resources males and females invest in their offspring. In a very few species (less than 1%) it is actually the males who provide the majority of parental care for offspring (seahorses, katydids). But in all other species, including all mammals, it is the female who is the higher-investing parent. As a result, the mating habits and preferences between the higher-investing and lower-investing sex vary. Specifically, the higher-investing sex (i.e., the one who stands to lose the most energy, time, and resources by having an offspring) is predicted to be more careful in choosing a mate. Alternately, the lower-investing sex (i.e., the one who stands to pass on genes without risking loss of resources) will have to compete to be chosen as a mating partner. The lesser-investing sex is predicted to be more competitive, more aggressive, and more willing to engage in sex, at lower cost, and with more partners (Alexander & Noonan, 1979).

As members of the mammalian class and primate order, where do humans fit into this picture? First, men in human societies throughout the world invest more in their wives and offspring than any other primate. In all other primates, males do not know whose offspring are theirs, and consequently they invest relatively little in specific offspring, but defend the troop as a whole. Female primates tend to their own offspring, assisted by female relatives, and gather food for themselves. As we shall discuss below, confidence in paternity among men in human societies is not a given. Nevertheless, men typically share resources with a long-term mate, and extend their care and protection to her children. Notwithstanding this parental care provided by men, women certainly qualify as the higher-investing sex and are therefore generally more likely than men to be more selective in their mate choice. In contrast, men, compared to women, have been demonstrated to be more interested in a variety of sex partners, let less time elapse before seeking sexual intercourse, lower their standards dramatically when pursuing short-term mates, have a larger number of extramarital affairs, are generally more competitive and aggressive, and engage in male-male competition (Buss, 2008).

If the human example, like all other species, is consistent with Trivers' theory, especially compelling evidence can be garnered from species where sex roles are reversed. According to parental investment theory, if males in certain species invest more highly in offspring and take on the heavier burden of parental care, then they would be more discriminating in mate selection and females would be more aggressive and engage more readily in sexual intercourse. In line with this expectation, it has been found that in so called "sex-role reversed" species, females are highly competitive for males and more readily seek sexual intercourse (Mormon crickets, water bugs, red-necked phalaropes, katydids, dance flies; Alcock, 2001a).

☐ Mate Selection

Humans vary in terms of mating strategies such as monogamy and polygamy as well as their reliance on time strategies such as long-term mating strategies and short-term mating strategies. In the following sections we discuss how each of these strategies may have evolved, their costs and benefits, and what determines which strategy an individual may use.

Both men and women who seek long-term relationships typically look for a loving and dependable partner who is physically attractive, has a pleasant disposition, and is in good health (Buss, 2008). Modern technology such as birth control and medical treatment has altered the consequences of sexual encounters, but our evolutionary past had a hand in shaping our preferences for a sexual partner. From an evolutionary perspective, mate preferences have evolved to solve different sets of adaptive problems.

In the International Mate Selection Project, David M. Buss (1989) and his colleagues presented men and women with a list of 18 characteristics that they might consider desirable in a long-term partner. The items included such things as love, chastity, good health, ambition, education, social status, attractiveness, and financial prospects. Over the course of 5 years, over 10,000 participants from 37 different cultures (spanning six continents and five islands) contributed data. The samples were diverse, representing different religions, ethnic groups, races, political systems, economic systems, and even different mating systems. Results from this massive study provided data about cross-cultural and gender similarities and differences. Gender differences that are prominent on a multicultural scale reveal evolutionary shaping based on unique biological pressures for males and females throughout time. In summary, Buss (1989) found that men and women were similar in their desires for many qualities. Both sexes wanted mates who were kind, understanding, intelligent, exciting, healthy, and dependable. However, he also found two clusters of sex differences that proved to be universal. Women, more than men, in all 37 cultures valued potential mates with good financial prospects. Men, more than women, universally agreed that youth and physical attractiveness (two hypothesized correlates of fertility and reproductive value) were of primary importance. These results provide a first wave of evidence that our evolutionary past may influence our current mate choices.

Female Preferences

Women everywhere can readily list ideal traits for a mate ranging from intelligence to brawny athleticism to successful financial standing and attentiveness to needs. According to current research, these women are not so far off from describing a man who would be ideal from an evolutionary perspective. Athleticism and physical attractiveness, for example, reveal a healthy strength and an ability to competently compete to acquire resources. In the EEA (environment of evolutionary adaptation), those with the resources are the ones who survive to pass on their genes. High social and financial standing are also necessary for a very similar reason. Men at the top of a social hierarchy, whether thousands of years ago or today, have priority of access to most of the resources necessary for comfort and survival. And, perhaps even of most importance is a man's attentiveness and generosity. An individual unwilling to share can have all of the resources in the world yet ultimately make a bad mate. According to Buss (2008), women have evolved a mate preference for a partner who has good financial prospects, high social status, older age, ambition, athletic ability, dependability, exhibits love and commitment cues, positively interacts with children, is emotionally stable, is physically attractive, and is kind.

Though today's Western social structure may preclude the cognitive desire or actual need for a man with financial prospects and social status, women have nonetheless evolved to find such traits attractive in a partner. Over thousands of generations, women have benefited by choosing mates who were able to provide the benefits of material provisions, social influence, reciprocal alliances, and protection of offspring. In ancestral times lacking in hospitals and modern medical care, women faced the same burdens of internal fertilization, a 9-month gestation, and lengthy lactation. Lack of birth control resulted in women spending much of their reproducing years burdened by cycles of pregnancy and suckling. They would have benefited greatly by selecting mates who possessed the social standing and material resources to provide for their needs and for the needs of their ever-growing family. Similar to current societies, individuals with social status and wealth have access to more nutritious food, better living environments, and superior health care. Greater social status and greater wealth allow children social opportunities that may be missed by children in lower-status families. Modern women are the descendants of these successful ancestors and thus have inherited their mate preferences.

Another study that demonstrated female preference for wealth and higher social standing in potential mates was conducted by Baize and Schroeder (1995), who found that women are significantly more likely to respond to personal ads from older men who indicated that they were highly educated and drew higher salaries. Similarly, Pawlowski and Koziel (2002) studied 551 male personal ads and found that men with higher levels of education, who were comparatively older, comparatively taller, and who offered more resources received more interested responses from women.

Many young men may not yet have reached their maximum level of wealth and social status. How, then, do women decide who has the most potential as the new crop of up and comers in society? One way that women have evolved to solve this problem is through attraction to older men (Pawlowski & Koziel, 2002; Rusu & Bencic, 2007). Older men have had the time to establish a degree of status yet unattainable to most of their younger counterparts. It has also been shown that women are attracted to signs of ambition and motivated individuals (Buss, 2008; Hatfield & Sprecher, 1995; Minervini & McAndrew, 2006). Such individuals will make use of any opportunities that come their way and have higher potential of attaining status and all of the benefits that come along with it.

A key to understanding mate choice in evolutionary terms requires not only cross-cultural similarities but also cross-species consistency.

Throughout the animal world, the importance of physical fitness is important to successful reproduction. Almost all offspring require protection at birth (though none as long term as a human child), and stronger males are more likely to be successful protectors of the young. A man's size, strength, physical prowess, and athletic ability are cues that signal solutions to the problem of protection. During human evolution, physical protection may have been one of the most important things a man could offer a woman (Barber, 1995). Therefore, women evolved a preference for men who are physically capable of protecting them (Bleske-Rechek & Buss, 2001; Geary & Flinn, 2001).

Good health is also a universally desired quality. An unhealthy mate would run the risk of premature death, transmission of disease, or other debilitation that would ultimately lead to lack of ability to provide for a mate and potential offspring. Such a mate could also infect potential children and/or pass on poor genes. Therefore, both men and women desire health in a long-term mate. Physical signs of health include good teeth, symmetrical proportions in the face and body, strong posture, muscle tone, and athletic ability.

A final, but not trivial, desire for women is a partner who is loving, compassionate, and committed to a long-term relationship, and to the offspring that result from the union. A man who holds resources and has good health has all of the requirements of a potentially successful mate, but if he were unwilling to share those resources, his children would not likely survive to reproductive age to pass on his genes. Therefore, men who are loving and compassionate with children are rated considerably more attractive than those who are not (Buss, 2008; Geary, Vigil, & Byrd-Craven, 2004).

Male Preferences

Men who invest their time and resources in a long-term partner certainly benefit by being selective themselves. If his strength, wealth, and status are to be solely invested in one partner and their offspring then what kind of partner is he going to choose to invest in? Will he seek the same qualities that his female counterparts are seeking? In part yes, but because the adaptive problems associated with reproductive success in males differ from those of females, males have evolved their own strategies. Some of the problems associated with female reproductive success do not apply. He does not have the burden of carrying a child and does not require protection and financial support during times of labor and intensive infant care. Other problems pertain uniquely to men. A key problem that is uniquely male involves *confidence of paternity*. If a child of a long-term mate is not the father's genetic offspring, he will be squandering his reproductive efforts by investing his resources in someone else's genes. Therefore long-term commitment to monogamous relationships for males would be expected to depend on his being reasonably sure that the child carries his own genetic makeup. It should not be a surprise to an evolutionist that men consider promiscuity and unfaithfulness to be the least desirable traits in a long-term mate, since they both serve to reduce confidence in paternity (Buss & Schmitt, 1993). Indeed, unfaithfulness in a wife is the most upsetting of any behavior for males—a finding for which there is widespread cross-cultural evidence (Betzig, 1986; Buss, 2008; Daly & Wilson, 1978).

If confidence of paternity is resolved, men, like women, can potentially benefit from a long-term relationship in several ways. A man who demonstrates a willingness to invest his time and resources will appear more appealing to women. He, therefore, will have a wider selection of women to choose from. In addition, his long-term investment increases the likelihood that his children will survive to a reproductive age and continue to pass on his genes. Children benefit not only from his physical protection, but also his role modeling and the extension of his alliances within the community. In modern societies, children with investing fathers have been shown to have higher academic achievement, better emotional regulation, and higher social competence (Cabrera, Tamis-LeMonda, Bradley, Hofferth, & Lamb, 2000; Lamb, 1997; Pleck, 1997). In hunter-gather societies, paternal investment is likewise related to decreased mortality and higher social status for the child (Hill & Hurtado, 1996). So, men as well as women (and, certainly, the child) can benefit from a long-term commitment such as marriage.

Similar to women, the International Mate Selection Project by David M. Buss (1989) demonstrates that men also seek a partner who is intelligent, kind, healthy, and who has similar attitudes, personalities, and religious and political beliefs. Beyond those common traits, however, men seek women who have high reproductive value and high fertility. A woman's reproductive value is her potential to bear children. If men seek women with a high reproductive value, then the woman's age in itself becomes an important criterion in selecting a mate, since a woman's lifetime childbearing potential decreases with age from a high of about three at age 20 to much less than one after age 40 (Buss, 2008).

Reproductive value can be distinguished from fertility which refers to actual reproductive performance. Thus a woman in her mid-20s has the highest potential to produce healthy offspring, whereas women in their young teens or those approaching old age have limited potential for immediate fertility. Reproductive value and fertility must be inferred by men, who rely on observable cues that may indicate that a woman is reproductively viable. Specifically, youth, beauty, and body shape serve as indicators to whether a woman would make a successful reproductive partner. Probably the most useful and direct indicator of

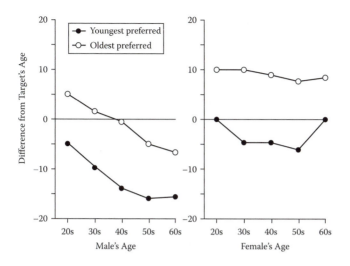

FIGURE 11.1   Men universally prefer young women as mates. As men age, they prefer women who are increasingly younger than they are (left). As women age they do not show this pattern (right). (From Kenrick & Keefe, 1992.)

reproductive potential is age. Young women have a greater likelihood of reproducing and their children are generally healthier and more likely to survive.

Two findings are of relevance to this hypothesized evolved preference. First, men do universally prefer young women. Even more revealing is the finding that as men age, they prefer women who are increasingly younger than they are, as shown in Figure 11.1.

So the pattern reveals that men desire mates who are not just a few years younger than they are at any age, but that they desire women who are close to their maximum reproductive value. In line with this evolutionary hypothesis are additional findings that reveal that some males prefer women who are older. Why would this be so? Kenrick and his colleagues decided that a strong test of the evolutionary hypothesis would be to ask teenagers what age they prefer in a dating partner. From the standpoint of reproductive value, male teens (12 to 19) should *not* prefer a younger partner, but a partner who is older. Results revealed that adolescent males expressed a desire for dates who were 3 to 5 years older on average (Kenrick, Keefe, Gabrieldis, & Cornelious, 1996).

Another key indicator of reproductive potential is health. While health is not always obvious to observe, many of its characteristics are. Women with clear skin and eyes, full lips, good muscle tone, strong long hair as well as a youthful gait, animated facial expressions, and high energy are likely to be perceived as more healthy and therefore having higher reproductive value. These characteristics, also associated with beauty, are widely accepted to be attractive in a mate (Symons, 1995). Similarly, symmetry of facial features as well as body structures is considered beautiful and has been found to indicate physical fitness (Gangestad & Scheyd, 2005; Hönekopp, Bartholomé, & Jansen, 2004; Rhodes, 2006). Asymmetries may indicate developmental problems, disease, or generally poor genes. This preference for beautiful faces, furthermore, seems not to require any cultural training. In a study attempting to determine if these features are learned or innate, Langlois, Roggman, and Reiser-Danner (1990) measured infants' responses to faces of varying "beauty." Interestingly, infants as young as 2 months gazed longer at attractive faces (as judged by adult evaluations of the faces) than those faces judged to be unattractive (see also Ramsey, Langlois, Hoss, Rubenstein, & Griffin, 2004).

In recent years there has been an accumulation of evidence that there are even subtle changes throughout a woman's menstrual cycle that impact her rated attractiveness by other adults (Oberzaucher et al., 2008; Saxton et al., 2008). For example, during the luteal phase women are rated as less attractive than they are when they are ovulating. Analysis shows that a woman's jaw is slightly broader and the distance between the eyes and eyebrows is larger during the luteal phase, giving her a more masculine appearance. During the ovulatory phase, however, when the woman is most fertile, the lips are fuller and the face is less robust and she is rated as more attractive, healthy, sexy, and likeable (Oberzaucher et al., 2008).

Finally, in cross-cultural research, a woman's body mass index (BMI) and body shape, as measured by her waist-to-hip ratio (WHR), were found to be important components in predicting her attractiveness to men. In general, men tend to prefer a lower BMI (slender woman) and a lower WHR (curvaceous figure) (Swami & Tovee, 2007; Swami, Neto, Tovee, & Furnham, 2007.) Beyond these general preferences, it has been found that ideal BMI varies by culture. For example, research has shown that men too have evolved a preference for the body type that is linked with higher status. If a larger woman is associated with higher social rank, then the men will be more attracted to a larger, more robust woman. If, on the other hand, thinness is a mark of social prestige, then thinness is preferred (Buss, 2008).

With respect to a woman's WHR, Singh (2004) found that there is a universal preference for a low (.70) ratio of a woman's waist and size of her hips (hour glass figure). Research has determined that a woman's WHR is an accurate indicator of a woman's reproductive status as well as a woman's long-term health status. Women with low to normal WHR (.67 to .80) are at a reduced risk for infertility, cardiovascular disease, and carcinoma (Singh, 1993). WHR rises during pregnancy, poor health, and with increasing age, perhaps signaling a poor reproductive partner. Though men's ideal weight for women varies throughout cultures, the ideal ratio generally remains the same. Specifically, regardless of overall body size, women with a lower WHR are generally deemed by men to be more attractive (Singh, 1993, 2004; Singh & Young, 1995). Illustrating further support of male attraction to youth and beauty, in the Baize and Schroeder (1995) personal ads study that was mentioned earlier, men preferentially responded to ads from women who reported being younger and who mentioned being physically attractive.

Of course, personal ads do not quite represent the features of the EEA that shaped sexual attraction. Initial sexual attraction deals mostly with the senses. Visual perception, audition, and olfaction can all contribute to the chemistry or initial attraction individuals feel when they encounter one another. In general, men and women are influenced by body shape, lack of disease and deformity, a high degree of symmetry, and a healthy body posture. The voice quality and movements, as well as the scent (natural or artificial) of the individual can also lead to attraction or repulsion. Pheromones, for example, are chemicals produced by an organism that transmit a message to other members of the same species. There are many types of pheromones. Among them, sex pheromones are documented in insects and their effects are currently being debated in humans and other primate groups (Laska, Wieser, & Hernandez Salazar, 2006; McClintock, 1983, 1999; Thornhill & Gangestad, 1999). Many researchers believe that pheromones may be the cause of the sense of instant "chemistry" or the feeling of instant attraction or dislike of another individual. These pheromones are released by the apocrine glands (e.g., sweat glands) that become fully functional after an adolescent reaches puberty, perhaps accounting for the marked increase of sexual attraction in this stage of development.

☐ Short-Term Mating Strategies

If a long-term strategy leads to increased confidence of paternity for the father and for increased safety and protection for the mother and the young, it remains evident that a long-term mating strategy is not the only strategy that exists, and so we must ask the evolutionary question, why are short-term couplings so prevalent in cultures throughout the world? How does it benefit a man to have a short-term mate? What are the benefits for a woman?

Male Short-Term Costs and Benefits

Once again, Trivers' parental investment theory provides the theoretical prediction that men will have evolved a stronger preference than women for multiple short-term sexual liaisons. This asymmetry arises from the fact that increasing short-term sexual encounters increases the number of offspring a man can produce, more than increasing the number of offspring per partner. Over the course of 12 short-term sexual encounters, a man can potentially produce 12 children. A woman in a similar situation can have 12 partners; yet can still only bear one child per 9-month period. Therefore, if men are designed to maximize their reproductive success, would they not seek multiple short-term mates?

Of course male and female strategies must be viewed as operating within a game strategic context where neither strategy can be executed without consideration of the other. So if the female strategy is to be highly selective and seek a male who is willing to commit to a long-term investment, a strict short-term tactic might limit the number and quality of women that a man will have access to. A man employing a short-term tactic would then need to lower his standards for his mate. Beyond this decrease in quality and possible risk of limiting his chances of finding a long-term mate (women may not want to marry a man who evidentially is unwilling to commit to a long-term relationship), a short-term tactic carries other potential risks for a man (Buss & Schmitt, 1993). An increased number of sexual partners increases the risk of sexually transmitted disease. Children produced in such a union may also have less chance of surviving to adulthood due to lack of paternal protection and connections. However, such encounters have ultimately proven relatively successful or else short-term couplings would not be evident in our society today. Though modern men may not engage in short-term sexual intercourse with the intention of having additional children (most men probably take precautions to prevent such an event), their ancestors who engaged in short-term affairs successfully passed down their genes and thus a short-term strategy exists in the gene pool today. Along with the risks of short-term relationships, there are additional dilemmas that men must solve to have productive short-term mating. First of all, we have established that women are looking for men who are willing to commit their time and resources to their families. During a short-term affair, the idea is to get in and out without sacrificing any resources. Men must find women who are willing to engage in sex without expectation of further investment by the male. (Why women would choose to fill this role will be discussed later in the chapter.) Men must also find women who demonstrate fertility (rather than those who merely have high reproductive value) who are more likely to reproduce from a single sexual encounter (Buss, 2008). Therefore, when seeking a short-term mate, men are more likely to be attracted to women who display signs of fertility as well as women who demonstrate easy accessibility.

According to Buss and Schmitt's (1993) sexual strategies theory, men and women possess psychological adaptations for a range of mating strategies, including short-term mating. However, men have additional characteristics that make them seem better suited to short-term tactics than women. Specifically, it has been established that men possess greater desire for short-term sexual relationships than women, men prefer larger numbers of sexual partners over time than women, and men require less time before consenting to sex than women (Schmitt, Shackelford, & Buss, 2001). So, despite potential obstacles, the benefit for men is still relatively obvious. They can pass on their genes without sacrificing any of their resources, even if a smaller percentage of these children survive to reproductive age.

The evolutionary basis for women to engage in short-term sexual relations is less obvious. On the surface, the costs for women appear to outweigh any potential benefits. Due to the prevalence of modern men who engage in short-term mating, however, there must have been women with whom they could propagate or else they would have been selected against. Therefore, there must be some benefit for women to engage in such behavior.

There have been several hypotheses proposed to explain women's engagement in short-term sexual relations during the EEA. These include the resource accrual hypothesis (Symons, 1979), the genetic benefit hypothesis (Fisher, 1958), the mate-switching hypothesis (Fisher, 1992), and the mate skill acquisition hypothesis (Greiling & Buss, 2000), to name a few.

The *resource accrual hypothesis* generally predicts that women may have engaged in short-term mating in exchange for goods and other resources. Not only could the woman have acquired material goods but she could have also obtained the additional protection of a male, at least on a short-term basis. If the woman's primary long-term mate was absent (perhaps on an extended hunting trip), the woman and her children may have been vulnerable and the added protection of an additional male could provide needed protection. The *genetic benefit hypothesis* increases the potential of enhanced fertility, variation in offspring, and access to superior genes. If a woman's primary mate was infertile or otherwise less than ideal, the woman could have increased the sexual appeal of future generations of her offspring by mating with a more attractive partner. She may also have produced genetically varied children, giving her genes a better chance of surviving in an unstable environment. A third hypothesis, the *mate-switching hypothesis*, says that women may have been able to expel an undesirable mate by either jeopardizing their current relationship by an extramarital affair or otherwise find a new mate through infidelity. And, finally, the *mate skill acquisition hypothesis*, which is encouraged in younger members of some cultures, is an experimental state where a woman may experiment with a variety of partners in order to hone her skills of seduction and attraction and also establish what she is looking for in a long-term mate (Buss, 2008).

All of these hypotheses postulate some benefit for the female. However, the costs for women were (and are) present as well. To begin with, the cost of investing 9 months of gestation and then another unspecified amount of time raising a child is a huge potential cost (especially throughout human evolution prior to recent introduction of birth control measures) of an uncommitted affair. Additional costs include reputation damage associated with promiscuity and lack of desirability as a long-term mate. Women without a long-term partner also lacked male physical protection and ran a greater risk for physical and sexual abuse. Also, women with a long-term partner risked his withdrawal of financial and physical resources due to lack of faithfulness.

In order to explore women's and men's desires for a long-term versus short-term mating strategy, Buss and Schmitt (1993) asked them to rate the importance of 67 characteristics for a short-term mate (e.g., a one-night stand) and for a long-term mate (e.g., marriage partner). They found that when looking for a long-term mate, male and female's standards were both relatively high. However, men's standards for a short-term mate were significantly lower than a woman's standards. Concurrent research by Kenrick and his colleagues confirmed that both sexes expressed high standards in a marriage partner, yet men's standards dropped dramatically for a short-term fling while women's standards remained consistently high (Kenrick, Sadalla, Groth, & Trost, 1990). Further research has demonstrated that, cross-culturally, women are more likely to choose characters described as stable, nonviolent, low in dominance and risk taking as preferred marriage partners but are more likely to choose characters described as dominant, aggressive, and confident for brief sexual affairs (Kruger, Kardum, Tetaz, Tifferet, & Fisher, 2008).

Schmitt (2005) undertook a parallel study to explore variation in cross-cultural mating strategies. Schmitt and colleagues developed the Sociosexual Orientation Inventory (SOI) in order to better understand the individual differences in human mating strategies. The SOI is a seven-item self-report measure of human sexuality and can be used to determine an individual's mating strategy. Low SOI scores signify that an individual follows a more monogamous mating strategy, whereas high SOI scores indicate that an individual has a more promiscuous mating strategy. In his study, Schmitt had the SOI administered to 14,059 people across 48 nations. Among Schmitt's findings was that gender differences in sociosexuality were generally large and demonstrated cross-cultural universality across all 48 nations. For example, in every culture the average man scored significantly higher on sociosexuality (more promiscuous) than the average woman. In addition, men and women significantly differed from one another in both sociosexual behaviors and attitudes in all but three cultures. Although culture certainly has an influence on which mating strategy an individual will choose, an individual's gender is a stronger predictor of behavior, regardless of culture (Schmitt, 2005). Besides confirming Trivers' parental investment theory, these results lend confirming evidence for several other evolutionary theories of human mating, including the sex ratio theory and the strategic pluralism theory.

Sex ratio theory (Pedersen, 1991) proposes that the predominant mating strategy within a culture will be determined by the ratio of marriage-age men to marriage-age women. In a culture where men are scarce, women must compete for a mating partner and therefore they are predicted to be more promiscuous and quicker to consent to sex. In an environment where women are scarcer, men must accommodate the female strategy and monogamy is predicted to be predominant. Schmitt's cross-cultural data supported this theory in that the sex ratio in a culture was significantly correlated with its sociosexuality level.

Schmitt's data also supported the strategic pluralism theory (Gangestad & Simpson, 1990). This theory proposes that humans possess a menu of alternate mating strategies that they can follow and that local environment influences which strategy they will choose. When the local environment is demanding and the difficulties associated with supporting and raising offspring is high, the predominant mating strategy will be monogamy. In this situation, both parents are needed to ensure the survival of their genes. In an environment where bi-parental care is less necessary for successful child-rearing, the people should tend to be more promiscuous and opt for short-term, more frequent mating. Schmitt's data found that quality of environment was significantly correlated with sociosexuality. Furthermore, it is generally the women who account for the majority of the shift in mating strategy. In harsh environments women are more selective and less willing to engage in casual, uncommitted sex. A harsh environment includes not only environments with limited resources but also environments where there is a prevalence of low-birth-weight infants, child malnutrition, or high infant mortality. In more comfortable environments, where bi-parental care is a less critical component in raising viable offspring, women are more willing to engage in short-term affairs.

☐ Chapter Summary

In sexually reproducing species, mating systems vary from perennial and serial monogamy to the prevalent polygyny and scarce polyandry. Among mammals where polygyny is by far the most widespread mating system, females not only invest more in the ovum, but also in the biological costs of internal fertilization and gestation, a prolonged pregnancy, and lactation. Each of the evolutionary achievements that define a mammal results inevitably in a more concentrated female investment in a decreasing number of offspring. In contrast, male mammals provide a tiny initial investment in the offspring. Moreover, in 95% of the 4000 species of mammals males provide no parental care after birth.

Men in human societies throughout the world invest more in their wives and offspring than any other primate. In all other primates, males do not know whose offspring are theirs, and consequently they invest relatively little in specific offspring, but defend the troop as a whole. Confidence in paternity among men in human societies is not a given. Nevertheless, men typically share resources with a long-term mate and extend their care and protection to her children. However, women certainly qualify as the higher-investing sex and are therefore generally more selective than men in their mate choice. Compared to women, men tend to be more interested in a variety of sex partners, let less time elapse before seeking sexual intercourse, lower their standards dramatically when pursuing short-term mates, have a larger number of extramarital affairs, are generally more competitive and aggressive, and engage in male-male competition.

Research has demonstrated that men and women seek many similar qualities in a mate. Men and women endorse preference for loving, healthy, dependable, and kind partners. However, gender differences emerge as well. According to the International Mate Selection Project, headed by David Buss, regardless of culture, women prefer men who have economic and physical resources, and who demonstrate a willingness to share such resources. Such qualities in a mate would help ensure material provisions, social influence, reciprocal alliances, quality genes for reproduction, and ultimate protection for future offspring. Men prefer women who are likely to be faithful, and who possess youth, beauty, and a pleasing body shape, qualities that are indicators of high reproductive value, good health, and high fertility. Long-term mating strategies in humans can benefit both men and women. Among other things, a long-term strategy can potentially lead to increased confidence of paternity for the father and increased safety and protection for the mother and the offspring.

Trivers' parental investment theory provides the theoretical prediction that men will have evolved a stronger preference than women for multiple short-term sexual liaisons. This asymmetry arises from the fact that increasing short-term sexual encounters increases the number of offspring a man can produce, more than increasing the number of offspring per partner. Over the course of 12 short-term sexual encounters, a man can potentially produce 12 children. A woman in a similar situation can have 12 partners, yet can still only bear one child per 9-month period. Benefits to women of short-term strategies may be explained by the resource accrual hypothesis, the genetic benefit hypothesis, the mate-switching hypothesis, and mate skill acquisition hypothesis.

David Schmitt undertook a comprehensive study to explore cross-cultural mating strategies. Using the Sociosexual Orientation Inventory (SOI), he found that gender was a key predictor of preferred mating strategy. His data support two evolutionary theories of human mating: (1) the sex ratio theory, and (2) the strategic pluralism theory. Overall, a nation's sex ratio was found to influence its sociosexuality.

☐ **For Further Inquiry**

Buss, D. M. (1989). Sex differences in human mate preferences: Evolutionary hypotheses testing in 37 cultures. *Behavioral and Brain Sciences, 12*, 1–49.

Miller, G. (2001). *The mating mind: How sexual choice shaped the evolution of human nature*. New York, NY: Anchor Books.

Schmitt, D. P. (2005). Sociosexuality from Argentina to Zimbabwe: A 48-nation study of sex, culture, and strategies of human mating. *Behavioral and Brain Sciences, 28*(2), 247–311.

Darwinian Medicine and Evolutionary Psychiatry

Two major trends in contemporary research explore issues of human mental and physical health from an evolutionary perspective. Medical anthropologists deal broadly with issues of biological and cultural adaptations that improve or worsen physical health, embracing evolution as a central theoretical concept (Brown, Barrett, & Padilla, 1998; Eaton, Shostak, & Konner, 1998). Similarly, Darwinian medicine (Nesse, 2005; Nesse & Williams, 1994) has elaborated evolutionary explanations for human vulnerabilities to diseases, including mental illness and psychopathology. This chapter draws upon each of these disciplines to understand both physical and mental health and illness from an evolutionary perspective.

One of the first systematic efforts to explain diseases from an evolutionary perspective was a collaboration between a physician, Randolph Nesse, and an evolutionary biologist, George Williams (Nesse & Williams, 1994). In their now classic work, entitled *Why We Get Sick*, they formulated six possible answers:

1. Novel environments
2. Infection
3. Genes
4. Defenses
5. Design compromises
6. Evolutionary legacies

☐ Novel Environments

A key idea uniting Darwinian approaches to disorder or malfunction is the concept of a mismatch between our genetic makeup and our current modern environment (Eaton, Shostak, & Konner, 1998). While the human organism was shaped by forces operating over millions of years to fit the lifestyle of paleolithic hunter-gatherers, we now live in a vastly different environment, often one that is at odds with our genetic makeup. The accumulation of cultural changes beginning with the advent of agriculture 10,000 years ago has outpaced the biological capacity for maintaining an adaptive fit to this "novel" environment. This has become especially true throughout the industrial revolution era spanning only 200 years and increasingly aggravated in the high-tech computerized society of the 21st century. Later in this chapter, we shall trace the outline of this mismatch by examining pandemics and chronic degenerative diseases that are pervasive in our modern civilization.

The cultural shift from a hunter–gatherer economy to an agriculturalist society introduced major changes that impacted human health. Without question, agriculture provided the foundation for a major leap forward in human civilizations, including the expansion of population sizes of human groups that were feasible in a given territory. But if the benefit of agriculture was a new capacity to sustain larger concentrations of humans, the cost to humans living in such urban centers in the Old World about 5000 years ago was the new challenge of dealing with contagious or infectious disease. Up until this time humans had lived in small, nomadic bands of hunter-gatherers who had very little cause for concern regarding these diseases. However, the increased size and density of agricultural communities resulted in an increased risk of parasitic and infectious diseases (Armelagos, 1998). Because the rise of preindustrial urban centers (only 2500 years ago in the New World) was recent in evolutionary terms, a specific genetic adaptation to any specific pathogen is highly unlikely. In our present context of a shrinking global village the spread of infectious diseases like Ebola, HIV, or avian bird flu can be almost instantaneous. Because of the speed of air travel an outbreak can move from a single point to anywhere on earth within 72 hours, much less time than the typical incubation period of most diseases.

Other consequences of the rise of agriculture were an increase in sedentary lifestyles and nutritional problems. Paradoxically, the risk for infectious diseases was often aggravated in agricultural societies because of nutritional deficiencies brought on by blight, drought, and overreliance on single crops. These same problems afflict billions of people living today as evidenced by United Nations and World Health Organization statistics on infant mortality, which can run as high as 50% in some African countries. Food shortages have likely been a recurring problem for human societies throughout our evolutionary history. Shortages of specific vitamins and minerals more likely arose after the spread of agriculture and herding economies (Nesse & Williams, 1994).

☐ Infection

Evolutionary biologists have made great strides in understanding the dynamics of host-pathogen relations, describing them as an arms race that will inevitably favor the more rapidly evolving and far more numerous bacteria or virus than its host. With each advance by the organism to combat them, bacteria and viruses escalate the arms race to new heights. This dynamic explains why we will not be able to eradicate all infectious diseases, a topic we shall treat in greater detail below in the case of pandemics like HIV/AIDS.

☐ Genes

Natural selection generally operates to reduce or eliminate defective genes created by mutations, but sometimes genes that cause disease are selected for because they also provide benefits. A classic example is the retention of a high frequency of genes that causes sickle-cell anemia in African populations that live in areas where malaria is prevalent. Individuals who are heterozygous for this gene benefit from its protection against malaria because it can speed the removal of infected cells. However, if an individual inherits the gene from both parents (homozygotes) then he or she gets sickle-cell anaemia, which in the past usually led to an early death before reaching reproductive age. This case illustrates a context-specific *heterozygous advantage* since this form is superior to both homozygous forms because it confers a resistance to malaria. Natural selection would reduce genes causing sickle-cell anemia in a population living in an ecology free of the threat of malaria. However, natural selection would not eliminate the gene entirely because it is recessive. Once the gene is relatively rare in a population (one in a thousand) the odds that random mating would lead to the deleterious homozygote are exceedingly rare (one in a million). Thus, as the frequency of the gene decreases, the power of natural selection to eliminate it decreases even faster.

☐ Defenses

Ewald (1994) and Nesse and Williams (1994) stress the distinction between symptoms of a disease that represent defects and those that constitute an adaptive response by the organism or a defense against the disease. In their example of pneumonia, a person may exhibit a change in skin color accompanied by frequent coughing. The bluish skin color is the result of a lack of oxygen in the hemoglobin, clearly a deficit caused by the disease. In contrast, the cough is a coordinated defense that has been shaped by natural selection because it serves an adaptive function, namely to expel mucus and rid the body of harmful bacteria. The implication is that confusing the body's naturally designed defenses with other symptoms may hamper recovery if a treatment suppresses the bodily defenses and has the effect of prolonging or aggravating the illness.

☐ Design Compromises

A cost-benefit analysis of different designs usually reveals an inevitable trade-off that makes a perfect design impossible. In World War II bombers could be designed with thick defenses against flak but they would suffer more hits because they were heavier, slower, and less maneuverable. In human evolution, a bipedal design gave us the ability to travel while carrying food and babies, but also predisposed us to back problems (Nesse & Williams, 1994).

☐ Evolutionary Legacies

Finally, designs that are gradually shaped by natural selection can be marvelous, but never perfect. As products of the blind forces of selection they are the best possible result of a process constrained by limited evolutionary pathways, design trade-offs, random effects, and imperfect reproduction. In short, nature's designs do not reveal divine perfection, just the relentless pursuit of adaptation.

☐ Host–Pathogen Arms Race

Throughout human evolution the body has had to ward off the unpleasant and sometimes fatal effects of infections caused by invasions of pathogens such as bacteria, viruses, and other parasites. As Ridley (1993) has argued in *The Red Queen*, this host–pathogen relationship may be likened to a continuous arms race where each side struggles to gain the upper hand. Essentially, the strategies of the pathogens are designed to replicate copies and spread them far and wide. Strategies of the host are designed to kill or expel the invading pathogens. Unpleasant symptoms of infectious diseases, like sneezing, coughing, fever, and diarrhea may be recast within this scenario as evolved strategies by the host organism or the pathogen in this arms race. Of course, the ultimate defense system of the host is the immune system, an ancient adaptation that first evolved in reptiles. To understand the body's various defense mechanisms it is first necessary to understand in more detail what they are defending us from.

A common class of pathogens are bacteria, tiny single-celled organisms that can exist both outside a host organism, and sometimes only inside a host. Many different forms of bacteria exist, involving quite different strategies and counterstrategies. An invading army of shigella bacteria causes the host to suffer from various forms of dysentery. The intestinal defense involves a series of contractions in the gut and diarrhea in order to flush out the bacteria as efficiently as possible. Studies show that some medicines like Lomotil can reduce these symptoms but prolong the infection (Oliwenstein, 1998).

In other cases, such as cholera, these same symptoms look more like a strategy designed by the bacteria to spread from one host to another. Cholera kills many of its hosts but since it induces severe diarrhea within hours of contagion it is able to survive and multiply by moving quickly from host to host. Cholera bacteria induce diarrhea by producing toxins that cause the gut to flush out both beneficial and cholera bacteria. In the case of cholera, everything possible must be done to halt the spread of the infection, including treating the symptom of diarrhea.

Many bacterial infections induce the body to raise its internal temperature and reduce the percentage of iron in the bloodstream by as much as 80%. These reactions cause the patient to feel listless and feverish, prompting medical treatments to reduce the fever and add iron into the blood. However, from the perspective of Darwinian medicine, both treatments aid the invading bacteria, which require iron to multiply and which cannot survive in higher body temperatures.

Besides the body's natural defenses against invasions of various bacteria, scientists have also developed medical techniques using antibiotics to combat them. The modern era of antibiotics really got underway when Alexander Fleming made a serendipitous observation in his laboratory in 1929. He noticed that the bacteria he was cultivating in petri dishes were negatively affected by nearby colonies of the mold *Penicillium*. This simple observation was soon developed into one of the greatest miracles of modern medicine as the newly invented penicillin vaccine to combat staphylococcal bacteria associated with wound infections saved millions of lives of wounded soldiers in World War II.

Antibiotics derived from mold have evolved over millions of years in fungi to attack bacteria while at the same time remaining nontoxic to the fungi. The use of such antibiotics together with other public health measures in the mid-20th century led to spectacular successes in reducing deaths from bacteria that cause tuberculosis, pneumonia, and many other infectious diseases. However, given the widespread use of antibiotics and enough time, bacteria have counterattacked with their own strategies. Here is a brief account of the fate of penicillin provided by Nesse and Williams (1994, p. 53):

> Consider staphylococcal bacteria, the most common cause of wound infection. In 1941 all such bacteria were vulnerable to penicillin. By 1944, some strains had already evolved to make enzymes that could break down penicillin. Today, 95% of staphylococcus strains show some resistance to penicillin. In the 1950s, an artificial penicillin, methicillin, was developed that could kill these organisms, but the bacteria soon evolved ways around this as well, and still new drugs needed to be produced. The drug ciprofloxacin raised great hopes when it was introduced in the 1980s, but 80% of the staphylococcus strains in New York City are now resistant to it. In an Oregon Veterans' Administration hospital the rate of resistance went from 5% to over 80% in a single year.

Currently, we are spending $40 billion a year on this particular arms race (Quammen, 2005). As these different cases demonstrate, an evolutionary perspective is a useful and necessary adjunct to conventional medicine for understanding, preventing, and treating infectious diseases.

Viral infections involve even smaller, simpler pathogens than bacteria. Viruses, however, can be extremely deadly agents, as most people today understand given the human immunodeficiency virus or HIV. Other viruses that have evolved strategies that rely on their host to disperse them within a population of similar hosts may be a nuisance, causing us to cough and sneeze. The common cold virus that exists throughout the world in about 100 different varieties (all of which are constantly evolving) is a good example of a simple RNA-type virus. It is not fatal to the host but just virulent enough to induce the host to pass it along to others. A single sneeze can contain as many as a million tiny droplets that settle to the ground very slowly. Although they would be dispersed very quickly in the open or killed by sunlight, indoors they can hang around for weeks. This makes enclosed spaces containing many people an excellent breeding ground or what Paul Ewald (1994) calls a *cultural vector* for airborne infectious diseases. What might be some common cultural vectors for spreading such disease? A daycare or school, airplane, nursing home, or hospital are all excellent candidates. In hospitals and nursing homes, patients are often confined for long periods of time, but medical personnel and equipment move from room to room and can unwittingly spread diseases if hygiene measures are not practiced diligently.

☐ Pandemics

Cultural vectors that combine enclosed spaces with long distance travel have caused and continue to cause a large proportion of the major epidemics that have wiped out hundreds of millions of people. In the second and third centuries, measles and smallpox epidemics spread along caravan routes killing a third of the people in those communities that had not already been exposed to such diseases. This phenomenon was revisited over a thousand years later when Europeans brought smallpox to the New World, unintentionally killing many more Native Americans than those who died from warfare. The bubonic plague was similarly spread from Asia, where it had long smouldered, to European port cities in Europe where it eventually spread to unexposed populations and killed one out of every three Europeans. All of these examples qualify as worldwide epidemics or *pandemics*.

Bubonic Plague

The Plague of Justinian in AD 541–542 is the first of three firmly recorded pandemics of bubonic plague, though there are suggestive reports recorded much earlier in biblical records and Greek writings. This outbreak is thought to have originated in Ethiopia or Egypt, coming by water to the huge city of Constantinople. Transport ships carrying massive amounts of grain, mostly from Egypt, were likely to have been the source of contagion for the city, aided by public granaries that nurtured the rat and flea population.

Bubonic plague is the most common form of plague and is primarily a disease of rodents. Human infection most often occurs when a person is bitten by a rat flea that has fed on an infected rodent. The disease becomes evident 3 to 7 days after the infection. Initial symptoms are chills, fever, diarrhea, headaches, and the formation of buboes. The buboes are formed by the infection of the lymph nodes, which swell and become prominent. If unchecked, the bacteria infects the bloodstream (septicemic plague) and can progress to the lungs (pneumonic plague).

In septicemic plague there is bleeding into the skin and other organs, which creates black patches on the skin, hence the name "black death." People who die from this form of plague often die on the same day symptoms first appear. With pneumonic plague infecting lungs comes the possibility of person-to-person transmission through respiratory droplets associated with coughing and sneezing.

At its peak the Plague of Justinian killed approximately 5000 people in Constantinople daily until 40% of the city's inhabitants succumbed. It went on to destroy up to a quarter of the human population of the eastern Mediterranean. Only a few years later in AD 588, a second major plague wave spread through the Mediterranean into what is now France, with estimates as high as 25 million dead.

An even more famous and deadly pandemic struck during the mid-14th century. In the early 1330s an outbreak of deadly bubonic plague occurred in China. Since China was one of the busiest of the world's trading nations, it was only a matter of time before the outbreak spread to western Asia and Europe. In October of 1347, several Italian merchant ships returned from a trip to the Black Sea, one of the key links in trade with China. When the ships docked in Sicily, many of those on board were already dying of plague. Within days the disease spread to the city and the surrounding countryside, despite efforts to contain it.

By the following August, the plague had spread as far north as England, where people called it "the black death" because of the black spots it produced on the skin. A merciless killer was loose across Europe, and Medieval medicine had nothing to combat it. In winter the disease seemed to disappear, but only because fleas—which were now helping to carry it from person to person—are dormant then. Each spring, the plague attacked again. With an estimated 237 million victims throughout the many years of infection, it constitutes the largest death toll from any known pandemic. In Europe alone, an estimated 25 million people out of a total population of 75 million died in less than 5 years between 1347 and 1352. A strong presence of the more contagious pneumonic and septicemic varieties increased the pace of infection, spreading the disease deep into inland areas. In the worst case, the lungs became infected and the pneumonic form was spread from person to person by coughing, sneezing, or simply talking. The time of infection to death was less than one week.

Even when the worst was over, smaller outbreaks continued, not just for years, but for centuries. The survivors lived in constant fear of the plague's return. Smaller plagues continued to strike parts of Europe from the 15th to the 17th century, with varying degrees of intensity. A third pandemic began in China in 1855, spreading the bubonic plague to all inhabited continents, and ultimately killing more than 12 million people in India and China alone. Like the two earlier pandemics, this pandemic was likely spread around the world through ocean-going trade, transporting infected persons, rats, and cargos harboring fleas. From port cities, a more virulent pneumonic strain spread to inland regions via a strong person-to-person contagion.

Since the 19th century changes in hygiene habits and strong public health and sanitation efforts have reduced the rate of infection from infectious diseases, including the plague. Throughout the 20th century, the World Health Organization reports 1000 to 3000 human cases of plague every year, with an average of 1670 per year between 1966 and 1993.

Spanish Flu

Unfortunately, other equally severe pandemics were recorded in the 20th century. At its worst, the bubonic plague killed approximately 5 million victims a year. As bad as that is, the worst human death rate ever recorded was the influenza of 1918 to 1919, right after World War I. The war killed 9 million men in 4 years, but the so-called Spanish flu was responsible for over 25 million deaths in one year alone.

The death toll in the United States was 850,000 people, making it an area of the world that was least devastated by this virus. However, eastern port cities were hit hard, with death tolls in Philadelphia estimated at 158 out of 1000 and similar prevalence rates in Baltimore and Washington, D.C. Luxury ocean liners from Europe would arrive in New York with 7% fewer passengers than they embarked with. The confined area of the ship was especially conducive to the spread of the disease.

In just a year and a half from the outbreak an estimated 25 to 40 million people died worldwide. Then, just 18 months after the flu appeared, it vanished. Only recently have scientists begun to unravel the mystery of its sudden outbreak and equally sudden disappearance. In 1997 researchers at the Armed Forces Institute of Pathology in Washington, D.C., isolated genetic material from the virus. Because there was no living virus available, they obtained material from lung specimens preserved in formaldehyde by army doctors in 1918. The researchers spent nearly two years extracting just 7% of the genetic code. Based on this evidence, it appears that the virus passed from birds to pigs and then to humans. The viruses tend to remain stable in the birds, but occasionally they infect pigs. Then the pig immune system is activated forcing the virus to mutate in order to survive. Both the Asian flu (1957) and the Hong Kong flu (1968), which killed between one and four million people, mutated from pig viruses.

In the 21st century an avian flu virus endemic in Asia appears to be evolving in ways that increasingly heighten the possibility of another pandemic. The H5N1 virus, a subtype of the avian influenza virus, is found in poultry. Since the initial outbreak, millions of chickens, ducks, and other birds in Asia and Africa have been slaughtered. Thus far the human death toll has been checked, but there is not yet a vaccine for the disease. Meanwhile the virus has undergone relentless genetic changes and become even more pathogenic. It now affects not only birds, but also cats, pigs, and even tigers.

There is some evidence that influenza pandemics occur on a regular cycle, with one every 20 to 30 years. Any potential pandemic is likely to emerge from developing countries with limited means to contain it. Migratory birds and domestic ducks may be responsible for its spread to other continents. These birds typically show no symptoms but excrete the highly pathogenic virus and play an important role in its transmission to other bird populations.

HIV/AIDS

Over the past 30 years we have witnessed the worldwide spread of the human immunodeficiency virus, which has resulted in the deaths of over 40 million people worldwide from AIDS. Unlike the viruses previously described, HIV does not attempt to escape detection by the immune system; it attacks it instead. The immune system's T-cells that coordinate the counterattack against the virus are continuously destroyed by the HIV virus. Following infection, an individual with HIV typically remains healthy for a time. During this period, the body produces enough T-cells to offset the losses to the HIV virus. But over time the system is overwhelmed and T-cells are eventually destroyed at a faster rate than they are produced. This leaves the body vulnerable to any other pathogens that may be around. Although these pathogens may cause only mild infections in healthy individuals they can be serious or fatal to an individual with an advanced case of HIV infection, producing an acquired immune deficiency syndrome, or AIDS.

From the initial outbreak of HIV/AIDS in the late 1970s this new pathogen spread rapidly.

> In Western countries, AIDS appeared initially as a disease mainly of male homosexuals because their large numbers of sex partners greatly accelerated sexual transmission, and of intravenous drug users because the drug user's needles were effective vectors. ... Conversely, the use of clean needles and condoms can not only curtail the transmission of the virus, *it can also cause the evolution of lower virulence.* (Nesse & Williams, 1994, p. 61)

Despite unparalleled large-scale public health measures and education, in 2005 there were approximately 5 million new cases of HIV, and approximately 3 million deaths from AIDS, all of which were preventable in principle. By far the region of the world most affected by the HIV/AIDS pandemic is sub-Saharan Africa where current rates of infection are 10 to 70 times higher than the rates of other regions.

☐ Evolutionary Psychiatry

The evolutionary logic outlined previously in relation to physical diseases can also be applied to mental illness. Mechanisms designed by natural selection to serve specific functions are not perfect and may under certain circumstances go awry. Such circumstances may be more frequent in novel environments that are far different than the human EEA. Like physical diseases, there may exist confusion between symptoms of the disease and evolved defense mechanisms that serve adaptive functions. Some scholars believe that an evolutionary perspective is not only helpful, but ultimately necessary, to properly distinguish abnormal behavior from behaviors that fall within the normal range.

The use of diagnostic criteria set forth in the official *Diagnostic and Statistical Manual of Mental Disorders (DSM)* to differentiate specific psychiatric disorders and estimate their prevalence rates has been increasingly called into question by evolutionary scholars (Troisi, 2008; Wakefield, 2005). Currently about 50% of Americans adults will be diagnosed with a psychiatric disorder during their lifetime (Kessler et al., 2005a). When applied to the 2004 U.S. Census residential population estimate for ages 18 and older, this figure translates to over 115 million people (U.S. Census Bureau, 2005).

Of course, the problem of defining mental and personality disorders, as distinct from the vast array of normal problems that people everywhere grapple with during the course of their everyday lives, is extremely difficult. Nevertheless, these data documenting implausibly high prevalence rates clearly necessitate a rethinking of the *DSM-IV* as a diagnostic tool. Indeed, another major revision of the *DSM* was currently underway in 2009. However, all previous revisions have led to a proliferation of the number of "distinct" disorders and ever-increasing life-time prevalence rates of total psychiatric disorders. These are trends that cannot continue.

In this book, we have emphasized developmental and evolutionary perspectives—both of which may be useful in remedying this situation. Following the harmful dysfunction analysis of Wakefield (1992, 2005), we shall present the view that any disorder must be

1) *Harmful, that is, negative as judged by social values*; and
2) *Caused by a dysfunction, that is, by failure of a psychological mechanism to perform its function, in the sense of biological function.* (Wakefield, 2005, p. 891)

This scheme involving two criteria implies that value judgments within any particular culture alone are insufficient to determine whether a given behavior is pathological, since a separate dysfunction criterion must also be met. This criterion serves as a check on an undesirable proliferation of different disorders or a spectacular rise in prevalence for any given disorder. Another check is provided by a third criterion. Most consider it as axiomatic that (3) *any psychiatric disorder is, by definition, relatively rare.*

According to these criteria it would not be possible for any society to label 20% of their citizens as schizophrenic on political grounds and hold them in hospitals against their will. In examining the question of what is harmful, one must ultimately consider for whom the "disorder" is harmful. Finally, following the logic of developmental psychopathology, I would add a fourth criterion for evaluating developmental disorders: (4) *harmful for the individual's present well-being or future development.* Thus, certain forms of anxious attachment might be classifiable as a psychiatric disorder because they are harmful to the present and future well-being of the child and dysfunctional from the standpoint of not serving the biological function for which the attachment system evolved. However, classifying one out of three infants as suffering from an attachment disorder, or one out of four boys as having attention-deficit hyperactivity disorder (ADHD) would not meet the criterion of relative rarity necessary for diagnosing a psychiatric disorder. As we shall see, these four postulates, while simple and straightforward, are likely to give rise to various controversies and debates. Such debates may be healthy and essential in keeping the number of different disorders and their prevalence rates from increasing to absurd levels and for eliminating disorders that are neither harmful to the individual nor dysfunctional in the biological sense.

Fear-Related Problems

Because many mental disorders are actually emotional problems or lead to emotional symptoms, we begin with a common group of affective disorders in order to illustrate the connection to evolved emotional responses. Elsewhere, I have argued that there is abundant behavioral evidence for an evolved fear system (LaFreniere, 2005). In this section I discuss stimuli that seem to arouse innate fears in humans and the behavioral/emotional systems that are connected to fear, including phobias, panic disorders, and anxiety.

Gray (1987) proposed five general principles to account for all fear stimuli: intensity, novelty, evolutionary dangers, social stimuli, and conditioned stimuli. Pain and loud noise are examples of intense stimuli, though animals respond in a variety of ways to pain, including anger-aggression as well as fear-avoidance. Bowlby (1969) considered that infant fears are caused by a combination of biology and experience and that infants would more readily respond with fear to events or situations that provided the infant with "natural clues to danger." Bowlby listed only four such cues: pain, being left alone, sudden changes in stimulation, and rapid approach. Gray expanded the list of the potential stimuli that might have an evolutionary basis to include fear of strangers, separation anxiety and fear of being alone, fear of open places, heights, falling or loss of support, fear of the dark, and fear of snakes or spiders.

At least four of these infant fears have been sufficiently researched to document characteristics consistent with an evolved domain-specific response system: stranger distress, separation anxiety, fear of heights, and fear of impending collision. Other fears that were once considered to be innate have now been demonstrated to be learned, but the learning of the fear response to some objects (but not others) is so reliable, fast, and permanent as to call for special explanation.

Prepotency and Preparedness

Prepotency refers to findings that show people to be faster at identifying fear-inducing objects (like snakes) from an array of objects that include non-fear-inducing objects (like flowers). It appears that our brains are prewired to be vigilant for certain dangers in our evolutionary environment of adaptation. We are also inclined to show specific responses to prepotent stimuli. Thus it is far easier to condition a fear response to a picture of a snake than to a picture of a flower or some other nonthreatening object. This predisposition to respond in certain ways to specific stimuli is referred to as *preparedness*. The other evolutionary solution to this adaptive problem is to provide the infant offspring with reflexes that quickly mature into adaptive responses and to hardwire into the neural circuitry of the organism certain innate fears.

Many common phobias resemble either or both of these evolutionary solutions. Some phobias make adaptive sense as a means of avoiding danger, such as fear of heights, but are considered phobic responses because they are so exaggerated that they become dysfunctional in everyday life. Other phobias show an ease of acquisition (e.g., fear of snakes) that is consistent with the concepts of prepotency and preparedness. Finally, phobias show a certain degree of permanence in that they are difficult to "unlearn." Although exposure treatment has been shown to be effective (Marks & Tobena, 1990), its effectiveness may consist of suppressing the fear response rather than unlearning the association.

Anxiety

Of all the major mental health disorders, anxiety disorders are the most prevalent. Estimates of one-year prevalence of anxiety disorders combining data from the Epidemiological Catchment Area study and the National Comorbidity Survey (NCS) put the prevalence at 16.4% (Kessler et al., 1993). Moreover, data from the NCS indicates that anxiety disorders are more chronic than either mood disorders or substance abuse disorders (Kessler et al., 1994). Given these data on prevalence and chronicity, anxiety disorders are associated with substantial costs, accounting for approximately 30% of total costs of mental health care, compared to 22% for mood disorders and 20% for schizophrenia (Rice & Miller, 1993). DuPont et al. (1996) estimated these costs in 1990 at $46.6 billion out of a total expenditure on mental illness of $147.8 billion for that year alone, or 31.5% of the total. Since the 1990s prevalence rates and their associated costs have continued to increase. The latest data available indicate that in 2005 approximately 40 million American adults ages 18 and older (18.1%) had an anxiety disorder. These numbers do not include an additional 9% of Americans estimated to have had a *DSM-IV* personality disorder (Samuels et al., 2002), which includes another cluster of anxious disorders (i.e., avoidant personality disorder, dependent personality disorder, and obsessive-compulsive personality disorder).

Among children and adolescence the combined prevalence of anxiety disorders is also higher than all other mental disorders (Costello et al., 1996). The one-year prevalence in children ages 9 to 17 is 13%, including separation anxiety disorder, generalized anxiety disorder, social anxiety disorder (social phobia), and obsessive-compulsive disorder. However, such discrete categories of anxiety disorders may be fictional, as the comorbidity between them can be as high as 90% (Klein & Pine, 2002), eliminating even the possibility of an empirical demonstration of discriminant validity. For example, in a study of anxiety disorders in over 2000 Dutch children the distinctions among the types of anxiety were not found to be valid (Ferdinand, Van Lang, Ormel, & Verhulst, 2006). A number of similar affective and cognitive processes appear to be common across the entire range of disorders, including hyperarousal, hypervigilance, narrow focus of attention, overestimation of risk, and avoidance of threat (Craske, 2003). In addition to this problem of pseudo comorbidity between various types of anxiety disorders, symptoms of anxiety very commonly co-occur with depression, with comorbidity estimates ranging from 30% to 50% (Curry, March, & Hervey, 2004).

From an evolutionary perspective anxiety makes adaptive sense in some circumstances. Unpredictable or threatening situations may give rise to anxiety, which takes the form of a heightened sensitivity to indicators of potential danger. Unlike fear, there is no clear and present danger, and no clear and immediate response, such as flight. Since the danger or threat is not clearly perceived, no precise course of action is warranted, but a generalized uneasiness persists. According to Nesse (2005), anxiety may have evolved as an inexpensive response system that protects against potentially costly dangers. Although they can be annoying and inconvenient, false alarms are less costly than failing to respond to a real crisis. Like other functional emotions that can be unpleasant (such as anger or sadness), dysfunctional anxiety must be defined within the context of an evolved emotional system.

Deficient anxiety (or deficient anger or sadness) could also be viewed as problematic, though hypophobias are rarely studied (Marks & Nesse, 1994). One example of potential dysfunction arising from a hypophobia involves a study that attempted to establish that fear of heights results from severe falls early in life. Instead they found adult fear of heights in just 3% of the group who suffered a fall early in life, compared to 18% in the control group, indicating that those with a deficient fear of heights early in life maintained this hypophobia decades later. Anxiety (like depression) may also be viewed as a disorder whose prevalence in contemporary society has increased due to the *mismatch* between our modern, fast-paced, competitive, and often impersonal society and our evolved tendencies for communal life in our ancestral environment. Natural selection may not have adequately prepared us for the stress of life in crowded cities of 20 million people where anxiety responses are frequent, but in which potential threats are never evaluated carefully enough to reduce their frequency.

Panic Attacks and Agoraphobia

Panic attacks and agoraphobia represent the extreme tips of such anxieties, and as psychiatric disorders, are relatively rare. For example, the prevalence rate of panic disorder is estimated at about 0.08%, affecting 6 of 1000 men and 10 of 1000 women. A panic attack consists of an overwhelming sense of anxiety that does not appear to have any specific "trigger." The individual who experiences such an unpredictable panic attack may suffer acutely for a half hour or so from symptoms like shortness of breath, sweating, flushing, dizziness, chest pain, and an irresistible need to "get out of here."

Most of the symptoms used to diagnose a panic attack involve behaviors related to an escape response. The main difference between the two responses is that for those suffering from panic disorder the response is triggered too easily and too often.

In agoraphobia, similar symptoms as a panic attack occur under specific conditions: the attack occurs in unfamiliar surroundings, wide open spaces, or crowds of strangers. These precipitating conditions make evolutionary sense since our hominid ancestors would be more readily exposed to dangers of all kinds under similar circumstances. Moreover, the typical response of agoraphobics to seek relief from their symptoms in their home with the company of family members is consistent with an evolutionary perspective, because here an escape response would be unnecessary.

Nesse (1987) proposes that if panic disorder and agoraphobia represent extreme forms of an evolved escape response, (1) they should show similar patterns across cultures, and (2) medications that block panic attacks would block other adaptive anxiety responses as well. In this view, medications should be designed to shift the threshold of the response towards the norm rather than prevent the response from occurring.

Depression

The adaptive function of sadness and depression appears to be less obvious than for fear and anxiety. Of what possible use to us are such emotions and moods? Several evolutionary explanations have been proposed and empirically supported over the years, but first it must be noted that many different types of depression exist and a number of different pathways to the disorder are possible. Indeed Sroufe and Rutter (1984) believe that the persistent search for a single cause for a disorder was one of the most troublesome myths that hindered research into the etiology of many mental disorders. Today recognition that different types of causes can lead to different types of depression is commonplace.

The *DSM* recognizes several distinct types of "mood disorders," including major depressive disorder, dysthymic disorder (chronic, mild depression), and bipolar disorder. Like many mental disorders, depression (or at least its diagnosis) has been increasing recently in Western societies at an alarming rate and may soon become the second biggest health-care problem after heart disease. Approximately 20.9 million American adults, or about 9.5% of the U.S. population age 18 and older in a given year, have a mood disorder (Table 12.1; Kessler, Chiu, Demler, & Walters, 2005b), and major depressive disorder is the leading cause of disability in the United States for those ages 15 to 44 (World Health Organization, 2004). Major depressive disorder affects approximately 14.8 million American adults, or about 6.7 percent of the U.S. population age 18 and older in a given year

TABLE 12.1 Annual Prevalence Rates
of Anxiety and Mood Disorders
in the United States

Anxiety Disorders (18%)	
Panic disorder	2.7%
Obsessive-compulsive disorder (OCD)	1%
Post-traumatic stress disorder (PTSD)	3.5%
Generalized anxiety disorder (GAD)	3.1%
Social phobia	6.8%
Agoraphobia	0.8%
Specific Phobia	8.7%
Mood Disorders (9.5%)	
Major depressive disorder	6.7%
Dysthymic disorder	1.5%
Bipolar disorder	2.6%
Suicide	.001%

(Kessler et al., 2005b), and it is more prevalent in women than in men, by nearly 2:1 (Crick & Zahn-Waxler, 2003; Kessler et al., 2003).

Clinicians recognize that reactive depression is a normal response to a particularly stressful event such as the death of a loved one. In contrast, clinically diagnosed depression may be unrelated to life events or it may be an unusually intense and protracted reaction to them. Symptoms include sadness, lethargy, social withdrawal, and suicidal ideation, though suicide itself is rare. Because it is such a frequent problem in humans, and because emotions of grief and bereavement are universal, evolutionary scholars have argued that sadness and inactivity may serve important adaptive problems, and depression has become a central topic in Darwinian psychiatry.

From a functionalist perspective emotions are viewed as arising from the pursuit of one's goals (Campos, Mumme, Kermoian, & Campos, 1994). Frustration and anger may arise when an important goal is blocked and the focusing of attention and energetic physiological component of these emotions is viewed as functional in overcoming obstacles. However, if persistent effort results in failure with respect to the goal, then low mood motivates disengagement (Nesse, 2005). This kind of "tactical withdrawal" has been called the *social navigational hypothesis* (Watson & Andrews, 2002). According to this view positive mood serves to increase initiative and risk taking when potential payoffs are high, while low mood motivates changing strategies when risks are high, thus avoiding wasteful expenditures of energy. When such goals are essential to the individual and no alternative strategy is found, depression may result (Klinger, 1975).

An earlier theory of depression that can be seen as a more specific instance of this general functionalist perspective was advocated by a British clinician, John Price (Price, 1967; Price, Sloman, Gardner, Gilbert, & Rohde, 1994). According to Price's *social competition hypothesis,* individuals who lose status after a failed hierarchy struggle may withdraw into a state of depression and inactivity as a result. Price views such a response as an evolved mechanism in social species that live within a dominance hierarchy. The function of the response is to reduce aggression and any potential threat and thus protect the individual from further attack. If indeed such a mechanism has evolved in social hierarchical species then homologous behaviors should be evident in these species.

Recent research in primates provides evidence of homology with respect to "yielding" in dominance struggles. In their research with vervet monkeys, McGuire and colleagues at UCLA have reported a positive association between mood and status that appears to be mediated by the neurotransmitter serotonin (McGuire, Troisi, & Raleigh, 1997). First, they found that the alpha males in each group of vervets had serotonin levels that were twice as high as subordinate males. When the alpha males lost their position they noted two responses: serotonin levels fell and their behavior changed dramatically. Previously confident high-status monkeys were subsequently observed to exhibit behaviors typical of depression in monkeys such as stereotypic rocking, huddling, and loss of appetite. Even more interesting, these behaviors were alleviated by giving the monkeys the antidepressant Prozac to artificially increase serotonin levels. Further experiments revealed that after removing the alpha male from a group, randomly chosen males who were given Prozac invariably rose to the top of the hierarchy (McGuire & Troisi, 1998; McGuire, Troisi, & Raleigh, 1997).

In humans, the picture may be more complex. However, Price's social competition hypothesis has been indirectly supported by findings of low levels of serotonin in many cases of depression and by data indicating that high-status, aggressive, and competitive men typically have high levels of serotonin. Current data regarding this hypothesis could not be directly applied to explaining depression in women; however, some theorists have suggested that their greater vulnerability to depression may arise from a perception of powerlessness (Gilbert, 1992) and/or be associated with their lower levels of serotonin production than men. At the present time the availability of monoamines in the brain, a group of neurochemicals including serotonin, dopamine, and norepinephrine, is widely accepted as the leading biological factor underlying clinical depression (Leonard, 1997). Antidepressant drugs typically increase serotonin availability in the synapse immediately, but because depressive symptoms persist for several weeks or more after the administration of antidepressant medication, a simple cause-effect hypothesis can be eliminated.

Other evolutionary theorists have suggested that female depression may have distinct causes and serve quite different functions in women. In the general functionalist sense, as for men, depression may signal that current strategies are failing and a new approach is needed. Failure to be accepted or sudden deterioration of close relationships, as opposed to loss of status, may be an important trigger of depressive episodes in women. Alternatively, several researchers view depression as a desperate form of social manipulation, what might be termed the *social bargaining theory* of depression. For example, behaviorist investigators have found that mothers may use depressive symptoms as a last resort to control interpersonal conflicts within the family, particularly if family members respond to the appearance of such symptoms with improved behavior. As a more extreme example of social bargaining, Hagen (2002) views postpartum depression as a "blackmail threat" to abandon the infant, although it is likely that acute postpartum depression is associated with decreased levels of estrogen caused by childbirth (Parry & Newton, 2001).

Finally, as with many mental disorders listed in *DSM-IV*, prevalence rates for depression are on the rise, particularly for young people, and in affluent Western societies (Nesse & Williams, 1994). One of the most significant aspects of an evolutionary perspective is to raise questions about features of contemporary society that create conditions for such widespread maladaptation. Many scholars (e.g., Nesse & Williams, 1994) discuss features of modern society that they view as potentially harmful to the modern psyche, particularly the relative absence of community.

Social support is a well-known *protective factor* for depression in that it reduces the probability of its onset whatever other risk factors may be operating. Conversely, social isolation is itself a *risk factor* for depression because it increases the probability of its onset. It follows that if more people today live in social isolation without effective social support, they are vulnerable to severe depression when the inevitable problems of life arise, whatever these precipitating stressful events may be. In this view, it is not the existence of stressful events per se that explains the increase in prevalence rates of depression, but the disintegration of supportive communities and the increased degree of social isolation. According to Robert Wright (1994), 25% of households in the United States consist of a single person, compared to 8% in 1940. It would be difficult to argue that the stresses of the widespread poverty of the Great Depression and the uncertainties and sacrifices of World War II were relatively insignificant stressors compared to the stress of contemporary American life. It would not be difficult to argue that the urban neighborhoods of that era provided more supportive networks of family and friends than those of today.

Evolutionary psychologists extend this same line of reasoning back in time to our ancestral past. Anthropological accounts of existing hunter-gatherer societies like the !Kung San of southern Africa or remote agrarian small-scale societies reveal a high degree of social cohesion and relative absence of depressive symptoms. In these relatively small groups that typify life in our ancestral past, people live in close contact with an extended family of kin and neighbors for most of their lives. They may move to a neighboring village and join a new family network upon marriage or return to their own if separated. From birth until death they remain immersed in a stable and supportive community. Rivalries and tensions may exist but they are generally open and frequently resolved in short order (Wright, 1994). Viewed from this perspective, we may be ill equipped by nature to live in a novel environment of millions of people living in close proximity and near complete anonymity, given that our inherited emotional and social predispositions prepared us for life in small, stable communities of extended kin. To the extent that individuals are able to create such communities within the wider ecological framework of their urban existence they may be expected to live healthier lives.

☐ Chapter Summary

Darwinian medicine has elaborated evolutionary explanations for human vulnerabilities to diseases, including mental illness and psychopathology. One of the first systematic efforts to explain diseases from an evolutionary perspective was a collaboration between a physician, Randolph Nesse, and an evolutionary biologist, George Williams. In their now classic work, entitled *Why We Get Sick*, they formulated six possible answers:

1. Novel environments
2. Infection
3. Genes
4. Defenses
5. Design compromises
6. Evolutionary legacies

Throughout human evolution the body has had to ward off the unpleasant and sometimes fatal effects of infections caused by invasions of pathogens such as bacteria, viruses, and other parasites. The metaphor of *The Red Queen* has been used to liken this host-pathogen relationship to a continuous arms race where each side struggles to gain the upper hand. Essentially, the strategies of the pathogens are designed to replicate copies and spread them far and wide. Strategies of the host are designed to kill or expel the invading pathogens. Unpleasant symptoms of infectious diseases like sneezing, coughing, fever, and diarrhea may be recast within this scenario as evolved strategies by the host organism or the pathogen in this arms race.

Viral infections involve even smaller, simpler pathogens than bacteria. Viruses, however, can be extremely deadly agents, as most people today understand given the human immunodeficiency virus or HIV. Other viruses that have evolved strategies that rely on their host to disperse them within a population of similar hosts may be a nuisance, causing us to cough and sneeze. Enclosed spaces containing many people provide an excellent breeding ground or what Paul Ewald (1994) calls a *cultural vector* for airborne infectious diseases. Cultural vectors that combine enclosed spaces with long distance travel have caused and continue to cause a large proportion of the major epidemics that have wiped out hundreds of millions of people in worldwide epidemics or *pandemics*.

Over the past 30 years we have witnessed another pandemic. The worldwide spread of HIV has resulted in the deaths of over 40 million people from AIDS. HIV does not attempt to escape detection by the immune system; it attacks it instead. The immune system's T-cells that coordinate the counterattack against the virus are continuously destroyed by the HIV virus. Over time the system is overwhelmed and T-cells are eventually destroyed at a faster rate than they are produced. This leaves the body vulnerable to any other pathogens that may be around. Although these pathogens may cause only mild infections in healthy individuals they can be serious or fatal to an individual with an advanced case of HIV infection, producing an acquired immune deficiency syndrome, or AIDS.

The evolutionary logic outlined previously in relation to physical diseases also applies to mental illness. Mechanisms designed by natural selection to serve specific functions are not perfect and may under certain circumstances go awry. Many believe that an evolutionary perspective is not only helpful, but ultimately necessary, to properly determine what is normal and what is abnormal. In this book we have also emphasized the necessary coordination of developmental and evolutionary perspectives—both of which are essential to defining normal versus abnormal.

Following the harmful dysfunction analysis of Wakefield (1992, 2005), we shall present the view that any disorder must have the following characteristics:

1. It must be harmful, that is, negative as judged by social values.
2. It must be caused by a dysfunction, that is, by failure of a psychological mechanism to perform its function, in the sense of biological function.
3. Any psychiatric disorder is, by definition, relatively rare.
4. It must be harmful for the individual's present well-being or future development.

Because many, if not most, mental disorders are actually emotional problems, we begin with a common group of affective disorders in order to illustrate the connection to evolved emotional responses. Some fears that were once considered to be innate have now been demonstrated to be learned, but the learning of the fear response to some objects (but not others) is so reliable, fast, and permanent as to call for special explanation. *Prepotency* refers to findings that show people to be faster at identifying fear-inducing objects (like snakes) from an array of objects that include non-fear-inducing objects (like flowers). We are also inclined to show specific responses to prepotent stimuli, referred to as *preparedness*. The other evolutionary solution to this adaptive problem is to provide the infant offspring with reflexes that quickly mature into adaptive responses and to hardwire into the neural circuitry of the organism certain innate fears.

Many common phobias resemble either or both of these evolutionary solutions. Some phobias make adaptive sense as a means of avoiding danger, such as fear of heights, but are considered phobic responses because they are so exaggerated that they become dysfunctional in everyday life. Other phobias show an ease of acquisition (e.g., fear of snakes) that is consistent with the concepts of prepotency and preparedness. Finally, phobias show a certain degree of permanence in that they are difficult to "unlearn."

Each year over 20 million Americans are diagnosed with a mood disorder, and major depressive disorder is the leading cause of disability in the United States. According to the social navigational hypothesis, positive mood increases initiative and risk taking when potential payoffs are high, while low mood motivates changing strategies when risks are high, thus avoiding wasteful expenditures of energy. When such goals are essential to the individual and no alternative strategy is found, depression may result. According to Price's social competition hypothesis, individuals who lose status after a failed hierarchy struggle may withdraw into a state of depression and inactivity as a result. The function of the response is to reduce aggression and any potential threat and thus protect the individual from further attack.

Some theorists believe depression in women has distinct causes and different functions. In the general functionalist sense, as for men, depression may signal that current strategies are failing and a new approach is needed. Failure to be accepted or sudden deterioration of close relationships may be an important trigger of depressive episodes in women. Alternatively, several researchers view depression as a desperate form of social manipulation, what might be termed the social bargaining theory of depression.

One of the most significant aspects of an evolutionary perspective is to raise questions about features of contemporary society that create conditions for such widespread maladaptation. Many scholars discuss features of modern society that they view as potentially harmful to the modern psyche, particularly the relative absence of community. Viewed from this perspective, we may be ill equipped by nature to live in a novel environment of millions of people living in close proximity and near complete anonymity, given that our inherited emotional and social predispositions prepared us for life in small, stable communities of extended kin. To the extent that individuals are able to create such communities within the wider ecological framework of their urban existence they may be expected to live healthier lives.

☐ For Further Inquiry

Nesse, R. M., & Stearns, S. C. (2008). The great opportunity: Evolutionary applications to medicine and public health. *Evolutionary Applications 1*(1), 28–48.

Nesse, R. M., & Williams, G. C. (1994). *Why we get sick: The new science of Darwinian medicine*. New York, NY: Vintage Books.

Trevathan, W. R. (2008). *Evolutionary medicine*, 2nd ed. New York, NY: Oxford University Press.

Troisi, A. (2008). Psychopathology and mental illness. In C. B. Crawford & D. Krebs (Eds.), *Foundations of evolutionary psychology*. New York, NY: Taylor & Francis.

CHAPTER

Altruism, Cooperation, and Competition

☐ Sociobiological Perspectives

During the heyday of sociobiology in the 1960s, 1970s, and 1980s the question of altruism rose to the forefront of evolutionary thinking and stirred up considerable debate. Indeed, it would be difficult to overestimate the theoretical importance of altruism in sociobiological accounts of behavior. Altruism appears to be deeply problematic from certain evolutionary perspectives because, by definition, it implies that an individual engages in behavior that benefits others at one's own expense and thus would be selected against. So the essential dilemma is this: how could truly altruistic behavior evolve in the egoistic universe envisioned by Darwin's theory? In this chapter we shall answer this question in three complementary ways. Apparently altruistic behavior could evolve if it turns out that it ultimately benefits the individual in terms of (1) inclusive fitness, or (2) delayed benefits resulting from reciprocity. Finally, altruism could also evolve if it ultimately benefits the group. This third mechanism is only possible if natural selection of competing groups trumps selection pressures operating against altruism within the group. We first examine mechanisms that enable cooperation within the selfish gene paradigm emphasizing the gene's level of selection.

Kin Selection

As many naturalists before him, Hamilton (1964) recognized that acts of altruism were most common between kin. This insight was captured in a remark by J. B. S. Haldane who commented, "I will jump into the river to save two brothers or eight cousins," anticipating Hamilton's more formal elaboration of the principle of *kin selection*. This elegant idea is that natural selection can favor cooperation if the donor and the recipient of an altruistic act are genetic relatives. He therefore devised a formula $c < rb$, where c equals the cost to the actor, r is the degree of genetic relatedness between the actor and the recipient, and b is the benefit. It is important to remember that both costs and benefits are calculated in the currency of reproductive success. The direct fitness of the individual (direct offspring) plus the gain in reproductive success from indirect fitness (the offspring of relatives weighted by their degree of relatedness) equals *inclusive fitness*. Rather than always behaving out of self-interest, evolutionists since Hamilton view animals as behaving in ways that maximize inclusive fitness.

Following Hamilton's rule, and maintaining a "selfish gene" perspective, evolutionists expect animals to help those with whom they share genes "by common descent." A coefficient of relatedness can be calculated so r in the formula can be assigned to different relatives. Identical twins share 100% their genes, parents share 50% with their offspring as do biological siblings and fraternal twins, grandparents-grandchildren, aunts/uncles-nieces/nephews share 25% and so on. The more genes that are shared, the greater the likelihood of altruism. When evaluating the inclusive fitness of the behavior induced by a certain gene, it is important to include the behavior's effect on kin who might carry the same gene. Therefore, in orthodox sociobiology, the "extended phenotype" of cooperative behavior is the consequence of "selfish genes" (Dawkins, 1976; E. O. Wilson, 1975).

Early sociobiologists used kin selection to reveal a hidden "genetic selfishness" underlying apparent acts of altruism and cooperation. If an individual carries the cooperator gene, its relatives are more likely to carry the gene. So if you are a cooperator, and you also know who your relatives are, you know individuals who are more likely to cooperate with you. And you do not even have to know exactly who your relatives might be. If you are an organism that tends to live its life near where it is born, you can be sure that those around you are more likely to be your close relatives. Even if an individual cooperator ends up worse off because it pays the costs of cooperation and gets no benefits, cooperator genes will be better off overall—a copy of the gene will also be carried by the individuals who get the benefit of cooperation.

But the less certain you are about who else carries a copy of your cooperator gene, the less effective kin selection is at evolving cooperation.

Remember Haldane's initial insight? It may often pay to cooperate with two brothers, but it is worth helping a first cousin only if the benefits produced by the cooperation outweigh the costs by at least eight times. This radiating network of cooperation is illustrated in Arab folk culture by the saying, myself versus my brothers, my brothers and I versus the village, our village versus the neighboring village, our village and neighboring villages versus other tribes, and so forth. Cooperation can be expected the closer the genetic relatedness, but defection creeps in as genetic relatedness dwindles. As a result, kin selection is a very poor mechanism for evolving widespread cooperation. Because relatedness is an imperfect indicator of common genes, cooperation can evolve via kin selection only where the benefits from cooperation far outweigh the costs.

Overall the concept of kin selection has been successful in explaining the limited degree of cooperation that exists among animals, since much of it occurs between relatives. The most common type is where parents provide food and protection to their genetic offspring. In cases where parents are not the only individuals that help rear offspring, invariably the details of the social ecology reveal the hand of kin selection. For example, in a number of communal bird species, eggs are incubated and chicks are fed by birds that are often not their parents. One species, the Mexican jay, lives in flocks of 5 to 15 in pine and oak woodlands. Each flock defends a territory as a group, actively excluding other flocks. At each nest various members of the flock help bring food to the young, and birds that are not parents typically bring about half of the food (J. L. Brown, 1970). Kin selection provides the answer for this apparent altruism. The individuals within each flock are highly related, and the cooperating birds are helping others that have a high likelihood of carrying their cooperator genes. High genetic relatedness is the rule within the cooperative hunting groups of African lions, wild dogs, and spotted hyenas, and within the groups of savannah baboons and many species of monkeys that collectively defend against predators (Corning, 1998).

Probably the most compelling demonstration of kin selection is the eusociality found in the insect world, considered by Wilson as one of the pinnacles of social evolution. The term *eusocial* was defined by E. O. Wilson (1975) to include those organisms having the following three characteristics:

1. Reproductive division of labor (with or without sterile castes)
2. Overlapping generations
3. Cooperative care of young

Eusociality is a challenge for biologists to understand because worker castes in eusocial species forgo individual reproduction but rear young that are not their own. Any theory about eusociality has to explain why selection acting on individuals does not lead some to undermine the colony by reproducing themselves. Despite the obvious advantages of eusociality, it appeared paradoxical even to Darwin since the presence of nonbreeding individuals within a species seemed to contradict his theory of evolution. How can individuals incapable of passing on their genes possibly evolve and persist in the population? Since they do not breed, their fitness should be zero and any alleles causing this condition should be quickly eliminated from the population. In *The Origin of Species*, Darwin called this behavior the "one special difficulty, which at first appeared to me insuperable, and actually fatal to my theory." Darwin anticipated that the resolution to the paradox would lie in finding close family relationships in these species, but conceptual advances like kin selection or inclusive fitness had to wait for Mendel's discovery of the mechanisms for genetic inheritance and the modern synthesis.

As Darwin suspected, the eusocial colonies in the Hymenoptera group of ants, termites, and bees are invariably formed of individuals that are closely related (E. O. Wilson, 1975). However, Wilson's current view about eusociality differs from the assessment in his seminal book *Sociobiology: The New Synthesis* (1975). Let us examine both of his views in the order that they were formulated.

According to his widely accepted earlier account, selection acting on individuals that are genetically related (kin selection), rather than on whole colonies, explains eusociality in Hymenoptera. Eusociality evolves in these species due to their haplodiploidy, which facilitates the operation of kin selection. Species of social bees, wasps, and ants have workers that do not go on to produce offspring, but help their sisters and brothers to produce offspring. Amazingly, a bee worker shares 75% of her genes with her sisters, whereas we share only 50% of our genes with our brothers or sisters. And the reason for this difference is that our reproduction is diploid, while bees are haplodiploid.

In *diploid* animals both the male and female have two sets of chromosomes; the female egg contains one of the two sets and the male sperm contains one of his two sets. So when fertilization occurs the fertilized egg again contains two sets of chromosomes; half from the male and half from the female. So the average degree of relatedness between siblings is 50%.

In *haplodiploid* animals the male has only one set of chromosomes because he develops from an unfertilized egg, so every sperm contains the same one set of chromosomes; in other words, he passes on 100% of his genes. The female, however, is diploid so has two sets of chromosomes, and each egg will contain one of these two sets. Because males develop from unfertilized eggs this means that sons share 100% of their genes with the queen. But the queen passes on only half her genes to her son so she is related to him by just 50%. The workers (females) have also inherited one set of the queen's two sets of chromosomes so they will be 50% related to her, and they will also have received the one set that the male has. Now let's do a little simple math. Each sister receives one of a possible two sets of chromosomes from the queen, and these make up half her genes, so there is a 50% chance that 50% of her genes will be the same as her sister's. So that's 50% × 50% = 25%. Then both sisters get the same set of genes from the male as he has only one set. So half their genes are exactly the same, and if you add this 50% to the 25% from the queen you get a relatedness of 75%. This mechanism of sex determination gives rise to what W. D. Hamilton termed *supersisters* who share 75% of their genes. From the selfish genes perspective, it is clearly more advantageous to raise sisters because the sterile workers are more closely related to their supersisters than to any offspring they might have if they were to breed themselves. Even if workers never reproduce, they are potentially passing on more of their genes (75%) by caring for their sisters than they would by having their own offspring (who share 50% of their genes). This unusual situation where females may have greater fitness when they help rear siblings rather than producing offspring was used by Wilson (1975) to explain the multiple independent evolutions of eusociality within the haplodiploid group, Hymenoptera.

Thirty years after his explanation of eusociality as kin selection, E. O. Wilson (Wilson & Hölldobler, 2009) now argues for a new perspective. Wilson reviewed recent findings that point to aspects of eusociality that the standard explanation has difficulty accounting for. Eusociality has evolved only a few times, and not all of them were in haplodiploid species. Furthermore, the vast majority of haplodiploid species are not eusocial. He then examines recent evidence that the eusociality found in some Hymenoptera (and rarely in other species), is a result of natural selection on nascent colonies of species possessing features that predispose them to colonial life. Wilson concludes that these features, principally progressive provisioning of larvae and behavioral flexibility that leads to division of labor, allow some species to evolve colonies that are maintained and defended because of their proximity to food sources. Ultimately, Wilson argues that selection acting on traits that emerge at a group level provides a more complete explanation for eusociality's rare instances than kin selection. Kin selection is, he writes, "not wrong" but incomplete. We shall explore this possibility of multiple levels of selection, including group selection, in more detail later in this chapter.

While Hamilton's inclusive fitness theory represents one of the most important theoretical advances since Darwin, it is quite clear that concepts beyond kin selection are required if we wish to explain social behavior fully. It is simply unsatisfactory to have a theory that only accounts for altruism and cooperation among relatives because we also observe such behavior between genetically unrelated individuals. This problem stimulated Harvard theorist Robert Trivers to work out an additional explanation for the existence of altruism within the model of the selfish gene. Rather than the widespread nepotism in animals where parents are observed to provide care and even sacrifice their lives for their offspring, Trivers focused his attention on human acts of altruism directed towards non-kin. How could these acts, which seem to contradict the selfish gene view of individual selection, be explained by evolutionary theory as well?

Reciprocal Altruism

Trivers (1971) began his analysis by borrowing Hamilton's rule and removing the "kin" from kin altruism. Thus the formula $c < rb$ reduces to $c < b$. In other words, for non-kin altruism to evolve the cost to the actor must be less than the benefit to the recipient. In sociobiology, *reciprocal altruism* is a form of altruism in which one organism provides a benefit to another without expecting any immediate payment or compensation. However, reciprocal altruism is not unconditional. Trivers stipulates that altruism must give rise to a surplus of cooperation, in the sense that the potential benefits must be perceived to be meaningfully larger than the costs to the benefactor. Moreover, the original beneficiary must reciprocate an act of altruism if the situation is later reversed. Failure to do so will usually cause the original benefactor to withdraw future acts of altruism.

Two other prerequisites are needed to establish Trivers' concept of reciprocal altruism. First, individuals must be able to recognize each other in order to "keep accounts." This allows the individual to reciprocate with "honest players" and to detect and punish "cheaters." Second, individuals should have a reasonably long lifespan to allow for the reciprocal relationship between two individuals to establish itself in repeated contacts. These prerequisites of reciprocal altruism make it unlikely that mosquitoes engage in reciprocal altruism. Although reciprocal altruism is observed in a few species like dolphins, birds, and primates, the consensus among zoologists is that such occurrences in animals are relatively rare (Slater, 1994). As Trivers recognized, however, reciprocity among humans is more the rule than the exception.

An interesting example of reciprocal altruism found in animals is food sharing in the South American vampire bat (Wilkinson, 1984). Each night the bats leave the shelter of hollow trees to search for large animals. If a bat finds an animal, it will attempt to feed on the animal's blood. Each night some bats will be successful, but no individual bat will always find and feed off an animal every night. Young inexperienced bats are unsuccessful about one night in three. A few bad nights in a row could spell death. This danger can be avoided if the bats that nest together share food. Those that have been successful regurgitate some blood for others that have missed out. Because all bats risk having bad nights in which they fail to get blood themselves, they can all benefit from this cooperation.

305 Altruism, Cooperation, and Competition

Careful observation of the bats revealed that any particular bat would give blood to some, but not to others. And those who got the blood were not necessarily close relatives, as would be expected if kin selection were operating. Those who were given blood were bats that had given the individual blood in the past. And those who were refused blood were those who had previously refused the individual blood. The bats knew each other as individuals, knew who were likely to reciprocate and who were not, and chose to give blood only to those who were likely to reciprocate.

Paradoxically, reciprocal altruism could not become established within the group unless members refuse to cooperate with individuals that fail to reciprocate. If an individual continues to do favors for others that do not return the favor, then nonreciprocators will win out. An individual that cheats by receiving favors but not repaying them will gain all the benefits of cooperation without paying any of the costs. If a cheat resides within a large population of cooperators, it will do extremely well, collecting favors and never returning them. In these circumstances, cheats will prosper, increasing in numbers in the population until all cooperators die out. In such a group, the most competitive strategy will be to accept favors but not reciprocate. Reciprocal altruism will not survive, even if its benefits outweigh its costs.

However, all this changes if the individuals live together for a long time, repeatedly have the opportunity to interact and exchange favors, and have the capacity to remember which individuals return favors and which do not. If these conditions are met, cheats will not be able to continually take benefits from the cooperators, because they will be recognized as cheats and excluded from further cooperation. Once this happens, they will not gain any of the benefits of cooperation. If they cooperate in this way, cooperators will out-compete cheats (Axelrod, 1984).

In summary, there are three minimal requirements for cooperation to evolve via reciprocal altruism:

1. There must be repeated interactions between the same pair of individuals.
2. Each partner must be able to retaliate against defection by the other.
3. Individual recognition must be possible (or the number of potential partners with whom an individual interacts must be small, preferably only one).

But it will rarely be this simple. It might pay cheats to look like cooperators to extract favors, then to quit while they are ahead. Or when they have gained a reputation for cheating in one group, they may move on to another group where they are unknown. To avoid being cheated, cooperators will have to get very good at detecting cheats (Martinez-Coll & Hirshleifer, 1991).

Well-documented cases of reciprocal altruism have been found only in a few species of animals such as vampire bats, dolphins, and elephants, and in some species of monkeys, baboons, and apes (Packer, 1977). In most of these cases, cooperation depends on individual recognition between pairs of individuals in the absence of any known genetic relationship between the pair. The relative rarity of reciprocal altruism is because the conditions under which it works are quite limited. How many species of animals live together for long periods, repeatedly have the opportunity to cooperate, are able to recognize each other, can remember how each individual behaved each time it had the opportunity to cooperate, and can keep track of favors owed and favors earned, and judge whether reciprocal favors are similar in value? The answer, of course, is humans—we are the species that meet these conditions to the highest degree and the theory of reciprocal altruism fits very well with many aspects of human relations. It works well for explaining cooperative relationships between people in small closely knit communities: tribes, villages of extended kin, teams, friendship networks, and other relatively small, stable social groups.

☐ Evolutionary Game Theory

Because of the hidden complexity of reciprocal altruism scientists have turned to mathematical models inspired by game theory to work out its various implications. In game theory, the "Nash equilibrium," initially proposed by John Nash in 1950, is a solution concept of a game involving two or more players in which no player has anything to gain by changing his or her strategy unilaterally. Nash's key innovation was to introduce the distinction between cooperative and noncooperative (zero-sum) games. Cooperative games allow for players to make enforceable agreements with other players, allowing a group to commit to a superior strategy than is otherwise possible among egoists. By broadening von Neumann's zero-sum games (which have little relevance to the real world) to include games that involve subtle blends of cooperation and competition, Nash succeeded in opening a world of real-life applications stemming from his mathematical solutions. Eventually game theory gained wide influence in economics, sociology, political science, and evolutionary biology. Because of this, Nash received the Nobel Prize in economics in 1994. A few years later his life story was brought to the screen in the film *A Beautiful Mind*, which won four Academy Awards in 2002, including Best Picture of the Year.

So what exactly is the Nash equilibrium? Stated simply, players are in *Nash equilibrium* if each one is making the best decision that they can, taking into account the decisions of the others. However, a Nash equilibrium does not necessarily mean the best cumulative payoff for all the players involved; in many cases all the players might improve their payoffs if they could somehow agree on a cooperative strategy different from the Nash equilibrium.

Let's follow this thinking using a concrete example: competing oil producers looking to sell their product in an open international market. If each oil producer has chosen a marketing strategy and no producer can benefit by changing his or her strategy while the other players keep theirs unchanged, then the current set of strategy choices and the corresponding payoffs constitute a Nash equilibrium. Buyers can exploit the competitive self-interest of each oil producer by buying only from the lowest priced seller, driving prices towards equilibrium in keeping with supply and demand. However, if enough oil producers can cooperate in a binding collective agreement to fix prices at a level of their choosing they can outplay any independent producer. They can, in the real world, form a cartel in order to maximize their profits. Of course many real-world contextual factors can enter into this equation, but Nash's hypothetical concept of an equilibrium point is central to any resolution of the game.

Evolutionary game theory provides an interesting vantage point from which to explore the interplay of competition and cooperation in humans. Although the importance of resource competition among individuals follows rather directly from evolutionary theory, as we have seen evolutionary logic is also compatible with the evolution of mechanisms enabling cooperative behavior. Unique benefits of cooperation to the individual can arise when a goal can be obtained by a cooperative pair or group, but impossible to achieve by any individual working alone (Charlesworth, 1982; Maynard Smith, 1982), or when a cooperative pair stands to gain more by working together than a noncooperative pair. The application of game theory to the problem of human cooperation was to get an important boost from a political scientist, Robert Axelrod, who combined forces with one of the leading evolutionary biologists of his era, William D. Hamilton (Axelrod & Hamilton, 1981).

☐ The Prisoner's Dilemma

Robert Axelrod's original interest in game theory arose during the Cold War era from a concern with international politics and especially the risk of nuclear war. He was especially intrigued by the iterated prisoner's dilemma game because it seemed to capture the tension between doing what is good for the individual and what is good for all. The prisoner's dilemma is a symmetric two-person game, in which the alternative plays are "cooperate" and "defect." The payoffs are shown in Table 13.1.

TABLE 13.1 The Prisoner's Dilemma Payoff Matrix

	Cooperation	Defection
Cooperation	R = 3	S = 0
	Reward for mutual cooperation	Sucker's payoff
Defection	T = 5	P = –1
	Temptation to defect	Punishment for mutual defection

Note that if player B cooperates, it pays A to defect; also, if player B defects, it pays A to defect. That is, it pays A to defect no matter what B does; similarly, it pays B to defect no matter what A does. Yet, if both defect, they do less well than if both cooperate; this is the dilemma.

Many strategies had been proposed to play this game effectively. Axelrod's interest in artificial intelligence led him to consider hosting a computer tournament to evaluate alternative strategies for the iterated prisoner's dilemma. This iterated prisoner's dilemma format tends to offer a long-term incentive for cooperation, even though there is a short-term incentive for defection. Axelrod invited game theory experts to submit their strategies in the form of computer programs. The entries were diverse and varied in complexity, initial hostility, capacity for forgiveness, etc. The winning program, submitted by Anatol Rapoport, was also the simplest. This was TIT FOR TAT: cooperate on the first move, and then cooperate or defect exactly as the other player did on the preceding move.

The results of the first tournament were published, and people were again invited to submit programs for a second tournament. The result was again a victory for TIT FOR TAT, even though everyone knew that this simple program would again be competing against them. Axelrod later showed that TIT FOR TAT is stable against invasion by any other possible strategy, provided that the sequence of games against each opponent is long enough. This demonstrates that cooperation based upon reciprocity can emerge in a population of egoists (with only a small cluster of reciprocators), and then resist invasion by predatory strategies. Importantly, Maynard Smith (1982) comments that kin selection may often provide the impetus needed for the initial spread of a trait that, once it is common, can be maintained by mutualistic effects alone. It is important to remember that because one mechanism is shown to be involved in sustaining cooperation, it does *not* logically follow that no other mechanism is involved.

Further computer analysis showed that if a succession of tournaments were played, with programs increasing in representation if they did well, then TIT FOR TAT ultimately displaced all others. The fact that TIT FOR TAT was the most numerous of all the surviving programs at the end of the evolutionary simulation led Axelrod to propose TIT FOR TAT as a suitable paradigm for exploring human cooperation across a wide range of contexts. In describing the success of TIT FOR TAT, Axelrod (1984, p. 54) states:

> What accounts for TIT-FOR-TAT's robust success is its combination of being nice, retaliatory, forgiving and clear. Its niceness prevents it from getting into unnecessary trouble. Its retaliation discourages the other side from persisting whenever defection is tried. Its forgiveness helps restore mutual co-operation. And its clarity makes it intelligible to the other player, thereby eliciting long-term co-operation.

Thus far we have examined kin selection and reciprocal altruism as two viable mechanisms that have enabled cooperation to evolve under specific conditions. This analysis provides some hints for a more general way of building cooperative organization out of self-interested individuals. Where they are effective, both mechanisms ensure that cooperators benefit from their cooperation. Where these mechanisms fail, they fail to the extent that cooperators do not gain any benefit from their cooperation. Kin selection is undermined when the individual helped by the cooperation does not carry the cooperator gene. Reciprocal altruism is undermined when a recipient of cooperation cheats by failing to return the favor. When this occurs, a cooperator will not enjoy the benefits of its cooperative act, only the costs, and will end up worse off than the cheat.

Moreover there are at least two further limitations of reciprocal altruism to establish cooperation in large, complex societies, even where cooperation produces substantial benefits (Axelrod, 1997). First, as previously discussed, reciprocal altruism will work only where cheats can be successfully excluded from future cooperation. This will not be the case if cheats can easily find other individuals to deal with who know nothing of their previous actions. However, this is precisely the context of modern large-scale economic markets. Individuals can readily leave a bad reputation behind them and find new individuals to deal with who are unaware of their previous actions. Reciprocal altruism is therefore not the mechanism that has produced the large-scale markets that organize economic exchanges across human societies.

The other great limitation of reciprocal altruism is that it is only effective where the benefits of cooperation can be neatly parcelled up, precisely valued, and swapped between individuals (Axelrod, 1997). Where the benefits of a cooperative act impact many individuals, reciprocal altruism cannot operate easily. This is especially true in our complex, differentiated societies, where most cooperative acts impact many others. It would be impossible to separate out the effects and keep track of them as favors that have to be returned. And if favors are not returned with acts of similar value, reciprocal altruism fails. To succeed, free riders, cheats, and thieves who contribute nothing to the cooperation must enjoy none of the benefits

created by cooperation. In conclusion, because kin selection and reciprocal altruism can explain only limited cooperation under restricted conditions, they are not likely to be the mechanisms that enabled the evolution
of the complex human organizations that we see today.

☐ Multilevel Selection Theory

Since the advent of agriculture, humans have lived in progressively larger
groups that depend upon progressively more complex forms of cooperation.
To explain human forms of cooperation we need a more comprehensive
theory that can explain the widespread existence of human ultrasociality.
Ultrasociality refers to a collective organization with full division of labor,
including individuals who gather no food but are fed by others, or who are
prepared to sacrifice themselves for the defense of others. Because complex
systems of cooperation and mutual support can be found in all human societies, from small tribes to huge nations, evolutionists saw the need to develop
a satisfactory explanation of how such social systems have emerged.

Everyone will agree that cooperation is in general advantageous for the
group of cooperators as a whole, even though it may curb some individual
freedoms. Cooperation can increase the fitness of the cooperators, when the
cooperators together can collect more resources than the sum of resources
collected by each of them individually. To take a simple example, a pack of
wolves can kill large animals (moose, elk, bison), that no individual wolf
would be able to kill. Yet, for each wolf separately the best strategy is to let
the other wolves take the risks while hunting and then come to eat from
their captures. But if all wolves acted like that, all advantages of cooperation
would disappear. The optimal strategy for the pack is to cooperate, but the
optimal strategy for each individual wolf is not to cooperate. This leads to
the problem of levels of selection. Since evolution first optimizes benefits at
the individual level, we need additional mechanisms to explain how evolution can optimize outcomes beneficial to the group. The possibility that
cooperation might evolve, not between individuals, but between groups has
been discussed since Darwin, but most notably by David Sloan Wilson and
colleagues (Wilson, 1975; Wilson & Sober, 1994; Wilson & Wilson, 2007).

Darwin's statement about group selection in humans in *The Descent of
Man* (1871) (quoted in Chapter 2) is the starting point for most arguments
in favor of multilevel selection theory. It is universally recognized that the
chief difficulty with the spread of altruistic genes within any group is that
genes for group advantageous behavior are seldom advantageous for the
individual who acts to benefit the group. Consequently they are generally
selected against within groups. For Darwin, the solution was to recognize
that natural selection could operate at more than one level, including the

level of selection between competing groups. In short, Darwin proposed that although *selfishness beats altruism within groups, altruistic groups beat selfish groups.* Thus, multilevel selection theory views natural selection as involving trade-offs in the selection of heritable traits at different levels of selection. At the within-group level, a trait for morality, which increases the fitness of other group members at the expense of the individual's own fitness, will decline to extinction over time within the group. Multilevel selection theory solves this dilemma by positing that the same trait could increase in the total population if groups possessing the trait are more likely to out-compete groups that do not possess the trait. Ultimately selection for the trait within the total population (species) will depend upon the relative speed and potency of within- and between-group selection.

Multilevel selection theory has also been invoked to explain what Maynard Smith and Szathmary (1995) refer to as "major transitions in evolution"—transitions that shift the unit of selection from solitary replicators to networks of replicators enclosed within compartments. A number of authors have explored the question of why lower-level selection did not disrupt the formation of the higher-level unit using multilevel selection theory (Frank 1999; Maynard Smith & Szathmary, 1995; Michod, 1997, 1999; Wilson & Wilson, 2007). The concept of such *superorganisms* or groups of cooperating organisms that transform themselves into a single organism has a long lineage (Wheeler, 1911) but it has re-emerged as a viable concept in recent years. Throughout the evolution of life forms, major transitions have involved shifts from independent genes to chromosomes, from prokaryotic cells to eukaryotic cells containing organelles, from unicellular to multicellular organisms, and from solitary organisms to colonies. Some of these transitions occurred in the distant evolutionary past, others much more recently. In each case, a number of smaller units, originally capable of surviving and reproducing on their own, coalesced into a single larger unit, thus generating a new level of biological organization. The challenge is to understand *why* it was advantageous for the lower-level units to cooperate with one another, and form a larger unit, not *whether* such transitions took place. Similarly, cooperation is widespread in humans and the challenge is to understand which factors promote and sustain it, not whether it could evolve.

☐ The Role of Punishment in Promoting Cooperation

Thus far we have argued for the role of reciprocity, kin selection, and group selection as possible mechanisms supporting the spread of genes favoring cooperation within a population. We have also pointed out that these three mechanisms are equally capable of acting in concert (multi-level selection) as well as acting independently. Regardless of the specific mechanism at work, the problem of cheating and its punishment is central to any theoretical model of cooperation. According to Nowak (2006), punishment can promote cooperative behavior but it is not a mechanism for the evolution of cooperation. By itself, punishment can only enhance the level of cooperation that is achieved in such models. Let us examine how this might work in human societies.

Maynard Smith (1982) has proposed that humans play a type of game that seems beyond the capacity of animals. This is the "social contract" game. If we suppose that some behavior, for example theft, is considered undesirable by members of a stable group, they can agree not to steal, and to punish any member of the group who does steal. This social contract does not, in itself, guarantee honesty, because the act of punishing is presumably costly, and therefore individuals would be tempted to accept the benefits of the contract but not the costs of enforcing it. Maynard Smith argues that the success of the social contract implies that refusal by an individual to participate in enforcing the contract should also be regarded as a breach to be punished. As culture evolves, enforcement is entrusted to a subgroup, who are compensated for carrying it out.

Trivers' theory of reciprocal altruism also predicts that people will have two great concerns in their relationships with others. First, they want to avoid being cheated by others, so they will want to know who can be trusted to return favors. Second, they will want others to see them as trustworthy, and not as a cheat who should be excluded from beneficial cooperation. Axelrod (1997) proposes that humans have many behaviors that serve to protect against cheating. For example, most people have great interest in judging other people's trustworthiness. A major part of gossip and other social communication involves exchanging information that helps people make these judgments. People tend to be reluctant to risk cooperating with strangers when they have no knowledge of their reputation and character. This is especially true when the stranger does not depend on them for future cooperative opportunities because they have little to lose if they ruin their reputation (Dunbar, 1997).

People are also generally concerned to protect their own reputation for trustworthiness and honesty, particularly within their group. People often react instantly and emotionally to any attack on their character. Most of us are also concerned to ensure that we are seen to treat our friends fairly whenever there are things to be shared and that we repay our obligations to people we know. And we do not want to enter into obligations with friends that we might not be able to repay.

We have seen that virtually all theorists agree that punishment against defection or cheating is an important ingredient for sustained cooperation in the prisoner's dilemma. This implies that cooperation cannot evolve in a species or be sustained in a social group unless a potential cooperator can effectively detect individuals who cheat, so that they can be excluded from future interactions in which they could exploit cooperators—effectively solving what is often referred to as "the free-rider problem." A "free-rider" is an individual who accepts a benefit (a ride) without satisfying the requirements (a ticket) for provision of the benefit. For reciprocal altruism to evolve in humans, natural selection must favor a complex psychology in each individual, regulating the tendency to cooperate, the tendency to cheat, and the response to others' acts of cooperation and cheating. What would such a psychology look like?

☐ Evolutionary Psychology of Cooperation

Evolutionary psychologists Cosmides and Tooby (1992) have proposed an evolutionary theory of cooperation that incorporates some of these ideas known as *social contract theory*. They reasoned that humans would need to evolve a set of five information-processing mechanisms in order to establish cooperative social contracts and deal effectively with the potential of cheating. As previously discussed, people must be able to

1. Recognize different individuals.
2. Remember the history of their interactions with them.
3. Communicate their values, needs, and desires.
4. Understand others' values, needs, and desires.
5. Represent the costs and benefits of the items exchanged.

Evidence from primatology and paleoanthropology suggests that our ancestors have engaged in social exchange for at least several million years, thus it qualifies as an enduring selection pressure on the hominid line. In particular, Cosmides and Tooby hypothesized that the evolved architecture of the human mind would include inference procedures that are specialized for detecting cheaters. To test their hypothesis, they chose an experimental paradigm called the Wason selection task (Wason, 1966; Wason & Johnson-Laird, 1972) that tests logical reasoning. In this task, the subject is asked to look for violations of a conditional rule of the form "If P then Q." Initially Wason used abstract but familiar conditionals involving letters and numbers. Participants were presented with four cards and given the rule: *If a card has a vowel on one side, then it has an even number on the other side.*

A   D   8   5

They were then instructed to indicate only those card(s) you definitely need to turn over to see if any card violates this rule. Simple enough, right?

From a logical point of view, the rule has been violated whenever a card with a vowel has an odd number on the other side. Hence the logically correct answer is to turn over the vowel card with the letter "A" to verify that there is not an odd number on the other side and to turn over the odd number card "5" to verify that there is not a consonant on the other side. The other two cards are irrelevant to the conditional rule, hence it does not matter what is on the other side.

More generally, for a rule of the form If P then Q, one should turn over the cards that represent the values P and not-Q since the conditional, *if p then q* is false only if the antecedent or p term is true and the consequent or q term is false. If the human mind develops reasoning procedures specialized for detecting logical violations of conditional rules, this would be intuitively obvious. But it is not. Wason and colleagues found that only 4 of 100 participants chose the correct response for the above task, so if you did not you are with the other 96%! Subsequent studies have confirmed that less than 25% of participants spontaneously choose the correct response since in a conditional reasoning task of the form, *if p then q.* Moreover, even formal training in logical reasoning does little to boost performance on descriptive rules of this kind (Cheng, Holyoak, Nisbett, & Oliver, 1986; Wason & Johnson-Laird, 1972). Indeed, a large literature exists that shows that people are not very good at detecting logical violations of if-then rules in Wason selection tasks, even when these rules deal with familiar content drawn from everyday life (Manktelow & Evans, 1979; Wason, 1983). But the results change dramatically when logical rules involve detecting violations of familiar social rules like the minimum age of 21 for drinking alcohol. Consider the following task:

Beer   Coke   16 years old   22 years old

Participants were presented with the rule *If a person is drinking alcohol they must be over nineteen years of age* and were asked to imagine themselves as police officers checking for under-age drinkers. Under these conditions most subjects correctly choose the p and not-q cards (beer, 16 years old).

For Cosmides and Tooby, the Wason selection task provides an ideal tool for testing hypotheses about reasoning specializations designed to operate on social conditionals, such as social exchanges, threats, permissions, obligations, and so on, because (1) it tests reasoning about conditional rules, (2) the task structure remains constant while the content of the rule is changed, (3) content effects are easily elicited, and (4) there was already a body of existing experimental results against which performance on new content domains could be compared.

In their view, demonstrating that people who ordinarily cannot detect violations of conditional rules can do so when that violation represents cheating on a social contract would constitute initial support for the view that people have cognitive adaptations specialized for detecting cheaters in situations of social exchange. Their research plan has been to use subjects' inability to spontaneously detect violations of conditionals expressing a wide variety of contents as a comparative baseline against which to detect the presence of performance-boosting reasoning specializations. By seeing what content-manipulations switch on or off high performance, the boundaries of the domains within which reasoning specializations successfully operate can be mapped.

The results of these investigations were striking. People who ordinarily cannot detect violations of if-then rules can do so easily and accurately when that violation represents cheating in a situation of social exchange (Cosmides, 1989; Cosmides & Tooby, 1989, 1992). This is a situation in which one is entitled to a benefit only if one has fulfilled a requirement (e.g., "If you take benefit B, then you must satisfy requirement R"). Cheating is accepting the benefit specified without satisfying the condition that provision of that benefit was made contingent upon.

When asked to look for violations of social contracts of this kind, the correct answer is immediately obvious to almost all subjects, who commonly experience a "pop out" effect. No formal training is needed. Whenever the content of a problem asks subjects to look for cheaters in a social exchange—even when the situation described is culturally unfamiliar and even bizarre—subjects experience the problem as simple to solve, and their performance jumps dramatically. In general, 65% to 80% of subjects get it right, the highest performance ever found for a task of this kind. They choose the "benefit accepted" card (e.g., "riding the bus") and the "cost not paid" card (e.g., "no ticket"), for any social conditional that can be interpreted as a social contract, and in which looking for violations can be interpreted as looking for cheaters.

Everywhere it has been tested people do not treat social exchange problems as equivalent to other kinds of reasoning problems. Their minds distinguish social exchange contents and reason as if they were translating these situations into representational primitives such as "benefit," "cost," "obligation," "entitlement," "intentional," and "agent." Indeed, the relevant inference procedures are not activated unless the subject has represented the situation as one in which one is entitled to a benefit only if one has satisfied a requirement.

Procedures activated by social contract rules don't look as if they were designed to detect logical violations per se; instead, they appear to be most useful for detecting cheaters, whether or not this corresponds to the logically correct selections. There are now a number of experiments comparing performance on Wason selection tasks in which the conditional rule either did or did not express a social contract. These experiments have provided evidence for a series of domain-specific effects as predicted by Cosmides and Tooby. Social contracts activate content-dependent rules of inference that appear to be specialized for processing information relevant to cheater detection. The programs involved do not operate so as to detect potential altruists (individuals who pay costs but do not take benefits), nor are they activated in social contract situations in which errors would correspond to innocent mistakes rather than intentional cheating. The pattern of results elicited by social exchange content is so distinctive that Cosmides and Tooby believe reasoning in this domain must be governed by computational units that are domain specific and functionally distinct: what they have called social contract algorithms (Cosmides, 1989; Cosmides & Tooby, 1992).

Despite the fact that empirical evidence for the evolutionary design of social contract algorithms is limited to conditional reasoning task performance, with no organic basis for modularity in neuroscience data, and no developmental data on the early emergence of this ability, the evolutionary logic is clear. The environment of evolutionary adaptedness (EEA) for the human species would favor evolutionary stable strategies (ESS) in which characteristically human cooperation and competition coevolve. In this environment and throughout a long period of human evolution, a "cheater-detection module" would be a definite advantage to inclusive fitness.

☐ Chapter Summary

Altruistic behavior can evolve if it benefits the individual in terms of (1) inclusive fitness, (2) reciprocal altruism, or (3) under special conditions if it ultimately benefits the group. Hamilton's concept of kin selection stipulates that natural selection can favor cooperation if the donor and the recipient of an altruistic act are genetic relatives. The direct fitness of the individual (direct offspring) plus the gain in reproductive success from indirect fitness (the offspring of relatives weighted by their degree of relatedness) equals inclusive fitness. Rather than always behaving out of self-interest, evolutionists view animals as behaving in ways that maximize inclusive fitness.

Kin selection has been successful in explaining the most common type of cooperation in animals where parents provide food and protection to their genetic offspring. For example, in a number of communal bird species, eggs are incubated and chicks are fed by birds that are often not their parents. The individuals within each flock are highly related, and the cooperating birds are helping others that have a high likelihood of carrying their cooperator genes. High genetic relatedness is the rule within the cooperative hunting groups of African lions, wild dogs, and spotted hyenas, and within the groups of savannah baboons and many species of monkeys that collectively defend against predators.

Probably the most compelling demonstration of kin selection is the eusociality found in the insect world, defined by E. O. Wilson (1975) to include those organisms having the following three characteristics:

1. Reproductive division of labor (with or without sterile castes)
2. Overlapping generations
3. Cooperative care of young

Concepts beyond kin selection are certainly required if we wish to explain human social behavior. This problem stimulated Harvard theorist Robert Trivers to develop the concept of reciprocal altruism in which one organism provides a benefit to another without expecting any immediate payment or compensation. However, reciprocal altruism is not unconditional. Trivers stipulates that altruism must give rise to a surplus of cooperation, in the sense that the potential benefits must be perceived to be meaningfully larger than the costs to the benefactor. Moreover, the original beneficiary must reciprocate an act of altruism if the situation is later reversed. Two other prerequisites are: (1) individuals must be able to recognize each other in order to "keep accounts," and (2) individuals should have a reasonably long lifespan to allow for the reciprocal relationship between two individuals to establish itself in repeated contacts.

Well-documented cases of reciprocal altruism have been found only in a few species of animals such as vampire bats, dolphins, and elephants, and in some species of monkeys, baboons, and apes (Packer, 1977). The relative rarity of reciprocal altruism is because the conditions under which it works are quite limited. Few species of animals live together for long periods, repeatedly have the opportunity to cooperate, are able to recognize each other, can remember how each individual behaved each time it had the opportunity to cooperate, and can keep track of favors owed and favors earned, and judge whether reciprocal favors are similar in value. Humans meet these conditions to the highest degree and the theory of reciprocal altruism fits very well with many aspects of human relations. It works well for explaining cooperative relationships between people in small closely knit communities: tribes, villages of extended kin, teams, friendship networks, and other relatively small, stable social groups.

Evolutionary game theory provides an interesting vantage point from which to explore cooperation in humans. Axelrod hosted a computer tournament to evaluate alternative strategies for the iterated prisoner's dilemma. The winning program named TIT FOR TAT simply cooperates on the first move, and then cooperates or defects exactly as the other player did on the preceding move. Axelrod believes it is a suitable paradigm for exploring human cooperation across a wide range of contexts. Axelrod (1984, p. 54) states:

> What accounts for TIT-FOR-TAT's robust success is its combination of being nice, retaliatory, forgiving and clear. Its niceness prevents it from getting into unnecessary trouble. Its retaliation discourages the other side from persisting whenever defection is tried. Its forgiveness helps restore mutual co-operation. And its clarity makes it intelligible to the other player, thereby eliciting long-term co-operation.

Because they can explain only limited cooperation under restricted conditions, kin selection and reciprocal altruism cannot be the sole mechanisms that enabled the evolution of the complex human organizations that we see today. We need a more comprehensive theory to account for the widespread existence of human ultrasociality. Ultrasociality refers to a collective organization with full division of labor, including individuals who gather no food but are fed by others, or who are prepared to sacrifice themselves for the defense of others. Darwin proposed a solution that involves two levels of natural selection: *selfishness beats altruism within groups, but altruistic groups beat selfish groups.* At the within-group level, a trait for morality, which increases the fitness of other group members at the expense of the individual's own fitness, will decline to extinction over time within the group. Multilevel selection theory solves this dilemma by positing that the same trait could increase in the total population if groups possessing the trait are more likely to out-compete groups that do not possess the trait.

Virtually all theorists agree that punishment against defection or cheating is an important ingredient for sustained cooperation in the prisoner's dilemma. This implies that cooperation cannot evolve in a species or be sustained in a social group unless a potential cooperator can effectively detect individuals who cheat, so that they can be excluded from future interactions in which they could exploit cooperators—effectively solving what is often referred to as "the free-rider problem." A "free-rider" is an individual who accepts a benefit (a ride) without satisfying the requirements (a ticket) for provision of the benefit. For reciprocal altruism to evolve in humans, natural selection must favor a complex psychology in each individual, regulating the tendency to cooperate, the tendency to cheat, and the response to others' acts of cooperation and cheating.

Evolutionary psychologists Cosmides and Tooby (1992) have proposed an evolutionary theory of cooperation that incorporates some of these ideas known as social contract theory. They reasoned that humans would need to evolve information-processing mechanisms in order to establish cooperative social contracts and deal effectively with the potential of cheating. Cosmides and Tooby believe reasoning in this domain must be governed by computational units that are domain specific and functionally distinct, what they have called social contract algorithms. Clearly the environment of evolutionary adaptedness (EEA) for the human species would favor the development of evolutionary stable strategies (ESS) in which characteristically human cooperation and competition coevolve. In this environment and throughout a long period of human evolution, a "cheater-detection module" would be a definite advantage to inclusive fitness.

☐ For Further Inquiry

Axelrod, R. (1997). *The complexity of cooperation: Agent-based models of competition and collaboration*. Princeton, NJ: Princeton University Press.

Axelrod, R. (2006). *The evolution of cooperation* (Rev. ed.) New York, NY: Basic Books.

Cosmides, L., & Tooby, J. (1992). Cognitive adaptations for social exchange. In J. Barkow, L. Cosmides, & J. Tooby (Eds.), *The adapted mind*. New York, NY: Oxford University Press.

Nowak, M. A. (2006). Five rules for the evolution of cooperation. *Science, 314*(5805), 1560–1563.

REFERENCES

Ahrens, R. (1954). Beitrag zur entwicklun des physionomie und mimikerkennens. *A.F. Exp. U. Angew, Psychologie, 2,* 599–633.

Ainsworth, M. D. (1967). *Infancy in Uganda: Infant care and the growth of love.* Baltimore, MD: Johns Hopkins University Press.

Ainsworth, M. D. S. (1977). Infant development and mother-infant interaction among Ganda and American families. In P. H. Leiderman, S. R. Tulkin, & A. Rosenfeld (Eds.), *Culture and infancy: Variations in the human experience.* New York, NY: Academic Press.

Ainsworth, M. D. S., Bell, S., & Stayton, D. (1974). Infant-mother attachment and social development: Socialization as a product of reciprocal responsiveness to signals. In M. Richards (Ed.), *The integration of the child into the social world.* Cambridge, UK: Cambridge University Press.

Ainsworth, M. D. S., Blehar, M., Waters, E., & Wall, S. (1978). *Patterns of attachment.* Hillsdale, NJ: Lawrence Erlbaum Associates.

Alcock, J. (2001a). *Animal behavior: An evolutionary approach* (7th ed.). Sunderland, MA: Sinauer.

Alcock, J. (2001b). *The triumph of sociobiology.* Oxford, UK: Oxford University Press.

Alexander, G. M., & Hines, M. (2002). Sex differences in response to children's toys in nonhuman primates (*Cercopithecus aethiops sabaeus*). *Evolution & Human Behavior, 6*(23), 467–469.

Alexander, R. D. (1979). *Darwinism and human affairs.* Seattle, WA: University of Washington Press.

Alexander, R. D. (1989). The evolution of the human psyche. In C. Stringer and P. Mellars (Eds.), *The Human Revolution* (pp. 455–513). Edinburgh, UK: University of Edinburgh Press.

Alexander, R. D., & Noonan, K. M. (1979). Concealment of ovulation, parental care, and human social evolution. In N. A. Chagnon & W. Irons (Eds.), *Evolutionary biology and human social behavior* (pp. 402–435). North Scituate, MA: Duxbury Press.

American Psychiatric Association. (1994). *Diagnostic and statistical manual on mental disorders* (4th ed.). Washington, DC: Author.

Amsterdam, B. (1972). Mirror self-image reactions before age two. *Developmental Psychobiology, 5,* 297–305.

Apter, T. (1990). Mothers on a seesaw: Friends and peers. In *Altered loves: Mothers and daughters during adolescence.* New York, NY: St. Martin's Press.

Arend, R., Gove, F., & Sroufe, L. A. (1979). Continuity of individual adaptation from infancy to kindergarten: A predictive study of ego-resiliency and curiosity in preschoolers. *Child Development, 50,* 950–959.

Argue, D., Donlon, D., Groves, C., & Wright, R. (2006). *Homo floresiensis*: Microcephalic, pygmoid, Australopithecus, or Homo? *Journal of Human Evolution, 51*(4): 360–374.

Armelagos, G. J. (1998). Health and disease in prehistoric populations in transition. In P. J. Brown (Ed.), *Understanding and applying medical anthropology* (pp. 59–69). Mountain View, CA: Mayfield Publishing.

Axelrod, R. (1984). *The evolution of cooperation.* New York, NY: Basic Books.

Axelrod, R. (1997). *The complexity of cooperation: Agent-based models of competition and collaboration.* Princeton, NJ: Princeton University Press.

Axelrod, R. (2006). *The evolution of cooperation* (Rev. ed.). New York, NY: Basic Books.

Axelrod, R., & Hamilton, W. D. (1981). The evolution of cooperation. *Science, 211,* 1390–1396.

Baize, H. R., & Schroeder, J. E. (1995). Personality and mate selection in personal ads: Evolutionary preferences in a public mate selection process. *Journal of Social Behavior and Personality, 10,* 517–536.

Baldwin, J. M. (1902). *Development and evolution.* New York, NY: Macmillan.

Banks, M. S., & Salapatek, P. (1981). Infant pattern vision: A new approach based on contrast-sensitivity function. *Journal of Experimental Child Psychology, 31,* 1–45.

Banks, M. S., & Salapetek, P. (1983). Infant visual perception. In P. H. Mussen (Ed.), *Handbook of child psychology* (Vol. 2, 4th ed.): *Infancy and developmental psychobiology.* New York, NY: Wiley.

Barber, N. (1995). The evolutionary psychology of physical attractiveness: Sexual selection and human morphology. *Ethology and Sociobiology, 16,* 385–424.

Bard, P. (1928). A diencephalic mechanism for the expression of rage with special reference to the sympathetic nervous system. *American Journal of Physiology, 84,* 490–513.

Barker, D. J. P. (Ed.). (1992). *Fetal and infant origins of adult disease.* London, UK: BMJ Books.

Barker, D. J. P. (1997). Maternal nutrition, fetal nutrition, and disease in later life. *Nutrition, 13,* 807.

Barkow, J. (Ed.). (2006). *Missing the revolution: Darwinism for social scientists.* Oxford, UK: Oxford University Press.

Barkow, J., Cosmides, L., & Tooby, J. (1992). *The adapted mind: Evolutionary psychology and the generation of culture.* New York, NY: Oxford University Press.

Baron-Cohen, S. (1995). *Mindblindness: An essay on autism and theory of mind.* Cambridge, MA: MIT Press/Bradford Books.

Baron-Cohen, S. (2005). The empathizing system: A revision of the 1994 model of the mindreading system. In B. J. Ellis & D. F. Bjorklund (Eds.), *Origins of the social mind: Evolutionary psychology and child development* (pp. 468–492). New York, NY: Guilford Press.

Barr, R. G. (1999). Infant crying behavior and colic: An interpretation in evolutionary perspective. In W. R. Trevathan, E. O. Smith, & J. J. McKenna (Eds.), *Evolutionary medicine.* New York, NY: Oxford University Press.

Barr, R. G., Konner, M., Bakeman, R., & Adamson, L. (1991). Crying in !Kung San infants: A test of the cultural specificity hypothesis. *Developmental Medicine and Child Neurology, 33*(7), 601–610.

Barrera, M. E., & Maurer, D. (1981a). Recognition of mother's photographed face by the three-month-old. *Child Development, 52,* 558–563.

Barrera, M. E., & Maurer, D. (1981b). The perception of facial expressions by the three-month-old infant. *Child Development, 52,* 203–206.

Barrett, K., & Campos, J. (1987). Perspectives on emotional development: 2. A functionalist approach to emotions. In J. Osofsky (Ed.), *Handbook of infant development* (2nd ed., pp. 555–578). New York, NY: Wiley.

Bates, J. E. (1980). The concept of difficult temperament. *Merrill-Palmer Quarterly*, *26*, 299–319.

Bates, J. E. (1987). Temperament in infancy. In J. D. Osofsky (Ed.), *Handbook of infant development* (2nd ed., pp. 1101–1149). New York, NY: Wiley.

Bates, J., Maslin, C., & Frankel, K. (1985). Attachment security, mother-child interaction, and temperament as predictors of behavior problem ratings at age three years. In I. Bretherton & E. Waters (Eds.), Growing points in attachment theory and research. *Monographs of the Society for Research in Child Development*, *50* (Whole No. 209), 167–193.

Bateson, P., & Martin, P. (1999). *Design for a life: How behaviour develops*. London, UK: Jonathan Cape.

Batki, A., Baron-Cohen, S., Wheelwright, S., Connellan, J., & Ahluwalia, J. (2000). Is there an innate gaze module? Evidence from human neonates. *Infant Behavior & Development*, *23*(2), 223–229.

Baumrind, D. (1967). Child care patterns anteceding three patterns of preschool behavior. *Genetic Psychology Monographs*, *75*, 43–88.

Bell, R. (1968). A reinterpretation of the direction of effects in studies of socialization. *Psychological Review*, *75*, 81–95.

Bell, S., & Ainsworth, M. D. S. (1972). Infant crying and maternal responsiveness. *Child Development*, *43*, 1171–1190.

Belsky, J. (1997). Attachment, mating, and parenting: An evolutionary interpretation. *Human Nature*, *8*, 361–381.

Belsky, J. (2005). Differential susceptibility to rearing influence: An evolutionary hypothesis and some evidence. In B. Ellis & D. Bjorklund (Eds.), *Origins of the social mind: Evolutionary psychology and child development* (pp. 139–163). New York, NY: Guilford Press.

Belsky, J., & Fearon, R. M. (2002). Early attachment security, subsequent maternal sensitivity, and later child development: Does continuity in development depend upon continuity of caregiving? *Attachment and Human Development*, *3*, 361–387.

Belsky, J., & Isabella, R. (1988). Maternal, infant, and social-contextual determinants of attachment security: A process analysis. In J. Belsky & T. Nezworski (Eds.), *Clinical implication of attachment* (pp. 41–94). Hillsdale, NJ: Erlbaum.

Belsky, J., Rovine, M., & Taylor, D. G. (1984). The Pennsylvania infant and family development project: 2. The origins of individual differences in infant–mother attachment: Maternal and infant contributions. *Child Development*, *55*, 718–728.

Belsky, J., Spritz, B., & Crnic, K. (1996). Infant attachment security and affective–cognitive information processing at age 3. *Psychological Science*, *7*, 111–114.

Belsky, J., Steinberg, L., & Draper, P. (1991). Childhood experience, interpersonal development, and reproductive strategy: An evolutionary theory of socialization. *Child Development*, *62*, 647–670.

Benenson, J. F. (1993). Greater preference among females than males for dyadic interaction in early childhood. *Childhood Development*, *64*, 544–555.

Bering, J. M., & Povinelli, D. J. (2003). Comparing cognitive development. In D. Maestripieri (Ed.), *Primate psychology: Bridging the gap between the mind and behavior of human and nonhuman primates* (pp. 205–233). Cambridge, MA: Harvard University Press.

Bertenthal, B., Campos, J., & Barrett, K. (1984). Self-produced locomotion: An organizer of emotional, cognitive, and social development in infancy. In R. Emde & R. Harmon (Eds.), *Continuities and discontinuities in development* (pp. 175–210). New York, NY: Plenum.

Betzig, L. (1986). *Despotism and differential reproduction: A Darwinian view of history.* Hawthorne, NY: Aldine.

Betzig, L. (1993). Sex, succession, and stratification in the first six civilizations. How powerful men reproduced, passed power on to their sons, and used power to defend their wealth, women, and children. In L. Ellis (Ed.), *A comparative biosocial analysis* (pp. 37–74). Westport, CT: Praeger.

Bjorklund, D. F., & Pelligrini, A. D. (2002). *The origins of human nature: Evolutionary developmental psychology.* Washington, DC: American Psychological Association.

Blakemore, J. E. O., Berenbaum, S. A., & Liben, L. S. (2008). *Gender development.* New York: Psychology Press.

Blakemore, J. E., LaRue, A. A., & Olejnik, A. B. (1979). Sex appropriate toy preference and the ability to conceptualize toys as sex-role related. *Developmental Psychology, 15,* 339–340.

Blehar, M., Lieberman, A., & Ainsworth, M. (1977). Early face to face interaction and its relation to later infant-mother attachment. *Child Development, 48,* 182–194.

Bleske-Rechek, A. L., & Buss, D. M. (2001). Opposite-sex friendship: Sex differences and similarities in initiation, selection, and dissolution. *Personality and Social Psychology Bulletin, 27*(10), 1310–1323.

Blumberg, S. H., & Izard, C. E. (1986). Discriminating patterns of emotion in 10- and 11-year-old children's anxiety and depression. *Journal of Personality and Social Psychology, 51*(4), 852–857.

Bogin, B. (1999). Evolutionary perspective on human growth. *Annual Review of Anthropology, 28,* 109–153.

Bokhorst, C. L., Bakermans-Kranenburg, M. J., Pasco Fearon, R. M., van IJzendoorn, M. H., Fonagy, P., & Schuengel, C. (2000). The importance of shared environment in mother-infant attachment security: A behavioral genetic study. *Child Development, 74,* 1769–1782.

Borgerhoff-Mulder, M. (1989). Early maturing Kipsigis women have higher reproductive success than late maturing women and cost more to marry. *Behavioral Ecology and Sociobiology, 24,* 145–153.

Borrello, M. E. (2005). The rise, fall, and resurrection of group selection. *Endeavour, 29,* 43–47.

Bouchard, T. J., Jr. (1996). The genetics of personality. In K. Blum & E. P. Noble (Eds.), *Handbook of psychoneurogenetics* (pp. 267–290). Boca Raton, FL: CRC Press.

Bouchard, T. J., Jr., Lykken, D. T., McGue, M., Segal, N. L., & Tellegen, A. (1990). Sources of human psychological differences: The Minnesota study of twins reared apart. *Science, 250,* 223–228.

Bowlby, J. (1951). *Maternal care and mental health.* Geneva, Switzerland: World Health Organization.

Bowlby, J. (1960). Grief and mourning in infancy and early childhood. *Psychoanalytical Study of Children, 15,* 9–52.

Bowlby, J. (1969). *Attachment and loss: Vol. 1. Attachment.* New York, NY: Basic Books.

Bowlby, J. (1973). *Attachment and loss: Vol. 2. Separation, anxiety, and anger.* New York, NY: Basic Books.

Bowlby, J. (1980). *Attachment and loss: Vol. 3. Loss*. New York, NY: Basic Books.

Bowlby, J. (1988). *A secure base: Parent–child attachment and healthy human development*. New York: Basic Books.

Boyd, R., & Richerson, P. J. (1992). Punishment allows the evolution of cooperation (or anything else) in sizable groups. *Ethology and Sociobiology, 13*(3): 171–195.

Boyd, R., & Richerson, P. J. (2002). Group beneficial norms spread rapidly in a structured population. *Journal of Theoretical Biology, 215*, 287–296.

Brazelton, T. B. (1969). *Infants and mothers*. New York, NY: Delacorte.

Bretherton, I. (1985). Attachment theory: Retrospect and prospect. In I. Bretherton & E. Waters (Eds.), Growing points of attachment theory and research. *Monographs of the Society of Research in Child Development, 50*.

Bridges, K. M. B. (1932). Emotional development in early infancy. *Child Development, 3*, 325–341.

Broude, G. J., & Greene, S. J. (1976) Cross-cultural codes on twenty sexual attitudes and practices. *Ethnology, 15*, 409–429.

Brown, B. B. (1990). Peer groups and peer culture. In S. S. Feldman & G. R. Elliot (Eds.), *At the threshold: The developing adolescent*. Cambridge, MA: Harvard University Press.

Brown, G. W., & Harris, T. O. (1978). *Social origins of depression*. New York, NY: Free Press.

Brown, G. W., Harris, T. O., & Hepworth, C. (1995). Loss, humiliation and entrapment among women developing depression: A patient and non-patient comparison. *Psychological Medicine, 25*, 7–21.

Brown, J. L. (1970). Cooperative breeding and altruistic behaviour in the Mexican jay. *Animal Behaviour, 18*, 366–378.

Brown, P., Sutikna, T., Morwood, M. J. et al. (2004). A new small-bodied hominin from the Late Pleistocene of Flores, Indonesia. *Nature, 431*, 1055–1061.

Brown, P. J., Barrett, R., & Padilla, M. (1998). Medical anthropologies: An introduction to the fields. In P. J. Brown (Ed.), *Understanding and applying medical anthropology* (pp. 10–17). Mountain View, CA: Mayfield Publishing.

Buss, A. H., & Plomin, R. (1975). *A temperament theory of personality development*. New York, NY: Wiley.

Buss, A. H., & Plomin, R. (1984). *Temperament: Early developing personality traits*. Hillsdale, NJ: Lawrence Erlbaum Associates.

Buss, D. M. (1989). Sex differences in human mate preferences: Evolutionary hypotheses testing in 37 cultures. *Behavioral and Brain Sciences, 12*, 1–49.

Buss, D. M. (1991). Evolutionary personality psychology. *Annual Review of Psychology, 42*, 459–491.

Buss, D. M. (1996). Social adaptation and five major factors of personality. In J. S. Wiggins (Ed.), *The five-factor model of personality: Theoretical perspectives* (pp. 180–207). New York, NY: Guilford Press.

Buss, D. M. (2000). Desires in human mating. *Annals of the New York Academy of Sciences, 907*, 39.

Buss, D. M. (Ed.). (2005). *The handbook of evolutionary psychology*. Hoboken, NJ: Wiley & Sons.

Buss, D. M. (2008). *Evolutionary psychology: The new science of the mind* (3rd ed.). Boston, MA: Allyn & Bacon.

Buss, D. M., & Schmitt, D. P. (1993). Sexual strategies theory: An evolutionary perspective on human mating. *Psychological Review, 100*, 204–232.

Buss, L. (1988). *The Evolution of Individuality.* Princeton, NY: Princeton University Press.

Byrne, R. W., & Whitten, A. (1988). *Machiavellian intelligence: Social expertise and the evolution of intellect in monkeys, apes and humans.* Oxford, UK: Oxford University Press.

Cabrera, N. J., Tamis-LeMonda, C. S., Bradley, R. H., Hofferth, S., & Lamb, M. E. (2000). Fatherhood in the twenty-first century. *Child Development, 71*(1), 127–136.

Cahill, L. (2006). Why sex matters for neuroscience. *Nature Reviews: Neuroscience, 7*(6), 477–484.

Caldera, Y. M., Huston, A. C., & O'Brien, M. (1989). Social interactions and play patterns of parents and toddlers with feminine, masculine, and neutral toys. *Child Development, 60,* 70–76.

Calkins, S. D., & Fox, N. A. (1992). The relations among infant temperament, security of attachment, and behavioral inhibition at twenty-four months. *Child Development, 63,* 1456–1472.

Call, J., & Tomasello, M. (2008). Does the chimpanzee have a theory of mind? 30 years later. *Trends in Cognitive Science, 12,* 187–192.

Calvin, W. H. (1983). *The throwing Madonna.* New York, NY: McGraw-Hill.

Campos, J. (1994). *The new functionalism in emotion.* SRCD Newsletter.

Campos, J. J., & Barrett, K. C. (1984). Toward a new understanding of emotions and their development. In C. E. Izard, J. Kagan, & R. B. Zajonc (Eds.), *Emotions, cognition, and behavior* (pp. 229–263). New York, NY: Cambridge University Press.

Campos, J., Campos, R., & Barrett, K. (1989). Emergent themes in the study of emotional development and emotional regulation. *Developmental Psychology, 25,* 394–402.

Campos, J. J., Emde, R., Gaensbauer, T., & Henderson, C. (1975). Cardiac and behavioral interrelationships in the reactions of infants to strangers. *Developmental Psychology, 11,* 589–601.

Campos, J. J., Hiatt, S., Ramsay, D., Henderson, C., & Svejda, M. (1978). The emergence of fear on the visual cliff. In M. Lewis & L. A. Rosenblum (Eds.), *The development of affect: Vol. I. Genesis of behavior* (pp. 149–182). New York, NY: Plenum.

Campos, J., Mumme, D., Kermoian, R., & Campos, R. (1994). A functionalist perspective on the nature of emotion. In N. Fox (Ed.), The development of emotion regulation: Biological and behavioral considerations. *Monographs of the Society for Research in Child Development, 59*(2/3, Serial No. 240).

Camras, L. A. (1992). Expressive development and basic emotions. *Cognition and Emotion, 6,* 269–283.

Camras, L., Holland, E., & Patterson, M. (1993). Facial expression. In M. Lewis & J. Haviland (Eds.), *Handbook of emotions* (pp. 199–208). New York: Guilford.

Cannon, W. (1927). The James-Lange theory of emotions: A critical examination and alternative theory. *American Journal of Psychology, 39,* 106–124.

Carroll, S. B. (2000). Endless forms: The evolution of gene regulation and morphological diversity. *Cell, 101,* 577–580.

Carroll, S. B. (2005). *Endless forms most beautiful: The new science of evo devo and the making of the animal kingdom.* New York, NY: Norton.

Carroll, S. B., Jennifer, K., Grenier, S. D., & Weatherbee, S. D. (2004). *From DNA to diversity: Molecular genetics and the evolution of animal design* (2nd ed.). New York, NY: Norton.

Cassidy, J., & Mohr, J. J. (2001). Unsolvable fear, trauma, and psychopathology: Theory, research and clinical considerations related to disorganized attachment across the life span. *Clinical Psychology: Science and Practice, 8,* 275–298.

Cattell, R. B. (1963). Theory of fluid and crystallized intelligence: A critical experiment. *Journal of Educational Psychology, 54,* 1–22.

Centers for Disease Control and Prevention. (2004, October 6). Prevalence of overweight and obesity among children and adolescents: United States, 1999–2002. Washington, DC: Author.

Chagnon, N. A. (1968). *Yanomamö: The fierce people.* New York, NY: Holt Rinehart & Winston.

Chagnon, N. A. (1979). Is reproductive success equal in egalitarian societies? In N. Chagnon, & W. Irons (Eds.). *Evolutionary biology and human social behavior.* North Scituate, MA: Duxbury Press.

Chagnon, N. A. (1988). Is reproductive success equal in egalitarian societies? In N. A. Chagnon & W. Irons (Eds.), *Evolutionary biology and human social behavior.* North Scituate, MA: Duxbury Press.

Chandler, M., Fritz, A., & Hala, S. (1989). Small-scale deceit: Deception as a marker of two-, three-, and four-year-olds' early theories of mind. *Child Development, 60,* 1263–1277.

Charlesworth, W. R. (1969). The role of surprise in cognitive development. In D. Elkind & F. Flavell (Eds.), *Studies in cognitive development* (pp. 257–314). London, UK: Oxford University Press.

Charlesworth, W. R. (1974). General issues in the study of fear: Section IV. In M. Lewis & L. A. Rosenblum (Eds.), *The origins of fear* (pp. 254–258). New York, NY: Wiley.

Charlesworth, W. R. (1982). An ethological approach to research on facial expressions. In C. E. Izard (Ed.), *Measuring emotions in infants and children.* Cambridge, UK: Cambridge University Press.

Charlesworth, W. R. (1992). Darwin and developmental psychology: Past and present. *Developmental Psychology, 28,* 5–16.

Charlesworth, W., & Dzur, C. (1987). Gender comparisons of preschoolers' behavior and resource utilization in group problem solving. *Child Development, 58,* 191–200.

Charlesworth, W. R., & Kreutzer, M. A. (1973). Facial expressions of infants and children. In P. Ekman (Ed.), *Darwin and facial expression: A century of research in review* (pp. 91–168). New York, NY: Academic Press.

Charlesworth, W. R., & LaFreniere, P. J. (1983). Dominance, friendship and resource utilization in preschool groups. *Ethology and Sociobiology, 4,* 175–186.

Cheng, P., Holyoak, K., Nisbett, R., & Oliver, L. (1986). Pragmatic versus syntactic approaches to training deductive reasoning. *Cognitive Psychology, 18,* 293–328.

Chevalier-Skolnikoff, S. (1973). Facial expression of emotion in nonhuman primates. In P. Ekman (Ed.), *Darwin and facial expression* (pp. 11–90). New York, NY: Academic Press.

Chiappe, D., & MacDonald, K. (2005). The evolution of domain-general mechanisms in intelligence and learning. *Journal of General Psychology, 132,* 5–40.

Chisholm, J. S. (1996). The evolutionary ecology of attachment organization. *Human Nature, 7*, 1–38.

Chomsky, N. (1968). *Language and mind.* New York, NY: Harcourt, Brace & World.

Chomsky, N. (1986). *Knowledge of language: Its nature, origin, and use.* New York, NY: Pantheon.

Christopherson, E. R. (1989). Injury control. *American Psychologist, 44*, 237–241.

Cicchetti, D., & Hesse, P. (1983). Affect and intellect: Piaget's contributions to the study of infant emotional development. In R. Phluchik & H. Kellerman (Eds.), *Emotion: Theory, research and experience: Vol. 2, Emotion in early development* (pp. 115–170). New York, NY: Academic Press.

Cicchetti, D., & Sroufe, L. A. (1976). The relationship between affective and cognitive development in Down's syndrome infants. *Child Development, 47*, 920–929.

Clutton-Brock, T. H. (1991). *The evolution of parental care.* Princeton, NJ: Princeton University Press.

Collaer, M. L., & Hines, M. (1995). Human behavioral sex differences: A role for gonadal hormones during early development? *Psychological Bulletin, 118*, 55–107.

Coop, G., Bullaughey, K., Luca., F., & Przeworski, M. (2008). The timing of selection at the human *FOXP2* gene. *Molecular Biological Evolution, 25*, 1257–1259.

Corning, P. (1998) The cooperative gene: On the role of synergy in evolution. *Evolutionary Theory, 11*, 183–207.

Cosmides, L. (1989). The logic of social exchange: Has natural selection shaped how humans reason? *Cognition, 31*, 187–276.

Cosmides, L., & Tooby, J. (1989). Evolutionary psychology and the generation of culture, Part II. Case study: A computational theory of social exchange. *Ethology and Sociobiology, 10*, 51–97.

Cosmides, L., & Tooby, J. (1992). Cognitive adaptations for social exchange. In J. Barkow, L. Cosmides, & J. Tooby (Eds.), *The adapted mind.* New York, NY: Oxford University Press.

Costa, P. T., & Widiger, T. A. (Eds.) (1994). *Personality disorders and the five-factor model of personality.* Washington, DC: American Psychological Association.

Costello, E. J., Angold, A., Burns, B. J., Stangl, D. K., Tweed, D. L., Erkanli, A., & Worthman, C. M. (1996). The Great Smoky Mountains Study of Youth. Goals, design, methods, and the prevalence of DSM-III-R disorders. *Archives of General Psychiatry, 53*, 1129–1136.

Cowan, G., & Avants, S. K. (1988). Children's influence strategies: Structure, sex differences, and bilateral mother-child influences. *Child Development, 59*, 1303–1313.

Craske, M. G. (2003). *Origins of phobias and anxiety disorders: Why more women than men?* London, UK: Elsevier.

Crews, D., Gore, A. C., Hsu, T., Dangleben, N. L., Spinetta, M., Schallert, T., Anway, M. D., & Skinner, M. K. (2007). *Transgenerational epigenetic imprints and mate preference.* Proceedings of the National Academy of Science, 104, 5942–5946.

Crick, F. H. C. (1968). The origin of hte genetic code. *Journal of Molecular Biology, 38*, 367–379.

Crick, N. R., & Zahn-Waxler, C. (2003). The development of psychopathology in females and males: Current progress and future challenges. *Development and Psychopathology, 15*, 719–742.

Crittenden, P. M. (1992). Treatment of anxious attachment in infancy and early childhood. *Development and Psychopathology, 4*(4), 575–602.

Crockenberg, S. (1981). Infant irritability, mother responsiveness, and social support influences on the security of infant-mother attachment. *Child Development, 52,* 857–865.

Crockenberg, S., & Litman, C. (1990). Autonomy as competence in 2-year-olds: Maternal correlates of child defiance, compliance, and self-assertion. *Developmental Psychology, 26,* 961–970.

Curry, J. F., March, J. S., & Hervey, A. S. (2004). Comorbidity of childhood and adolescent anxiety disorders. In T. H. Ollendick & J. S. March (Eds.), *Phobic and anxiety disorders in children and adolescents: A clinician's guide to effective psychosocial and pharmacological interventions.* Oxford, UK: Oxford University Press.

Daly, M., & Wilson, M. (1978). *Sex, evolution and behavior.* North Scituate, MA: Duxbury Press.

Daly, M., & Wilson, M. (1988). *Homicide.* New York: Aldine Transaction.

Daniels, D., & Plomin, R. (1985). Origins of individual differences in infant shyness. *Developmental Psychology, 21*(1), 118–121.

Dannemiller, J. L., & Stephens, B. R. (1988). A critical test of infant pattern preference models. *Child Development, 59,* 210–216.

Darwin, C. (1859). *The origin of species.* London, UK: Murray.

Darwin, C. (1958). Barlow, N. (Ed.), *The autobiography of Charles Darwin 1809–1882. With the original omissions restored. Edited and with appendix and notes by his granddaughter Nora Barlow,* London, England: Collins.

Darwin, C. (1871/1896). *The descent of man and selection in relation to sex.* New York, NY: Appeltin.

Darwin, C. R. (1872/1965). *The expression of emotions in man and animals.* Chicago, IL: University of Chicago Press.

Davidson, R. J., Ekman, P., Saron, C., Senulis, R., & Friesen, W. V. (1990). Approach-withdrawal and cerebral asymmetry: 1. Emotional expression and brain physiology. *Journal of Personality and Social Psychology, 58,* 333–341.

Davidson, R. J., & Fox, N. A. (1982). Asymmetrical brain activity discriminates between positive versus negative affective stimuli in human infants. *Science, 218,* 1235–1237.

Dawkins, R. (1976). *The selfish gene.* New York, NY: Oxford University Press.

Dawkins, R. (1982). *The extended phenotype.* New York, NY: Oxford University Press.

Dawkins, R. (1986). *The blind watchmaker.* New York, NY: Norton.

Dawkins, R., & Krebs, J. R. (1978). Animal signals: Information or manipulation? In J. R. Krebs & N. B. Davies (Eds.), *Behavioral ecology* (pp. 282–309). Oxford, UK: Blackwell Scientific Publishers.

Delgado, J. (1969). Offensive-defensive behavior in free monkeys and chimpanzees induced by radio stimulation of the brain. In S. Garattini & E. B. Sigg (Eds.), *Aggressive behavior.* Amsterdam, the Netherlands: Excerpta Medica.

Denham, S. A., & McKinley, M. (1993). Sociometric nominations of preschoolers: A psychometric analysis. *Early Education and Development, 4,* 109–122.

Denham, S. A., McKinley, M., Couchoud, E. A., & Holt, R. (1990). Emotional and behavioral predictors of preschool peer ratings. *Child Development, 61,* 1145–1152.

de Peretti, E., & Forest M. G. (1976). Unconjugated dehydroepiandrosterone plasma levels in normal subjects from birth to adolescence in human: The use of a sensitive radioimmunoassay. *Journal of Clinical Endocrinolology Metabolism, 43*(5), 982–991.

de Waal, F. (1982). *Chimpanzee politics: Power and sex among apes.* New York: Harper & Row.

de Waal, F. (1986). Deception in the natural communication of chimpanzees. In R. W. Mitchell & N. S. Thompson (Eds.), *Deception: Perspectives on human and nonhuman deceit.* Albany, NY: State University of New York Press.

de Waal, F. (1996). *Good natured: The evolution of right & wrong in umans and other animals.* Cambridge, MA: Harvard University Press.

DiPietro, J. A. (1981). Rough and tumble play: A function of gender. *Developmental Psychology, 17,* 50–58.

Dobzhansky, T. (1973). Nothing in biology makes sense except in the light of evolution. *American Biology Teacher, 35,* 125–129.

Douvan, E., & Adelson, J. (1966). *The adolescent experience.* New York, NY: Wiley.

Draper, P., & Harpending, H. (1982). Father absence and reproductive strategy: An evolutionary perspective. *Journal of Anthropological Research, 38*(3), 255–73.

Drickamer, L. C. and Vessey, S. H. (1973). Group-changing behavior among male rhesus monkeys. *Primates, 14,* 359–368.

Duarte, C., Maurício, J., Pettitt, P. B., Souto, P., Trinkaus, E., van der Plicht, H., & Zilhão, J. (1999). The early Upper Paleolithic human skeleton from the Abrigo do Lagar Velho (Portugal) and modern human emergence in Iberia. *Proceedings of the National Academy of Sciences, 96*(13), 7604–9.

Dunbar, R. I. M. (1997). *Grooming, gossip and the evolution of language.* Cambridge, MA: Harvard University Press.

Dunbar, R. I. M., & Barrett, L. (Eds.). (2007). *The Oxford handbook of evolutionary psychology.* Oxford, UK: Oxford University Press.

Dunn, J., & Kendrick, C. (1982). *Siblings.* Cambridge, MA: Harvard University Press.

DuPont, R. L., Rice, D. P., Miller, L. S., Shiraki, S. S., Rowland, C. R., & Harwood, H. J. (1996). Economic costs of anxiety disorders. *Anxiety, 2,* 167–172.

Durrett, M. E., Otaki, M., & Richards, P. (1985). Attachment and mother's perception of support from the father. *International Journal of Behavioral Development, 7,* 167–176.

Eagly, A. H., & Crowley, M. (1986). Gender and helping behavior: A meta-analytic review of the social psychological literature. *Psychological Bulletin, 100,* 283–308.

Easterbrooks, M. A., & Lamb, M. E. (1979). The relationship between quality of infant-mother attachment and infant competence in initial encounters with peers. *Child Development, 50,* 380–387.

Eaton, S. B., & Eaton, S. B., III. (1999). Breast cancer in evolutionary context. In W. R. Trevathan, E. O. Smith, & J. J. McKenna (Eds.), *Evolutionary medicine* (pp. 429–442). New York, NY: Oxford University Press.

Eaton, S. B., Eaton, S. B., III, & Konner, M. J. (1999). Paleolithic nutrition revisited. In W. R. Trevathan, E. O. Smith, & J. J. McKenna (Eds.), *Evolutionary medicine* (pp. 313–332). New York: Oxford University Press.

Eaton, S. B., Shostak, M., & Konner, M. (1998). Stone-agers in the fast lane: Chronic degenerative diseases in evolutionary perspective. In P. J. Brown (Ed.), *Understanding and applying medical anthropology* (pp. 21–32). Mountain View, CA: Mayfield Publishing.

Eaton, S. B., Shostak, M., & Konner, M. (1988). *The Paleolithic prescription.* New York, NY: Harper & Row.

Eaton, W. O., & Yu, A. P. (1989). Are sex differences in child motor activity level a function of sex differences in maturational status? *Child Development, 60,* 1005–1011.

Eder, D., & Hallinan, M. (1978). Sex differences in children's friendships. *American Sociological Review, 43,* 237–250.

Egeland, B., & Farber, E. (1984). Infant–mother attachment: Factors related to its development and changes over time. *Child Development, 55,* 753–771.

Egeland, B., & Sroufe, L. A. (1981). Developmental sequelae of maltreatment in infancy. In D. Cicchetti & R. Rizley (Eds.), *Development approaches to child maltreatment: New directions for child development* (pp. 77–91). San Francisco, CA: Jossey-Bass.

Ehrhardt, A. A. (1985). The psychobiology of gender. In A. S. Rossi (Ed.), *Gender and the life course.* New York, NY: Aldine.

Ehrhardt, A. A., & Baker, S. W. (1974). Fetal androgens, human central nervous system differentiation, and behavioral sex differences. In R. C. Friedman, R. M. Rickard, & R. L. Van de Wiele (Eds.), *Sex differences in behavior.* New York, NY: Wiley.

Eibl-Eibesfeldt, I. (1972). Similarities and differences between cultures in expressive movements. In R. A. Hinde (Eds.), *Nonverbal communication* (pp. 297–311). Cambridge, MA: Cambridge University Press.

Eibl-Eibesfeldt, I. (1973). The expressive behavior of the deaf-and-blind-born. In M. Von Cranach & I. Vine (Eds.), *Social communication and movement* (pp. 163–194). New York, NY: Academic Press.

Eibl-Eibesfeldt, I. (1989). *Human ethology.* New York, NY: Aldine de Gruyter.

Eibl-Eibesfeldt, I. (1995). The evolution of familiality and its consequences. *Futura, 4,* 253–264.

Ekman, P. (1992). An argument for basic emotions. *Cognition and Emotion, 6,* 169–220.

Ekman, P., & Friesen, W. V. (2003). *Unmasking the face.* Cambridge, MA: Malor Books.

Eldredge, N., & Gould, S. J. (1972). Punctuated equilibria: An alternative to phyletic gradualism. In T. J. M. Schopf (Ed.), *Models in paleobiology* (pp. 82–115). San Francisco, CA: Freeman.

Ellis, B. J. (2004). Timing of pubertal maturation in girls: An integrated life history approach. *Psychological Bulletin, 130,* 920–958.

Ellis, B. J., & Bjorklund, D. J. (Eds.). (2005). *Origins of the social mind: Evolutionary psychology and child development.* New York, NY: Guilford Press.

Ellis, B. J., & Garber, J. (2000). Psychosocial antecedents of variation in girls' pubertal timing: Maternal depression, stepfather presence, and marital and family stress. *Child Development, 71,* 485–501.

Emde, R., & Koenig, K. L. (1969). Neonatal smiling and rapid eye movement states. *American Academy of Child Psychiatry, 8,* 57–67.

Emde, R. N., Izard, C., Huebner, R., Sorce, J. F., & Klinnert, M. (1985). Adult judgments of infant emotions: Replication studies within and across laboratories. *Infant Behavior and Development, 8,* 79–88.

Emde, R. N., McCartney, R. D., & Harmon, R. J. (1971). Neonatal smiling in REM states, Part 4. Premature study. *Child Development, 42*, 1657–1661.

Emde, R. N., Plomin, R., Robinson, J. A., Corley, R., DeFries, J., Fulker, D. W., Reznick, J. S., Campos, J., Kagan, J., & Zahn-Waxler, C. (1992). Temperament, emotion, and cognition at fourteen months: the MacArthur Longitudinal Twin Study. *Child Development, 63*(6):1437–55.

Engen, T. L., Lipsitt, L., & Peck, M. B. (1974). Ability of newborn infants to discriminate sapid substances. *Developmental Psychology, 10*, 741–744.

Erikson, E. H. (1963). *Childhood and society* (2nd ed.). New York, NY: Norton.

Erickson, M., Egeland, B., & Sroufe, L. A. (1985). The relationship between quality of attachment and behavior problems in preschool in a high risk sample. In I. Bretherton & E. Waters (Eds.), Growing points in attachment theory and research. *Monographs of the Society for Research in Child Development* (Whole No. 209, 147–186).

Eswaran, V., Harpending, H., & Rogers, A. R. (2005). Genomics refutes an exclusively African origin of humans. *Journal of Human Evolution, 49*(1), 1–18.

Eudald, C., de Castro, J. M. et al. (2008). The first hominin of Europe. *Nature, 452*, 465–469.

Ewald, P. (1994). *Evolution of infectious disease.* New York, NY: Oxford University Press.

Eysenck, H. J. (1967). *The biological basis of personality.* Springfield, IL: Charles C. Thomas.

Fabes, R. A., Eisenberg, N., & Miller, P. (1990). Maternal correlates of children's vicarious emotional responsiveness. *Developmental Psychology, 26*, 639–648.

Fagen, R. M. (1981). *Animal play behavior.* New York, NY: Oxford University Press.

Fagen, R. M. (1995). Animal play, games of angels, biology and Brian. In A. D. Pelligrini (Ed.), *The future of play theory.* Albany, NY: State University of New York Press.

Fagot, B. I., Leinbach, M. D., & Hagan, R. (1986). Gender labeling and the adoption of sex-typed behaviors. *Developmental Psychology, 22*, 440–443.

Faust, M. S. (1960). Developmental maturity as a determinant of prestige in adolescent girls. *Child Development, 31*, 173–184.

Feinman, S., & Lewis, M. (1983). Social referencing and second order effects in ten-month-old infants. *Child Development, 54*, 878–887.

Feldman, R. S., Jenkins, L., & Popoola, O. (1979). Detecting of deception in adults and children via facial expressions. *Child Development, 50*, 350–355.

Ferdinand, R. F., Van Lang, N. D., Ormel, J., & Verhulst, F. C. (2006). No distinctions between different types of anxiety symptoms in pre-adolescents from the general population. *Journal of Anxiety Disorders, 20*, 207–221.

Field, T., & Fogel, A. (1982). *Emotion and early interaction.* Hillsdale, NJ: Lawrence Erlbaum Associates.

Figueredo, A. J., & King, J. E. 1996. The evolution of individual differences in behavior. *Western Comparative Psychological Association Observer, 2*(2), 1–4.

Fisher, H. H. (1992) Anatomy of love. New York: Norton.

Fisher, R. A. (1958). *The genetical theory of natural selection* (2nd ed.). New York, NY: Dover.

Flavell, J. H., Green, F. L., & Flavell, E. R. (1986). Development of knowledge about the appearance-reality distinction. *Monographs of the Society for Research in Child Development, 51* (Serial No. 212).

Flavell, J. H., Shipstead, S. G., & Croft, K. (1978). Young children's knowledge about visual perception: Hiding objects from others. *Child Development, 49,* 1208–1211.

Flinn, M. V. (2004). Culture and developmental plasticity: Evolution of the social brain. In K. MacDonald and R. L. Burgess (Eds.), *Evolutionary perspectives on human development* (Chapter 3, pp. 73–98). Thousand Oaks, CA: Sage.

Flinn, M. V., Geary, D. C., & Ward, C. V. (2005). Ecological dominance, social competition, and coalitionary arms races: Why humans evolved extraordinary intelligence. *Evolution and Human Behavior, 26,* 10–46.

Fouts, R. (1997). *Next of kin: What chimpanzees have taught me about who we are.* New York, NY: William Morrow.

Fox, N. A., Henderson, H. A., Rubin, K. H., Calkins, S. D., & Schmidt, L. A. (2001). Continuity and discontinuity of behavioral inhibition and exuberance: Psychophysiological and behavioral influences across the first four years of life. *Child Development, 72,* 1–21.

Fox, N. A., Kimmerly, N. L., & Schafer, W. D. (1991). Attachment to mother/attachment to father: A meta-analysis. *Developmental Psychology, 62,* 210–225.

Frank, S. (1999). *Foundations of Social Evolution.* Princeton, NJ: Princeton University Press.

Freedman, D. (1965). An ethological approach to the genetic study of human behavior. In S. Vanderberg (Ed.), *Methods and goals in human behavior genetics* (pp. 141–162). New York, NY: Academic Press.

Freedman, D. (1974). *Human infancy: An evolutionary perspective.* Hillsdale, NJ: Lawrence Erlbaum Associates.

Freire, A., Eskritt, M., & Lee, K. (2004). Are eyes windows to a deceiver's soul? Children's use of another's eye gaze cues in a deceptive situation. *Developmental Psychology, 40*(6), 1093–1104.

Fridland, A. J. (1994). *Human facial expression: An evolutionary view.* San Diego, CA: Academic Press.

Frisancho, A. R., Matos, J., Leonard, W. R., & Yaroch, L. A. (1985). Developmental and nutritional determinants of pregnancy outcome. *American Journal of Physical Anthropology, 66,* 247–262.

Gallup, G. G. (1977). Self-recognition in primates: A comparative approach to the bi-directional properties of consciousness. *American Psychologist, 32,* 329–338.

Gangestad, S. W., & Scheyd, G. H. (2005). The evolution of human physical attractiveness. *Annual Review of Anthropology, 34,* 523–548.

Gangestad, S. W., & Simpson, J. A. (1990). Toward an evolutionary history of female sociosexual variation. *Journal of Personality, 58,* 69–96.

Ganong, W. F. (1997). Review of medical physiology (18th ed.). Stamford, CT: Appleton & Lange.

Gardner, D., Harris, P. L., Ohmoto, M., & Hamazaki, T. (1988). Japanese children's understanding of the distinction between real and apparent emotion. *International Journal of Behavioral Development, 11*(2), 203–218.

Gardner, R. A., and Gardner, B. T. (1969), Teaching sign language to a chimpanzee, *Science, 165,* 664–672.

Gazzaniga, M. S. (1985). *The social brain: Discovering the networks of the mind.* New York, NY: Basic Books.

Geary, D. C. (1998). *Male, female: The evolution of human sex differences.* Washington, DC: American Psychological Association.

Geary, D. C. (2005). *The origin of mind: Evolution of brain, cognition, and general intelligence*. Washington, DC: American Psychological Association.

Geary, D. C. (2006a). Sex differences in social behavior and cognition: The utility of sexual selection for hypothesis generation. *Hormones and Behavior, 49,* 273–275.

Geary, D. C. (2006b). Evolutionary developmental psychology: Current status and future directions. *Developmental Review, 26,* 113–119.

Geary, D. C., & Flinn, M. V. (2001). Evolution of human parental behavior and the human family. *Parenting: Science and Practice, 1,* 5–61.

Geary, D. C., & Huffman, K. J. (2002). Brain and cognitive evolution: Forms of modularity and functions of mind. *Psychological Bulletin, 128,* 667–698.

Geary, D. C., Vigil, J., & Byrd-Craven, J. (2004). Evolution of human mate choice. *Journal of Sex Research, 41*(1), 27–42.

Gerhart, J., & Kirschner, M. (1997). *Cells, embryos and evolution*. Oxford, UK: Blackwell Science.

Gewirtz, J. L. (1965). The course of infant smiling in four child-rearing environments in Israel. In B. M. Foss (Ed.), *Determinants of infant behavior* (Vol. 3, pp. 205–248). London, UK: Methuen.

Gibbs, F. A., Gibbs, E. L., & Fuster, B. (*1948*). Psychomotor epilepsy. *Archives of Neurological Psychiatry, 60,* 331–339.

Gilbert, P. (1992). *Depression: The evolution of powerlessness*. New York, NY: Guilford Press.

Gilbert, P. (2000). Varieties of submissive behavior as forms of social defense: Their evolution and role in depression. In L. Sloman & P. Gilbert (Eds.), *Subordination and defeat: An evolutionary approach to mood disorders and their therapy* (pp. 3–46). Mahwah, NJ: Lawrence Erlbaum Associates.

Ginsburg, H. J., & Miller, S. M. (1982). Sex differences in children's risk-taking behavior. *Child Development, 53,* 426–428.

Goldberg, L. R. (1990). An alternative "description of personality": The big-five factor solution. *Journal of Personality and Social Psychology, 59,* 1216–1229.

Goldman, B., & Cullinan, J. (2000). Evolutionary perspectives on human reproductive behavior. *Annals of the New York Academy of Sciences, 907.*

Goldsmith, H. H. (1993). Temperament: Variability in developing emotion systems. In M. Lewis & J. M. Haviland (Eds.), *Handbook of emotion* (pp. 353–364). New York, NY: Guilford Press.

Goldsmith, H. H., & Campos, J. J. (1986). Fundamental issues in the study of early temperament: The Denver twin temperament study. In M. E. Lamb, A. L. Brown, & B. Rogoff (Eds.) *Advances in developmental psychology* (Vol 4, pp. 231–283). Hillsdale, NJ: Erlbaum.

Goldsmith, H. H., & Gottesman, I. I. (1981). Origins of variation in behavioral style: A longitudinal study of temperament in young twins. *Child Development, 52,* 91–103.

Goldsmith, H. H., Losoya, S. H., Bradshaw, D. L., & Campos, J. J. (1994). Genetics of personality: A twin study of the five factor model and parental-offspring analyses. In C. Halverson, R. Martin, & G. Kohnstamm (Eds.), *The developing structure of temperament and personality from infancy to adulthood* (pp. 241-265). Hillsdale, NJ: Lawrence Erlbaum Associates.

Goodall, J. (1971). *In the shadow of man*. New York: Houghton Mifflin.

Goodall, J. (1986). *The chimpanzees of Gombe*. Cambridge, MA: Belknap Press.

Goodman, M. (1963). Man's place in the phylogeny of primates as reflected in serum proteins. In S. L. Wasburn (Ed.), *Classification and human evolution* (pp. 204–234). Chicago, IL: Aldine.

Gosling, S. D., & John, O. P. (1999). Personality dimensions in nonhuman animals: A cross-species review. *Current Directions in Psychological Science, 8*(3), 69–75.

Gould, S. J. (1989). *Wonderful life*. New York, NY: W. W. Norton.

Gould, S. J., & Eldridge, N. (1977). Punctuated equilibria: The tempo and mode of evolution reconsidered. *Paleobiology, 3*, 115–151.

Gould, S. J., & Lewontin, R., (1979). *The spandrels of San Marco and the Panglossian paradigm: A critique of the adaptationist programme*. Proceedings of the Royal Society of London, *205*, 281–288.

Gowers, W. R. (1881). *Epilepsy and other chronic convulsive diseases: Their causes, symptoms, and treatment*. New York, NY: William Wood.

Gray, J. A. (1982). *The neuropsychology of anxiety*. Oxford, UK: Oxford University Press.

Gray, J. A. (1987). *The psychology of fear and stress*. Cambridge, UK: Cambridge University Press.

Graziano, W. G., & Ward, D. (1992). Probing the big five in adolescence: Personality and adjustment during a developmental transition. *Journal of Personality, 60*, 425–439.

Greeno, C. G. (1989). *Gender differences in children's proximity to adults*. Unpublished doctoral dissertation, Stanford University, Stanford, CA.

Greiling, H., & Buss, D. M. (2000). Women's sexual strategies: The hidden dimension of short-term extra-pair mating. *Personality and Individual Differences, 28*, 929–963.

Griffin, J. E., & Ojeda, S. R. (Eds.). (2004). *Textbook of endocrine physiology*. Oxford, UK: Oxford University Press.

Gross, D., & Harris, P. L. (1988). False beliefs about emotion: Children's understanding of misleading emotional displays. *International Journal of Behavioral Development, 11*, 475–488.

Grossman, K., Grossman, K., Huber, F., & Wartner, U. (1981). German children's behavior toward their mothers at 12 months and their fathers at 18 months in Ainsworth's Strange-Situation. *International Journal of Behavioral Development, 4*, 157–181.

Grossmann, K., Grossman, E. E., Spranger, G., Suess, G., & Unzer, L. (1985). Maternal sensitivity and newborn orienting responses as related to quality of attachment in northern Germany. In I. Bretherton & E. Waters (Eds.), Growing point in attachment theory and research. *Monographs of the Society for Research in Child Development* (Whole No. 209, pp. 233–356).

Guillemin, R. (2005). Hypothalamic hormones a.k.a. hypothalamic releasing factors. *Journal of Endocrinology, 184*, 11–28.

Gunnar, M., Mangelsdorf, S., Larson, M., & Herstgaard, L. (1989). Attachment, temperament, and adrenocortical activity in infancy: A study of psychoendocrine regulation. *Developmental Psychology, 25*, 355–363.

Hagen, E. H. (1999). The functions of post-partum depression. *Evolution and Human Behavior, 20*, 325–359.

Hagen, E. H. (2002). Depression as bargaining: The case postpartum. *Evolution and Human Behavior, 23*, 323–336.

Hagen, E. H. (2005). Controversial issues in evolutionary psychology. In D. M. Buss (Ed.), *The handbook of evolutionary psychology* (pp. 145–173). New York, NY: Wiley.

Hala, S., Chandler, M., & Fritz, A. S. (1991). Fledgling theories of mind: Deception as a marker of three-year-olds' understanding of false belief. *Child Development, 62*(1), 83–97.

Hales, C. N., & Barker, D. J. (1992). Type 2 (non-insulin-dependent) diabetes mellitus: The thrifty phenotype hypothesis. *Diabetologia, 35*, 595–601.

Hamilton, W. D. (1964). The genetical evolution of social behaviour. I and II. *Journal of Theoretical Biology, 7*, 1–52.

Hamilton, W. D., & Zuk, M. (1982). Heritable true fitness and bright birds: A role for parasites? *Science, 218*, 384–387.

Harlow, H. F. (1958). The nature of love. *American Psychologist, 13*, 673–685.

Harlow, H. F. (1959). Love in infant monkeys. *Scientific American, 200*, 68–74.

Harlow, H. F. (1969). Age-mate or peer affectional system. In D. S. Lehrman, R. A. Hinde, and E. Shaw (Eds.), *Advances in the study of behavior* (Vol. 1, pp. 335–383). New York, NY: Academic Press.

Harlow, H. F. (1971). *Learning to love*. San Francisco, CA: Albion.

Harlow, H. F., & Harlow, M. K. (1966). Learning to love. *American Scientist, 54*, 244–272.

Harlow, J. M. (1868/1963). Recovery from the passage of an iron bar through the head. Reprinted in *History of Psychiatry, 4*, 274–281.

Harmon, R. J., & Emde, R. N. (1972). Spontaneous REM behaviors in a macrocephalic infant. *Perceptual and Motor Skills, 34*, 827–833.

Harris, J. R. (1998). *The nurture assumption: Why children turn out the way they do*. New York, NY: Free Press.

Harris, P. L. (1989). *Children and emotion: The development of psychological understanding*. Oxford, UK: Basil Blackwell.

Harris, P. L., Brown, E., Marriot, C., Whittall, S., & Harmer, S. (1991). Monsters, Ghosts, and witches: Testing the limits of fantasy–reality distinctions in young children. *British Journal of Developmental Psychology, 9*, 105–123.

Harris, P. L., & Gross, D. (1988). Children's understanding of real and apparent emotion. In J. W. Astington, P. L. Harris, & D. R. Olson (Eds.), *Developing theories of mind* (pp. 295–314). Cambridge, UK: Cambridge University Press.

Harris, P. L., Johnson, C., Hutton, D., Andrews, G., & Cooke, T. (1989). Young children's theory of mind and emotion. *Cognitive and Emotion, 3*(4), 379–400.

Harvey, P. H., & Clutton-Brock, T. H. (1985). Life history variation in primates. *Evolution, 39*, 559–581.

Hatfield, E., & Sprecher, S. (1995). Men's and women's preferences in marital partners in the United States, Russia, and Japan. *Journal of Cross-Cultural Psychology, 26*, 728–750.

Hauser, M. D. (1997). *The evolution of communication*. Cambridge, MA: MIT Press.

Haviland, J. M., & Lelwica, M. (1987). The induced affect response: 10-week-old infants' responses to three emotional expressions. *Developmental Psychology, 23*, 97–104.

Hawks, J. (2005). http://johnhawks.net/weblog/reviews/genetics/mtdna_migrations

Hawks, J., Cochran, G., Harpending, H. C., & Lahn, B. T. (2008). A genetic legacy from archaic Homo. *Trends in Genetics, 24*(1), 19–23.

Hawks, J., & Wolpoff, M. H. (2003). Sixty years of modern human origins in the American Anthropological Association. *American Anthropologist, 105*(1), 87–98.

Hayden-Thomson, L., Rubin, K. H., & Hymel, S. (1987). Sex preferences in sociometric choices. *Developmental Psychology, 23*, 558–562.

Hayward, C., Killen, J. D., Wilson, D. M., Hammer, L. D., Litt, I. F., Kraemer, H. C., et al. (1997). Psychiatric risk associated with early puberty in adolescent girls. *Journal of the American Academy of Child and Adolescent Psychiatry, 36*, 255–262.

Hazen, C., and Shaver, P. (1987). Romantic love conceptualised as an attachment process. *Journal of Personality and Social Psychology, 52*(3), 511–524.

Hebb, D. (1946). On the nature of fear. *Psychological Review, 53*, 259–276.

Henry, J. P. (1986). Neuroendocrine patterns of emotional response. In R. Plutchik & H. Kellerman (Eds.), *Emotion: Theory, research and experience* (Vol. 3). New York, NY: Academy Press.

Hill, J. P. (1980). *Understanding early adolescence: A frame-work*. Chapel Hill, NC: Center for Early Adolescence.

Hill, K., & Hurtado, A. M. (1996). *Ache life history*. New York, NY: Aldine De Gruyter.

Hinde, R. A. (1974). *Biological bases of human social behavior*. New York, NY: McGraw-Hill.

Hinde, R. A., Titmus, G., Easton, D., & Tamplin, A. (1985). Incidence of friendship and behavior toward strong associates versus nonassociates in preschoolers. *Child Development, 56*, 234–245.

Hönekopp, J., Bartholomé, T., & Jansen, G. (2004). Facial attractiveness, symmetry, and physical fitness in young women. *Human Nature, 15*(2), 147–167.

Hood, B. M., Willen, J. D., & Driver, J. (1998). Adult's eyes trigger shifts of visual attention in human infants. *Psychological Science, 9*(2), 131–134.

Hopkins, W. D. (1996). Chimpanzee handedness revisited: 55 years since Finch (1941). *Psychonomic Bulletin and Review, 3*, 449–457.

Huebner, R. R., & Izard, C. E. (1988). Mothers' responses to infants' facial expressions of sadness, anger and physical distress. *Motivation and Emotion, 12*(2), 185–196.

Humphrey, N. K. (1976). The social function of intellect. In P. P. G. Bateson & P. A. Hinde (Eds.), *Growing points in ethology*. Cambridge, UK: Cambridge University Press.

Humphreys, A. P., & Smith, P. K. (1987). Rough and tumble, friendship, and dominance in school children: Evidence for continuity and change with age. *Child Development, 58*, 201–212.

Hunziker, U. A., & Barr, R. G. (1986). Increased carrying reduces infant crying: A randomized controlled trial. *Pediatrics, 77*(5), 641–648.

Huxley, J. S. (1966). A discussion on the ritualization of behavior in animals and man. *Philosophical Transcripts of the Royal Society* (London), *251*, 249–271.

Hwang, C. P. (1986). Behavior of Swedish primary and secondary caretaking fathers in relation to mother's presence. *Developmental Psychology, 22*, 749–751.

Isabella, R. (1993). Origins of attachment: Maternal interactive behavior across the first year. *Child Development, 64*, 605–621.

Isabella, R. A., & Belsky, J. (1991). Interactional synchrony and the origins of infant-mother attachment: A replication study. *Child Development, 62*, 373–384.

Izard, C. E. (1991). *The psychology of emotions.* New York, NY: Plenum Press.

Izard, C. E., Hembree, E. A., & Huebner, R. R. (1987). Infants' emotion expressions to acute pain: Developmental change and stability of individual differences. *Developmental Psychology, 23,* 105–113.

Jacklin, C. N., & Maccoby, E. E. (1978). Social behavior at 33 months in same-sex and mixed-sex dyads. *Child Development, 49,* 557–569.

Jackson, E. D., Payne, J. D., Nadel, L., & Jacobs, W. J. (2005). Stress differentially modulates fear conditioning in healthy men and women. *Biological Psychiatry, 59,* 516–522.

Jacobson, J. L., & Willie, D. E. (1986). The influence of attachment pattern on developmental changes in peer interaction from the toddler to the preschool period. *Child Development, 57,* 338–347.

Janson, C. H., & van Schaik, C. P. (1993). Ecological risk aversion in juvenile primates: Slow and steady wins the race. In M. R. Pereira & L. A. Fairbanks (Eds.), *Juvenile primates* (pp. 57–74). New York, NY: Oxford University Press.

Jersild, A. T. (1968). *Psychology* (6th ed.). Englewood Cliffs, NJ: Prentice-Hall.

Johanson, D. C., & Edey, M. E. (1981). *Lucy: The beginnings of humankind.* New York, NY: Simon & Schuster.

John, O., Caspi, A., Robins, R. W., Moffitt, T. E., & Sthouthamer-Loeber, M. (1994). The "Little Five": Exploring the nomological network of the five-factor model of personality in adolescent boys. *Child Development, 65,* 160–178.

Josephs, I. (1993). *The regulation of emotional expression in preschool children.* New York, NY: Waxmann Verlag.

Josephs, I. (1994). Display rule behavior and understanding in preschool children. *Journal of Nonverbal Behavior, 18,* 301–326.

Joshi, M. S., & MacLean, M. (1994). Indian and English children's understanding of the distinction between real and apparent emotion. *Child Development, 65,* 1372–1384.

Jürgens U. (1995). Neuronal control of vocal production in non-human and human primates. In: Zimmerman E, Newmann JD, Jürgens U, (Eds.) *Current topics in primate vocal communication* (pp. 199–206). New York: Plenum Press.

Kagan, J. (1971). *Change and continuity in infancy.* New York: Wiley.

Kagan, J., Keasley, R. B., & Zelazo, P. R. (1978). *Infancy: Its place in human development.* Cambridge, MA: Harvard University Press.

Kalat, J. W. (1999). *Introduction to psychology* (5th ed.). Pacific Grove, CA: Brooks/Cole.

Karen, R. (1994). *Becoming attached: Unfolding the mystery of the infant-mother bond and its impact on later life.* New York, NY: Warner Books.

Keeley, J. H. (1977). The functions of Paleolithic flint tools. *Scientific American, 237,* 108–127.

Keltner, D. (2007). *Evolutionary approaches to emotion.* Berkeley, CA: University of California Press.

Kenrick, D. T., & Keefe, R. C. (1992). Age preferences in mates reflect sex differences in reproductive strategies. *Behavioral and Brain Sciences, 15,* 75–133.

Kenrick, D. T., Keefe, R. C., Gabrielidis, C., & Cornelius, J. S. (1996). Adolescents' age preference for dating partners: Support for an evolutionary model of life history strategies. *Child Development, 677,* 1499–1511.

Lyons-Ruth, K., Repacholi, B., McLeod, S., & Silva, E. (1991). Disorganized attachment behavior in infancy: Short-term stability, maternal and infant correlates, and risk-related subtypes. *Development and Psychopathology, 3*(4), 377–396.

Lytton, H. & Romney, D. M. (1991). Parents' differential socialization of boys and girls: A meta-analysis. *Psychological Bulletin, 109*, 267–296.

Maccoby, E. E. (1988). Gender as a social category. *Developmental Psychology, 24*, 755–765.

Maccoby, E. E. (1990). Gender and relationships: A developmental account. *American Psychologist, 45*, 513–520.

Maccoby, E. E. (1998). *Two sexes: Growing up apart, coming together.* Cambridge, MA: Belknap Press.

Maccoby, E. E., & Jacklin, C. N. (1974). *The psychology of sex differences.* Stanford, CA: Stanford University Press.

Maccoby, E., & Martin, J. (1983). Socialization in the context of the family. In E. M. Hetherington (Ed.), *Handbook of child psychology: Socialization, personality, and social development* (Vol. 4, pp. 1–101). New York, NY: Wiley.

MacDonald, K. B. (1983). Stability of individual differences in behavior in a litter of wolf cubs *(Canis lupus). Journal of Comparative Psychology, 2*, 99–106.

MacDonald, K. B. (1991). A perspective on Darwinian psychology: Domain-general mechanisms, plasticity, and individual differences. *Ethology and Sociobiology, 12*, 449–480.

MacDonald, K. (1992). Warmth as a developmental construct: An evolutionary analysis. *Child Development, 63*, 753–773.

MacDonald, K. B. (1995). Evolution, the five-factor model, and levels of personality. *Journal of Personality 63*, 525–567.

MacDonald, K. B. (1997). The coherence of individual development: An evolutionary perspective on children's internalization of cultural values. In J. Grusec & L. Kuczynski (Eds.), *Parenting strategies and children's internalization of values: A handbook of theoretical and research perspectives* (pp. 321–355). New York, NY: Wiley.

MacDonald, K. B. (1999). Love and security of attachment as two independent systems underlying intimate relationships. *Journal of Family Psychology, 13*(4), 492–495.

MacDonald, K. B. (2008). Effortful control, explicit processing and the regulation of human evolved predispositions. *Psychological Review, 115*(4), 1012–1031.

MacDonald, K. B., & Parke, R. D. (1986). Parent-child physical play: The effects of sex and age of children and parents. *Sex Roles, 15*, 367–378.

MacLean, P. D. (1952). Some psychiatric implications of physiological studies on frontotemporal portion of limbic system (visceral brain). *Electroencephalography and Clinical Neurophysiology, 4*, 407–418.

MacLean, P. D. (1990). *The triune brain in evolution: Role in paleocerebral functions.* New York, NY: Plenum Press.

MacLean, P. D. (1993). Cerebral evolution of emotion. In M. Lewis & J. M. Haviland (Eds.), *Handbook of emotions* (pp. 67–86). New York, NY: Guilford Press.

Main, M., & Solomon, J. (1990). Procedure for identifying infants as disorganized/disoriented during the Ainsworth Strange Situation. In M. Greenberg, D. Cicchetti, & M. Cummings (Eds.), *Attachment in the preschool years: Theory, research, and intervention* (pp. 121–160). Chicago, IL: University of Chicago Press.

344   References

Main, M., & Weston, D. R. (1982). The quality of the toddler's relationship to mother and father as related to conflict behavior and readiness to establish new relationships. *Child Development, 52,* 932–940.

Malthus, T. R. (1798/1826). *An essay on the principle of population, as it affects the future improvement of society* (6th ed.). London, UK: Murray

Mangelsdorf, S., Gunnar, M., Kestenbaum, R., Lang, S., & Andreas, D. (1990). Infant proneness-to-distress temperament, maternal personality, and mother-infant attachment: Associations and goodness of fit. *Child Development, 61,* 820–831.

Manktelow, K., & Evans, J. St. B. T. (1979). Facilitation of reasoning by realism: Effect or non-effect? *British Journal of Psychology, 70,* 477–488.

Marcus, G. (2004). *The birth of the mind: How a tiny number of genes creates the complexities of human thought.* New York, NY: Basic Books.

Marcus, J., Maccoby, E. E., Jacklin, C. N., & Doehring, C. H. (1985). Individual differences in mood in early childhood: Their relation gender and neonatal sex steroid. *Developmental Psychobiology, 18,* 327–340.

Margulis, L. (1970). *Origin of eukaryotic cells: Evidence and research implications for a theory of the origin and evolution of microbial, plant, and animal cells on the Precambrian earth.* New Haven, CT: Yale University Press.

Marks, I. (1987). *Fears, phobias, and rituals: Panic, anxiety, and their disorders.* Oxford, UK: Oxford University Press.

Marks, I. M., & Nesse, R. M. (1994). Fear and fitness: An evolutionary analysis of anxiety disorders. *Ethology and Sociobiology, 15,* 247–261.

Marks, I. M., & Tobena, A. (1990). Learning and unlearning fear: A clinical and evolutionary perspective. *Neuroscience and Biobehavioral Reviews, 14,* 365–384.

Marler, P. (1984). Animal communication: Affect or cognition? In K. R. Scherer & P. Ekman (Eds.), *Approaches to emotion* (pp. 345–365). Hillsdale, NJ: Lawrence Erlbaum Associates.

Marlowe, F. W. (2003). The mating system of foragers in the Standard Cross-Cultural Sample. *Cross-Cultural Research: The Journal of Comparative Social Science, 37*(3), 282–306.

Marth, G., Schuler, G., Yeh, R., Davenport, R., Agarwala, R., Church, D., Wheelan, S., ... Sherry, S. T. (2003). Sequence variations in the public human genome data reflect a bottlenecked population history. *Proceedings of the National Academy of Sciences USA, 100,* 376–381.

Martin, R. D. (1989). Primate origins and evolution: A phylogenetic reconstruction. London: Chapman & Hall.

Martin, R. D., Maclarnon, A. M., Phillips, J. L., & Dobyns, W. B. (2006). Flores hominid: New species or microcephalic dwarf? *The Anatomical Record. Part A, Discoveries in Molecular, Cellular, and Evolutionary Biology, 288*(11), 1123–1145.

Martinez-Coll, J. C., & Hirshleifer, J. (1991) The limits of reciprocity. *Rationality and Society, 3,* 35–64.

Martorell, R. (1995). Promoting healthy growth: rationale and benefits. In P. Pinstrup-Anderson, D. Pelletier, & H. Alderman (Eds.), *Child growth and nutrition in developing countries: Priorities for action* (pp. 15–31). Ithaca, NY: Cornell University Press.

Matas, L., Arend, R., & Sroufe, L. (1978). Continuity of adaptation in the second year: The relationship between quality of attachment and later competence. *Child Development, 49,* 547–556.

Matheny, A. (1989). Children's behavioral inhibitions over age and across situations: Genetic similarity for a trait change. *Journal of Personality, 57,* 215–235.

Matias, R., & Conn, J. (1993). Are max-specified infant facial expressions during face to face interaction consistent with differential emotions theory? *Developmental Psychology, 29,* 524–531.

Maurer, D., & Salapetek, P. (1976). Developmental changes in the scanning of faces by young infants. *Child Development, 47,* 523–527.

Maynard Smith, J. (1976). Group selection. *Quarterly Review of Biology, 51,* 277–283.

Maynard Smith, J. (1982). *Evolution and the theory of games.* Cambridge, UK: Cambridge University Press.

Maynard Smith, J., & Szathmary, E. (1995). *The major transitions in evolution.* Oxford, UK: Oxford University Press.

Mayr, E. (1970). *Population, species, and evolution.* Cambridge, MA: Harvard University Press.

Mayr, E. (1974). Behavior programs and evolutionary strategies. *American Scientist, 62,* 650–659.

Mayr, E. (1982). *The growth of biological thought: Diversity, evolution, and inheritance.* Cambridge, MA: Harvard University Press.

Mazur, A., & Booth, A. (1998). Testosterone and dominance in men. *Behavioral and Brain Sciences, 21,* 353–397.

McClintock, M. K. (1983). Pheromonal regulation of the ovarian cycle: Enhancement, suppression, and synchrony. In J. G. Vandenbergh (Ed.), *Pheromones and reproduction in mammals* (pp. 113–149). New York, NY: Academic Press.

McClintock, M. K. (1999). Pheromones and regulation of ovulation. *Nature, 401,* 232–233.

McClintock, M. K., & Herdt, G. (1996). Rethinking puberty: The development of sexual attraction. *Current Directions in Psychological Science, 6,* 178–183.

McCrae, R. R., Costa, P. T., Terracciano, A., Parker, W. D., Mills, C. J., De Fruyt, F., & Mervielde, I. (2002). Personality trait development from age 12 to age 18: Longitudinal, cross-sectional, and cross-cultural analysis. *Journal of Personality and Social Psychology, 83,* 1456–1468.

McElwain, N. L., Cox, M. J., Burchinal, M. R., & Macfie, J. (2003). Differentiating among insecure mother–infant attachment classifications: A focus on child–friend interaction and exploration during solitary play at 36 months. *Attachment and Human Development, 5,* 136–164.

McGaugh, J. L. (2004). The amygdala modulates the consolidation of memories of emotionally arousing experiences. *Annual Review of Neuroscience, 27,* 1–28.

McGrew, W. C. (1972). *An ethological study of children's behavior.* New York, NY: Academic Press.

McGuire, M., & Troisi, A. (1998). *Evolutionary psychiatry.* Cambridge, MA: Oxford University Press.

McGuire, M., Troisi, A., & Raleigh, M. M. (1997). Depression in an evolutionary context. In S. Baron-Cohen (Ed.), *The maladapted mind* (pp. 225–282). Hove, UK: Psychology Press.

Mendelson, C. R. (2004). Mechanisms of hormone action. In J. E. Griffin, & S. R. Ojeda (Eds.), *Textbook of endocrine physiology* (pp. 49–88). Oxford, UK: Oxford University Press.

Meyer-Balburg, H. F., Dolezal, C., Baker, S. W., Carlson, A. D., Obeid, J. S., & New, M. I. (2004). Prenatal androgenization affects gender-related behavior but not gender identity in 5-12-year-old girls with congenital adrenal hyperplasia. *Archives of Sexual Behavior, 33,* 97–104.

Michod, R. (1997). Cooperation and conflict in the evolution of individuality. I. Multilevel selection of the organism, *American Naturalist 149*(4), 607–645.

Michod, R. (1999). *Darwinian dynamics.* Princeton, NJ: Princeton University Press.

Miller, G. (2001). *The mating mind: How sexual choice shaped the evolution of human nature.* New York, NY: Anchor Books.

Mineka, S., and Cook, M. (1988). Social learning and the acquisition of snake fear in monkeys. In T. R. Zentall & B. G. Galef (Eds.), *Social learning: Psychological and biological perspectives* (pp. 51–73). Hillsdale, NJ: Lawrence Erlbaum Associates.

Mineka, S., & Cook, M. (1993). Mechanisms involved in the observational conditioning of fear. *Journal of Experimental Psychology. General, 122,* 24–38.

Minervini, B. P., & McAndrew, F. T. (2006). The mating strategies and mate preferences of mail order brides. *Cross-Cultural Research: The Journal of Comparative Social Science, 40*(2), 111–129.

Mitani, J. C., Gros-Louis, J. & Richards, A.. (1996). Sexual dimorphism, the operational sex ratio, and the intensity of male competition among polygynous primates. *American Naturalist, 147,* 966–980.

Mitchell, G. & Brandt, E. M. (1970). Behavioral differences related to experience of mother and sex of infant in the rhesus monkey. *Developmental Psychology, 3*(1), 149.

Miyake, K., Chen, S., & Campos, J. (1985). Infant temperament, mother's mode of interaction, and attachment in Japan. In I. Bretherton & E. Waters (Eds.), Growing points in attachment theory and research. *Monographs of the Society for Research in Child Development, 50*(1/2, Serial No. 209), 276–297.

Money, J., & Ehrhardt, A. A. (1972). *Man and woman, boy and girl.* Baltimore, MD: Johns Hopkins University Press.

Monod, J., Changeux, J. P., & Jacob, F. (1963). Allosteric proteins and cellular control systems. *Journal of Molecular Biology 6,* 306–329.

Morwood, M. J., Soejono, R. P., Roberts, R. G., Sutkina, T., Turney, C. S. M., Westaway, K. E., Rink, W. J., … Fifield, L. K. (2004). Archaeology and age of a new hominin from Flores in eastern Indonesia. *Nature, 431,* 1087–1091.

Murdock, G. P. (1981). *Atlas of world cultures.* Pittsburgh, PA: University of Pittsburgh Press.

Müller, G. B., & Newman, S. A. (Eds.). (2005). Special issue: Evolutionary innovation and morphological novelty. *Journal of Experimental Zoology. Part B: Molecular and Developmental Evolution, 304B,* 485–631.

Munson, J. A., McMahon, R. J., & Spieker, S. J. (2001). Structure and variability in the developmental trajectory of children's externalizing problems: Impact of infant attachment, maternal depressive symptomatology, and child sex. *Development and Psychopathology, 13,* 277–296.

National Center for Health Statistics (2008). Prevalence of overweight, obesity, and extreme obesity among adults: United States, trends 1976–80 through 2005–2006.

Nelson, C. A. (1987). The recognition of facial expression in the first two years of life: Mechanisms of development. *Child Development, 58*, 889–909.

Nelson, C. A., & De Haan, M. (1997). A neurobehavioral approach to the recognition of facial expressions in infancy. In J. A. Russell & J. M. Fernández-Dols (Eds.), *The psychology of facial expression*. Cambridge, England: Cambridge University Press.

Nesse, R. M. (1987). An evolutionary perspective on panic disorder and agoraphobia. *Ethology and Sociobiology, 8*, 573–583.

Nesse, R. M. (2000). Is depression an adaptation? *Archives of General Psychiatry, 57*, 14–20.

Nesse, R. M. (2005). Natural selection and the regulation of defenses: A signal detection analysis of the smoke detector principle. *Evolution and Human Behavior, 26*, 88–105.

Nesse, R. M., & Stearns, S. C. (2008). The great opportunity: Evolutionary applications to medicine and public health. *Evolutionary Applications 1*(1), 28–48.

Nesse, R. M., & Williams, G. C. (1994). *Why we get sick*. New York, NY: Times Books Random House.

Nettle, D. (2004). Evolutionary origins of depression: A review and reformulation. *Journal of Affective Disorders, 81*, 91–102.

NICHD Early Child Care Research Network. (1997). The effects of infant child care on infant–mother attachment security: Results of the NICHD Study of Early Child Care. *Child Development, 68*, 860–879.

NICHD Early Child Care Research Network. (2006). Infant–mother attachment classification: Risk and protection in relation to changing maternal caregiving quality. *Developmental Psychology, 42*, 38–58.

Nishizawa, S. et al. (1997). Differences between males and females in rates of serotonin synthesis in the human brain. *Proceedings of the National Academy of Sciences USA, 94*, 5308–5313.

Noble, W., & Davidson, I. (1996). *Human evolution, language and mind*. Cambridge, UK: Cambridge University Press.

Nowak, M. A. (2006). Five rules for the evolution of cooperation. *Science, 314*(5805), 1560–1563.

Oberzaucher, E., Blantar, I., Schmehl, S., Holzleitner, I., Katina, S., & Grammer, K. (2008, July). *The myth of hidden ovulation: How the face changes during the menstrual cycle*. Paper presented at the XIX Biennial Conference of the International Society for Human Ethology, Bologna, Italy.

O'Connor, T. G., & Croft, C. M. (2001). A twin study of attachment in preschool children. *Child Development, 72*, 1501–1511.

Odom, R., & Lemond, C. (1972). Developmental differences in the perception and production of facial expressions. *Child Development, 43*, 359–369.

Okasha, S. (2001). Why won't the group selection controversy go away? *British Journal for the Philosophy of Science, 52*, 25–50.

Okasha, S. (2004). *Multi-level selection and the major transitions in evolution*. Paper presented in Philosophy of Science Assoc. 19th Biennial Meeting Austin, Texas.

Okasha, S. (2005). Maynard Smith on the levels of selection question. *Biology and Philosophy, 20*(5), 989–1010.

Okasha, S. (2006). *Evolution and the levels of selection*. New York, NY: Oxford University Press.

Oliwenstein, L. (1998). Dr. Darwin. In P. J. Brown (Ed.), *Understanding and applying medical anthropology* (pp. 33–37). Mountain View, CA: Mayfield Publishing.

Oller, D. K. (2000). *The emergence of the speech capacity*. Mahwah, NJ: Lawrence Erlbaum Associates.

Oller, D. K. (2004). Underpinnings for a theory of communicate evolution. In D. K. Oller & U. Griebel, G. (Eds.). *Evolution of communicative systems: A comparative approach*. Cambridge, MA: The MIT Press.

Oller, D. K., & Griebel, U. (Eds.). (2004). *Evolution of communication systems: A comparative approach*. Cambridge, MA: MIT Press.

Oller, D. K., & Griebel, U. (2005). Contextual freedom in human infant vocalization and the evolution of language. In R. L. Burgess & K. MacDonald (Eds.), *Evolutionary perspectives on human development*. Thousand Oaks, CA: Sage Publications.

Oller, D. K., & Griebel, U. (2008). *Evolution of communicative flexibility*. Cambridge, MA: MIT Press.

Oster, H., Hegley, D., & Nagel, L. (1992). Adult judgments and fine-grained analyses of infant facial expressions: Testing the validity of a priori coding formulas. *Developmental Psychology, 28*, 1115–1131.

Owings, D., & Morton, E. S. (1998). *Animal vocal communication: A new approach*. New York, NY: Cambridge University Press.

Packer, C. (1977). Reciprocal altruism in Papio anubis. *Nature, 265*, 441–443.

Packer, C., & Heinsohn, R. (1996). Lioness leadership. *Science 271*, 1215–1216.

Paley, V. G. (1984). *Boys and girls: Superheroes in the doll corner*. Chicago, IL: University of Chicago Press.

Palmer, R. A. (2004). Symmetry breaking and the evolution of development. *Science, 306*, 828–833.

Panksepp, J. (1993). Neurochemical control of moods and emotions: Amino acids to neuropeptides. In M. Lewis & J. M. Haviland (Eds.), *Handbook of emotions* (pp. 87–107). New York, NY: Guilford Press.

Panksepp, J. (1998). *Affective neuroscience: The foundations of human and animal emotions*. New York, NY: Oxford University Press.

Panksepp, J., & Panksepp, J. B. (2000). The seven sins of evolutionary psychology. *Evolution and Cognition, 6*(2), 108–131.

Panksepp, J., Siviy, S., & Normansell, L. (1984). The psychobiology of play: Theoretical and methodological perspectives. *Neuroscience & Biobehavioral Reviews, 8*, 465–492.

Papez, J. W. (1937). A proposed mechanism of emotion. *Archives of Neurology and Psychiatry, 79*, 217–224.

Paquette, D., & LaFreniere, P. J. (1994). Relations mere-enfant, culture et socialisation. *Review Canadienne de Psycho-Education, 23*(1), 17–41.

Parke, R. D., & Slaby, R. G. (1983). The development of aggression. In P. H. Mussen (Series Ed.) & E. M. Hetherington (Vol. Ed.), *Handbook of child psychology: Vol. 4. Socialization, personality, and social development* (pp. 547–641). New York, NY: Wiley.

Parke, R. D., & Stearns, P. (1993). Fathers and childrearing: A historical analysis. In G. Elder, Jr., J. Modell, & R. D. Parke (Eds.), *Children in time and place: Developmental and historical insights*. New York: Cambridge University Press.

Parry, B. L., & Newton, R. P. (2001). Chronobiological basis of female specific mood disorders. *Neuropsychopharmacology, 25*(5S), S102–S108.

Pascalis, O., de Haan, M., & Nelson C. A. (2002). Is face processing species-specific during the first year of life? *Science. 296*, 1321–1323.

Pawlowski, B., & Koziel, S. (2002). The impact of traits offered in personal advertisements on response rates. *Evolution and Human Behavior, 23*, 139–149.

Pedersen, F. A. (1991). Secular trends in human sex ratios: Their influence on individual and family behavior. *Human Nature, 2*, 271–291.

Pelletier, D., & Alderman, H. (Eds.). (1995). *Child growth and nutrition in developing countries. Priorities for action.* Ithaca, NY: Cornell University Press.

Pellicano, E., & Rhodes, G. (2003). The role of eye-gaze in understanding other minds. *British Journal of Developmental Psychology, 21*, 33–43.

Penfield, W., & Jasper, H. (1954). *Epilepsy and the functional anatomy of the human brain.* Boston, MA: Little, Brown.

Peters-Martin, P., & Wachs, T. D. (1984). A longitudinal study of temperament and its correlates in the first 12 months. *Infant Behavior and Development, 7*, 285–298.

Piaget, J. (1952). *The origins of intelligence in children.* New York, NY: Routledge & Kegan Paul.

Piaget, J. (1962). *Play, dreams and imitation in childhood.* New York, NY: Norton.

Piaget, J. (1967). *The mental development of the child.* In D. Elkind (Ed.), *Six psychological studies by Piaget.* New York, NY: Random House.

Pinker, S. (2002). *The blank slate: The modern denial of human nature.* London, UK: Allen Lane.

Pinker, S. J. (1994). *The language instinct.* New York, NY: William Morrow & Co.

Pinker, S. (1997). *How the mind works.* London: Allen Lane.

Pleck, J. H. (1997). Paternal involvement: Levels, sources, and consequences. In M. E. Lamb (Ed.), *The role of the father in child development* (3rd ed.). Hoboken, NJ: Wiley.

Plomin, R. (1994). *Genetics and experience: The interplay between nature and nurture.* Thousand Oaks, CA: Sage Publications.

Plomin, R., Chipuer, H. M., & Loelin, J. C. (1990). Behavioral genetics and personality. In L. A. Pervin (Ed.), *Handbook of personality* (pp. 225–243). New York, NY: Guilford Press.

Plomin, R., DeFries, J. C., & McClearn, G. E. (1990). *Behavioral genetics: A primer.* New York, NY: W. H. Freeman.

Plomin, R, Emde, R. N, Braungart, J. M., Campos, J., Corley, R., Fulker, D. W., Kagan, J., Reznick, J. S., Robinson, J. & Zahn-Waxler, C. (1993). Genetic change and continuity from fourteen to twenty months: The MacArthur Longitudinal Twin Study. *Child Development, 64*(5):1354–76.

Plutchik, R. (1980). *Emotion: A psychoevolutionary synthesis.* New York: Harper & Row.

Pons, F., Harris, P. L., & de Rosnay, M. (2004). Emotional comprehension between 3-11 years: Developmental periods and hierarchical organization. *European Journal of Developmental Psychology, 1*(2), 127–152.

Popper, K. (1965). *The logic of scientific discovery* (2nd ed.). New York, NY: Harper & Row.

Povinelli, D. J. (2000). *Folk physics for apes: The chimpanzee's theory of how the world works.* New York, NY: Oxford University Press.

Povinelli, D. J., Bierschwale, D. T., & Cech, C. G. (1999). Comprehension of seeing as a referential act in young children, but not juvenile chimpanzees. *British Journal of Developmental Psychology, 17*, 37–60.

Povinelli, D. J., & Eddy, T. J. (1996). What young chimpanzees know about seeing. *Monographs of the Society for Research in Child Development, 61* (2, Serial No. 247).

Povinelli, D. J., Perilloux, H. K., Reaux, J. E., & Beirschwale, D. T. (1998). Young and juvenile chimpanzees' (Pantroglodytes) reactions to intentional versus accidental and inadvertent actions. *Behavioral Processes, 42,* 205–218.

Povinelli, D. J., Reaux, J. E., Bierschwale, D. T., Allain, A. D., & Simon, B. B. (1997). Exploitation of pointing as a referential gesture in young children, but not adolescent chimpanzees. *Cognitive Development, 12,* 423–461.

Powlishta, K. K., & Maccoby, E. E. (1990). Resource utilization in mixed-sex dyads: The influence of adult presence and task type. *Sex Roles, 23*(5/6), 223–240.

Prabhakar, S., Visel, A., Akiyama, J., Shoukry, M., Lewis, K., Holt, A., Plajzer-Frick, I., ... Noonan, J. (2008). Human-specific gain of function in a developmental enhancer. *Science, 321,* 1346–1350.

Pratt, C. & Bryant, P. (1990). Young children understand that looking leads to knowing (so long as they are looking into a single barrel). *Child Development, 61*(4), 973–982.

Premack, D. (1988). Does the chimpanzee have a theory of mind? Revisited in R. W. Byrne & A. Whiten (Eds.), *Machiavellian intelligence: Social expertise and the evolution of intelligence in monkeys, apes, and humans.* Oxford, UK: Oxford University Press.

Premack, D., & Woodruff, G. (1978). Does the chimpanzee have a theory of mind? *Behavioral and Brain Sciences, 1,* 515–526.

Price, J. S. (1967). Hypothesis: The dominance hierarchy and the evolution of mental illness. *Lancet, 2,* 243–246.

Price, J. S., & Sloman, L. (1987). Depression as yielding behavior: An animal model based on Schjelderup-Ebb's pecking order. *Ethology and Sociobiology, 8,* 85–98.

Price, J. S., Sloman, L., Gardner, R., Gilbert, P., & Rohde, P. (1994). The social competition hypothesis of depression. *British Journal of Psychiatry, 164,* 309–335.

Pryce, C. R. (1993). The regulation of maternal behavior in marmosets and tamarins. *Behavioral Processes, 30,* 201–224.

Pryce, C. R. (1995). Determinants of motherhood in human and nonhuman primates: A biosocial model. In C. R. Pryce, R. D. Martin, & D. Skuse (Eds.), *Motherhood in human and nonhuman primates: Biosocial determinants* (pp. 1–15). Basel, Switzerland: Karger.

Quammen, D. (2005). Was Darwin wrong? *National Geographic Magazine,* 7–33.

Quinlan, R. J. (2007). Human parental effort and environmental risk. *Proceedings of the Royal Society B: Biological Sciences, 274*(1606), 121–125.

Ramsey, J. L., Langlois, J. H., Hoss, R. A., Rubenstein, A. J., & Griffin, A. M. (2004). Origins of a stereotype: Categorization of facial attractiveness by 6-month-old infants. *Developmental Science, 7*(2), 201–211.

Rauch, E. M., Sayama, H., & Bar-Yam, Y. (2003). Dynamics and genealogy of strains in spatially extended host-pathogen models. *Journal of Theoretical Biology, 221,* 655–664.

Relethford, J. H. (1998). Genetics of modern human origins and diversity. *Annual Review of Anthropology, 27,* 1–23.

Rhodes, G. (2006). The evolutionary psychology of facial beauty. *Annual Review of Psychology, 57,* 199–226.

Rice, D. P., & Miller, L. S. (1993). The economic burden of affective disorders. In R. M. Scheffler, L. F. Rossiter, & T.-W. Hu (Eds.), *Advances in health economics and health services research* (Vol. 14, pp. 37–53). Greenwich, CT: JAI Press.

Richman, N., Stevenson, J. S., & Graham, P. J. (1982). *Preschool to school: A behavioral study.* London: Academic Press.

Ridley, M. (2004). *The red queen: Sex and the evolutional of human nature.* London, UK: Penguin.

Ridley, M. (1996). *Evolution* (3rd ed.). Cambridge, MA: Blackwell Science.

Ridley, M. (2003). *Nature via nurture: Genes, experience, and what makes us human.* New York, NY: HarperCollins.

Rodin, J. (1977). Bidirectional influences of emotionality, stimulus responsivity, and metabolic events in obesity. In J. D. Maser & M. E. P. Seligman (Eds.), *Psychopathology: Experimental models.* San Francisco, CA: Freeman.

Rosenblum, L. A., Coe, L. L., & Bromley, L. J. (1975). Peer relations in monkeys: The influence of social structure, gender, and familiarity. In M. Lewis & L. A. Rosenblum (Eds.), *Friendship and peer relations.* New York, NY: Wiley.

Rossano, M. (2003). *Evolutionary psychology: The science of human behavior and evolution.* New York, NY: Wiley.

Rothbart, M. (1989). Temperament in childhood: A framework. In G. Kohnstamm, J. Bates, & M. Rothbart (Eds.), *Temperament in childhood* (pp. 59–73). New York: Wiley.

Rothbart, M. K. (1981). Measurement of temperament in infancy. *Child Development, 52,* 569–578.

Rothbart, M. K., & Bates, J. E. (1998). Temperament. In N. Eisenberg (Ed.), *Handbook of child psychology* (Vol. 3, pp. 105–176). New York, NY: Wiley.

Rowe, D. C. (1994). *The limits of family influence: Genes, experience, and behavior.* New York, NY: Guilford Press.

Rowe, D. C. (2000). Environmental and genetic influences on pubertal development: Evolutionary life history traits? In J. L. Rodgers, D. C. Rowe, & W. B. Miller (Eds.), *Genetic influences on human fertility and sexuality.* Boston, MA: Kluwer.

Rubin, R. T., Reinisch, J. M., & Haskett, R. F. (1981). Postnatal gonadal steroid effects on human behavior. *Science, 211*(4488), 1318–1324.

Rumbaugh, D. M. (Ed.). (1977). *Language learning by a chimpanzee.* New York, NY: Academic Press.

Rumbaugh, D. M., Beran, M. J. & Savage-Rumbaugh, E. S. (2004). Language. In D. Maestripieri (Ed.), *Primate psychology* (pp. 395–423). Cambridge, MA: Harvard University Press.

Rusu, A. S., & Bencic, A. (2007). Choosing a mate in Romania: A cognitive evolutionary psychological investigation of the personal advertisements market. *Journal of Cognitive and Behavioral Psychotherapies, 7*(1), 27–43.

Rutter, M. (2006). *Genes and behavior: Nature-nurture interplay explained.* Oxford, UK: Blackwell.

Rutter, M., & Garmezy, N. (1983). Developmental psychopathology. In P. H. Mussen (Ed.), *Handbook of child psychology* (4th ed., Vol. 4, pp. 776–911). New York, NY: Wiley.

Sackett, G. P. (1966). Monkeys reared in isolation with pictures as visual input: Evidence for an innate releasing mechanism. *Science, 154,* 1468–1470.

Samuels, J., Eaton, W., Bienvenu, J. et al. (2002). Prevalence and correlates of personality disorders in a community sample. *British Journal of Psychiatry, 180,* 536–542.

Sander, L. (1975). Infant and caretaking environment. In E. J. Anthony (Ed.), *Explorations in child psychiatry* (pp. 129–165) New York: Plenum.

Sarich, V., & Wilson, A. C. (1967). Immunological time scale for hominid evolution. *Science, 158,* 1200–1203.

Savage-Rumbaugh, E. S. (1986). *Ape language: From conditioned response to symbol.* New York, NY: Columbia University Press.

Savage-Rumbaugh, E. S., & Lewin, R. (1996). *Kanzi: The ape at the brink of the human mind.* New York, NY: Wiley.

Savin-Williams, R. C. (1987). *Adolescence: An ethological perspective.* New York, NY: Springer-Verlag.

Saxton, T., Gao, T., Burriss, R., Rowland, H., Havlicek, J., & Roberts, S. C. (2008, July). *Changes in attractiveness across the menstrual cycle are detectable in multiple modalities.* Paper presented at the XIX Biennial Conference of the International Society for Human Ethology, Bologna, Italy.

Scarr, S. (1992). Developmental theories for the 1990's: Development and individual differences. *Child Development, 63,* 1–19.

Scarr, S., & McCartney, K. (1983). How people make their own environments: A theory of genotype-environment effects. *Child Development, 54,* 425–435.

Scarr, S., & Salapatek, P. (1970). Patterns of fear development during infancy. *Merrill-Palmer Quarterly, 16,* 53–90.

Schmitt, D. P. (2005). Sociosexuality from Argentina to Zimbabwe: A 48-nation study of sex, culture, and strategies of human mating. *Behavioral and Brain Sciences, 28*(2), 247–311.

Schmitt, D. P., Realo, A., Voracek, M., & Allik, J. (2008). Why can't a man be more like a woman? Sex differences in Big Five personality traits across 55 cultures. *Journal of Personality and Social Psychology, 94,* 168–182.

Schmitt, D. P., Shackelford, T. K., & Buss, D. M. (2001). Are men really more "oriented" toward short-term mating than women? *Psychology, Evolution, & Gender, 3,* 211–239.

Schore, A. N. (1994). *Affect regulation and the origin of self: The neurobiology of emotional development.* Hillsdale, NJ: Lawrence Erlbaum Associates.

Schultz, T. R., & Cloghesy, K. (1981). Development of recursive awareness of intention. *Developmental Psychology, 17*(4), 465–471.

Schuurman, R., Nijhuis, M., van Leeuwen, R., et al. (1995). *Rapid changes in human immunodeficiency virus type 1 RNA load and appearance of drug-resistant virus populations in persons treated with Lamivudine (3TC).* Chicago, IL: University of Chicago Press.

Schwartz, G. M., Izard, C. E., & Ansul, S. E. (1985). The 5-month-old's ability to discriminate facial expression of emotion. *Infant Behavior and Development, 8,* 65–77.

Seligman, M. E. P. (1975). *Helplessness: On depression development and death.* San Francisco, CA: Freeman.

Seligman, M. E. P., & Peterson, C. (1986). A learned helplessness perspective on childhood depression: Theory and research. In M. Rutter, C. E. Izard, & P. B. Read (Eds.), *Depression in young people* (pp. 223–249). New York, NY: Guilford.

Selye, H. (1950). *Stress: The physiology and pathology of exposure to stress.* Montreal, CA: Acta.

Semenza, C., Pasini, M., Zettin, M., Tonin, P., & Portolan, P. (1986). Right hemisphere patients' judgements on emotions. *Acta Neurologica Scandinavica, 74,* 43–50.

Serbin, L. A., Moller, L. C., Gulko, J., Powlishta, K. K., & Colburne, K. A. (1994). The emergence of gender segregation in toddler playgroups. In C. Leaper (Ed.), *Child gender segregation: Causes and consequences* (pp. 7–17). San Francisco, CA: Jossey-Bass.

Serbin, L. A., Powlishta, K. K., & Gulko, J. (1993). The development of sex typing in middle childhood. *Monographs of the Society for Research in Childhood Development, 58* (No. 2, Serial No. 232).

Sergent, J., Ohta, S., & MacDonald, B. (1992). Functional neuroanatomy of the face and object processing: A positron emission tomography study. *Brain, 115,* 15–36.

Seyfarth, R. M., & Cheney, D. L. (1997). Some general features of vocal development in nonhuman primates. In C. Snowden & M. Hausberger (Eds.), *Primate communication.* Cambridge, UK: Cambridge University Press.

Shea, B. T. (1985). The ontogeny of sexual dimorphism in the African apes. *American Journal of Primatology, 8,* 183–188.

Sherif, M., Harvey, O., White, B., Hood, W., & Sherif, C. (1961). *Intergroup conflict and cooperation: The Robbers Cave experiment.* Norman, OK: University of Oklahoma Press.

Shors, T. (2002). Opposite effects of stressful experience on memory formation in males versus females. *Dialogues in Clinical Neuroscience, 4,* 139–147.

Shultz, T. R., & Cloghesy, K. (1981). Development of recursive awareness of intention. *Developmental Psychology, 17,* 465–471.

Silbereisen, R., Petersen, A., Albrecht, H., & Kracke, B. (1989). Maturational timing and the development of problem behavior: Longitudinal studies in adolescence. *Journal of Early Adolescence, 3,* 247–268.

Simmons, R. G., Blyth, D. A., & McKinney, K. L. (1983). The social and psychological effects of puberty on white females. In J. Brooks-Gunn & A. C. Petersen (Eds.), *Girls at puberty: Biological and psychosocial perspectives* (pp. 229–272). New York, NY: Plenum Press.

Singh, D. (1993). Adaptive significance of waist-to-hip ratio and female physical attractiveness. *Journal of Personality and Social Psychology, 65,* 293–307.

Singh, D. (2004). Mating strategies of young women: Role of physical attractiveness. *Journal of Sex Research, 41(1),* 43–54.

Singh, D., & Young, R. K. (1995). Body weight, waist-to-hip ratio, breasts, and hips: Role in judgments of female attractiveness and desirability for relationships. *Ethology and Sociobiology, 16,* 483–507.

Sinha, C. (2004). The evolution of language: From signals to symbols to systems. In D. K. Oller & U. Griebel (Eds.), *Evolution of communication systems: A comparative approach.* Cambridge, MA: MIT Press.

Slater, J. S. B. (1994). Kinship and altruism. In J. S. B. Slater & T. R. Halliday (Eds.), *Behaviour and evolution.* Cambridge, UK: Cambridge University Press.

Smith, C. A., & Lazarus, R. S. (1990). Emotion and adaptation. In L. A. Pervin (Ed.), *Handbook of personality: Theory and research.* New York, NY: Guilford Press.

Smith, P., & Dalgleish, L. (1977). Sex differences in parent and infant behavior in the home. *Child Development, 48,* 1250–1254.

Smith, R., & LaFreniere, P. (2008). *Development of theory of mind from ages four to eight.* Paper presented at the XIX Biennial Conference of the International Society for Human Ethology, Bologna, Italy.

Snowden, C. T. (2004). Social processes in the evolution of complex cognition and communication. In D. K. Oller & U. Griebel (Eds.), *Evolution of communication systems: A comparative approach.* Cambridge, MA: MIT Press.

Snyder, S. (1985, October). The molecular basis for communication between cells. *Scientific American,* 132–141.

Sober, E. (1984) *The nature of selection.* Chicago, IL: University of Chicago Press.

Sober, E., & Wilson, D. S. (1998). *Unto others.* Cambridge, MA: Harvard University Press.

Sodian, B., & Schneider, W. (1990). Children's understanding of cognitive cuing: How to manipulate cues to fool a competitor. *Child Development, 61(3),* 697–704.

Sodian, B., Taylor, C., Harris, P. L., & Perner, J. (1991). Early deception and the child's theory of mind: False trails and genuine markers. *Child Development, 62,* 468–483.

Sorce, J. F., Emde, R. N., Campos, J., & Klinnert, M. D. (1985). Maternal emotional signaling: Its effect on the visual cliff behavior of 1-year-olds. *Developmental Psychiatry, 21,* 195–200.

Spalding K. L., Arner, E., Westermark, P. O., Bernard, S., Buchholz, B., et al. (2007). Dynamics of fat cell turnover in humans. *Nature 453,* 783–787.

Spitz, R. A., Emde, R. N., & Metcalf, D. R. (1970). Further prototypes of ego formation: A working paper from a research project on early development. *Psychoanalytic Study of the Child, 25,* 417–441.

Sroufe, L. A. (1979). Socioemotional development. In J. D. Osofsky (Ed.), *Handbook of infant development* (pp. 462–516). New York, NY: Wiley.

Sroufe, L. A. (1983). Infant-caregiver attachment and patterns of adaptation in preschool: Roots of maladaption and competence. In M. Perlmutter (Ed.), *Minnesota symposia on child psychology, 16.* Hillsdale, NJ: Lawrence Erlbaum Associates.

Sroufe, L. A. (1985). Attachment classification from the perspective of infant–caregiver relationships and infant temperament. *Child Development, 56,* 1–14.

Sroufe, L. A. (1989). Relationships, self, and individual adaptation. In A. J. Sameroff & R. N. Emde (Eds.), *Relationship disturbances in early childhood: A developmental approach.* New York: Basic Books.

Sroufe, L. A. (1996). *Emotional development: The organization of emotional life in the early years.* New York, NY: Cambridge University Press.

Sroufe, L. A. (1997). Psychopathology as an outcome of development. *Development and Psychopathology, 9,* 251–268.

Sroufe, L. A., Egeland, B., Carlson, E. A., & Collins, W. A. (2005). *The development of the person: The Minnesota Study of risk and adaptation from birth to adulthood.* New York, NY: Guilford Press.

Sroufe, L. A., Fox, N. E., & Pancake, V. R. (1983). Attachment and dependency in developmental perspective. *Child Development, 54,* 1615–1627.

Sroufe, L. A., & Rutter, M. (1984). The domain of developmental psychopathology. *Child Development, 55,* 17–29.

Sroufe, L. A., & Wunsch, J. P. (1972). The development of laughter in the first years of life. *Child Development, 43*, 1326–1344.

Steinberg, L. D., & Hill, J. P. (1978). Patterns of family interaction as a function of age, the onset of puberty, and formal thinking. *Developmental Psychology, 14*, 683–684.

Stenberg, C. R., & Campos, J. J. (1990). The development of anger expressions in infancy. In N. Stein, B. Leventhal, & T. Trabasso (Eds.), *Psychological and biological approaches to emotion* (pp. 247–282). Hillsdale, NJ: Lawrence Erlbaum Associates.

Story, A. E., Walsh, C. J., Quinton, R. L., & Wynne-Edwards, K. E. (2000). Hormonal correlates of paternal responsiveness in new and expectant fathers. *Evolution and Human Behavior, 21*, 79–95.

Strayer, F. F., & Strayer, J. (1976). An ethological analysis of social agonism and dominance relations among preschool children. *Child Development, 47*, 980–989.

Stringer, C. (2002). *The evolution of modern humans: Where are we now?* London, UK: The Natural History Museum.

Stringer, C., & Andrews, P. (1988). Genetic and fossil evidence for the origin of modern humans. *Science, 239*, 1263–1268.

Stringer, C., & McKie, R. (1996). *African exodus: The origins of modern humanity.* New York, NY: Henry Holt.

Strober, M. (1985). Depressive illness in adolescence. *Psychiatric Annals, 15*(6), 375–378.

Strumpf, E. (2004). *The obesity epidemic in the United States: Causes and extent, risks and solutions,* The 2004 Commonwealth Fund/John F. Kennedy School of Government Bipartisan Congressional Health Policy Conference, The Commonwealth Fund.

Suomi, S. J. (2000). A biobehavioral perspective on developmental psychopathology: Excessive aggression and serotonergic dysfunction in monkeys. In A. J. Samaroff, M. Lewis, & S. Miller (Eds.), *Handbook of developmental psychopathology.* New York, NY: Springer.

Suomi, S. J. (2003). *Gene–environment interactions and the neurobiology of social conflict.* Annals of the New York Academy of Sciences, *1008*, 132–9.

Suomi, S. J. (2005). Mother-infant attachment, peer relationships, and the development of social networks in rhesus monkeys. *Human Development, 48*, 67–79.

Swami, V., Neto, F., Tovee, M. J., & Furnham, A. (2007). Preferences for female body weight and shape in three European countries. *European Psychologist, 12*(3), 220–228.

Swami, V., & Tovee, M. J. (2007). Perceptions of female body weight and shape among indigenous and urban Europeans. *Scandinavian Journal of Psych*ology, *48*, 43–50.

Swisher, C. C., Rink, W. J., Anton, S. C., Schwarcz, H. P., Curtis, G. H., & Suprijo, A. (1996). Latest *Homo erectus* of Java: Potential contemporaneity with *Homo sapiens* in Southeast Asia. *Science, 274*, 1870–1874.

Symons, D. (1979). *The evolution of human sexuality.* New York, NY: Oxford University Press.

Symons, D. (1995). Beauty is in the adaptations of the beholder: The evolutionary psychology of human female sexual attractiveness. In P. R. Abramson & S. D. Pinkerton (Eds.), *Sexual nature, sexual culture* (pp. 80–118). Chicago, IL: University of Chicago Press.

Tanner, J. M. (1990). *Fetus into man: Physical growth from conception to maturity.* Cambridge, MA: Harvard University Press.

Tanner, J. M., Wilson, M. E., & Rudman, C. G. (1990). Pubertal growth spurt in the female rhesus monkey: Relation to menarche and skeletal maturation. *American Journal of Human Biology, 2,* 101–106.

Tattersall, I. (2000). Paleoanthropology: The last half-century. *Evolutionary Anthropology, 9,* 2–16.

Taylor, S. E. (2006). Tend and befriend: Biobehavioral bases of affiliation under stress. *Current Directions in Psychological Science, 15,* 273–277.

Tellegen, A., Lykken, D. T., Bouchard, T. J., & Wilcox, K. J. (1988). Personality similarity in twins reared apart and together. *Journal of Personality & Social Psychology, 54,* 1031–1039.

Termine, N. T., & Izard, C. E. (1988). Infants' responses to their mothers' expressions of joy and sadness. *Developmental Psychology, 24,* 223–229.

Thomas, A., & Chess, S. (1977). *Temperament and development.* New York: Brunner/Mazel.

Thompson, R. A. (1990). *Emotion and self-regulation. Nebraska Symposium on Motivation* (pp. 367–467). Lincoln, NE: University of Nebraska Press.

Thompson, R. A., & Lamb, M. E. (1983). Individual differences in dimensions of socio-emotional development in infancy. In R. Plutchik & H. Kellerman (Eds.), *Emotion: Theory, research and experience: Vol. 2. Emotions in early development.* New York: Academic Press.

Thompson, R. A., & Lamb, M. E. (1984). Assessing qualitative dimensions of emotional responsiveness in infants: Separation reactions in the strange situation. *Infant Behavior and Development, 7,* 423–445.

Thornhill, R., & Gangestad, S. W. (1999). The scent of symmetry: A human sex pheromone that signals fitness? *Evolution and Human Behavior, 20,* 175–201.

Tinbergen, N. (1951). *The study of instinct.* London, UK: Oxford University Press.

Tinbergen, N. (1963). On aims and methods of ethology. *Z. Tierpsychol., 20,* 410–433.

Tinbergen, N. (1964). The evolution of signaling devices. In Etkin, W. (Ed.). *Social behavior and organization among vertebrates,* Chicago, IL: University of Chicago Press.

Tomasello, M. (2008). *Origins of human communication.* Cambridge, MA: MIT Press.

Tomasello, M., & Call, J. (1997). *Primate cognition.* Oxford, UK: Oxford University Press.

Tooby, J., & Cosmides, L. (1990). On the universality of human nature and the uniqueness of the individual: The role of genetics and adaptation. *Journal of Personality, 58,* 17–68.

Tooby, J., & Cosmides, L. (1992). Psychological foundations of culture. In J. Barkow, L. Cosmides, & J. Tooby (Eds.), *The adapted mind* (pp. 19–136). New York, NY: Oxford University Press.

Tooby, J., & Cosmides, L. (1995). Mapping the evolved functional organization of mind and brain. In M. Gazzaniga (Ed.), *The cognitive neurosciences.* Cambridge, MA: MIT Press.

Tooby, J., & Cosmides, L. (2005). Conceptual foundations of evolutionary psychology. In D. M. Buss (Ed.), *The handbook of evolutionary psychology* (pp. 5–67). New York, NY: Wiley.

Trivers, R. (1971). The evolution of reciprocal altruism. *Quarterly Review of Biology, 46,* 35–57.

Trivers, R. L. (1972). Parental investment and sexual selection. In B. Campbell (Ed.), *Sexual selection and the descent of man 1871-1971*. Chicago, IL: Aldine.

Trivers, R. L. (1974). Parent-offspring conflict. *American Zoologist, 14*, 249–264.

Troisi, A. (2008). Psychopathology and mental illness. In C. B. Crawford & D. Krebs (Eds.), *Foundations of evolutionary psychology*. New York, NY: Taylor & Francis.

Tronick, E. Z. (1989). Emotions and emotional communication in infants. [Special issue]. *American Psychologist, 42(2)*, 112–119.

Tronick, E. Z., Morelli, G. A., & Ivey, P. K. (1992). The Efe forager infant and toddler's pattern of social relationships: Multiple and simultaneous. *Developmental Psychology, 28*, 568–577.

Troy, M., & Sroufe, L. A. (1987). Victimization among preschoolers: Role of attachment relationship history. *Journal of the American Academy of Child and Adolescent Psychiatry, 26*, 166–172.

UNAIDS/WHO AIDS epidemic update: December 2005 http://www.unaids.org/epi/2005/doc/report_pdf.asp

Uniform Crime Reports (1997). Washington, DC: Federal Bureau of Investigation.

U.S. Census Bureau. (2005, June 5). Population Estimates by Demographic Characteristics. Table 2: Annual Estimates of the Population by Selected Age Groups and Sex for the United States: April 1, 2000 to July 1, 2004 (NC-EST2004-02). Washington, DC: Author.

van den Boom, D. C. (1991). The influence of infant irritability on the development of the mother-infant relationship in the first six months of life. In J. K. Nugent, B. M. Lester, & T. B. Brazelton (Eds.), *The cultural context of infancy* (Vol. 2, pp. 63–89). Norwood, NJ: Ablex.

van den Boom, D. C. (1994). The influence of temperament and mothering on attachment and exploration: An experimental manipulation of sensitive responsiveness among lower-class mothers with irritable infants. *Child Development, 65*, 1457–1477.

van den Boom, D. C., & Hoeksma, J. B. (1994). The effect of infant irritability on mother-infant interaction: A growth-curve analysis. *Developmental Psychology, 30*, 581–590.

van Gennep, A. (1960). *The rites of passage*. Chicago, IL: Chicago University Press.

van Hooff, J. A. R. A. M. (1972). A comparative approach to the phylogeny of laughter and smiling. In R. A. Hinde (Ed.), *Nonverbal communication*. New York, NY: Cambridge University Press.

van IJzendoorn, M. H., Juffer, F., & Duyvesteyn, M. G. C. (1995). Breaking the intergenerational cycle of insecure attachment: A review of the effects of attachment-based interventions on maternal sensitivity and infant security. *Journal of Child Psychology and Psychiatry, 36*, 225–248.

Van IJzendoorn, M. H., & Kroonenberg, P. M. (1988). Cross-cultural patterns of attachment: A meta-analysis of the Strange Situation. *Child Development, 59*, 147–156.

van IJzendoorn, M. H., Schuengel, C., & Bakermans-Kranenburg, M. J. (1999). Disorganized attachment in early childhood: Meta-analysis of precursors, concomitants, and sequelae. *Development and Psychopathology, 11*, 225–249.

van Oosterzee, P., & Morwood, M. (2007). *A new human: The startling discovery and strange story of the "hobbits" of Flores, Indonesia*. London, UK: Collins.

Vaughn, B., Egeland, B., Waters, E., & Sroufe, L. A. (1979). Individual differences in infant-mother attachment at twelve and eighteen months: Stability and change in families under stress. *Child Development, 59,* 971–975.

Vaughn, B., & Sroufe, L. A. (1979). The temporal relationship between infant HR acceleration and crying in an aversive situation. *Child Development, 50,* 565–567.

Vaughn, B. E., Lefever, G. B., Seifer, R., & Barglow, P. (1989). Attachment behavior, attachment security, and temperament during infancy. *Child Development, 60,* 728–737.

Wade, M. J. (1977). An experimental study of group selection. *Evolution, 31,* 134–153.

Wade, N. (2006). *Before the dawn: Recovering the lost history of our ancestors.* New York, NY: Penguin.

Wahler, R. G. (1967). Infant social attachments: A reinforcement theory interpretation and investigation. *Child Development, 38,* 1079–1088.

Wakefield, J. C. (1992). The concept of mental disorder: On the boundary between biological facts and social values. *American Psychologist, 47,* 373–388.

Wakefield, J. C. (2005). Biological function and dysfunction. In D. M. Buss (Ed.), *The handbook of evolutionary psychology.* Hoboken, NJ: Wiley.

Walden, T. A., & Ogan, T. A. (1988). The development of social referencing. *Child Development, 59,* 1230–1240.

Walker, A., & Leakey, R. (1993). The postcranial bones. In A. Walker & R. Leakey (Eds.), *The Nariokotome Homo erectus skeleton.* Berlin, Germany: Springer.

Wallen, K. (1996). Nature needs nurture: The interaction of hormonal and social influences on the development of behavioral sex differences in rhesus monkeys. *Hormones and Behavior, 30,* 364–378.

Wang Y., & Beydoun, M. (2007). The obesity epidemic in the United States—Gender, age, socioeconomic, racial/ethnic, and geographic characteristics: A systematic review and meta-regression analysis. *Epidemiological Review, 29:* 6–28.

Washburn, S. L. (1960). Tools and human evolution. *Scientific American, 203,* 3–15.

Wason, P. (1966). Reasoning. In B. M. Foss (Ed.), *New horizons in psychology.* Harmondsworth: Penguin.

Wason, P. (1983). Realism and rationality in the selection task. In J. St. B. T. Evans (Ed.), *Thinking and reasoning: Psychological approaches.* London: Routledge.

Wason, P., & Johnson-Laird, P. (1972). *The psychology of reasoning: Structure and content.* Cambridge, MA: Harvard University Press.

Watson, P. J., & Andrews, P. W. (2002). Toward a revised evolutionary adaptationist analysis of depression: The social navigation hypothesis. *Journal of Affective Disorders, 72,* 1–14.

Watters, E. (2006). DNA is not destiny: The new science of epigenetics rewrites the rules of disease, heredity, and identity. *Discover Magazine.* http://discovermagazine.com/2006/nov/cover

Wcislo, W. T. (1989). Behavioral environments and evolutionary change. *Annual Review of Ecology and Systematics, 20,* 137–169.

Weisfeld, G. E. (1997). Puberty rites as clues to the nature of human adolescence. *Cross-Cultural Research, 31,* 27–54.

Weisfeld, G. E. (1999). *Evolutionary principles of human adolescence.* New York, NY: Basic Books.

Weisfeld, G. E., & Billings, R. L. (1988). Observations on adolescence. In K. B. MacDonald (Eds.), *Sociobiological perspectives on human development.* New York, NY: Springer-Verlag.

Weiskrantz, L. (1956). Behavioral changes associated with ablation of the amygdalois complex in monkeys. *Journal of Comparative and Physiological Psychology, 49*, 381–391.

Weismann, A. (1893). *The germ-plasm theory: A theory of heredity.* London, UK: Walter Scott.

Wellman, H. M. (1990). *The child's theory of mind.* Cambridge, MA: MIT Press.

Wellman, H. M., & Wooley, J. (1990). From simple desires to ordinary beliefs: The early development of everyday psychology. *Cognition, 35*, 245–275.

Werfel, J., & Bar-Yam, Y. (2004). The evolution of reproductive restraint through social communication. *Proceedings of the National Academy of Sciences USA, 101*, 11019–11020.

West-Eberhard, M. J. (2003). *Developmental plasticity and evolution.* Oxford, UK: Oxford University Press.

Westergaard, G. C., Liv, C., Haynie, M. K., & Suomi, S. J. (2000). A comparative study of aimed throwing by monkeys and humans. *Neuropsychologia, 38*, 1511–1517.

Wheeler, W. M. (1911). The ant colony as an organism. *Journal of Morphology, 22*, 307–325.

Whiten, A., & Byrne, R. W. (1988). Tactical deception in primates. *Behavioral and Brain Sciences, 11*, 233–273.

Whiting, B. B., & Edwards, C. P. (1988). *Children of different worlds.* Cambridge, MA: Harvard University Press.

Wilkinson, G. S. (1984). Reciprocal food sharing in the vampire bat. *Nature, 308*, 181–184.

Williams, G. C. (1966). *Adaptation and natural selection.* Princeton, NJ: Princeton University Press.

Wilson, D. S. (1975). A theory of group selection. *Proceedings of the National Academy of Sciences USA, 72*, 143–146.

Wilson, D. S. (1994). Adaptive genetic variation and human evolutionary psychology. *Ethology and Sociobiology 15*, 219–235.

Wilson, D. S. (2006). Human groups as adaptive units: Toward a permanent consensus. In P. Carruthers, S. Laurence, & S. Stich (Eds.), *The innate mind: Culture and cognition.* Oxford, UK: Oxford University Press.

Wilson, D. S., & Sober, E. (1994). Re-introducing group selection to the human behavioral sciences. *Behavioral and Brain Sciences, 17*, 585–654.

Wilson, D. S., & Wilson, E. O. (2007). Rethinking the theoretical foundation of sociobiology. *The Quarterly Review of Biology, 82(4)*, 327–348.

Wilson, E. O. (1975). *Sociobiology.* Cambridge, MA: Harvard University Press.

Wilson, E. O. (1992). *The diversity of life.* Cambridge, MA: Harvard University Press.

Wilson, E. O. (2005). Kin selection as the key to altruism: Its rise and fall. *Social Research, 72(1)*, 159–166.

Wilson, E. O. & Hölldobler, B. (2009). *The superorganism: The beauty, elegance, and strangeness of insect societies.* New York: W. W. Norton.

Wilson, M., & Daly, M. (1985). Competitiveness, risk taking, and violence: The young male syndrome. *Ethology and Sociobiology, 6*, 59–73.

Wimmer, H., & Perner, P. (1983). Beliefs about beliefs: Representation and constraining function of wrong beliefs in young children's understanding of deception. *Cognition, 13*, 103–128.

Wizeman, T. M., & Pardue, M. (2001*). Exploring the biological contributions to human health: Does sex matter?* Washington, DC: National Academy Press.

Wolff, P. (1963). Observations on the early development of smiling. In B. M. Foss (Ed.), *Determinants of infant behavior* (Vol. 1). London, UK: Methuen.

Wolpoff, M. H., & Caspari, R. (1996). *Race and human evolution: A fatal attraction.* New York, NY: Simon & Schuster.

Wolpoff, M. H., Hawks, J., Frayer, D. W., & Huntley, K. (2001). Modern human ancestry at the peripheries: A test of the replacement theory. *Science, 291,* 293–297.

Wolpoff, M. H., Thorne, A. G., Smith, F. H., Frayer, D. W., & Pope, G. G. (1994). Multiregional evolution: A world-wide source for modern human populations. In M. H. Nitecki & D. V. Nitecki (Eds.), *Origins of anatomically modern humans* (pp. 175–199). New York, NY: Plenum Press.

Woodruff, G., & Premack, D. (1979). Intentional communication in the chimpanzees: The development of deception. *Cognition, 7,* 333–362.

Wooley, S. C., & Garner, D. M. (1991). Obesity treatment: The high cost of false hope. *Journal of the American Dietetic Association, 91,* 1248–1251.

World Health Report (2004). Changing history, annex table 3: Burden of disease in DALYs by cause, sex, and mortality stratum in WHO regions, estimates for 2002. Geneva, Switzerland: WHO.

Wrangham, R. W. (1987). The significance of African apes for reconstructing human evolution. In W. G. Kinzey (Ed.), *The evolution of human behavior: Primate models* (pp. 51–71). Stony Brook, NY: SUNY Press.

Wray, G. A., & Babbitt, C. C. (2008). Enhancing gene regulation. *Science, 321,* 1300–1301.

Wright, R. (1994). *The moral animal: The new science of evolutionary psychology.* New York, NY: Pantheon Books.

Wright, S. (1932). The roles of mutation, inbreeding, crossbreeding, and selection in evolution. In *Proceedings of the VI International Congress of Genetics* (Vol.1, pp. 356–366).

Wynne-Edwards, V. C. (1962). *Animal dispersion in relation to social behaviour.* Edinburgh, Scotland: Oliver & Boyd.

Wynne-Edwards, V. C. (1986). *Evolution through group selection.* London, UK: Blackwell.

Youngblade, L. M., & Belsky, J. (1992). Parent-child antecedents of five-year-olds' close friendships: A longitudinal analysis. *Developmental Psychology, 28*(4), 700–713.

Younge-Browne, G., Rosenfeld, H. M., & Horowitz, F. D. (1977). Infant discrimination of facial expressions. *Child Development, 48,* 555–562.

Zelazo, P. R., & Komer, M. J. (1971). Infant smiling to non-social stimuli and the recognition hypothesis. *Child Development, 42,* 1327–1339.

Zerjal,T., Xue, Y., Bertorelle,G., Wells, R. S., Bao, W., et al. (2003). The genetic legacy of the Mongols. *American Journal of Human Genetics, 72,* 466–482.

Ziabreva, I., Poeggel, G., Schnabel, R. & Braun, K. (2003). Separation-induced receptor changes in the hippocampus and amygdala of Octodon degus: Influence of maternal vocalizations. *Journal of Neuroscience, 23,* 5329–5336.

GLOSSARY

ACTH: A hormone produced by the pituitary gland that stimulates the adrenal cortex to produce its hormones, notably cortisol and other corticosteroids or "stress hormones."

action potentials: Neural impulses; consisting of discrete, all-or-nothing electrical bursts that begin at one end of the axon on a neuron and travel to the other end.

active genotype–environment interaction: The notion that genotypes affect the types of environments that people prefer and will seek out.

adaptation: Close functional fit between a character and aspects of the environment achieved gradually by a process of natural selection.

adaptationist approach: In evolutionary psychology, a strategy involving the search for adaptive design; adaptations "designed" by natural selection to solve problems of organism–environment interaction.

adaptive problem: In evolutionary psychology, any of numerous problems arising from organism–environment interactions, the solution to which results in enhancement or facilitation of reproduction of the organism.

adaptive radiation: Extensive evolutionary diversification from a parental taxon into several new taxa having different adaptations (e.g., several new species originating from one ancestral population, as in Darwin's finches or New World warblers).

adrenarche: The first phase of puberty in which the adrenal cortex produces an increase in adrenal androgens, around age 7. This increase helps launch the growth spurt and the appearance of pubic and axillary hair.

alleles: Different genes that occupy the same locus on a pair of chromosomes and thus can potentially pair with one another.

allometry: Normal body proportionality.

altricial: Species that are relatively immature at birth and require substantial parental care for survival.

amygdala: An almond-shaped structure that is part of the limbic system. Experimental lesions of this region have been shown to produce profound emotional changes, leading some researchers to consider it to be the emotion center of the brain.

anagenesis: Gradual transformation of a species by natural selection. Compare with *cladogenesis*

analogy: An ethological term for similar characteristics in two different species, where the similarity is achieved through convergent evolution (i.e., similar adaptation) rather than through descent from a common ancestral form. Compare *homology*

anthropomorphic: The attribution of human form or personality to a nonhuman.

antidepressant: A drug used to treat depression by making certain transmitter substances, such as serotonin, more available for use at synapses.

appearance–reality tasks: In these tasks children are shown objects that look like other objects, such as a sponge that looks like a rock, requiring an understanding that appearances can sometimes be misleading and not an accurate representation of reality.

appraisal: Evaluation of a salient event in a given context. Many theorists view appraisals as central to the process of determining the individual's emotional response to the event.

arousal: Alert state, with the autonomic nervous system activated, and the body prepared for action.

attachment: An enduring emotional bond that leads the infant to experience pleasure, joy, and safety in the principal caregiver's company and distress when temporarily separated.

autonomic nervous system (ANS): The portion of the peripheral nervous system inside the body of vertebrates that innervates smooth muscles and glands.

axon: The process of a neuron conducting impulses away from the cell body.

Baldwin effect: Incorporation (hardwiring) into the brain of behavioral traits via the differential survival of individuals who learn to respond appropriately to novel, adverse, and recurring environment conditions.

basic emotions: A small set of emotions including fear, joy, and anger that is considered primary because of these emotions' (1) universal expression, (2) quick onset, (3) comparable expressions in other animals, (4) emotion-specific physiology, (5) universal antecedent events, (6) coherence in response systems, (7) brief duration, (8) automatic appraisal mechanism, and (9) unbidden occurrence. See *primary emotions*

behavioral approach systems (BAS): Refers to a cluster of tendencies involving dominance/sensation-seeking, risk taking, and impulsivity.

behavioral ecology: The study of the evolutionary functions of behavior.

behavioral inhibition: A temperamental characteristic reflecting one's tendency to withdraw from unfamiliar people or situations.

behavioral inhibition systems (BIS): Refers to a cluster of tendencies involving fear, wariness, caution, and safety seeking.

behavior genetics: The scientific study of how one's hereditary endowment interacts with environmental influences to determine such attributes as intelligence, temperament, and personality.

belief–desire psychology: A developmental model in which desire psychology emerges first and refers to the ability to explain and predict another person's behavior based on assumptions about their desires, prior to understanding the relation between beliefs and action.

biological function: The relatively immediate consequence or end accomplished by an individual's behavior or other characteristic. Compare *fitness*

bonobo: A pygmy chimpanzee.

catch-up growth: If deprived of adequate nutrition, once normal nutrition is restored, growth greatly accelerates, even supernormally. This catch-up growth may completely compensate for the period of growth retardation, but permanent stunting can occur if the nutritional deficiency was bad enough.

causation: Unless further modified, used here to mean proximate causation, one of Tinbergen's four questions; underlying mechanism.

central nervous system (CNS): The outermost, newest in evolutionary terms, and (in humans) by far the largest portion of the brain; it is divisible into two hemispheres (right and left), and each hemisphere is divisible into four lobes—the occipital, temporal, parietal, and frontal.

chromosomes: The structures within the cell nucleus that contain the genetic material (DNA).

cladogenesis: The evolution of reproductively isolated populations into distinct species. See *speciation*

classical conditioning (or Pavlovian conditioning): Learning to associate a neutral stimulus with something pleasurable or painful.

clique: Close-knit groups of mutual friends who spend a great deal of time interacting and do not readily allow others to join them.

closed system: A system that is isolated from the matter in its environment. Although energy can be exchanged, matter cannot (as in a closed pot of water over heat).

coevolution: Evolution of two or more entities (species; variants within a species; organism and habitat/environment) that are joined as a system.

conspecific: Member of the same species.

constraint: Applied to both development and evolution, a factor or set of factors that either restricts particular changes from happening or makes them more likely.

control evolution: The development of similar traits that have similar functions from differing evolutionary origins.

control parameter: In dynamic systems theory, a parameter to which the system is particularly sensitive.

corpus callosum: A large fiber tract that connects the two cerebral hemispheres.

corpus luteum: A hormone-secreting structure that develops in an ovary after an ovum has been discharged but degenerates after a few days unless pregnancy has begun.

cortex: The most recently evolved outer layer of the forebrain of mammals that is so prominent in humans; sometimes referred to as the neocortex or cerebral cortex.

cortisol: The primary stress hormone produced by the *hypothalamic-pituitary-adrenocortical (HPA) system*. This system is a *neuroendocrine* system that is regulated by outputs from the amygdala to the hypothalamus, which in turn regulates the production and release of stress hormones into the bloodstream.

critical period: A brief period in the development of a human being or animal that is the optimal time of readiness for responding to particular stimuli or acquiring particular skills or abilities.

critical realism: Philosophical foundation of classic ethology that assumes that species-typical adaptations mirror external reality because the organism's perceptual faculties evolved in response to those features of external reality critically involved in the organism's survival and reproduction.

cross-foster: The experimental procedure of fostering the young of one strain (or species) onto a mother from a second strain (or species).

crowd: A larger collective of same-sex cliques.

cultural vector: Enclosed spaces containing many people provides an excellent breeding ground for airborne infectious diseases.

cybernetics: The scientific study of methods of control and communication common to organisms and certain machines like computers.

Darwinism: The evolutionary theory proposed by Charles Darwin that all currently living organisms have evolved from earlier forms in accordance with the principle of natural selection.

deception cues: Inadvertent expressive behaviors that inform the receiver that deception may be occurring, but do not reveal the concealed information.

developmental plasticity: Phenomenon by which any given genotype can give rise to a range of different physiological or morphological types in response to different environmental conditions during development.

dendrites: The thin, tube-like extensions of a neuron that typically branch repeatedly near the neuron's cell body and are specialized for receiving signals from other neurons.

dimorphism: Two variants of a characteristic found in a population; most often used with respect to sexual dimorphism.

display rules: A theoretical term implying that a particular society has implicit rules about what emotions can be displayed to others, and when.

dizygotic twins: Fraternal twins who share only 50% of their genotype. Compare *monozygotic twins*

DNA: Deoxyribonucleic acid; a molecule that is capable of self-replication during cell division as well as the regulated replication (transcription) of small portions of itself onto RNA as a step in protein synthesis.

domain-general: Mechanisms thought to govern all aspects of the mind, including reasoning, learning, memory, and language assumed to operate uniformly, according to unchanging principles, regardless of content.

domain-specific: Mechanisms involving evolved reasoning and regulatory circuits that are functionally specialized to organize the way we interpret experience critical to our adaptation.

dominant: In Mendelian genetics, the allele that is expressed in the heterozygous condition.

Duchenne smiles: Broad smiles readily identified by others as expressions of happiness that involve the action of multiple muscles and include the crinkling of the eyes as the mouth is pulled into a grin. They are called Duchenne smiles after the French scientist who first described them.

dynamic systems theory: Modern systems theory that postulates qualitative changes in systems and nonlinear causation. See also *organizational approach*

electroencephalography (EEG): A technique used to measure electrical activity emanating from the cerebral cortex or outer layer of the brain.

electromyography (EMG): A technique used to record muscle activation of posed and spontaneous facial expressions.

emergency reaction: The fight-or-flight response triggered by the hypothalamus.

emergent: A property of one level in a system that arose from interactions of elements at a lower level but that cannot be identified in those elements, taken either singly or collectively.

emotion: A state usually caused by an event of importance to the subject. It typically includes (1) a conscious mental state with a recognizable quality of feeling; (2) a bodily sensation and physiological change of some kind; (3) recognizable expressions of the face, tone of voice, and gesture; and (4) a readiness for certain kinds of action.

emotional dissemblance: The lack of correspondence between the internal affective state and its outward expression; may be divided into two broad categories, cultural display rules and nonverbal deception.

emotion regulation: The ability to regulate one's own emotions is thought to be shaped by the child's closest relationships. Development begins with dyadic regulation in which the caregiver predominates, then grows into guided self-regulation where the toddler's own self-regulation is guided by the caregiver, and finally emerges as true self-regulation.

endocrine system: Glands that are specialized to secrete hormones into the circulatory system.

endogenous smiles: The earliest smiles to appear in the neonate, they are spontaneous or reflexive and seem to depend on the infant's internal state. These first smiles, which involve simply turning up the corners of the mouth, do not occur when the infant is awake, but only when the infant is asleep, most often in periods characterized by low levels of cortical activity.

environment of evolutionary adaptedness (EEA): The ancestral human environment in which selection pressures caused the design of a particular adaptation to be favored over alternatives.

epigenesis: The conception of development as qualitative change, not reducible to genes or programs in genes, involving interactions within and among many levels of the organism and its external milieu.

ethogram: A general profile of species-typical behavior patterns that have evolved to promote the organism's adaptation to its ecological niche.

ethology: The scientific study of animal behavior, including humans, especially under natural conditions. Aims at understanding development, causation, function, and evolution of species-typical behavior patterns.

eukaryotic cells: Cells that contain many membrane-bound organelles; small membrane-bound structures inside the cell that carry out specialized functions. Compare *prokaryotic cells*

evocative genotype–environment interaction: The notion that our heritable attributes will affect others' behavior toward us and thus will influence the social environment in which development takes place.

evolutionary developmental biology (EDB): Branch of biology that addresses the evolution of embryonic development; how modifications of developmental processes lead to the production of novel features; and the role of developmental plasticity in evolution.

experimentation: Procedures undertaken to make a discovery, test a hypothesis, or demonstrate a known fact.

eyebrow flash: A momentary raising of the eyebrows, lasting about one-sixth of a second, which is a nonverbal sign of greeting in cultures throughout the world.

facial feedback hypothesis: The idea, introduced by Darwin and developed by Tomkins and Ekman, that information from facial movements creates or intensifies emotions.

false-belief tasks: Tasks in which children are told stories in which the protagonist is led to believe that an object has been hidden in one place while they themselves know it has been hidden elsewhere. By the age of four, children generally understand that false beliefs will guide their behavior.

fertility: A woman's potential for immediate and successful reproductive performance.

fitness: A measure of response to natural selection in an individual, stated in terms of probable contribution to future gene pools.

five-factor model (FFM): The view that the major dimensions of personality can be accounted for by just five factors. These "big five" personality dimensions are usually named for one end of the continuum they represent.

fixed action pattern: In classical ethology, a term for a behavior that occurs in essentially identical fashion among most members of a species (though it may be limited to one sex or the other), is elicited by a specific environmental stimulus, and is typically more complex than a reflex.

gametes: Egg cells and sperm cells.

game theory: An ethological model for conceptualizing conditional strategies in which the optimal strategy is not fixed, but requires a consideration of the strategies most likely to be encountered by other game players.

gender identity: The recognition by an individual of his or her own gender as an enduring quality of the self.

gene: A construct used to explain heredity, variously defined as a unit of inheritance identified by an associated phenotype, a location on a chromosome, and a transcribable sequence of nucleotides within a DNA molecule.

general adaptation syndrome: Bodily adjustments that take similar form in response to different stressors. The hypothalamus produces a hormone that affects the pituitary which produces ACTH, a hormone that stimulates the adrenal cortex to produce its hormones, notably cortisol and other stress hormones that cause various adjustments such as increased blood glucose and blood volume.

genetic benefit hypothesis: Women may engage in short-term mating to increase the potential of enhanced fertility, variation in offspring, and access to superior genes.

genomics: The study of genomes using DNA sequence data.

genotype: The complete set of genes possessed by an individual.

genotype–environment interactions: The notion that genotypes influence the environment in which an individual develops. See *active, evocative, and passive genotype–environment interaction*

germ plasm theory: Weismann's view that inheritance only takes place by means of the germ cells or gametes All of the other cells of the body—somatic cells—do not function as agents of heredity. Genetic information thus cannot pass from soma to germ plasm and on to the next generation, as Lamarck proposed. This state of affairs is referred to as the Weismann barrier and is a central component of the modern evolutionary synthesis.

glucagon: Pancreatic hormone that breaks glycogen into glucose.

glycogen: A complex carbohydrate stored in the liver and skeletal muscles that is the first reservoir tapped after blood glucose is exhausted.

gonadotropic releasing hormone (GnRH): Hormones secreted by the pituitary that stimulate the activity of the gonads.

growth hormone (GH): A hormone secreted by the pituitary gland that stimulates growth in animal cells.

habitat: The effective environment of an animal described in terms of resources and challenges that affect survival and reproduction.

heredity: The sum of the qualities and potentialities genetically derived from parents.

heritability: The extent to which a pattern of behavior is attributable to hereditary factors.

heritability coefficient: A measure of heritability, which can vary from 0 (no heritability) to 1 (complete heritability); defined as variance due to genes divided by total variance.

heterozygous advantage: Occasionally genes that cause disease are selected for because they also provide benefits. A classic example are genes that cause sickle-cell anemia in African populations that live in areas where malaria is prevalent. If individuals are heterozygous for this gene, they benefit from its protection against malaria because it can speed the removal of infected cells.

However, if an individual inherits the gene from both parents (homozygotes), then they get sickle-cell anemia.

homology: An ethological term for structures (or behavioral patterns) that have descended from a common ancestral structure or pattern, owing any similarity to that fact. Compare *analogy*

hormone: A chemical substance that travels in the blood to affect the brain or other parts of the body.

hunter-gatherer society: A small nomadic group of humans that relies on hunting animals and gathering plants for its food supply.

hypothalamic-pituitary-adrenocortical (HPA) system: Neuroendocrine system that is regulated by outputs from the amygdala to the hypothalamus, which in turn regulates the production and release of stress hormones into the bloodstream.

hypothalamus: Part of the forebrain responsible for controlling the autonomic nervous system and the pituitary gland; also implicated in species-characteristic behaviors of eating, drinking, sex, and attack.

imprinting: An instinctual restriction of social responses to familiar objects that is learned during a critical period in infancy of some species. Lorenz illustrated imprinting by demonstrating that goslings will follow and become attached to large moving objects.

inclusive fitness: The fitness of an individual combined with the fitness of its relatives, weighted by the extent of genetic sharing between the individual and its relatives.

inheritance of acquired characteristics: Lamarck's view that evolution was driven by the use and disuse of characters during the lifetime of an organism.

innate: Characteristics that are present at birth and assumed to be genetically predetermined.

instinct: Species-typical behavior that is unlearned and genetically programmed.

insulin: A pancreatic hormone that converts blood glucose into glycogen. Insulin also converts fatty acids into fat for storage in fat cells.

integration: The progression toward increased organization of more complex structures as development proceeds.

internal working model: Cognitive representations of the self and others that infants construct from interactions with their caregiver. The internal working model of their relationship is thought to be revealed in the infant's behavior in the strange situation.

intersexual selection: Members of one sex choose as mates members of the other sex whose phenotypes differ in some heritable fashion.

intrasexual selection: Competition of members of the same sex for mates.

kindchenschema: An ethological term (literally "baby-schema") used to refer to the relatively large head, large eyes, and soft, rounded features of the typical infant's face, which are thought to elicit an emotionally based care-giving response from the adult.

kin selection: An evolutionary term whereby natural selection favors traits that improve the reproductive success of relatives, mediated by shared genes.

lateralization: Greater representation of a function on one side of the brain than on the other.

law of economy: Because the body has only so much metabolic energy, and must allocate this energy adaptively to its various systems, the law of economy explains why animals tend to rest when they can, and why movements become more economical with practice.

leakage: In Ekman's theory of nonverbal deception, leakage refers to the inadvertent betrayal of withheld information.

learned helplessness: A feeling of helplessness arising from a lack of control over situations, due to previous exposure to uncontrollable events in similar situations.

leptin: Hormone produced by the body's fat cells that regulates body weight.

lesion: Damage to a part of the brain.

limbic system: Part of the forebrain, including the amygdala, which is thought to be especially important for emotions.

localization of function: The concept that different, localizable parts of the brain serve different, specifiable functions in the control of mental experience and behavior.

luteinizing hormone: A hormone secreted by the anterior pituitary gland that stimulates ovulation in females and the synthesis of androgen in males.

magnetic resonance imaging (MRI): A technique that uses magnetic detectors to measure the amounts of hemoglobin, with and without oxygen, allowing scientists to study the living brain by viewing it at different depths as if in slices.

magnetoencephalograph (MEG): A brain imaging technique that provides a color image of the brain at work that is based on electromagnetic fields that are created as electrochemical information passes between neurons.

major transitions in evolution: Transitions that shift the unit of selection from solitary replicators to networks of replicators enclosed within compartments (e.g., the evolution of the eukaryotic cell).

mate skill acquisition hypothesis: Women may engage in short-term mating to experiment with a variety of partners in order to hone skills of seduction and attraction and also establish what they are looking for in a long-term mate.

mate switching hypothesis: Women may engage in short-term mating to expel an undesirable mate or secure a new mate.

polyandry: The mating system in which females mate with more than one male.

polygamy: The mating system in which individuals mate with more that one partner at a time. See *polyandry* and *polygyny*

polygyny: The mating system in which males mate with more than one female.

polymorphism: The existence of more than one qualitatively distinct variant of a trait (or type) in a population.

positron emission tomography (PET scan): A brain imaging technique that provides a color image of brain activity on the screen of a computer monitor that is based on the uptake of a radioactive form of oxygen into active areas of the brain.

precocial: Species that are relatively mature at birth. Compare *altricial*

primary emotions: The small set of emotions present at birth in rudimentary form and emerging early in the first year that evolutionary theorists believe to be biologically programmed in terms of early expression and recognition. See *basic emotions*

prokaryotic cells: Prokaryotic cells are found in simple organisms like bacteria and do not have the distinct nucleus or the complex organization of the eukaryotes.

prolactin: A hormone released from the anterior pituitary gland that stimulates milk production after childbirth.

protective factors: Factors that reduce the probability of onset of a disorder whatever other risk factors may be operating.

prototype: In an organizational approach, a characteristic example of a concept.

proximate explanations: Explanations of behavior that state the immediate environmental conditions or the mechanisms within the individual that cause the behavior to occur. Compare *ultimate explanations*

puberty: The activation of sex hormones that marks the onset of adolescence and produces dramatic morphological changes. These changes include growth spurts (timed earlier for girls, but more extensive in boys), qualitative changes in physical appearance, the emergence of primary and secondary sex characteristics, and a general increase in sexual dimorphism related to male and female reproductive strategies.

punctuated equilibrium: Model that views evolution in terms of long stable eras punctuated with abrupt periods of change, often as a consequence of speciation, with major changes occurring after populations are separated geographically and genetically.

recessive: In Mendelian genetics, the allele that is expressed only in the homozygous condition (i.e., when paired with its counterpart).

to enhancing survival and reproduction. For example, the theory predicts that males will generally pursue relatively high-risk strategies compared to females.

parent–offspring conflict: From the standpoint of maximizing inclusive fitness an inevitable conflict of interest arises between the parent and the offspring.

parsimony: A criterion for evaluating the scientific merit of theories; a parsimonious theory is one that uses relatively few explanatory principles to explain a wide range of facts.

passive genotype–environment interaction: The concept that the rearing environments that biological parents provide are influenced by the parents' genes and, hence, are correlated with the child's own genotype.

peptide: A substance with large molecules made up of several amino acids that diffuses to affect the function of the brain or other parts of the body.

peripheral: In neuroanatomy, this term is used in contrast to "central"; thus, the peripheral nervous system is made up of the nerves running from the brain or spinal cord to muscles, and from the sensory endings to the brain or spinal cord.

peripheral nervous system: The entire set of cranial and spinal nerves that connect the central nervous system (brain and spinal cord) to the body's sensory organs, muscles, and glands.

phenotype: An observable, measurable feature of an individual that identifies its correlated genotype; a trait; a characteristic.

phylogenetic adaptation: Adaptations that have been retained because they provide some advantage or function for survival during our evolutionary past, such as reflexes.

phylogenetic approach: The conception that if all organisms are related to one another by common evolutionary descent, similarities should be expected between closely related species such as humans and their closest primate relatives.

phylogenetic comparison: To identify trends and common characteristics across a group of closely related species in order to discern the probable characteristics of their common ancestor.

phylogeny: The genealogy of a species (or other taxon) or of a trait; evolutionary history; one of Tinbergen's four questions.

physiology: The branch of biology that deals with the normal *functions* of living organisms and their parts.

pituitary gland: An endocrine gland having a vascular connection to the hypothalamic region of the brain, from which it receives regulatory hormones. Hormones produced by the pituitary, in turn, regulate many other glands in the body.

neurohormone: A chemical substance that is similar to a neurotransmitter in that it is secreted from the axon terminals of neurons, but is classed as a hormone because it is secreted into blood vessels rather than onto other neurons.

neuron: A nerve cell, the fundamental functional unit of nervous tissue.

neurotransmitter: A chemical substance released from the axon terminal of a neuron, at a synapse, that influences the activity of another neuron, a muscle cell, or a glandular cell; also called a transmitter.

normative development: Refers to the general or idealized developmental sequences that describe the average growth patterns in a given area (e.g., cognition, emotion) without reference to individual differences.

nurturance/love system: Refers to a cluster of tendencies involving the psychological basis for relationships of intimacy and other long-term relationships.

ontogeny: A synonym for development; one of Tinbergen's four questions.

open system: A system that can exchange both matter and energy with its environment.

organizational approach: An approach based on systems theory that emphasizes the role of emotions as regulators and determinants of both intrapersonal and interpersonal behaviors. It highlights the adaptive role of emotions by considering their meaning to the individual within a given context.

orienting reflex: An involuntary behavioral and physiological response to a sudden, novel, or unexpected event that includes a wide range of instrumental responses, such as heightened sensitivity of the sense organs, directing sense receptors toward stimuli, rapid inhibition of ongoing behaviors, and changes in respiration and heart rate (HR).

ovarian follicle: A fluid-filled structure in the mammalian ovary within which an ovum develops before ovulation.

oxytocin: A hormone released by the pituitary gland that causes increased contraction of the uterus during labor and stimulates the ejection of milk into the ducts of the breasts.

pandemic: A worldwide epidemic.

parasympathetic division of the ANS: A system composed of neurons linking the spinal cord to the internal organs. Its function is to maintain the body's state in nonemergency situations. Compare *sympathetic division of the ANS*

parental investment theory: In evolutionary psychology, the theory that gender differences in personality systems may be understood as evolved affective-motivational systems that represent a range of alternative strategies for attaining universal human goals related

maturation: Developmental changes in the body or behavior that result from the aging process rather than from learning, experience, or some specific environmental agent.

mismatch hypothesis: The present-day environment of humans has radical changes from that of our EEA, thus some mechanisms may actually be a source of maladaptation.

mitochondrial DNA (mtDNA): Typically passed on only from the mother; thus mitochondria are clones. Because the only source of change in the mtDNA from generation to generation is mutation, mtDNA can be used as a molecular clock to estimate the degree of relatedness between different populations.

monogamy: A mating system in which individuals mate with one partner at a time and share the raising of the young.

monozygotic twins: Identical twins that have the same genotype; they share 100% of their genes. Compare *dizygotic twins*

morphology: The branch of biology that deals with the form of living organisms and the relationship between their structures. Contrast with *physiology*

Mullerian inhibiting substance (MIS): A testicular hormone that suppresses development of the incipient female internal genitalia: the uterus, oviducts, and proximal vagina.

multiregional origin hypothesis: This hypothesis holds that genetic variation between contemporary human races is partly attributable to genetic inheritance from either Homo sapiens subspecies or other hominid species that were widely dispersed geographically prior to the evolution of modern Homo sapiens. Compare *single origin hypothesis*

naturalistic observation: Any data-collection procedure in which the researcher records subjects' ongoing behavior in a natural setting, without interfering with that behavior.

natural selection: Darwin's explanation of evolution based on the differential reproductive success or survival of individuals or groups possessing characteristics that promoted adaptation to the environment.

neocortex: See *cortex*

neonate: A newborn infant from birth to approximately 1 month of age.

neoteny: A particular type of heterochrony in which the juvenile form of some character is retained in adulthood.

neurochemicals: A genetic term for substances such as transmitters, peptides, and hormones that affect nerve function.

neurocultural theory: Ekman's theory of biologically based emotions and cultural display rules.

neuroendocrine system: See *endocrine system*

to enhancing survival and reproduction. For example, the theory predicts that males will generally pursue relatively high-risk strategies compared to females.

parent–offspring conflict: From the standpoint of maximizing inclusive fitness an inevitable conflict of interest arises between the parent and the offspring.

parsimony: A criterion for evaluating the scientific merit of theories; a parsimonious theory is one that uses relatively few explanatory principles to explain a wide range of facts.

passive genotype–environment interaction: The concept that the rearing environments that biological parents provide are influenced by the parents' genes and, hence, are correlated with the child's own genotype.

peptide: A substance with large molecules made up of several amino acids that diffuses to affect the function of the brain or other parts of the body.

peripheral: In neuroanatomy, this term is used in contrast to "central"; thus, the peripheral nervous system is made up of the nerves running from the brain or spinal cord to muscles, and from the sensory endings to the brain or spinal cord.

peripheral nervous system: The entire set of cranial and spinal nerves that connect the central nervous system (brain and spinal cord) to the body's sensory organs, muscles, and glands.

phenotype: An observable, measurable feature of an individual that identifies its correlated genotype; a trait; a characteristic.

phylogenetic adaptation: Adaptations that have been retained because they provide some advantage or function for survival during our evolutionary past, such as reflexes.

phylogenetic approach: The conception that if all organisms are related to one another by common evolutionary descent, similarities should be expected between closely related species such as humans and their closest primate relatives.

phylogenetic comparison: To identify trends and common characteristics across a group of closely related species in order to discern the probable characteristics of their common ancestor.

phylogeny: The genealogy of a species (or other taxon) or of a trait; evolutionary history; one of Tinbergen's four questions.

physiology: The branch of biology that deals with the normal *functions* of living organisms and their parts.

pituitary gland: An endocrine gland having a vascular connection to the hypothalamic region of the brain, from which it receives regulatory hormones. Hormones produced by the pituitary, in turn, regulate many other glands in the body.

polyandry: The mating system in which females mate with more than one male.

polygamy: The mating system in which individuals mate with more that one partner at a time. See *polyandry* and *polygyny*

polygyny: The mating system in which males mate with more than one female.

polymorphism: The existence of more than one qualitatively distinct variant of a trait (or type) in a population.

positron emission tomography (PET scan): A brain imaging technique that provides a color image of brain activity on the screen of a computer monitor that is based on the uptake of a radioactive form of oxygen into active areas of the brain.

precocial: Species that are relatively mature at birth. Compare *altricial*

primary emotions: The small set of emotions present at birth in rudimentary form and emerging early in the first year that evolutionary theorists believe to be biologically programmed in terms of early expression and recognition. See *basic emotions*

prokaryotic cells: Prokaryotic cells are found in simple organisms like bacteria and do not have the distinct nucleus or the complex organization of the eukaryotes.

prolactin: A hormone released from the anterior pituitary gland that stimulates milk production after childbirth.

protective factors: Factors that reduce the probability of onset of a disorder whatever other risk factors may be operating.

prototype: In an organizational approach, a characteristic example of a concept.

proximate explanations: Explanations of behavior that state the immediate environmental conditions or the mechanisms within the individual that cause the behavior to occur. Compare *ultimate explanations*

puberty: The activation of sex hormones that marks the onset of adolescence and produces dramatic morphological changes. These changes include growth spurts (timed earlier for girls, but more extensive in boys), qualitative changes in physical appearance, the emergence of primary and secondary sex characteristics, and a general increase in sexual dimorphism related to male and female reproductive strategies.

punctuated equilibrium: Model that views evolution in terms of long stable eras punctuated with abrupt periods of change, often as a consequence of speciation, with major changes occurring after populations are separated geographically and genetically.

recessive: In Mendelian genetics, the allele that is expressed only in the homozygous condition (i.e., when paired with its counterpart).

reciprocal altruism: Concept by which the original beneficiary of an act of altruism reciprocates later. Failure to do so will usually cause the original benefactor to withdraw future acts of altruism. Used by Trivers to explain non-kin cooperation in humans where individuals recognize each other in order to "keep accounts" across repeated contacts.

reciprocal determinism: The conception that the flow of influence between children and their environments is a two-way street; the environment may affect the child, but the child's behavior will also influence the environment.

recognitory assimilation: When the infant is presented with a challenging stimulus, such as a stationary face, there is strong effort leading to assimilation of the schema, followed by tension release and smiling. If there is no successful assimilation, the infant may turn away or cry.

reductionism: An explanatory mode that seeks to explain phenomena at one level of a system in terms of events and components at lower levels.

reflex: A fairly discrete action, based on a neural pathway that connects a stimulus to a response.

reification: A fallacy in scientific thought wherein the naming of a concept has the effect of making it seem like a concrete thing.

REM (rapid eye movement) sleep: The recurring stage of sleep during which the EEG resembles that of an alert person, rapid eye movements occur, the large muscles of the body are most relaxed, and true dreams are most likely to occur.

reproductive effort: Involves three different costs: (1) *mating* (including competing for mates), (2) *parenting* (including feeding, care, and protecting offspring), and (3) in some species, such as humans, *nepotism* (helping relatives to survive and reproduce more successfully).

reproductive value: A woman's potential to bear children.

resource accrual hypothesis: Women may engage in short-term mating in exchange for goods and other resources.

risk factor: Factor that increases the probability of onset of a disorder.

rites of passage: The rituals in some traditional societies that mark the transition into adulthood. They involve (1) an initial phase of isolation, (2) a phase of intentional confusion in which the identity of the adolescent is broken down, and (3) a phase of reinstatement in which the adolescent is incorporated into the adult community.

ritualization: An ethological term for the process by which signals evolved from incidental and involuntary expressions of emotions (i.e., facial expression or erection of hair or feathers).

rouge test: A test of infants' self-recognition; if they have achieved self-recognition, infants whose faces are marked with rouge will, when placed before a mirror, touch their own faces rather than the mirror image.

selection pressure: Any condition or process that causes some individuals to leave more descendants than others as a result of differences in genetic makeup.

self-conscious emotions: The feelings of guilt, shame, embarrassment, and pride that are linked to thoughts about the self or one's own actions in reference to internalized standards.

separation anxiety: A wary or fretful reaction that infants and toddlers often display when separated from the persons to whom they are attached, especially in an unfamiliar environment.

sex ratio theory: Proposes that the predominant mating strategy within a culture will be determined by the ratio of mature men to mature women.

sexual attraction: The attraction to other members of the same species for reproduction.

sexual dimorphism: Distinct difference in size and appearance between the sexes of an animal in addition to the differences in the sexual organs themselves.

sexual selection: The specific form of natural selection that arises from the advantage that certain individuals have over other individuals of the same sex and species in exclusive relation to reproduction.

sexual strategies theory: According to Schmitt and Buss, men and women possess psychological adaptations for a range of mating strategies.

shared environmental influence: An aspect of environment that is experienced (shared) by people living together that is often assumed to make them similar to one another.

sign stimulus: Ethologists' term for a stimulus that reliably elicits a behavior that occurs in essentially identical fashion among most members of a species (though it may be limited to one sex).

single-origin hypothesis (out-of-Africa model): One of two current theories regarding the origin of anatomically modern humans, that H. sapiens evolved from a single ancestral hominid population whose descendants ultimately replace all other species of hominids without interbreeding. Compare *multiregional origin hypothesis*

skin conductance: An electrical measurement of the minute amounts of sweat being produced by the skin. It indicates changes in the autonomic nervous system, which, in turn, indicate emotional changes.

social bargaining theory: Several researchers view depression as a desperate form of social manipulation, what might be termed the social bargaining theory of depression.

social competition hypothesis: Individuals who lose status after a failed hierarchy struggle may withdraw into a state of depression and inactivity as a result. Price viewed this as an evolved mechanism in social species that live within a dominance hierarchy, which functions to protect the individual from further aggression.

socialization: The process by which children acquire the beliefs, values, and behaviors considered desirable or appropriate by the society to which they belong.

social navigational hypothesis: According to this view, positive mood serves to increase initiative and risk taking when potential pay-offs are high, while low mood motivates changing strategies when risks are high, thus avoiding wasteful expenditures of energy.

social referencing: The use of other's emotional expressions to infer the meaning of otherwise ambiguous situations.

sociobiology: The comparative study of social organization in animals, including humans, especially with regard to its genetic and evolutionary history.

sociometric measures: Assessments of the network of relationships that exists in a stable group by asking the children themselves about their preferences for peer group members. Three basic techniques may be employed: rating scales, paired comparisons, and nominations.

speciation: The evolution of reproductively isolated populations into distinct species. See also *cladogenesis*

species: A population of organisms that can in principle reproduce with one another but that are reproductively isolated from those in other populations. This definition does not cover all populations that one would, on other grounds, want to designate as species.

species-characteristic pattern: An extended pattern of goal-directed behavior that is acquired genetically and is characteristic of a species.

standard social science model (SSSM): The prevailing notion that the contents of human minds are social constructions, and the view that the social sciences are autonomous and disconnected from any evolutionary or biological foundation.

stranger anxiety: A wary or fretful reaction that infants and toddlers often display when approached by an unfamiliar person.

strange situation: A laboratory test situation developed by Ainsworth to examine infants' reactions to separation from and reunion with their caregivers in order to determine the quality of their attachments to the caregivers.

strategic pluralism theory: Proposes that humans have a menu of alternate mating strategies that they can follow and that the condition of the local environment influences the strategies they will choose.

striatal system: The part of the forebrain concerned with scheduling daily activities.

subcortical: Relating to or involving nerve centers below the cerebral cortex.

sympathetic division of the ANS: The set of motor neurons that act upon visceral muscles and glands and mediate many of the body's responses to stressful stimulation, preparing the body for possible "fight or flight." Compare *parasympathetic division of the ANS*

synapse: The space between the axon terminal of one neuron and the dendrites of its neighbor across which a nervous impulse jumps from one neuron to another.

tabula rasa: The conception of the mind of an infant as a "blank slate" and that all knowledge, abilities, behaviors, and motives are acquired through experience.

tactical deception: The term used by ethologists to distinguish a conscious strategy of deception from other types of deception employed by animals (e.g., based on instinct or conditioning).

temperament: An individual's characteristic mode of response or disposition that is constitutional in origin, shows stability over time, and has a genetic basis.

temporal lobe: The lobe of the cerebral cortex that lies in front of the occipital lobe and below the parietal and frontal lobes that contains the auditory area of the brain.

thalamus: Brain nuclei providing the major source of inputs to the cortex.

theory: A set of concepts and propositions designed to organize, describe, and explain an existing set of observations.

theory of mind (TOM): The attribution of an unobservable mental state (e.g., a belief, a desire, or knowledge) to another individual.

trait: An aspect of personality that shows some stability over time and across situations.

transmitter substance: A chemical substance secreted by nerve cells to communicate with other nerve cells that may diffuse outside synapses to affect nerve cells over a local region.

tree of life: A branching representation depicting the relatedness of different species based on comparison of the composition of their DNA.

twin study: A study in which sets of twins differing in zygosity (kinship) are compared to determine the heritability of an attribute or attributes.

ultimate explanations: Functional explanations of behavior that state the role that the behavior plays or once played in survival and reproduction; that is, explanations of why the potential for the behavior was favored by natural selection. Compare *proximate explanations*

vagal tone: An index based on the time period between heartbeats, rather than heart rate, that measures the number of heartbeats per minute. This more precise measure takes into consideration the rhythmic increase and decrease of heart rate with respiration.

vagus: A complex system of bidirectional neural pathways linking the brain stem to various bodily organs, such as the heart and the digestive system.

Washoe: The first chimpanzee to master sign language, trained by Roger Fouts.

INDEX

A

Action potential, 104
Active effect, 58, 70
Adaptive design
  brain, 123
  evidence of, 46–47
  example of, 3–4
  functionalist perspective, 45
Adaptive radiation, 13
Adenine, 53
Adenosine triphosphate (ATP), 51
ADHD, *see* Attention-deficit hyperactivity
      disorder
Adrenal corticosteroids, 130
Adrenarche, 143
Agoraphobia, 290, 291
AIDS (acquired immune deficiency
      syndrome), 15, 284, 295
Alcohol consumption, 211
Allometry, 134
Allo-parenting, 133
Altruism, cooperation, and competition,
      299–319
  artificial intelligence, 308
  cheater-detection module, 319
  environment of evolutionary
      adaptedness, 316, 319
  eusociality, 301, 317
  evolutionary game theory, 306–307
  evolutionary psychology of
      cooperation, 313–316
  evolutionary stable strategies, 316, 319
  free-rider problem, 313, 318
  inclusive fitness, 300
  kin selection, 301
  logical reasoning, test of, 313
  major transitions in evolution, 311
  multilevel selection theory, 310–311,
      318
  one special difficulty, 302
  "pop out" effect, 315
  prisoner's dilemma, 307–310
  reciprocal altruism, 313
  role of punishment in promoting
      cooperation, 311–313

"selfish gene" perspective, 300
social contract algorithms, 316, 319
social contract theory, 313, 319
sociobiological perspectives, 299–306
  kin selection, 300–304
  reciprocal altruism, 304–306
summary, 316–319
superorganisms, 311
supersisters, 303
ultrasociality, 318
Wason selection task, 313
American Sign Language, 223
Amino acid(s)
  coding for production of, 53
  essential, 135
  meat, 139
  Neanderthal sample, 85
Amygdala, 102
Androgen, 130, 133
Anger, definition of, 174
ANS, *see* Autonomic nervous system
Antidepressants, 104
Anxiety, 288–289
  agoraphobia, 290
  -arousing experiences, 246
  deficient, 289
  disorders, 291
  dysfunctional, 289
  prevalence, 289, 291
  separation, 176, 177, 287
  stranger, 178
Appearance-reality tasks, 229
Ardipthecus ramidus, 75
Artificial intelligence, 308
ATP, *see* Adenosine triphosphate
Attachment, *see* Infancy, attachment in
Attention-deficit hyperactivity disorder
      (ADHD), 286
Australopithecus
  afarensis, 75, 76, 95
  africanus, 76
  anamensis, 75
  garhi, 76
Autonomic nervous system (ANS), 102,
      113, 124
Avoidant attachment, 190